THE SCARS YOU CAN'T SEE

Blessings
to a great friend
And fantastic historian.
Blessings to you & yours

Jennifer
Nashville

The Scars You Can't See

Finding Wholeness from the Trauma of Near Death

Natalie Zeleznikar

ISBN 13: 978-1-63489-475-3

Library of Congress Catalog Number has been applied for.
Printed in the United States of America
First Printing: 2022

26   25   24   23   22   5   4   3   2   1

Cover design by Zoe Norvell
Interior design by Patrick Maloney

Wise Ink Creative Publishing
807 Broadway St. NE
Suite 46
Minneapolis, MN 55413

Contents

Introduction

OST OF MY LIFE I have been skipping down my yellow brick road, simply enjoying life. Don't get me wrong, my life is not perfect—but I love to smile and I love to make others smile. In fact, I like *The Wizard of Oz* so much that my friends and colleagues have given me necklaces with all the best one-liners from the film.

So when I received my diagnosis of stage 1 invasive ductal carcinoma breast cancer in March 2015, it was like a paver popped up on my yellow brick road. Or perhaps it was more like a steady stream of dominoes falling down before my eyes and I just didn't know it yet.

I guess I shouldn't have been shocked—one out of eight women will be diagnosed with breast cancer in their lifetime—but I was. After I had my biopsy, I walked through the hospital parking ramp and finally found my car, climbed in, and sobbed. I cried and talked to myself for a while, blurting out, "Why now? Maybe it isn't cancer. Maybe it's just a fibroid cyst." I realized these thoughts were being yelled into a dashboard, and I realized I needed to pull myself together. I was late for a meeting.

As the days moved forward and reality set in, I viewed my case as a low-risk one because I had a low score of stage 1. Breast cancer is scored 0–4. If you have stage 0, it is noninvasive, you have abnormal cells, and physicians will likely recommend having the tumor removed. If you have stage 1, this is the earliest stage of invasive breast cancer. The tumor is two centimeters or smaller, and it may or may not be in your lymph nodes. Stage 2 means the tumor is between two and five centimeters, and the cancer may or may not be in the lymph nodes. Stage 3 typically means the cancer has spread to the lymph nodes. Stage 4 is the most serious level, as it means the cancer is metastatic. It has spread beyond the breast and nearby lymph nodes. So in my mind, having a low score of 1 was a blessing. I felt that those with higher scores really had something to worry about, and I should feel lucky.

What I did not foresee happening were several surgeries due to unfortunate circumstances that resulted in years of medical bills and time away from work. I would go on to be a survivor of sepsis, a severe infection that causes approximately 270,000 deaths annually in the United States. In recent years, the Centers for Disease Control and Prevention (CDC) has begun educating the public on the risks and signs of sepsis. I could have easily been one of those 270,000.

The reality is that one in three patients who die in a hospital have sepsis. In 2018 an article called "The Centrality of Sepsis: A Review on Incidence, Mortality, and Cost of Care" was published in the journal *Healthcare* and described the severity of the problem of sepsis in medicine today.[1] The article highlights several case studies that point to significant increases in sepsis over the past three decades. Among Medicare-aged patients, sepsis ranked second only behind heart failure among reasons for a readmission into a hospital within thirty days from previous hospital admission. Sepsis continues to be extremely expensive to treat, especially if there is multiple organ failure and several days or weeks of hospitalization or intensive-care-unit stays. Post-sepsis syndrome symptoms may include long-term cognitive and functional disabilities requiring medical interventions. Sepsis Alliance is a national 501(c)3 nonprofit with a mission to save lives and reduce suffering by improving sepsis awareness and care. The organization provides free sepsis education for patients, survivors, caregivers, and medical professionals across the continuum of care, which is phenomenal to see.

I do feel lucky to be alive today, and I'm even luckier to be able to share my story in hopes that it will prevent unnecessary deaths for those who face medical challenges and adversity. I am thankful for the support of my husband, sons, daughter-in-law, parents, and numerous family and friends. It was not an easy chapter in our lives, and the support we had made the moments bearable. Thank you for your unconditional love.

---

[1]   This article, by Jihane Hajj, Natalie Blaine, Jola Salavaci, and Douglas Jacoby, is available at ncbi.nlm.nih.gov, which is the website of the National Center for Biotechnology Information (NCBI). The NCBI "advances science and health by providing access to biomedical and genomic information."

1 ∾ Time Stops

THERE ARE SIGNIFICANT MOMENTS in life when you remember exactly where you were. For happy events, such as weddings, births, and graduations, I usually remember all the laughter, happiness, and fun of the events. For sad events and especially sudden tragedies, I remember different details, such as the weather and where I was standing, sitting, or driving. What I remember most is the time, for in these moments, it truly feels as though time has stopped.

When time stops, it feels like the world is moving all around you and you are literally frozen. Imagine being at an amusement park, sitting on a bench with all the people walking around and all the rides, noises, and lights. You are part of something, but your body, mind, and soul feel trapped, watching the scene from the outside.

Time stood still when I lay on the exam table during a breast biopsy and watched the ultrasound technician complete the procedure. I tasted salt from the tears rolling down my cheeks. The room was awkwardly silent. One of the health-care team members told me not to be surprised if they said I had cancer when they called next week. While lying on the exam table, my body was absolutely stiff. I was afraid to turn my head and see the monitor. After years of working as a healthcare administrator, I knew the protocol of what information an ultrasound technician could share with me. As it turned out, this woman was the only person who empathized with my emotion during the medical procedure. She humanized the sterile procedure, as my tears hit her hand while she moved the ultrasound wand.

What? A lump filled my throat. I felt the weight of the world on me for that moment. My mind raced, wondering if this meant they had seen a large mass, medium mass, or small mass. There was no way to know, because there is no one to ask until someone calls with the results. It is a waiting game of hell.

As I waited on the table for the biopsy to happen, the room felt intensely chilled. It felt like a Minnesota winter storm with ice hitting my face as tears kept flowing down my cheeks. My mind felt numb. My heart was breaking. The stainless-steel table I was on was meant to be sterile, sturdy, and freezing cold. I felt lifeless and wished this stainless steel could wrap me up in a cocoon and become my shield.

After the procedure, I dressed myself in a white robe and walked like a zombie down the hall. I looked at all the women in the waiting area and wondered who had cancer and who was there for a routine mammogram. *I bet they all know I have cancer,* I thought. Women are intuitive.

Years ago, I had been sitting in this very spot waiting for my name to be called when I saw a woman crying and walking to her locker. I was so sad for her. I thought about going over to console her—it felt odd to do that for a stranger, but doing nothing seemed odder to me, because I am a person who generally cares and hurts when others hurt. I feel bad that I did not reach out to her that day—instead, I put my head down in my magazine, pretended I never saw her tears, and drank my coffee. When I left the mammogram office later that day, my routine visit had turned out fine, and I prayed for the woman I never knew who had received news she never planned on that would change her life. She would have been all alone in a dressing room, unprepared, doing the routine like all the years before. Except this time it would be different. And life would never be the same again.

Years later I, too, walked the same hallway she and many others had walked. Everyone wore white robes, read magazines, and drank coffee, like it was a spa. Until you get to the boob-squishing part, or the part where you get a biopsy and bad news. The crowd looked the same as it always did, but this time I put on my white robe and became one of the statistics. Now I was the one in eight who had breast cancer. That was the only part that changed.

As I walked by the waiting room with fresh tears and a face full of running mascara, the air felt thick with helplessness—no one knew what to do. I felt their pain. I had been in their shoes before, so I smiled, went to my cube, and tried to remember how to get dressed while my brain was still in a fog.

When I was dressed, I did not want to unlock my door, because on the other side I had to deal with it. I wanted to stay in this cube for as long as I could. I did not want to tell anyone—my husband, my kids, my parents, my friends and family, and those I work with every day in my business.

Someone finally knocked on the door, and I said I would be out soon. I sat on the bench in the dressing room. Sitting longer didn't change anything, and I finally just had to find the strength to open the door and deal with it.

Now what? I did not want anyone worrying about me—in my mind every time I hear the word *cancer* I worry about death. I didn't want to put them through that. I didn't want to answer their questions because I would have no answers. It would be the first time in my life that I would choose not to tell those closest to me important information the moment I knew it. Suddenly the one who was born to be a caregiver might need care.

I looked in the office's waiting area and for the first time I saw all the pink cancer symbols that I had never noticed before while getting a routine mammogram. My mindset before the coming diagnosis was about how great it was to see nice gestures for other people. Now "other people" included me. *This can't be right*, I thought. *I can't have this. I feel great—they must have this wrong.*

I had convinced myself it was likely a benign fibroid cyst, like my mother has had many times. It was just a procedure, and I wouldn't know my real results for four to five days. I decided to hope for the best and mentally put this aside until I really knew. But as hard as I tried, my gut felt sick, and I wasn't able to sleep at all that night because deep down I already knew. Like I said, women are intuitive.

So I decided to tell my husband. I waited until he was in bed watching television. I walked into our bedroom and blurted, "I had the biopsy, and I don't know if it is cancer" as I walked to the adjacent bathroom. He didn't hear me, but at least I could say I told him. I wasn't ready to look anyone in the eye and say it. The entire conversation was one I didn't want to have unless forced to.

"What did you say?" he asked.

"They found a lump at my mammogram," I said. "They biopsied it and I have to wait to see if it is cancer. I feel like it will be a benign tumor, like my mom has had several times."

"They probably caught it early," my husband said. He reminded me that the technology is awesome today, so even if I did have cancer, it surely could be treated. "Let's not worry. You are going to be fine."

As a hockey mom with a senior in high school, I was distracted with our youngest son's team going to the state hockey tournament for his school in Hermantown, Minnesota, where we live. After all, the entire town of Hermantown empties to attend this tournament, and I wanted to be 100 percent focused as a Hawks fan and proud mom. So I knew I was not going to tell anyone, since the topic of cancer didn't go well with the joy of a state tournament. Many things have to wait when you are a hockey parent, and so could cancer.

It sounded so reasonable. Still, I was surprised I could not sleep at night, and I found myself wide awake many nights thinking through the what-ifs. Logically, it was a great plan, and I prayed every night. But when you are the one diagnosed, it takes a while to find your own sense of peace. It may take days or months. For me it took a few years. Time had stopped. The reality of the possibility of being taken out of the game of life had hit me, and I knew that would change everything.

Then the call came. Now, I had definitive results. I wasn't ready to tell anyone, not even my husband. So I kept it to myself for as long as I could. I needed time to process my feelings. I was scared. I was at work as the CEO of an assisted living facilities company where I had become the sole owner just four months earlier. Sitting in my office alone, I answered the call, thinking I would be able to take a deep breath and resume life as I knew it. I was waiting patiently for the doctor to say I had a benign fibroid cyst. But that did not happen. Instead, the doctor said I had cancer, stage 1 invasive ductal carcinoma. I went into solution mode, like I often do as a CEO, and asked what was next. The doctor said I would meet with a surgeon very soon to determine a treatment plan.

After I hung up the phone, I sat numbly in my office. I could not move. I would not be able to easily pretend this was not happening for the rest of the workday. But I put on my best face, like every CEO learns to do. Burying this emotion seemed like the best approach for me as a leader.

Being told I had cancer hit me like a freight train with emotions of past life events. I was caught off guard. Buried emotions resurfaced, bringing back a familiar pain that had gnawed at my chest when they happened.

In only three other moments in my life had time stopped, when I was flooded with such emotion. Suddenly, with these submerged feelings returning, my mind and body began to prepare for a paralyzing feeling I had felt before.

When we face tragedy, emotions are sometimes buried within us at various levels. It is different for everyone, but our bodies, minds, and souls are deeply connected—they remember past trauma to give us fortitude for things to come. As a way of protecting me, my mind went back to those three moments when time had stopped:

1. *January 3, 1997*

After months of bed rest, and then a long labor, our baby was delivered unresponsive. Since this was my second delivery, I was waiting for the baby to be placed on my chest. Instead, the emergency button was pushed, and a team rushed him to the NICU (neonatal intensive care unit). I knew something was wrong because his arms and legs dangled with no reflex.

My mom was crying in the room, and I asked her if the baby was OK. I had been on bed rest since my sixth month of pregnancy. Prior to my induced labor, I had seen a neonatologist weekly, who told me the baby had all the characteristics of Down syndrome.

Could all the medical reports be wrong? I wondered after he was taken to the NICU. I had been advised to read books on Down syndrome children and I chose not to. I would love this child like I loved my first child regardless, so why would I need to label this baby? Instead, I took my own approach and prayed. I prayed that he had his hands and that the medical reports that did not see his fingers would be wrong. I prayed that his bones were correctly formed, and that God would prepare us as parents no matter the outcome.

Throughout the pregnancy, I thought I was having a girl because the experience was very different from my first pregnancy. The babies had different heart rates, and many books I had read correlated baby heart rates with either a boy or a girl. With the first pregnancy, I had terrible acne and I gained 80 pounds. I could not believe it was humanly possible to go from 120 to 200 pounds in nine months. This time around I had no excess weight gain and no acne, so I assumed it must be a girl.

When we had our firstborn, we waited until the birth to know we were having a son. We didn't do the same with our second pregnancy because I was feeling anxious and needed peace of mind.

During a routine ultrasound, the technician told us it was a boy. *Thank God!* I thought. I was relieved, because in my heart I felt the baby would be fine. Our firstborn was huge—he was off the charts for weight, chest, head circumference, and bone measurements. At ten months old he weighed thirty pounds and the doctor told me he had childhood obesity. I cried and called my mother. "Honey, he is healthy and a great eater," she said. "Don't worry, he will grow into his body." And he did. This thirty-pound baby grew to be six feet two . . . and is not obese.

Preparing for the birth of our second son meant getting things ready at work too. At that time, I was an assistant administrator at a nursing home in Duluth, Minnesota. It was a large nursing home, with 247 residents and more than 300 employees. I was the acting administrator, too, so I had more stress than usual because of my dual role.

As with all twenty-four-hour operations, at all times someone in leadership has to be on call for emergencies. Every day, a leader in the organization must be available to resolve issues and concerns from employees, residents, or families of residents. Like most days, I had several meetings booked back-to-back. It was November—three months before my due date—and I was waddling down the hallways. I felt nauseated and had stomach pain but no contractions, and my office assistant advised me to call the doctor. I wanted to get to one more meeting and cross one more thing off the list. Eventually, it got too bad—when I called the doctor, they said to come in immediately.

I was surprised I was in labor this early. My contractions were ten minutes apart. The doctors stopped my labor and told me to immediately stop work and go on bed rest. "Let's hope to get you to your February due date," they said when they gave me medication called terbutaline to stop my labor.

Obviously, there was nothing I could do except return to work and lay out a new plan with the leadership team. Now I would be in bed, and likely not back for several months.

This was 1996, before cell phones. Technology and computerization were not in place like today. Most systems were manual, and offices were stacked with paper everywhere.

I often think now how grateful I am that cell phones did not exist then. This was a period of time when your workday actually stopped when you went home. When my kids were young and I came home, I changed clothes and played with them. We went to the park and played tag. We went exploring and I learned about their days. I was on their time. I thank God that I did not have to manage balancing and triaging all the emails and texts that a twenty-four-hour operation means today.

Perhaps there have been times in life when I have taken myself and life events too seriously. Sometimes my brain can't shut down. After all the years of running twenty-four-hour operations, I have been conditioned to be ready for something—anything—to happen at any time. (Later, when I was having so many unexpected surgeries after my cancer diagnosis, I came to appreciate the role of anesthesia. During surgery my mind could not race or plan multiple projects simultaneously. I would be completely at rest and my mind would slow down. I would joke with the anesthesia team, asking them to make sure they didn't slow me down *too* much. I've never been much of a nap person, so now would be my time to catch up.)

Parents feel certain stressors from time to time. Like every new mom, I had moments when I questioned decisions my husband and I had made. My profession is so highly regulated that I could not take ten years off and then re-enter the field easily, so we decided early on that I would not be a stay-at-home mom. I felt confident I could be a good mom while still working out of the home.

It was a hard enough decision to make as a couple, but it was even harder to be judged by others. I never judged anyone else, and I believe this is a personal decision for every mother. Still, the judgment I received was striking. Once, at a health-care convention, a male colleague in his thirties said to me, "I bet you are excited for your baby to be born." I said yes, and we began some small talk. When I asked if he had kids, too, he told me he did and his wife had chosen to stay home and give up her profession, as she realized she had her whole life to work.

I ended up calling my grandma from a pay phone, tears running down my cheeks. I don't know if it was just hormones, or if that was truly the meanest thing anyone had said to me. But I had to call Grandma Hazel. She had been a stay-at-home mom and I wanted to know if she thought I was making a mistake. "Natalie, God gives us all different talents, and he has given you the ability to do both," she said. "Don't ever listen to nonsense like this. Your mom was a working mom and raised three wonderful kids."

That was all I needed to hear. I knew I was OK if I had her blessing. She was a devout Methodist who had encouraged and supported her son and daughter in college. She had supported her daughter as a stay-at-home mom and her daughter-in-law as a working mom. Now her granddaughter was a working mom. None of this mattered to her. I realized at that moment how amazing she was. "I know your heart, soul, and mind, and it will all be fine, honey," she said. I had unconditional love, and I learned that this would be the most important gift I could have as a young woman. She cried for me that day too.

While we waited for the birth of our second son, our two-year-old would play with cars on my stomach while I was on bed rest. During those months, I listened to Luther Vandross's Christmas album and memorized every song. I did not know who Luther Vandross was, but when I watched him perform on *The Oprah Winfrey Show*, his voice brought me to tears. To this day, his music makes me feel the holiday spirit. The holidays are not the holidays to me without hearing the peacefulness of Luther Vandross. This was a great diversion to watching *Barney*, which our two-year-old loved. We watched *Barney* over and over and I listened to Luther Vandross over and over. Fair, right?

The holidays had passed, and my amniotic fluid levels were getting dangerously high. The baby was floating around and was not positioned down, and the umbilical cord was wrapping around his neck. Ultrasounds showed the baby was at a safe weight for birth, so we set an inducement date for January 3, 1997. As luck would have it, there was a blizzard happening and it was making the roads treacherous in Duluth.

After hours of labor and dilation, the doctor was called. I was hoping the storm did not mean the resident on duty would be the one delivering our baby. I stared at the clock—it was taking forever. Finally, the doctor arrived and I was told to push. The labor was very painful, which I later learned was because my tailbone broke in the process.

I was scared when the baby did not cry after delivery. The baby wasn't put on my chest immediately, so I knew something was wrong. The baby was quickly taken to an incubator. I turned my head to see the baby's arms dangling, his body looking limp. There was commotion everywhere and the baby was taken to the NICU. My husband kissed my forehead and my mom said, "Honey, the baby is alive."

I prayed to God to save our son. I sobbed, my legs shaking uncontrollably because I had lost so much fluid. My mom and husband left to be with the baby, and I was all alone. I wanted them to be with him, yet I was so scared. I had been on an emotional and physical roller coaster for months.

When I finally visited the NICU (neonatal intensive care unit), I felt helpless. Our baby looked gigantic there at seven pounds seven ounces. Some of the other babies were so small and so compromised. Every baby was hooked up to IVs, including our own. He was big, but his lungs were not fully developed, and back then I had not gotten a shot to help this happen. His heart had stopped beating at one point and he did not have a sucking reflex, so nursing was difficult. He would not be able to leave the NICU until he could take in liquids on his own, and I was extremely stressed. Soon I was told the baby did not have Down syndrome.

I had nursed our first baby, and I felt pressure to do the same now. But this time around I had a two-year-old who had spent little time with his mom the past three months because she had been bedridden. I felt torn. My mom sensed it too. "Honey, if you feel you want to bottle-feed the baby, it is fine," she said. "I bottle-fed you and your siblings, and you turned out fine." I knew I needed another woman just to give me permission to bottle-feed. I was tired, and I wanted to be able to care for both kids.

Leaving the NICU was a unique feeling. I had never been in a place like this. There were so many tiny babies. Grandma Hazel had always told me about how my cousin was born in 1969 weighing less than three pounds and went on to be an engineer, so I knew to take it moment by moment. Now was not the time to be weak.

2. October 18, 2014

After spending years of weekends at hockey rinks, my husband and I finally had a date night with two lifelong friends at our river cabin. After going four-wheeling in the woods, we had steak on the grill and wine waiting.

Later that Friday night, we played cards while streaming a game of our twenty-year-old son playing junior hockey in Canada. We laughed at how amazing technology was.

Suddenly, during the game, the action stopped. I saw a hockey player behind the net lying on the ice. The camera zoomed in and I caught a glimpse of what looked like a familiar mustache. I felt sick and helpless. We prayed with our friends, "Please, God, let our son be OK." There was an eerie feeling in the room as the camera panned away from the player and the bench, so we could not figure out who it was. My husband said he didn't think it was our son, but I somehow just knew in my gut. I knew what I had seen.

The game was delayed longer than I had ever seen after years of watching both our sons play hockey. Never had I witnessed a player not moving on the ice for thirty to forty minutes. And when the cameras are not showing the players, you know something is *very* wrong. Fans at the game were throwing blankets on the ice to cover his body. Apparently, the ambulance was in the mountains, and as they waited for it the audience could hear him screaming in pain. The rink had laughing gas, which they used to alleviate some of his pain in the meantime.

Forty-five minutes after the injury, we got the call we had been waiting for. I felt numb and on the verge of throwing up. Despite being someone who can usually talk a mile a minute and speak twenty thousand words a day, I was speechless. The man who called my cell phone said he was the trainer for the Langley Rivermen team, and our son had been hurt on the ice. We quickly learned they were unsure whether it was his hip or femur, and he was being transported to a hospital in Trail, British Columbia.

I felt the cold chill of October air as I walked outside and threw up over and over. My husband's brother, an ER doctor, was at the neighboring cabin and we called him over to be available when the ER doctor called from Canada. The ER doctor later confirmed that our son had a broken femur. Our son was on morphine and was waiting in the hallway until the Canadian government could approve his surgery.

I hoped we could get our son moved by air ambulance to a bigger city such as Vancouver for his surgery, but the physician in Trail said he was not stable enough and they would be unable to relocate him. The surgery would have to be in this remote area. Pain and anxiety overwhelmed me. If his femur moved in the wrong way, it could sever his femoral artery and he could bleed out and possibly die.

The hockey team had another game the next day, Saturday, so the team would be leaving for another city. My husband and I had to figure out a way to get one or both of us on a flight to our son as soon as possible. We left the cabin with nothing and drove home in the middle of the night, frantically searching for flights from Duluth to Trail. I prayed, "Please, God, let him live." My husband got me a flight right away from Duluth to Minneapolis and Minneapolis to Spokane, Washington. I cried the whole way.

I felt delirious from crying and full of anxiety because the clock was ticking down to our son's surgery time, and I did not want him to be there alone. I had planned to rent a car in Spokane and drive the four hours to Trail. As I said my name at the rental counter, the customer representative said, "I'm sorry, but we can't rent you a car." The representative said my driver's license was expired as of September 9. She did not show any care about my situation, which turned me from a normally polite person into a fierce grizzly bear mama. I had visions of jumping over the counter for the keys. My ability to reason was gone.

Utterly panicked, I sobbed at the counter. Other customers tried to help me figure out a plan. Giving up on assistance at the car rental counter, I ran outside and asked a cab driver how much it would cost to drive me to Trail. He looked at me like I was not thinking straight.

"One way?" he asked, and I said yes. "I will have to call and ask," he said.

After ten minutes on the phone, he found out it would be $500, so I said I would go find a cash machine.

"There is one other problem," he said. "Who will pick you up?" The driver told me the taxi service had recently shut down in Trail, and he could only take me as far as the border. I said that was perfect. The cab driver said, "No it's not. We are not allowed to drop you off there without a destination."

"Look, I will walk then," I said.

"You can't do that. It could be dangerous."

I felt like I was in the making of *Planes, Trains and Automobiles*. I was one thread from a nervous breakdown. Then I called my sister-in-law, who lived with her husband four hours away. They quickly boarded their dog and began Operation Rescue Natalie. They drove me four hours through a mountain chain to Trail. I was grateful not to be the one driving because the mountains were nail-biting for me as we weaved around switchback mountains. Thankfully, her husband's race car driving experience came in handy.

As we arrived at the hospital, I could not wait to get to him. All I wanted was to see him, hold him, and hug him. We were directed to his room, which he shared with two other people. The minute I saw him, he smirked, and I just hugged him. Before I had gone into the hospital, my brother had called and said, "Look, I know you are a wreck, but stay strong. He needs to see you not crying right now, as his world is upside down. You can do this."

I sobbed on the phone with him, but as I got to our son's room, I pulled myself together. There was no need to ask, "How are you?" I simply told him that I knew this sucked and I was sorry.

He had had surgery by the time we arrived, and the surgeon told me it was a success. He looked very pale, and it was strange to see a young man with a catheter bag. He had low hemoglobin from losing blood during the surgery. They would watch this carefully because he needed higher hemoglobin to be able to try standing and begin walking before being discharged.

This took a few days, as he was initially on oxygen and simply too weak. He soon showed me his leg and the surgical site. I took photos to send to his uncle, who is a physician, to confirm the surgical site looked OK. He had a long surgical scar area, and a rod had been placed inside his femur. I later learned the rod in his leg was too small to hold his height and weight. So when we returned home he had a new, bigger rod placed in his leg, six months after the initial surgery. While this was less than ideal, I was grateful the first surgeon kept him alive and stabilized him after a severe trauma-related surgery.

My sister-in-law and brother-in-law stayed a few days and then returned back home. I knew I could go day by day before making my own plans to go home. Somehow this small town felt like where I grew up in St. Francis, Minnesota, with kind and neighborly people everywhere. I soon discovered how connected the town was. Everyone knew that a Minnesota boy had been hurt on the ice. The community reached out and helped me in ways that made this tragedy bearable.

The kindness shown to me was unmatched, as I needed rides back to the motel after my family left. One night, someone visiting their own family member at the hospital walked the halls looking for the Minnesota mom. When they found me, they said, "I am going home and can drop you off." This went against all my teachings to not ride with strangers, but circumstances sometimes call for new rules, so off I went. The next night, a housekeeper found me and said her shift was over, so she could bring me home. Another night, I left with the coach of the Trail team himself.

Strangers took us to the airport when our son was strong enough to board a plane to get back to Vancouver. Our son played hockey for a junior team in Langley, British Columbia, and Vancouver was the closest airport. His hockey coaches picked us up and brought us to his billet family home. Billet families host hockey players in their homes while the players play juniors.

The camaraderie within the hockey community is amazing. When something bad happens to a player, people rally together. Before we left the hospital in Trail, the hockey player who had accidentally injured our son visited with his whole team and brought us food. I have always been impressed by the respectful nature of hockey players.

The next day, discharge day, Trail's hockey team owner drove us to the airport. As he drove his SUV onto the tarmac, workers were pushing a manual ramp up to the plane. The plane was surprisingly small—only a ten-passenger. The kindness displayed by the Trail community has been stamped into my brain forever.

Once we landed in Vancouver and got to Langley, his healing would begin. His dreams for Division I hockey were now over, and he was disappointed. No words could change the situation, but I thanked God he was not paralyzed. His billet mom was in Las Vegas when we arrived, so we were at his billet home alone for a few days. Before long, his team came over to visit. I stayed with him for two weeks in Langley until he was strong enough to fly back to Minnesota. I gathered all of his items and packed them in his car, which would now be shipped back to Minnesota. Naturally I forgot to pack the most important items—his multiple hockey sweatshirts. Thankfully, he is accustomed to a mother not known for attention to detail.

Years prior, a mom had told me that you literally feel the pain of your children when you are a parent. "You are as happy as your most unhappy child," she said. Now I got it. Until I felt the horror of fearing I could lose our son at birth, and that I could lose our son to a hockey injury, I never truly understood the love between a mother and a child. After all, this is a child you have loved and cared for with everything you have. Once you hold your child, you can't imagine life without them. This paralyzing feeling is known by moms who have endured miscarriages, life-threatening tragedies, or the death of their child. As a mother, there is an innate feeling to protect your child. Sometimes life events throw curve balls, so as mothers we adjust and recalibrate to the here and now.

3. *September 11, 2001*

As I drove to work in my four-door Subaru sedan, I stopped at the newspaper office in Two Harbors, Minnesota. Inside, people were crying and the room held an eerie feeling. When I asked what had happened, someone said the United States was under attack.

When I got to the nursing home where I worked, fellow employees and I watched the TV in the dining room and cried as we saw people jumping out of burning buildings. *This can't be reality*, I thought. *It has to be a television series.*

Sadly this was the first time I felt a level of indescribable pain from the tragedy of watching desperate people jump to their death. How terrible it had to be to make that choice, and to be unable to say goodbye to their families. I was full of fear and helplessness. Time had stopped again.

I spent the rest of the day frozen to a screen like a robot, watching this tragedy unfold. It made no sense to go back to work as if everything was normal, when nothing felt normal at all. Many of the residents watching TV with me were World War II veterans. "We are at war," one of them muttered. Seeing their tears and the horror in their eyes made me truly comprehend their pain and the sacrifices they had made after Pearl Harbor was attacked.

I never paid close attention to history lessons in school, but sitting with elderly men and women who lived it is the best history lesson I ever had. For me, history classes really started in 1991 when, in my profession to serve the elderly, I began as a licensed nursing home administrator. My career began as an assistant administrator and then administrator in long-term care. Ten years later I started in assisted living as an administrator, and eventually developed a business plan to develop and build small-setting assisted livings. After thirty years of this work, being with people in the last chapter of their life, I have learned what resiliency, hope, and empathy look like. While my life experiences will never compare to the sacrifices they made for my freedom, or the multiple lives lost for my freedom, I developed a deep and profound interest in their life stories. Their stories reinforced for me the importance of knowing how to endure hardship and knowing how to heal.

So when I faced my personal tragedies with my sons, the United States being attacked, and my personal cancer diagnosis, I knew life would march on. Those I had served the past thirty years taught me that. They taught me how to live through hardship and tragedy, as they modeled how to do it with God's grace. When times were tough for me, I would reflect on how many of the seniors I cared for had stood in bread lines during the Great Depression, lost everything, and rebuilt their lives many times, and how they knew that all things are possible with love and God. So through their wisdom, I dropped all feelings of fear and chose faith to direct my path.

Getting my cancer diagnosis triggered many emotions I had stuffed to the back of my brain from trauma I had faced at different moments in life. You may be surprised by how past emotions resurface, and I think it may be because we are all so busy that the emotion never was totally processed when it occurred. If this happens for you, too, it may be helpful to write down your thoughts and feelings so your mind can release some of the data it has stored. If you are like me, your mind may not be in the same place as your emotions, and that is why other life events resurface. So often, we don't want to be preoccupied with negativity, and we want to move on. Our emotions sometimes take longer to process when our mind has put the topic on a back shelf.

Emotions are different for everyone. This new unplanned event generated anxiety and fear in me. The anxiety triggered my mind to remember other events and buried emotions, which my mind had been waiting for my body to process. It was catch-up time. As I began to work through my emotions, I relived past tough times, and I reassured myself that I could be resilient again. This process helped me release the fear that came with hearing the word *cancer,* which is a word no one wants to hear, but we are forced to when diagnosed.

More than ever, now was a time I needed to give my mind positive thoughts, so I surrounded myself with those who had inspired me my entire life. My husband has always been a rock of support in my career, and we jointly did everything for our boys, so I had no concerns with my stability at home. But I knew I also needed my friends and family to hold my hand. As a woman with breast cancer, I was grateful to have friendships with women who were a tremendous sisterhood for me during my cancer surgeries.

Together, these relationships with family and friends

made all the difference in my healing. I had made a plan for my physical healing, but I needed my network for my emotional healing. I am grateful for those unconditional angels in my life. When time stops, or when you are in a time of need, I hope you, too, will have an army of angels at your disposal. If ever you can be an angel for someone else, I promise it will inspire you, and you will gain more than you give each and every time.

You may experience moments where silence from visitors comforts you more than words; a hand held is worth a thousand words.

2 ∾ D-Day

WHEN I GOT THE results of my breast biopsy, my hope while waiting turned to fear. I heard the "c" word, and decisions had to be made. All I could think of was D-Day—the day the Allied powers invaded the beaches of Normandy, France, in 1944. Perhaps this stemmed from years of caring for seniors who served in World War II and hearing their stories. These stories were on my mind, and as I felt my own pain now, somehow I felt their pain too. I was understanding only a piece of their anguish from those years, but suddenly I was feeling fear at levels I had never endured before.

After leaving the hospital the day of the biopsy, I had gone into autopilot mode, blocking the entire event out of my mind. I kept telling myself I had nothing concrete to react to yet. The results were still pending, so why waste these next four to five days crying and not sleeping?

Driving away from the biopsy, my mind had been blank—and I mean *blank*. I passed vehicles and scenery, yet I saw nothing. Nothing mattered. Nothing looked familiar. It was as though the fog of Lake Superior had fully engulfed my entire body. I was scared.

Then I had to go home and do something I am horrible at and pretend everything is fine and tell no one what my day was like. It was hard to know I had a biopsy and only tell my husband. The hard part was communicating on the phone with my mom and friends and consciously trying to sound the same when my mind was a million miles away while waiting for the results. Women are intuitive, so I hoped no one called, especially my mom. She would know by my voice right away that something was wrong. When my friends called, too, I texted them back so they couldn't hear my voice. This bought me some time. Oh, how I wanted to be able to truly buy time for real.

I did not do well pretending to be joyful with my usually high energy level around my husband and our sons. I am not a good liar. My internal compass forces me to tell the truth, so I was at odds with myself. The reality was that I was afraid to have the conversation regarding cancer. I hated—and still hate—the word *cancer* altogether. I did not want to lie, but I did not want to tell them anything either and have them worry. I have spent my life being a caregiver, so there was no point to worrying anyone until facts are known. I would carry the knowledge I had alone until I truly knew. This was emotionally draining.

I could not get my mind to shut down. I did not sleep well. I used Vicks VapoRub, a childhood wonder, in my nose to help relax my mind so I could try to sleep. I was on hyper alert, worrying about my family and our business. At work, I tried to pretend everything was normal too. People asked if I was OK. "Yes, I just have a lot on my mind," I'd say. Clearly, I was not a good actress.

My biopsy results arrived on February 26, 2015, while I was at work. Thankfully, when I got the call, I was by myself. I listened with a sick feeling in my stomach as the voice on the other end said what no one wants to hear: "You have cancer." I know there was more conversation than that, but I was too numb to remember any of it.

It was the first time in my life that I had no response. What was there to say? I just cried. The flood gates opened. I wasn't really shocked—my anxiety had already been imagining the worst. "Smile and make the best of any situation" was what I was taught as a young girl. Now that motto would be tested.

I spent many hours thinking about the "right" way to communicate the message of having cancer. Prior to a cancer diagnosis, I would often talk about women's health issues with my mom or girlfriends. This was different. So, when the biopsy came back with a cancer diagnosis, I told only my husband for the first week or more. Then later, as I was ready, I began telling others in a planned order: our sons, parents, siblings, extended family, friends, and those on my leadership team at work. I also called my pastor and asked for prayers. Once I had said it to everyone, I found a new level of peace.

But now what? I wanted to go to our youngest son's state high school hockey tournament and enjoy it all and never talk about cancer. And that's what we did. My husband and I decided we would tell the boys after the hockey season ended.

I was extremely emotional at the tournament. It was the senior year for many other moms, so my tears blended in with the crowd. I cried when the national anthem was played and the band came out. I cried when our son's picture was on the big screen as they called his name. I cried when the entire community cheered for the team. And still, I did the Hawk dance with the band and enjoyed every single moment of the tournament. I was with our community, and we were watching our kids play a game we loved. Life was good. Big decisions could come after hockey. Sometimes life just has to wait, and I've learned as a mom that it waits for hockey many times.

While all of this was going on around me, I was still processing the diagnosis. How could I make everything work? My doctors had recommended I have surgery within one month, but I had so many roles to play: wife, mom, and employer. I had four weeks to figure out a plan to put everything in place before surgery. At work, I had more than 400 employees and 350 seniors entrusted to my care, and soon I would be away from the operation for six to eight weeks.

One month is not enough time to put together a plan when you are talking about surgery. I have approached many things in life with a plan A and a plan B, and sometimes I just wing it, but this was different. Usually I know when I have scheduled vacations, so I can plan ahead. My longer absences, such as my pregnancies, had been planned with more advanced notice. But this of course was unplanned. Who plans for cancer?

Soon my stress was going to become the stress of my family and business. My mind felt like hamsters running nonstop in a Habitrail. I had a lot to figure out fast, and I did not know how this would happen. Time forced my hand, and I had to start telling people sooner than I wanted to. I had to protect everyone who depended on me to the best of my ability. I ended up taking out a $300,000 credit line for the business. As the CEO, I had an active role in community relations and marketing efforts to ensure sufficient admissions in our settings. There was no one to replace me, so I needed to protect the business in the event admissions and subsequently revenue declined in my absence.

The optimistic side of my personality kept reminding me that while I had invasive ductile carcinoma in my left breast, it was stage 1. When my mind went into solution mode, I naturally turned to Google, as does every patient diagnosed with cancer. I am not sure whether the Google world of research comforted or scared me more. Ignorance can be bliss at certain stages in life. After all, I could not change where I was at this point. But somehow, my cancer diagnosis wasn't like anything else. So when physicians told me I was lucky this was just stage 1, part of me agreed. On the other hand, this was still cancer, and no other diagnosis seems to receive a grading system, especially with a diagnosis so closely associated with death.

As I reviewed my biopsy information, I researched what I could before my next physician appointments. I felt confident the cancer had been caught early and that I would be a relatively simple case. From my research, my options seemed to be either:

1. A lumpectomy, where the cancerous tumor in the left breast would be removed, followed by daily radiation for a number of weeks, then followed by hormone therapy.

2. A double mastectomy, followed by hormone therapy. Some women elect a double mastectomy to eliminate all

future risks of more breast cancer. Others choose it to avoid radiation as part of their treatment plan.

My first appointment post-diagnosis was with a surgeon. As I listened to my surgeon review my biopsy, which included nothing found in my lymph nodes, the surgeon advised I get a lumpectomy with radiation and hormone therapy. I asked if I was able to have a double mastectomy. Hesitating, the physician said, "Yes, but there is no advantage to a double mastectomy. A lumpectomy is just as effective." I went home to think about it. I often wonder why I was not presented with both options until I asked.

I had reservations about a lumpectomy because a friend of mine, also in her forties, had the same cancer in the same breast, stage 0. She elected to have a lumpectomy with radiation, but a few months later cancer showed up in the other breast, and she elected to have a double mastectomy. She had told me how hard radiation was for her and it became a major worry for me. My friend was also a licensed nursing home administrator who ran twenty-four-hour operations in assisted living communities. She had a level of responsibility similar to mine, and we both knew how difficult it is to have the CEO of any organization out for a significant period of time. She was a great resource to share her journey with me when I was in decision-making mode.

After reviewing my options with my husband, family, friends, and several professionals, I elected to have a double mastectomy. I'd played enough tug-of-war with my mind to know that I wanted a level of peace that I would get only from a double mastectomy. That would mean I could put breast cancer behind me and move on without fear.

When I scheduled my surgery, I had a vacation to Mexico planned following the state hockey tournament with a few close friends and their sons. My physician said to enjoy the trip and that we would do the surgery at the end of April 2015.

The conversations had to happen, so I put on my big girl pants and made it happen. As I began to tell others I had cancer, there was no set script. It was pure raw emotion with tears every time. It might seem easy, but for me telling people I had cancer did not ever feel right. It was scary and awful. I did not want to tell them, but I did not want to keep secrets either. And, as a modest person, I really did not want to talk about cancer, least of all breast cancer. But the conversations had to happen, so I put on my big girl pants and made it happen.

My mom knows my tone of voice. I always say when I am sick that I am glad she lives in Florida because she can tell in my eyes if I am not well. It's easier to tell her a fib from a distance. But there is no way to fib about cancer. When I called her, I rattled off the facts as they were. It was hard to hear my mom cry—she wanted to take away my pain. We cried together and I tried to say it would all be great because we caught it early. My mom was as overwhelmed as I was. She simply wished she and my dad still lived closer to me.

For the first time, I understood how she felt. Now that I was a mother, I understood what it felt like knowing your child has health issues. Regardless of how old you are as a parent, you are always thinking of your children.

As a mom of boys, I wondered how I would bring this topic up. I did not want them to hear about my breast cancer from someone else. I decided to say it like every other conversation—matter-of-factly. They were eighteen and twenty years old, no longer young kids.

So after dinner one night, I told them what was happening. I can still remember where they were sitting in the living area off our kitchen.

I figured the last thing boys want to discuss is their mother's breasts, so I told them I had had a biopsy of my chest wall, which found a small tumor that needed to be removed. But I hadn't factored in the instant availability of the internet. Moments later, while still sitting in front of the television, they spoke. They asked me if this was breast cancer, and I said yes. With my boys, our conversations are always short. Honestly, that made it easier. They had only one question. They asked me, "Are you going to be OK?" I said what all moms say, and that was yes, of course. For the first time, our roles were reversed, and they were worried about me.

Once I told more people, natural responses followed: *Have you had a second opinion? Will you be at the place that can give you the best treatment plan?* I assured everyone that I truly felt I had little to worry about because this should be a relatively easy procedure. At least, that was how I was looking at it.

Having the option to have no chemo or radiation felt great to me. Because of that, it was easy to convince people not to worry about me. They were just concerned about how I would balance everything, as they know my personality and how I don't like to drop the ball. With cancer, things would be a little different. Unlike with a pregnancy, I did not have nine months to plan for a work transition time.

When it was time to tell my work team what was happening, I gathered everyone in our corporate office. The mood was somber. I took my typical spot at the head of the table, just like John Sr. on *The Waltons*. This time, my message was short. I didn't ramble like usual. "I have breast cancer," I said simply. Then I cried, because I was worried about the business and the added stress my departure would potentially create for my team.

The team was strong, and I knew they would work together to do their best during my absence. What I still didn't know for sure was how my surgery and recovery would go. I was also counting on strength and teamwork to get me through it all.

You will recognize that bad things happen to good people. Adversity is something we will all face at one time or another.

3 ❧ Choosing Where to Receive Care

S OME PEOPLE ASKED IF I had thought about going to the Twin Cities or to the Mayo Clinic in Rochester, Minnesota, for medical treatment. I hadn't, for two reasons. First, I had been a patient for more than twenty-five years at the same medical system in Duluth and had had excellent outcomes there in orthopedics, ENT, urology, neurology, and allergy. So I had a comfort level that had been established over twenty-five years. My second reason was the convenience of local medical treatment. My husband and boys could be closer to me when I had my surgery. My husband worked at the hospital so he would be able to come see me while still maintaining his work schedule during my surgery and any follow-up appointments.

Even though I've spent my life in health care, I did not fully understand what I needed for breast cancer treatment. In the initial moments of post-diagnosis shock, I completely entrusted my care to the hands of my health-care team where I had received care for decades.

In addition, as a leader of my own business, I believed I should trust the leadership team of my medical care in the same way I had been entrusted with the lives of the frail and elderly by families to receive care from my employees. Without trust, you can't find a place of peace. Plus, what kind of leader would I be if I did not practice what I preach?

Hindsight is always 20/20. Now that it is 2021 and I am more than five years removed from the initial shock of my diagnosis, things are clearer to me. I based my decision about which surgeon to use for my breast cancer on past successes from physicians in other specialty departments. I regret that decision.

My cancer experience ended up being radically different than the six- to eight-week leave of absence I expected. In a perfect world, surgeries and procedures go as planned. But that is not always the reality—complications occur from time to time. When that happens, it is critical for every patient to know the following:

- Which physician will be following you?
- Which physician will be taking the lead of your care?
- When will surgery be set up?
- How is the patient handled when things do not go as planned? Is your primary physician updated as part of your care plan team? As a patient, you may be like me and assume everything will be OK. This was a hard lesson to learn in my own health care and leadership as well. The true defining qualities of leadership show up when things do not go as planned.
- Who will be your advocate? Who will be in your room with you at the hospital to make sure your blood pressure is not taken on the arm where lymph nodes were taken

from? Who will know your normal blood pressure? Who will make sure you have compression stockings on your calves if you are bedridden?

• Who will make sure you have anticoagulant therapy, such as heparin, to prevent blood clots if you are bedridden for days?

• Who will make sure your pain is under control?

I now know the importance of a backup plan like this before *any* surgery. We can't assume a surgery will be without complications. This was what made me vulnerable. I almost died from complications, not breast cancer. It never crossed my mind, and now I believe a checklist is wise for us all at any age.

I believe many systems of basic communication broke down in my situation. After I had my mastectomy, I had pain in the noncancerous side and communicated this to the general surgeon, and it was dismissed. I had very low blood pressure documented with the oncologist after the mastectomy, and it was dismissed. Low blood pressure is one sign of sepsis. Pain in a surgical area is another sign of sepsis in the first thirty days after a surgery.

Following my double mastectomy, I assumed everything I felt was just part of the experience of that surgery. After all, I had never had a double mastectomy. I expected to have pain, and I had seen several physicians following the surgery who had access to my current concerns and past medical history. Since my medical team was not concerned, I kept silencing my innate gut instinct. This gut instinct is what I believe is our God-given personal alarm system. I believe we all have this gut instinct that tells us something is just not right. This alarm system within us keeps asking questions when answers don't match how we feel or what we know as our medical history.

I was hospitalized for the second time for a sepsis diagnosis fewer than thirty days from the initial mastectomy. This then resulted in one of the expanders in my left breast being removed related to a severe infection area. I would be hospitalized for a third time just days after my hospital discharge for sepsis diagnosis/expander removal. On my third admission, I had severe calf pain, which was the same feeling as when I had a blood clot in my other calf years prior following a knee surgery. This time, following an ultrasound, no blood clot was found, and I was diagnosed with CRPS (Complex Regional Pain Syndrome). When I googled this, I learned it was rare, with fewer than 200,000 cases in the United States per year. I also learned there is no cure, and it is chronic, which means the pain could last forever. This was my final straw, the point at which I was strong enough to use my gut instinct and press for a second opinion.

This would mean signing a release for all of my medical records for me to bring to the Mayo Clinic in Rochester, Minnesota. It also allowed me to have my records to review myself, as I had many questions and many opinions about what had gone wrong.

Now I could confirm the facts and establish timelines and connect the dots of what happened on what date. I was disillusioned by how many details had been missed, so I decided to write this book to help others know what to look for.

In what would be the start of extensive complications

and setbacks following my double mastectomy surgery, I was admitted to the hospital thirty days afterward with a life-threatening infection known as sepsis. When I arrived in the emergency room (ER) less than thirty days after my mastectomy, the on-call physician for the plastic surgery department was not the plastic surgeon who had done my original surgery. Nevertheless, without having seen me before, they did the admitting paperwork to get me onto the hospital's admitting floor in the middle of the night. To make matters worse, my chart with my original plastic surgeon may not have been reviewed at all, because it was stored off-site in a separate, unaffiliated building. When I was hospitalized, a hospitalist rounded to see me instead of my internal medicine physician or my primary plastic surgeon.

Even though I was in a hospital I had used many times over the last twenty-five years, somehow no one there had read my medical records. These clearly noted many times that I had one prior blood clot, a surgery-related clot following a knee meniscus repair. At a time in history when electronic medical records exist, I was shocked. Systems of basic communication had broken down. I was truly vulnerable for the first time in my health-care experience. All my years of understanding medical records, medical terminology, and triaging care were of no value—I was too sick to monitor myself. I was too sick to ask the questions my primary physicians would have asked if they had been present. My husband worked for the hospital in IT—he knew how the system works and he, too, had entrusted my care to the professional team.

While reviewing my medical records after the fact, I was

shocked by how I had fallen through the cracks. Multiple professionals had not questioned the following details in my chart, beginning in March 2015 with my biopsy and through my subsequent surgeries:

- Patient bedbound approximately thirty days post-surgery
- Abnormal EKG
- Lymph nodes removed in left armpit, therefore no blood draws or blood pressures can be done on left arm
- IV moved to multiple areas on right side, ultimately ending in right foot (I had no expander on my calf to prevent deep vein thrombosis (DVT), or blood clots)
- Patient did not have compression device on calves after surgery, possibly related to IV placed in right foot
- Patient did not have low-dose blood thinner, such as heparin, which may have been a possible treatment option and common protocol for those diagnosed with sepsis to prevent a blood clot
- Patient had a history of one blood clot from a prior knee surgery with long-term implications. This resulted in post-thrombotic syndrome, a long-term complication of a blood clot (as a patient, I had told health-care professionals multiple times prior to surgery about my need for a blood thinner).

In the five years since my ordeal with complications including sepsis, I have talked with many others with breast cancer who suffered setbacks. Those who had phenomenal experiences had care teams with a physician as the definitive leader when things went wrong. They did not have multiple physicians playing the blame game, but rather a clear path of who was in charge of the current medical need. The physician-patient relationship is vital, and ultimately someone needs to explore what happened when things go wrong. This is what all leaders do. I remember that before every surgery I signed a form stating that I was aware that possible outcomes included death. If you don't sign the form, the surgery will not happen. Patients have no other option but to sign the form. This has made me reevaluate our system, because patients are basically consenting to bad outcomes, including their own deaths.

In addition, I have wondered why our surgeons and anesthesiologists wouldn't have breathalyzer tests done as a part of shift reports. If an element of risk that includes the possibility of death exists, it made me wonder about an analogy with the risk and responsibility commercial pilots have. Since a plane could crash and ultimately kill passengers if a pilot was impaired, I know I am comforted that there are systems in place prior to flights. Would a physician ever be scheduled or randomly tested for drugs/alcohol when reporting to hospitals on-call, or would surgeons/anesthesiologists?

The *Journal of the American Medical Association* noted in 2013 that alcohol, narcotic, and sedative addictions are as common among physicians as the general public. Although I have no reason to believe I was cared for by an impaired physician or nurse, it did make me ask questions about protocols and the reality of being 100 percent vulnerable.

When I was diagnosed, I was convinced I was low-risk and did not review any of the websites related to breast cancer. Once I had surgical setbacks, I began asking questions

I wished I had asked initially. But the train had left the station. Now, years later, I have been able to use multiple websites and research sites to get myself to a place of healing. Writing is therapeutic for me and allows me to share and to educate others so that solutions can be found. We can all learn from what goes wrong for others. There are life lessons everywhere, and my situation is just one example. It is a teaching moment.

You will realize that life is given and taken away. Living requires the acceptance of both.

4 ∾ No Peace of Mind; a Piece of Hell

FTER MY DIAGNOSIS, I considered other options that would require traveling two to five hours from home, but I elected to stay in Duluth, Minnesota, for my double mastectomy surgery. I felt confident that the hospital where I had been a patient several times could successfully treat me for stage 1 cancer. I had noticed that the Breast Center had a plaque on the wall stating they were a regional breast center, with prestigious award recognition, when I went to my first appointment to see the general surgeon. Now they are part of the National Accreditation Program for Breast Centers, or NAPBC. Since I have not been there for years, I don't know if they still have the plaque on the wall as a regional breast center.

I assumed that a regional breast center specialized in breasts. After all, I was moved through the regional breast center by the breast center navigator, who coordinated everything. As it turned out, my surgeon was a general surgeon who also did appendix, hernia, and various other surgeries. I did not understand this until after my surgery was over and I ended up with an infection related to the double mastectomy surgery. I felt betrayed, shocked, and angry. I had chosen to remain close to home based on my confidence in the regional breast center award recognition on the wall when I went to see the general surgeon.

As a newly diagnosed cancer patient, the designation "regional breast center" meant to me that my surgeon would have performed higher volumes of breast surgeries. My assumption was wrong, and I did not have a surgeon who focused on only or mostly breast cancer. I have no idea how many surgeries like mine the surgeon had completed prior to mine. My assumption that practice makes perfect was not relevant in this situation.

Again, hindsight is 20/20. I should have gone to Healthgrades.com and reviewed each physician on my care team's specialty and how frequently they performed the surgery I needed. I should have asked friends who had mastectomy surgeries about their experiences and which physicians they recommended. This is where networking and talking with others is more valuable than blind trust and not sharing your diagnosis. I could have asked for suggestions from others on Facebook or reviewed sites like Reddit to get information and feedback, but that never crossed my mind.

Multiple aspects of my experience of post-surgery complications were deeply disturbing to me. I hadn't asked enough questions before my surgery, but as soon as I became infected after the first surgery, I sure did. I called the hospital numerous times. I was told they did not track infection rates. I left numerous messages. I called the plastic surgeon to ask the same question and was told the same thing.

I reviewed my medical records and wrote a letter to the hospital administrator to let them know that every physician dismissed my low blood pressure during the first thirty days after surgery at office visits, before I was admitted for sepsis. My letter also let them know that multiple phone calls were never returned to answer my questions. I felt that the top administration should review these physicians and my chart to determine how basic medical interventions had been missed. I wanted to make sure my situation would never be the reality for another woman with a double mastectomy. In addition, I wanted the administration to recognize the immense health setbacks and financial implications for the patient. I felt there should be some accountability and believed the hospital should compensate me for the errors that resulted in additional surgeries and years of added personal financial expenses.

The hospital responded with what appeared to be a standard canned response. Having spent my life in health care, this was surprising. I contacted my insurance company and reviewed every item that was coded by the hospital for billing, and every item the physicians and hospital were paid for. The hospital and physicians were paid the same amount they would have been paid for a perfect outcome. I had to meet my deductible each year and also pay large bills for my percentage for multiple surgeries that could have been avoided.

I was surprised to see that my hospital discharge papers indicated that I had sepsis, but the insurance billing and coding did not list this. I called my health insurance company and asked if they tracked sepsis occurrences for those hospitalized and how many patients are infected thirty days post-mastectomy surgery, but they didn't track those numbers at all. I began to wonder what drives positive patient outcomes for those who are under the Medicare eligibility age. What systems are in place to track infections post-surgery? Where is the accountability, and where is the education for the patient on sepsis signs and symptoms?

Hospitals are reimbursed for much of their work by the federal Medicare program. They must hit certain quality benchmarks in order to receive the complete reimbursement from Medicare. If this does not occur, or if someone on Medicare is hospitalized within thirty days of the surgery, a reimbursement penalty may occur. This means the hospital will be reimbursed less than the total possible reimbursement amount, so there is a strong incentive for positive outcomes. If you are not on Medicare, the reimbursement will be 100 percent regardless of the outcome to you, the patient. If you are not on Medicare, the reimbursement from private health insurance is *not* tied to patient outcomes.

This is why I want to shed some light on this topic. It seemed illogical to me that sepsis cases would not be tracked, since it kills more than 270,000 people in the US and 8,000,000 people worldwide annually. Many of these people are under sixty-five years of age and have a future they hope to live.

After caring for seniors my entire life, I was surprised to learn no tracking of negative outcomes occurs for patients under sixty-five. I asked the insurance company if the physicians and hospitals were paid 100 percent of the allowable billable charges, even if the charges resulted from negative outcomes from a prior surgery. The answer was yes. I wondered how much additional revenue is generated for hospitals because of preventable errors. If outcomes were measured, and payment was tied to those outcomes, would things be different? I believe the answer is yes. If you are over sixty-five and on Medicare, your provider should be paid less for negative outcomes that Medicare believes were preventable.

With every question I asked my original surgical team, I felt as though the physicians were playing the blame game. After a while, I knew I would never get a clear answer. Maybe I expected too much. Physicians refer patients to each other and share interest in being protected, and there is a professional bond.

I also realized that I had never seen an ad in the paper or on television from an attorney asking the public if they had been neglected or maltreated in a hospital. Yet working in assisted living and nursing home settings, I have seen these ads frequently for years. I began to wonder if there was a gap of missing data for people under sixty-five years of age who acquired sepsis within thirty days post-surgery. I felt as though, as a forty-eight-year-old in the hospital, my life did not matter. If I was sixty-five and on Medicare, the hospital would likely track a sepsis outcome related to a surgery in the first thirty days.

I also wondered whether surgery patients should be counted as vulnerable adults to encourage more account-ability for their treatment. The status of vulnerable adult generally refers to those eighteen years and older who receive certain care services from a qualified provider or, regardless of services received, those who possess physical, mental, or emotional infirmity or dysfunction. It can also refer to one who is unable to protect themselves against significant harm or exploitation.

As a bedbound surgical patient under anesthesia, I would describe myself as situationally equally vulnerable. Vulnerability should not apply only to seniors and people with certain disabilities. A person is vulnerable when they are unconscious, very ill, or undergoing surgery. Everyone's life matters and should be treated with special care, whether or not they are sixty-five and older, and through all their days.

It also mattered to me that if I had died, my death certificate would not have told the true story. Because I had cancer, it would have likely referenced a cancer complication. However, it would never state the complications that were likely preventable, such as an infected expander from my initial surgery, which resulted in sepsis and also a missed blood clot. This felt like a lie and haunted me and was a large part of why I decided to tell the whole story myself. I knew my outcome should never have happened—and numerous physicians who reviewed my chart agreed. Not one of the involved physicians audited my chart to find out what went wrong, what could have been done differently, or what was missed, and not one documented the sepsis and blood clot for quality measures.

For healthy adults with no outlying factors, like myself, reasonable quality monitoring for physicians and hospitals should be automatic. Basic quality-check systems should be in place to prevent infections and blood clots. Hospitals have other basic systems in place, like assuring my wristband was scanned every time anyone came into the room to give me medication or take a supply for a dressing change, which likely generated a charge. This makes patients feel like a billable object. It seems reasonable that professionals could be auditing for outcomes as well.

I knew sepsis and blood clot prevention were not new topics. So I was very curious to read every article I could on the topics of hospital protocols to prevent sepsis and blood clots. I found numerous articles and research papers on both topics by googling the following sets of words:

- Preventing sepsis post-surgery
- Preventing blood clots post-surgery
- Does sepsis increase risk for blood clots
- Treatment standards for blood clots
- Sepsis related blood clots
- Hospital protocols to prevent sepsis

During this research, I found the information from Johns Hopkins University to be very informative. I learned that many initiatives at hospitals are focused on reducing instances of sepsis and blood clots through early detection. Dr. Elliott Haut from Johns Hopkins has written many articles about this. It involves basic prevention practices for hospitalizations and ER visits, such as low-dose heparin, using proper compression devices on the patient's calves, and compression socks. Unfortunately, this was not my experience.

After I decided to have a double mastectomy, I focused

on the reconstruction part of the recovery, which involved the plastic surgeon. The initial surgery involved two surgeons. The first surgeon completed the double mastectomy. Then, once complete, the plastic surgeon entered the surgery room to complete the procedure. As I mentioned, I did not research the surgeon who would do the mastectomy portion. I figured it could not be that hard to cut and scoop out breast tissue. This was a mistake, as I now realize this is a specialty that requires precision too.

The plastic surgeon then inserted expanders into my breast area and sewed me up. The expanders are temporary plastic devices that help the area expand to make room for implants at a later date. They are filled with fluid weekly, and it takes months before you are ready for the implants.

After the surgery, I asked my plastic surgeon at a follow-up appointment why one of my breasts was discolored and not healing like the other breast. I assumed there would be some bruising, but I was puzzled about why the noncancerous side looked so different and appeared bruised. Matter-of-factly, the surgeon used the analogy of the rind of an orange. He explained that sometimes the general surgeon goes too deep and takes too much breast tissue out of one breast. I was told there was nothing that could be done when the plastic surgeon entered to insert the expanders. I could not believe I was listening to an orange analogy about my breasts. I wondered why the plastic surgeon continued to insert the expander and close me up, fully knowing too much tissue was taken. "Now," the plastic surgeon stated, "we will hope the tissue on your noncancerous side does not die." Tissue without a strong blood supply can die. This was not bruising, as I had assumed.

The surgeon did not mention any risk of sepsis or other life-threatening concerns. I later learned that if the tissue dies, it becomes a perfect environment for an infection to brew, which can often lead to sepsis. Sepsis often leads to blood clots, and the surgery train continues. This is exactly what happened to me. The double mastectomy was a failure. The initial surgery resulted over the next several years in several more surgeries, stress on my body, wound care, and endless healing, all related to an infection resulting from the double mastectomy. These negative outcomes could have been prevented.

I will never really know exactly what went wrong. The plastic surgeon had taken photos of me before my surgery, so it was known my breasts were not originally the same size. I wondered if the surgeons had carefully analyzed the actual amounts of tissue "scooped" out of each breast. I knew what my body looked like prior to the double mastectomy, but now I wasn't sure what to expect with surgical healing on my breasts. I now know that if you lose blood supply the tissue will die, and infection can create a sepsis storm in your body.

In the first two weeks following my mastectomy, I had very low blood pressure readings at routine clinic visits. This was a red flag, since I was in the window of fewer than thirty days since my first surgery. As I neared the thirty-day post-surgery mark, my body suddenly became weak, and I was re-hospitalized due to sepsis. Suddenly, my right chest wall had significant holes in my chest that showed the surgical mesh, a material placed during surgery to help healing. These holes tunneled to my ribcage, leaving disturbing visuals. The open wounds would later heal to have tremendous scar tissue in a layered pattern of thick scar tissue. This distortion of my body left me feeling extremely botched, like something very poorly done. I did not look human. I had a left breast area with an expander and the nipple was two inches higher than it was located prior to surgery. The right breast area had no expander and open wounds from an infected and removed expander with no nipple. As the wounds closed on the right breast area, the scar tissue created tight, rigid lines on my ribs. This rigidness made it painful to breathe and move and was very sensitive to touch.

My mind continued to wonder what went on the day of my surgery. I had so many questions: Who looks into things when surgeries go wrong? Are there cameras in the operating rooms for a medical director to review if a complaint occurs? Does anyone audit the surgeries? Was there video of the exact tissue amounts taken out and weighed from each breast when my biopsies were performed? If I elected to have my surgery videotaped, would I be able to do this? What could I reasonably expect?

I called JCAHO, the Joint Commission on Accreditation of Health Care Organizations, and the organization that accredits hospitals. I found all the information on jointcommission. org and began to educate myself. The Joint Commission is considered the gold standard for health care. Specialty-trained health-care professionals who are experts in their field visit hospitals to review how their staff do the following:

- Provide a safe environment for your care
- Educate you about the risks and options for your diagnosis and treatment

- Protect your rights as a patient, including your right to privacy
- Evaluate your condition before, during, and after diagnosis and treatment
- Protect you against infection
- Plan for emergency situations

When I contacted the Joint Commission, they asked me to fill out a new patient safety event or concern online. When filling out this form online, you are asked to outline your concerns. I did just that, and I signed my name so the hospital could do quality assurance on my case. When I followed up on the status of my complaint, I was told on a phone call with the Joint Commission that my case was closed. They had determined that there were no concerns to be investigated and nothing would be done. At least this is how I interpreted it. My formal complaint asked them to review several questions with the hospital, including why I was not given heparin with a sepsis diagnosis, and why standard care practices were not done for me to prevent a blood clot. The Joint Commission sent me no details of any action taken, nor did anyone contact me.

I asked JCAHO if they had received complaints about this or any other hospital, and the answer was yes, but they were not allowed to reveal how many. When I asked if JCAHO tracked post-surgery infection rates for mastectomies, the representative on the phone told me to ask my hospital. But I had already done that, to no avail. So I felt deflated and at another dead end.

Next I reached out to the Minnesota Hospital Association

(MHA). I wanted to inquire about the health-care system's double standards for caring for vulnerable adults in a hospital versus a nursing home. It was disturbing to me that no one monitors data if someone dies of sepsis or a blood clot at age forty-eight. Hospitals decide their own quality indicators, the MHA representative said. I kept asking myself, Wouldn't a hospital or surgeon want to know how many of their patients have sepsis or are hospitalized after the first surgery? This seemed like a basic quality measure that should be tracked.

As the months continued, I felt like Erin Brockovich, determined to solve a mystery of why people were dying too young. As patients move through the medical system, trying to determine the best path for their care and services, how does one determine what quality indicators to use for hospitals and physicians? Are quality indicators and surgery outcomes tracked at satellite independent surgical centers who partner with a hospital? If complications arise and a hospital-acquired infection occurs, why don't we hear more about these statistics?

Sepsis is a costly and deadly issue across the country. According to the National Institute of General Sciences, one million people develop sepsis annually, and 13 to 30 percent (about 270,000 people) die of it annually. I was shocked to learn that one in three hospital deaths are from sepsis. The Centers for Disease Control and Prevention (CDC) has multiple initiatives on their website that note sepsis as a significant concern for all patients. Patients are often not given information on sepsis on their patient discharge summary. Millions of sepsis diagnoses occur annually, and this has a significant price tag for treatment whether Medicare or private health insurance pays the bill.

When I went into surgery, I planned for success. I am an eternal optimist, and that mentality has generally served me well in my life. Even in perfect situations, it is better to pre-plan about plans A, B, and C. I thought my worst-case scenario would be eight weeks out of work versus six weeks out of work. I was way off and ended up with plan F. Once sepsis occurs, your healing process takes months. In my case, wounds had to be packed for months, and I would end up having eight total surgeries between 2015 and 2020.

I soon discovered Sepsis Alliance, an organization with several people who have stories of surviving sepsis and several stories of those who did not survive sepsis. I cried when I clicked on the "Faces of Sepsis™," as I could feel their pain. I suddenly realized how sick I really was following my infection from the double mastectomy and how lucky I was to be alive. I reached out to a board member and could not wait to just hear her story myself. I realized many of my symptoms during the healing process and lingering symptoms were likely associated with the sepsis diagnosis. These included difficulty sleeping and PTSD with anxiety and panic attacks that did not subside until I switched from the original health-care provider where the sepsis was diagnosed. It was helpful to realize others experienced the same emotions. After hours of reading about this nonprofit, I was moved to want to help educate as many people as possible about the signs and symptoms of sepsis. I loved their campaign "It's about TIME™." The pneumonic reminds people about major symptoms of sepsis to watch out

T = Temperature
I = Infection
M = Mental state
E = Extremely ill

for: T = is your temperature higher or lower than your baseline? I = is your surgical site or injured area showing any signs of redness or infection? M = is your mental state changing—do you feel foggy or confused? And E = do you feel extremely ill, with severe pain or shortness of breath? This acronym would have helped me. I had every single letter happening to me, yet had no clue it could be sepsis.

Now I had the opportunity to try and share my story, to assure that others could learn and have knowledge I wish I had then. After all, if you are like me, you may know someone who has died of sepsis or come close to death from sepsis. This is something that affects all ages. As Sepsis Alliance works hard on their education initiatives, I will do my part and offer a percentage of the book sale proceeds to this nonprofit.

Several people I have spoken with who had breast cancer also faced multiple setbacks, and some faced serious infections too. And this is just in Duluth, Minnesota. It is too easy to dismiss a sepsis diagnosis, blood clot, or another complication as a result of a cancer diagnosis. To date, the data around these cases is still not available for patient or public review. In comparison, if a patient dies of COVID-19 at any age, data is being tracked regardless of whether the patient had underlying pre-existing medical conditions such as Alzheimer's, congestive heart failure, lung diseases, obesity, or other relevant conditions. We know the ability to track reasons for death at all ages is possible, because the government is requiring hospitals to do it now for COVID-19. As a reference, COVID-19 has killed 3.3 million people as I write this, and sepsis kills 8 million worldwide annually.

Another difficult aspect of my experience was the frequent taking of photos of my breasts. Before my first surgery in 2015, I had pre-op pictures taken—it was my first nude photo shoot. My anxiety about taking nude photos was almost as overwhelming as my cancer diagnosis. As a modest person, I had a huge struggle ahead, as breast photos were taken throughout the process. I cried most of these days. These days were worsened by the fact that my post-surgery breasts did not turn out to look like any of the plastic surgery photos I had been shown. The book of before and after photos made me feel excited and hopeful for my reconstruction. But reality set in after my mastectomy, and I was unprepared for how it felt to see pictures of myself nude with no boobs, and with new scars. It was such a strange feeling to undress in front of a camera. I felt dirty. I did not feel like a lady. I did not even feel like a woman.

Each time I had to undress and put on a hospital gown, it reminded me that everything had changed. Even after it was really truly over, sometimes the disappointment still hits me. I still cry, or I laugh and refer to my new breasts as two bocce balls. I never got the cleavage I had hoped for, and my new breasts do not have nipples. Instead, they have scars and tattoos.

I decided it was time to get my first tattoos to create the illusion of a nipple, so I could feel complete. I elected to fly to New Jersey, a few years into my surgical procedures, to see an expert in nipple tattoos for women with breast cancer. My brother and dad met me and drove me to Vinnie Myers's tattoo office. I decided to listen to my brother, who had many tattoos, and go to the best of the best for my nipple tattoos. I have never regretted that decision. To this day, I have many physicians and other breast cancer patients who want to learn about Vinnie Myers and the work he does for women. This was a trip worth taking, and the professionalism and sensitivity shown by this man was truly amazing.

I have learned to see my scars and the tattoos as reminders that life went on for me—and it truly did. My journey may not have ended with the new boobs I had hoped for, but life moves on. Boobs don't have to matter that much.

You may realize that your setback is really becoming a setup for great things to happen in your life that you never anticipated or expected.

5 ∾ Be Careful What You Wish For

MY LEFT BREAST (CANCEROUS side) was larger than my right breast (non-cancerous side) and my plastic surgeon said the implants would look very natural and that I had great skin for surgery. Apparently, this was referencing the elasticity in my skin. I elected for silicone implants over saline ones, as the texture felt more natural.

In my younger years, I always thought that someday I would get a boob job and be a C cup. "I wish I had bigger boobs," I always said. My cancer diagnosis provided a natural opportunity for this. Now I could get something I always wanted (bigger boobs) from something I never wanted (cancer). Maybe this was the silver lining of breast cancer.

The next decision was how big I wanted them to be. Having always been an A or B cup, I wondered if I should consider being bigger. This was not the question to ask my husband, who responded that I should consider a D cup. As it ended up, I never picked the size—the size was picked for me, due to a loss in skin supply related to the infected expander's removal. After the surgery, I was probably an AA or A cup, the smallest possible size with the tissue and skin I had to work with.

In addition to size, I had another decision to make: Should I keep my nipples or have them removed and get tattoos that look like nipples? Here was another research project, which led me to learn about nipple sparing. Nipple sparing is where the surgeon leaves the nipple in place when the breast tissue is removed under the skin. I decided to elect for nipple sparing, but first I had to confirm the surgeon from the Breast Center could perform this. She said she could, especially if my lymph node biopsies during surgery came back clear. Another decision made. Check.

Before going into the operating room, I felt at ease, as I truly felt I was lucky to have stage 1 breast cancer. I kissed my husband and approached the surgery like an item to check off my to-do list. I went to the surgery praying my lymph nodes would be clear, and that the cancer would not be further advanced than stage 1. Even though I felt lucky, a part of me was apprehensive simply due to fear of the unknown once surgery started.

The day of my double mastectomy arrived on April 27, 2015, and my journey began. I was told the surgery went well by both the general surgeon and the plastic surgeon. Although I heard their words, something felt off. I had a higher degree of pain and bruising on my right breast area, the noncancerous side, which seemed odd, but I figured my body was just dealing with the surgery trauma differently. After all, it is hard to know what normal should feel like when you have never encountered something like this before. The hospital discharged me on April 30, 2015, three days after my surgery. I left the hospital wrapped in bandages and gauze like a mummy. I was very sore and in a great deal of pain. But I expected to have pain, as I figured it was a major surgery and with each day I would improve. Later I learned that normal is only a setting on a washing machine, and the pain I discounted as normal was far from normal.

As the weeks went on, it became obvious the right breast was not healing the same as the left breast. It was clearly discolored, with a dark blue/blackish coloring similar to a bruise. At my follow-up appointment with the surgeon on May 14, 2015, I voiced my concerns, including the continued pain, and I had a low blood pressure reading of 87/62. Low blood pressure is one indicator of sepsis. I was scheduled for my follow-up with the general surgeon on May 12, 2015, but I was called to reschedule till the 14th, as the doctor had a sick child. While at the May 14 appointment, I was told I would no longer have appointments with her, and my future follow-ups would be with the plastic surgeon only.

On May 22, 2015, I saw the oncologist for my review of my hormone test findings. I was told I was Er+, Pr+, and HER-. The hormone tests for each category are either + or -. Depending on the combination, this determines the treatment plan after the mastectomy. In my situation, Er+ meant estrogen positive. Estrogen helps cancer grow, and it would need to be suppressed as I still had my ovaries. So, I had monthly shots in oncology to stop my ovaries from producing estrogen, until I was able to have my ovaries removed. At this appointment, I explained I did not feel well, and I asked what my blood pressure was. I was told it was 80/60. I told the physician that is low for me and when it is that low, I have an infection. The physician told me he did not believe the reading was accurate, but the physician never did another blood pressure check. The oncologist did not examine my chest, which is normal. I was never advised to see my internal medicine physician, to see my plastic surgeon, or to go to the ER. I simply went home, trusting everything must be normal.

When I saw the plastic surgeon a few weeks after the mastectomy and insertion of expanders, he noted the discoloration and changes in my right nipple. He said he hoped my skin would stay alive and that the nipple would survive. Days later, I noticed my right nipple had completely fallen off, just like a baby's umbilical cord. I wanted to cry, but I had no more tears. I had not fully realized the magnitude of what was happening. When my surgeon had said, "I hope your skin lives," I knew this meant that my tissue was probably dying and brewing with infection.

What would have happened if someone had questioned this? My infection could have possibly been debrided and I could have avoided a long surgical journey. I will never know. But patients have nowhere to go, no one to tell them they are sorry for their error. In any other business, that is not the case.

After my right nipple fell off, the pain continued on that side. I assumed the pain was just my body adjusting to the expanders put inside my body. The expanders were temporary and would be removed during the second reconstruction surgery in the future. I knew it would take four to six weeks for the expanders to be filled weekly with small amounts of fluid to stretch the chest wall slowly. This is done to prepare for the expanders to be removed after the four to six weeks of filling, and then the permanent implants could be done. So I expected, with everything going well, that it would likely be a three-month process before I would have my reconstruction surgery date scheduled. I was looking forward to this three-month mark, anticipating being completely done, with the expanders removed and implants placed inside my chest wall.

After all, my doctors were not concerned. So I kept convincing myself I was being over-the-top, and that I should trust the doctors and not my husband or my gut instinct. A big mistake.

One month after my first surgery, two of my girlfriends came over to celebrate with me. We were celebrating my return to work in coming days. When they arrived, they noticed I was acting "off" and not my normal chatty self. I told them I had woken up at 4:00 a.m. with chest pain and took a pain pill to get back to sleep. I had not used pain pills for weeks, so I was worried. When I called the plastic surgeon's office at 9:00 that morning with my pain concerns, I was told the nurse was in surgery and they would call when done.

By lunchtime, I had still not received a call back, so I called again. This time a nurse took my call and advised me to take four ibuprofen pills for my chest pain. The nurse stated I probably just did too much because I was feeling better and strained the muscle. This seemed logical, so I continued to rest all day.

Since I didn't feel right later in the afternoon, I decided

to look at my hospital discharge guidelines after taking my ibuprofen. The guidelines had directions on what to look for as signs and symptoms. At that moment, I had no fever and no drainage, which were two things noted as concerns. I did not have a blood pressure cuff at home, so I did not know what my blood pressure was since my last clinic visit. The symptom I had mentioned at previous appointments of low blood pressure was dismissed, so I was not concerned about my blood pressure or getting a home blood pressure kit.

My girlfriends had come over around 6:00 p.m. and brought me dinner. We planned to share a glass of wine together to toast the one month since my surgery. For the next three hours, I visited with them, and I was truly going through the motions. I felt off, but I did not have a fever. I just felt like I had no energy all of a sudden. According to my friends, my coloring was off and I appeared pale. Before they left, I showed my girlfriends what my chest looked like. But it had changed drastically since I had last seen it in the morning. The red area on my right breast had expanded and was deep red. The area around my nipple had broken open and the surgical mesh appeared to have tunneled a hole into my chest. I was horrified—it looked like I had a flesh-eating disease. My girlfriends were shocked and said there were holes in my chest and they could see the surgical mesh. I was truly shocked. They both started to walk to my bedroom, as my husband was watching television there. I showed my husband and he said, "Get dressed—I need to get you to the hospital immediately." As I walked into our bedroom with my robe on, I needed to change into clothes to get to the ER. While standing by the bed, I could feel a faint feeling overtaking me. I suddenly was struggling to get my leg into my pants. I could feel my body heating up suddenly. I was finding it hard to breathe. My husband yelled for our son to start the truck, and my husband quickly drove me to the emergency room entrance where the ambulances drive in. I was very weak, and within a thirty-minute period since leaving our home, I had a high fever and severe chest pains. It came on that fast.

As my husband scrambled to find hospital staff to help me get out of the truck, I was soon taken right to an exam room in the ER area. Within minutes I became unable to speak. I remember hearing a hospital employee say, "It is a good thing you brought her in tonight, as she would have been dead by the morning if you would not have."

Years later, after reviewing my electronic health records while finally being treated elsewhere, I would discover that I had an abnormal EKG when I was admitted to the ER. This was the first moment I knew my abnormal EKG included having identified heart issues. I now believe the chest pain I felt at 4:00 a.m. the day I was admitted for sepsis was likely related to my heart and not mastectomy pain. By 9:00 p.m., I was having a mild heart attack and possibly having a pulmonary embolism pass through from a blood clot.

My symptoms presented much like the seniors I care for. Thirty days post-surgery I had discoloration on both breasts but especially the right, with a darker skin tone there, low blood pressure, and a history of one blood clot. This created a perfect storm. From my own research on the Johns Hopkins Medicine and CDC websites, I've discovered that there are numerous protocols for sepsis awareness. For one, people with cancer have a higher risk for sepsis, which would have been helpful information in my discharge papers.

Pulmonary embolisms and sepsis kill people of all ages daily, some with cancer some without, and following surgeries or other injuries at all stages of life. I was haunted by a recent tragedy that had struck close to home just one month before my first surgery. A family friend had lost his wife on their twenty-fifth anniversary. She had an infection in her finger and was being treated with antibiotics. She went to bed and never woke up—she died in her sleep from a heart attack. She was in her early forties, with five children. She was healthy, and no one expected a young woman to die from a finger infection. Her infection turned into sepsis, and ultimately the sepsis caused system failure and her heart stopped.

Once a body goes into sepsis, the train has left the station. Timing is crucial. You can go from no fever to a high fever in minutes, and in my case this happened. In my case, I had early signs of sepsis that my medical team ignored and dismissed: low blood pressures, discoloration, and pain. Practiced protocols need to be in place for all specialty physicians as well as the emergency room, because the body can crash once sepsis starts. We may think this could never happen to us or someone we love, but the risks for everyone are higher than we realize.

I learned in my research that sepsis can lead to blood clots (also called thrombosis). In the US, there are 100,000-300,000 deaths per year, which is greater than the total number of people who lose their lives each year to AIDS, breast cancer, and motor vehicle crashes combined, as outlined by www.stoptheclot.org. According to www. worldthrombosisday.org, one in four people are dying from conditions caused by thrombosis (blood clots). Therefore, worldwide Thrombosis Day is October 13 to raise awareness. These organizations provide amazing resources for education. They also let patients know to ask for D-dimer, which is a specific blood test, ultrasound of arm or leg to look for possible deep vein thrombosis, or a CAT scan of the chest, if there is a suspected pulmonary embolism, a piece of blood clot in the lungs that may cause chest pain. The above tests can determine if a blood clot is present.

When my husband had gotten me to the emergency room lobby triage center, I buckled over in pain. As soon as my husband told them I had chest pain, I went directly to an examination room. They quickly got me in a gown and a team arrived to hook me up to an IV. I usually hate needles, but my temperature was above 102 and I felt unresponsive and foggy. My normal temperature is 96.8.

Despite drifting in and out, I was still present enough to be scared. Somehow, I realized that I was in the same room my father-in-law had been in last November, two days before his death.

My body was crashing and I knew it. I had been hooked to numerous IVs and had several blood tests and an EKG, and it was clear I had sepsis. Now all I could do was pray that they could identify the bacteria and successfully treat me before my body shut down. I said the Lord's Prayer several times and prayed to my father-in-law and grandparents to please help me. I prayed that all my relatives in heaven would gather the angels to save me from dying. I was only forty-eight.

The hospital admitted me that night, May 26, fewer than thirty days after my double mastectomy. Within twenty-four hours, a tissue culture had identified a staphylococcus, or staph, infection on my right breast, and I was hooked up with a strong concoction of medications through my IV, including vancomycin. The medical team had matched me with an IV medication that could successfully treat the staph infection that surrounded my right breast expander and caused the sepsis. I felt hopeful because they identified a medication that would work for my particular bacterial strain.

For three days I shared a room with other patients while I had open wounds on my chest. My biggest fear was my infection risk. My open wounds required multiple bandage dressing changes daily. While the bandages were being changed, the open wounds on my chest would be exposed. I knew that all people have some amount of staph on their skin, and I also knew that staph is found on many surfaces in a hospital. The hospital staff are trained on infection control and proper handwashing. However, I could not be sure the guests of my roommates would follow proper handwashing. I could not control whether children who entered the room would touch my bed and linens as they crawled under the cubicle curtain toward my bed. Many times, I redirected the small children, but often I was sleeping when they entered the room. I was very sick and very weak.

Normally, I would love to share a room and have someone to talk to. This situation was different, and I was surprised I was placed with a roommate. I was in a room with a woman who was bedbound from a back surgery and hollered for me to help her to the bathroom. I explained I was in a bed and I would call the nurses to come help her. I was hooked up to IVs, bedbound, and weak from sepsis and the infection and it did not seem like a great place for small children to be. I had a cubicle curtain between us, but it was not my place to ask for the other patient to have no visitors. So I said nothing. I had zero interest in being labeled a problem patient.

Three days later, on May 29, I was scheduled for surgery to remove the infected expander on my right side. Each day I was hospitalized, I felt like I was weaker than many frail elderly people whom I have cared for the past thirty years. I was unable to look out for myself, read my vital signs, or know what meds I was on. After surgery, I was horrified to see myself. My husband said, "You look like you were slaughtered by a chainsaw." I had two open wounds on my right side, which required twice daily wet-to-dry wound packing for the next three months. The wounds were so deep that my ribs were extremely sensitive to touch.

When I expressed my disappointment with my infection and care, I was told, "Well at least you are alive." That response still angers me to this day. If I had ever needed wound care when I had a hysterectomy, I don't believe anyone would ever say that. So why would someone say that to someone with a cancer diagnosis? I did not expect a stage 1 cancer to bring me close to death. I knew people with stage 3 and 4 cancer who were in better shape than I was. They had radiation and chemotherapy and had better outcomes than I did. I felt like I was treated as an unjustified complainer. I was truly boiling at this point, as I believed I had reasonable justification to expect different care outcomes. I was beyond disappointed. I was now clearly in the anger phase of healing.

My simple case had become very complicated. I wished I had never wanted reconstructive surgery. *Be careful what you wish for* echoed in my head like a warning label phrase. It was too late to go back.

You will realize you have a choice to become bitter or to be a blessing to others even after you were diagnosed with a word associated with death.

6 ∾ Way Beyond Plan B

MY STAY IN THE hospital while being treated for sepsis lasted days. I never thought this could be possible—I felt like a shell of my former self. Nothing I remembered of Natalie was left. I was too weak to care for myself after having the expander removed. I was almost thankful I was so weak—maybe my constant sleepiness prevented a deep depression from setting in. I never got to that dark place, and I thank God for that. *This is just today, not forever*, I kept telling myself.

On June 8, I was hospitalized for a third time. In a routine appointment with my plastic surgeon, I commented that my leg was red, blotchy, and painful when I stood. He suspected a blood clot and had me readmitted to the hospital. At this point, my mom flew back from Florida to be available to care for me once I was discharged, as she knew I was weak.

Although I was a forty-eight-year-old adult, my mother's daughter was now as dependent as a young child. I was grateful to have her with me—I needed someone to get my medications, pack my wounds, and prepare my meals once I got home. I couldn't believe how vulnerable I was—too sick to stay awake, and too tired to do much of anything else.

My mom did a great job keeping the feel in our home normal during abnormal times. Mothers or mothers-in-law may not always be able to live in an adult child's home for weeks. But my mother's attention to detail was a welcome addition for my husband. After all, they are two peas in a pod, and together they took on home remodeling projects. My husband had someone to talk to while I was hospitalized and when discharged home.

I later learned there were moments they cried together too. Especially when I was discharged on June 8, 2015, with a Complex Regional Pain Syndrome (CRPS) and recommended to have a nerve block. The handouts given to me at discharge described a condition with no cure, and you would have the worst pain of your life, and possibly be disabled and in a wheelchair. Although I knew what I read, I never believed it. My mom and husband were concerned and did not know what to think. When they picked me up at the hospital entrance, we drove immediately to Rochester, Minnesota, for a second opinion.

When I returned from Mayo Clinic for a second opinion and I was home recovering, the kids would tell me, "Dad is so happy when Tuffy (as her grandchildren call my mother) is here, because things are done right." It was fun to laugh with the kids. While my husband and I have always been two very strong and driven personalities, it is well known that we are opposites. He would describe us as two thoroughbred horses. He would also describe me as the tornado in the relationship, and he would be the orderly one in our partnership. So being with my mom was a gift for him when dealing with a tornado type living through one crisis after another with my health care.

My husband always teased me that I was just like my dad, and that is true. He and I have our own style of organized chaos. Yet there is a definite side of my mom in me too. Like my mom, I'm one to bake hundreds of dozens of cookies at Christmas. She was one of eleven siblings, so baking in large quantities is normal for her. She always gave baked goods to everyone in the neighborhood and helped many whenever she could. I would say I have my mom's spitfire nature, too, when needed. Like all kids, I would say I got a perfect mix of both parents in me.

Like my mom and dad, opposites do attract, and together my husband and I always covered everything that happened in our lives together. My husband always encouraged me to take a chance with career changes, or I would probably be at the first job I ever had. I am very loyal, and breaking away from established relationships is never easy on me. My husband, on the other hand, always knew my capabilities before I did. He would nudge me to go for it, and I would do the same for him. As different as we are, our passion and commitment to working hard was never in doubt for either of us.

In the aftermath of my latest stay in the hospital, our bedroom looked like a surgical suite. My husband had an eight-foot-long table of medications and wound-packing products. I was grateful to have the organized and detailed person in our relationship as my partner. My new bed was a recliner we had moved into our bedroom. I needed to elevate my legs, and my ribs were still so sore that the recliner was the best option for sleeping. If my mom was not there, my husband was the perfect person to pack my wounds, as he had total attention to detail, and I appreciated it. For months, I was not able to be the partner he was accustomed to. He was used to chaos living with me, and now it was in the form of a medical tornado of concern. I guess this was the part of our vows where they mention "in sickness and in health."

During this time, getting dressed was exhausting and a big activity for my day. I had no energy, and if I was up for an hour, I quickly went back to sleep for hours. My mom tracked my medications, ensured I ate, and kept me hydrated while my husband was at work.

When my husband came home from work, he would kiss my forehead and go outside to work on our five-acre lot. He always had a project, and that summer he had more than usual because our youngest son had just graduated high school and we needed to prepare for his graduation party. Since I was still so weak at the end of June, I could not decorate the garage, or get the photos from his childhood ready, or work on the plan for decorating I had in my mind. Every mom knows what they envision for a specific holiday or special event, as they often play a critical role in making it happen. This time, I was not able to contribute anything. I wanted to make sure our youngest son's 2015 graduation was the same wonderful party as our oldest son's had been two years earlier.

Thanks to my husband, mom, and friends, it all happened. Together, they decorated the garage beautifully, and all the tables had the school colors with photos from his life. My husband made a video of several photos, which was just as I had hoped. We threw our son a decorated graduation party, and I was strong enough to stand and greet everyone. I wanted to be there so much, because I had missed his ceremony earlier that June while I was in the hospital. As a mom, this was something that mattered to me. No, the decorations and the photos were not critical items. But to me they were.

The months following my hospital discharge from the sepsis infection were often a blur. Aside from my son's party, I remember feeling like I didn't care that I was missing everything else. That is not normal for an extrovert like me. I typically don't miss events—I love to be at the party, and even host it. But now I simply wanted to be in my bedroom, surrounded by my Croatian lavender diffuser and taupe paint. I didn't watch TV or read a single book, and all the projects I thought I would do turned out to be totally unrealistic.

Many did not understand how I was perfectly content to do nothing during this time, but I was sick. I had *never* been this sick. I lost weeks, months of my life. Sometimes I still cry when I think about how sick I was.

After caring for frail seniors for years, I thought I understood how the body acts in recovery. After all, I had dedicated my entire life to this profession. But I had never experienced it myself—until now. Now I, too, got exhausted from having guests or visitors. I was thrilled to have a comfortable blanket and pillow. Peace and quiet had a whole new meaning to me. For the first time in my life, I truly understood that sometimes there is a time for *no* activity. Sometimes it is OK to miss events. It is OK to miss church. It is OK to take time for you so that you can truly heal.

My mom knew how sick I was, and her priority was that I was alive and getting stronger. So she protected me from myself. All that mattered to her was her girl. She took my phone away because she knew I would check my emails and texts and return endless calls at all hours. I remember on one of my many hospital stays her saying, "Hand over your phone," and I would sheepishly have to pull the charging cord that I had requested that the housekeeper weave through the back of my bed to reach the outlet so I could charge it 24/7. I was trying to do it all and failing miserably. When I cried, she would say, "Natalie, somehow it will all work out." And it did.

Minute by minute, I managed. I always wondered where my breaking point would be. I joked with my friends and coworkers that if I was in a catatonic position, please come visit me and make me laugh. They assured me I wouldn't crack.

The recovery from my double mastectomy was supposed to be six weeks, but it turned into a three-month ordeal with an infection, sepsis, and blood clot. The reconstruction process took longer because of the infection and blood clot to follow. I had to wait a year after the mastectomy date before I was strong enough to get the implants put in. Since I had severe complications, the healing process from the double mastectomy took over one year, from start to finish. Then other surgeries followed. In the end it was a process of five years and eight surgeries.

Initially, I thought of my double mastectomy as a minor surgery and approached it as a mini vacation. I learned fast that having a mastectomy and further complications is never a vacation. It began to feel like a trip to hell when I faced complications and multiple surgeries. I felt like everything had been sucked out of me. I was scared. When would I ever feel like me again? Even once my body had finally healed, it still took months for my mind, body, and soul to process what had happened and to heal. I did heal. I had changed. I was now stronger in body, mind, and soul than before.

The third time is not always a charm. On June 8, 2015, I was hospitalized a third time, just days after my discharge from sepsis and the removal of my expander. The plastic surgeon was concerned I had a blood clot when I voiced concern about lower leg pain and red blotchy skin. This time, the ultrasound and MRI showed no blood clot. Despite this diagnosis, I strongly believed I had a blood clot. I had taken photos of my leg, but I was treated as though I was an annoying patient whenever I tried to show them to my medical team. Later, when I read my medical records, "patient takes photos of leg" was documented there. If my medical reports did not match the photos I was showing, why didn't anyone do another ultrasound? My photos showed the red webbing and swelling on my back calf, which only happened when I walked to the bathroom. During these times, the hospitalist was not there, which was the reason I took the photos.

When you elevate your leg in bed, the pain of a blood clot is lessened. When you walk and the leg displays red webbing and swelling, taking photos helps document symptoms that the medical team may not be present to see. Taking photos of symptoms also helps to document when you experienced them. After going through multiple surgeries, I would advise anyone to take photos daily post-surgery so you can measure your swelling and healing progress.

Once I knew the medical team did not believe I had a blood clot, it was time for me to get a second opinion. In order to get discharged, I had to get my blood pressure to a normal level, as it was running low. I had a friend bring me Gatorade and a big bag of Lay's classic potato chips. Consuming the potato chips raised my blood pressure, and the Gatorade surely helped hydrate me. Now I could be discharged without going against medical advice. I learned the potato chip trick from a dear elderly friend Lou, who always had me bring him potato chips so he could keep his low blood pressure at a more normal level. I am grateful for all the tricks I have learned from the elderly, as this trick worked like a charm.

My husband and mom picked me up at the hospital in Duluth and drove me straight to the Mayo Clinic in Rochester. I brought my X-rays with me and checked in at the hotel next to the hospital. I'd made an appointment for a second opinion with a plastic surgeon there when my complications began after the sepsis diagnosis and expander removal, and I was determined to get that second opinion.

My mom wheeled me there because I could not walk, and the plastic surgeon quickly determined I needed to go to the ER to find the source of my leg pain before anything else could be coordinated for my breast reconstruction.

So off I went. The physician reviewed all the tests I'd had in Duluth and offered to give me an outside read. This meant another radiologist would read my prior X-ray results.

Immediately, these results were sent to the vascular department at Mayo. The radiologist noted that my veins were not viewable, which the vascular surgeon said is a red flag to call for another ultrasound immediately, which the Duluth hospital hadn't done. Fortunately, the doctor reviewing my case had also treated me for my blood clot ten years ago, and I was immediately worked into a packed schedule for my second ultrasound.

This one didn't take long. The ultrasound technician worked the wand down my right calf and said, "Don't move. I need to update your cardiovascular doctor at Mayo." I felt like my world had turned upside down, and I was just spinning like a top. I was terrified—what did they find? Did I have cancer somewhere else? One of my uncles had recently died of bone cancer and another had died of leukemia years prior, and I worried it was one of these.

But it was neither. The cardiovascular doctor confirmed I had an active blood clot exactly where my pain was. Finally, a diagnosis. I was beginning to think I had lost my mind. I found myself grateful for the one thing I begged my medical team to prevent: another blood clot. But it sure beat the alternative of having cancer in my bones. The good news was that the blood clot had been found; the bad news was that I had a clot. Because I now had two documented blood clots, I needed to take Coumadin in addition to heparin shots.

I continued appointments at the Mayo Clinic and got my second opinion from the plastic surgeon. When I unrobed for the doctors to see my chest, they were speechless. "This is so unfortunate. You should have been an easy case," they said. The physician agreed that my first surgeon had taken too much skin and gone too deep. They said it would take three months to heal my wounds, and then they wanted one year to pass before I had another surgery. I needed to heal and be stronger.

At this point of my journey, my decisions were all about trust. My trust had been broken. I could not go under the knife again without peace of mind. Once you lose trust in a physician and a hospital, it is impossible to mentally consider another surgery there.

At the Mayo Clinic, I felt I found physicians who operated on people who had complications like me. They could feel my pain. I was not just another patient, and for the first time, I felt hope. I felt human again.

With Mayo as my new medical home, my mind tried to process how I would run a twenty-four-hour business as a CEO while traveling four and a half hours one way to Mayo for appointments, while also preparing for another major surgery. "Why me?" I began to ask, before realizing, "Why not me?" After all, God gave me the tremendous advantage of family and friends to help carry me through this journey. I remembered Grandma Hazel's favorite Bible verse, Proverbs 3:5–6: "Trust in the Lord with all your heart, and lean not on your own understanding; In all your ways acknowledge Him, and He shall direct your path."[2] My medical

---

2   New King James Version.

situation was way beyond plan B, and once I had trust in a new treatment plan, I was able to have faith that a new plan, even if it was plan F, would be just fine. Fine it was.

You will feel a sense of urgency but realize that patience is a gift learned so you can endure the healing process of your diagnosis.

7 ∾ When Mom Is Sick

MY SONS WERE EIGHTEEN and twenty when I got sick. I was grateful for their age, because I was too sick to chase or watch after young boys. When graduation day arrived for our youngest son, I was hooked up to IVs and could not be discharged from the hospital to attend the ceremony. *Moms don't miss their kid's graduation*, I thought. *This will never happen again, and I am not there.* I felt guilty. I felt like a failure as a mom. I knew I could not get these days back. I thanked God for what I had and tried to hold on to smaller moments in time. Hour by hour. Sometimes taking it a day at a time was just too much.

Sometimes I felt like I would crack in a moment that I would not see coming. I am super sentimental, so things like graduations rank *way* up there for me. I had been looking forward to taking family photos with my son in his graduation gown.

Luckily, my mother is only seventeen years older than me, so she was my stand-in for the photos. Friends posted comments on Facebook that I looked great. I laughed and commented, "That's my mom."

Our son comforted me by making sure I knew I wasn't

missing anything great by reminding me how hot and sweaty graduations are. Rather than me celebrating at a graduation ceremony with our son, our son was trying to comfort me. Deep down I know he knew I was heart-broken, and he felt bad for me. He was quick-witted and let me know I was lucky to miss a hot, long, miserable event. His sense of humor kills me. I love the joy of boys and their honest, realistic perspectives. Thankfully, they had cell phones, so I could send a quick text to let them know I was thinking of them as they gathered for commencement. As a mom of boys, all I needed back was a short and sweet response, which I had come to know as normal.

While they would always be my boys, I now had young men, but they were great about coming to see me in my bedroom when they returned from school or events. They would watch television with me, and sometimes our king bed had all four of us in it to recap hockey, hockey, and more hockey. Thankfully, my husband and sons were all great about giving me my various injections when I needed them. I am the only one in our family who hates blood, needles, and horror movies. Now I would be forced to deal with blood, and they dealt with the injections with all the needles.

I am quite sure my sons and husband have all watched the movie *The Proposal* enough times to recite it word for word. Now when I ask them to watch it again, it is a hard "no." I could still watch it again.

Once I returned home following the third hospitalization, our community had organized a month-long meal train for me. I had never heard of a meal train, but what would be delivered each night became our favorite evening topic. Every day a different vehicle came up our driveway and left food in a cooler by our front door. The kids were interested to see the notes from the families who sent the meals. The thoughtfulness was overwhelming. I felt like I was back in my small hometown—neighbors caring for neighbors, people taking the time to care about you and your family.

When our son's graduation party rolled around, I still had drainage tubes and was in my wheelchair. The kids had not seen me out of my bedroom for more than eight weeks. I rotated between my bed and my recliner. One day, my son's girlfriend (now his wife) and a friend baked me cupcakes and frosted them both to look like boobs. We had a good laugh. I love to bake so it was a perfect gift.

The boys were old enough to be fairly independent, but I still felt like I was missing moments I could never get back. I was sleeping so much and felt like time was slipping through my fingers. I can't even remember where we spent some of the holidays those years when I was so sick. I love traditions—they are part of the fabric of being a mom. Being out of the game of life put me out of sync with doing things for the holidays with everyone I love. I missed so many events then that my life now is all about cherishing every single opportunity.

There were so many other big and small ways that people showed up for me when I got home from hospitalizations. My dear next-door neighbor walked over to check on me daily. My Rotary sisters made a peace garden in my front yard for me to enjoy from the window. My best friend from high school planted all the flowers and helped my husband with the gardening.

Nature had new meaning to me during this time. I noticed the birds more and listened to their songs. The birds gave me great entertainment, and I watched them at the feeders for hours. Being a busy mom with two sons in hockey for the past fifteen years, I had not really paid attention to the calming effect of birds.

Once, I asked my husband if he knew what kind of bird was making a particular song. He had a birdsong app on his phone and recorded it to figure out what bird it was. When it turned out to be a robin, I laughed and said I had a lot to learn. Now we have several feeders, and watching the birds is something we enjoy together. Birdwatching never gets old.

This era of my life felt like being trapped in a time capsule. I lost so much time with my family, and I felt guilty about it. I missed out on big events in my sons' lives and wasn't able to help my husband as much as I wanted to. Every member of a family feels pain when someone is sick. Every day, each person is affected differently, and their emotions transfer to each other in different ways. Sometimes you want to be quiet or sleep more. Sometimes you are bitter for doing more than your fair share. Sometimes you are jealous of others for being able to have fun. Sometimes you just want to feel normal again, whatever that means. Sometimes you just need to take a deep breath and take it minute by minute.

You will realize
being vulnerable is a
valuable lesson taught to
your kids when you
are sick.

8 ⁓ In Good Times and in Bad, in Sickness and in Health

IN THE MONTHS FOLLOWING my surgery, I felt like one of the women you see on the reality television show *Botched*, which features people with plastic surgery "gone wrong." With this new mental image of myself, it was hard to imagine a romantic moment with my husband would ever be the same. I had read that many couples divorced after an illness and this scared me. I was like a young teenager on an awkward first date. I felt incomplete in so many ways, but this was something I had to deal with because this was the new normal for me and my husband.

Although most men like bigger boobs, I knew my husband was accustomed to a woman who did not fit that profile. But now I would be boobless. That made me feel very awkward. After the double mastectomy, I had to wait a year before I could have the implants put in. So I was a woman with a deflated plastic expander on one side with scarring. On the other side, I had two wounds that had healed with scar tissue on top of my ribs, and no boob. I was embarrassed and nervous to be undressed in front of my husband. I just could not imagine how to lie next to him and feel like a woman again. In these healing months, I could not have a conversation with my husband because I was simply not ready. I did not understand that then. I needed many years to pass before I understood my emotions well enough to articulate them in any meaningful way with my husband.

You don't realize how strange your body feels without boobs, until they have been completely removed. No one can really prepare you for that. Boobs had never mattered to me prior to my mastectomy, but that changed after my surgery. I never realized how much breasts define a woman. They meant little to me before cancer, but not having them at all made me feel "so past sexy." I honestly felt like wearing a shirt that simply stated the reality that I was "so PAST sexy."

Yes, I was alive—and grateful to be—but I had to adjust to an awkward healing phase and redefining myself as a woman.

One day as I was lying next to my husband, he said, "I miss your boobs."

"So do I," I said. We laughed, which felt good for a moment.

Then I started second-guessing my decision to have the double mastectomy. Just acknowledging that we both missed my boobs triggered me to have a lot of guilt. This began the road of second-guessing. Maybe I should have had the lumpectomy and radiation on my left breast instead, like my husband had originally suggested. Maybe then I would still have two normal breasts. But it was too late. I wondered if all this could have been avoided if I had never had a double mastectomy. I was angry at myself for the decision I made. I had to forgive myself and move on. I had to learn how to communicate how I felt with my spouse in a healthy way. I had to realize my husband was hurting too.

I had heard my husband's feedback, but at the time of my diagnosis, I felt that the anxiety of wondering when the cancer would move to the other breast was worse. Ultimately, I had to make a choice. Like every other choice I have made in life, I learned that looking backward is never healthy.

In the months and years to come, I would wonder if I had done the right thing for myself. As things played out, I would discover that I had made the best decision at that moment in time. I needed to accept the choice I made and let it go.

It is so strange at forty-something to feel awkward about your body and with your husband, worrying that your marriage might not survive because you no longer have boobs. *OK, this is us now,* I thought. Life is not always packaged with a bow. When I visited with our pastor, months before he married our son and his wife, I remembered talking about all my husband and I went through in the twenty-eight years of married life. Soon the pastor commented, "Well at least he stayed," and I knew what he meant. I knew that he likely knew couples who divorced after a mastectomy. Somehow it was good to know that while we did not always handle things perfectly, we were together and we had grown as a couple.

Body image had never mattered to me before—I am not sure why. I have often been asked, for example, if it bothered me that my mom was thinner than me. The first time I heard that question, I was shocked—it had never even entered my head. After years of being a secure woman, I found myself feeling insecure about my body image. I had scars everywhere and I did not feel whole as a woman.

Once, between one of my many surgeries, I was sitting outside my office in my truck. It had been a stressful day. I prayed and cried, hanging my head over the steering wheel, and I said Grandma Hazel's name several times. I asked her to send me a sign that everything would be OK. Then I regained my composure and went back to work.

A few days later, I was on the phone with my cousin, who was helping my uncle prepare for his mother's estate sale. He wanted to know what Grandma Hazel's wedding ring looked like. His mother, who had the ring in her possession, had passed away unexpectedly and I was supposed to get the ring next. I tried to describe it: a simple ring with a worn-out wedding band, one main stone in the middle and a smaller stone on the side, with a white gold setting.

So off he went to look for this ring. He looked in every drawer, jewelry box, and purse. There was no ring. I was devastated. I knew Grandma Hazel wanted the ring to keep getting passed down in the family. But I didn't want anyone to feel bad, because there was nothing we could do. It was just one of those things. I had years of memories with her, and I didn't need a thing. I had to let it go.

A few days later, I was leaving work on a wet spring day. Before I stepped into my vehicle, I glanced down and something caught my eye. Right before me was a shiny ring on the ground of the parking lot. It was white gold, one stone in an old setting with smaller diamonds on the side, almost exactly like Grandma Hazel's ring. I could not believe it. It was no coincidence that I had found this ring.

In that moment, I knew everything was going to be OK. This ring was there for me to put on my hand so I could remind myself of that every day. And I did just that.

I couldn't wait to call my cousins and tell them to forget about the other ring. It did not matter—this was as good as the other one, in my mind. Everything would work out the way it needed to. I had the ring on my finger for life now.

You will realize that your path for healing from your diagnosis or setbacks may not match the path of healing for your spouse or those that love you.

9 ∾ How Can We Help?

As A ROTARIAN, I spent many hours gathering items for annual fundraisers. Each year, the Rotary Club distributed thousands of dollars to programs that helped people in need, from infants to adults.

My appreciation for how important fundraising is grew once I was in a situation of an actual need. I was now around many women with many stories of multiple clinic and hospital visits. One of the number-one reasons cited for divorce is conflict over money issues. Now my treatment plan would cost at minimum the $7,000 annual deductible, plus expenses to travel out of town for various medical appointments.

Before I had cancer, I never fully comprehended the need for fundraisers such as benefits held for people with cancer or other medical setbacks, or nonprofit fundraisers to benefit a charity in need. If you have health insurance, everything should be covered after your deductible, right? If you look at financial costs only through the lens of your medical bills, that may be true. Unfortunately, the real costs go well beyond the deductible expenses of just medical bills.

My insurance plan, for example, has a maximum

out-of-pocket expense limit. For many plans, this easily costs $7,000 or more each year. Other costs include the possible loss of a second income, out-of-network costs for care or second opinions, and caregiving costs when you are sick. For those who have built their lives dependent on a second income, or for anyone living on a single stream of income, financial devastation can occur quickly. Financial stress only worsens your health at a time you are told to de-stress in order to heal.

For those under retirement age, the Family Medical Leave Act (FMLA) grants people twelve weeks of unpaid leave without losing their jobs, if they have worked for their employer for at least one year. But even if everything goes as planned, many people do not have enough money in savings to cover their lost wages while out of work for surgery, radiation, or chemotherapy.

It is not uncommon to know people who have been diagnosed with a serious illness in their thirties, forties, or fifties. For many of them, these are child-rearing years. Regardless of whether they are single parents or dual-income families, when faced with a cancer diagnosis and treatment plan, many people face the negative effects of this loss of income.

Cancer has a way of focusing all of someone's energy on their immediate health needs. It is all-consuming to deal with the immediate health-care needs for the diagnosed person and their family. So, I strongly suggest accepting help from others to help care for yourself, your family, and your life.

Giving someone with a cancer diagnosis your time,

presence, and emotional or financial support is one of the greatest gifts for helping someone find the stability they need to heal. Most people with a serious illness are uncomfortable asking for help, so be creative with your offers to lend support. Thoughtfulness can come in many ways, depending on the situation.

When you first find out someone you know has cancer, shock and sadness fills your body. Sometimes these emotions paralyze our normal ability to reach out to a newly diagnosed friend or family member.

The rawness of the shock makes the first few weeks awkward for everyone. The newly diagnosed cancer patient doesn't want to worry those they love. Family and friends don't want to cry in front of them and cause more stress or pain. They want to be cheerleaders, so they try to stifle their stress and reflect only positive energy. In these beginning weeks, a text, email, Facebook message, or phone call is a wonderful way to show support.

Once cancer treatment begins, there are many thoughtful acts one can consider. You may give of your time, talent, or money. Maybe you have the ability to give in multiple areas.

Here are a few ways to give your time:

- Driving the person to and from appointments
- Sitting with them during treatments
- Continuing regular friend time, like having pedicures, coffee or wine, and movies at home
- Babysitting young children
- Transporting children to sporting events and other

activities, and coordinating their schedules during treatment months

- Cleaning the person's home and doing their laundry
- Shopping for their groceries
- Coordinating meal trains or deliveries to their home
- Organizing a prayer chain
- Decorating their home for the holidays
- Shopping for and wrapping birthday gifts for children
- Dropping off beer or wine for their partner with a note to let them know you are thinking of them too
- Helping children with homework and school-related items
- Coordinating an outing for the spouse or significant other: golf, shopping, a brewery, sporting event, walk, or something else to let them know you are thinking of them too

How to give your talent:

- Preparing meals
- Fixing things at their home
- Helping with their yard care, such as shoveling snow, mowing their lawn, landscaping, and gardening
- Caring for their pets or walking their dog
- House-sitting and bringing in their mail if they are out of town for appointments

How to give your money:

- Sending a gift card. Prepaid Visas or MasterCards are perfect, as they can use them for what they need most, or cash/check

- Delivering a bouquet of flowers
- Setting up a GoFundMe page to crowdfund their medical bills
- Coordinating a benefit or fundraiser on their behalf

Whatever you choose to do will make a difference. The most important thing to remember is the value of thoughtfulness. Each of us has our own unique way to connect with those we care about. Take a moment to selflessly hit the pause button and delay your own projects and needs to tend to someone else's.

When we do this in genuine and timely ways, we carry burdens together as family and friends. In these moments, we recognize that the person who gives benefits as much as the person who receives. These moments of caring become the fabric of our relationships. There is no greater gift than compassion and generosity.

When someone is diagnosed with cancer, the reality of death quickly comes to the forefront of your mind. People associate cancer with death, regardless of the stage—and no one wants to be stage 4. But no matter how advanced the cancer is, the surgical risks are still a reality for everyone. Even with a simple procedure, the risk of infection is there. Understanding your health-care needs and risks inside and out is vital for your life, so it is important to thoroughly research your surgical team. Have a backup plan in case your anticipated recovery period becomes more complicated.

Backup plans can include:

- Using your employer's supplemental insurance policies for short-term disability

- Purchasing other supplemental insurance plans, via companies such as Aflac
- Consider restructuring your home mortgage to reduce monthly payments if you receive a cancer diagnosis, in case your family is reduced to one income

Once your cancer treatments and surgeries end, there are usually still years of oncology visits and other medication regimes to prevent the possibility of cancer spreading to another area. Most breast cancer survivors are on medications for five to ten years after their mastectomy. Taking a medication to prevent any further cancers is information that is stored in your mind. From each day forward, your life choices will likely be approached differently. I felt initially that once I had the mastectomy, all my fears would be over. Then after the mastectomy, I realized I would be taking medications to prevent any residual cancer cells in my breast tissue area from attaching to other cells and creating cancer in another area of my body. For a while I worried about this, and then I decided worry did me no good, and I gave the worries to God.

I was asked many times if I felt like cancer changed me. Absolutely. I lost two and a half prime years of my life, and now I recognize how fast life really goes by. With or without a cancer diagnosis, each decade goes faster. Prior to cancer, I was running my race in life. My race was as busy as anyone else's. Now my race is still busy, but I hit the pause button more consciously to make sure I treasure certain moments in my life.

Cancer was a good slap across the face in my late forties

to make me evaluate myself. I needed to ensure I took a balanced approach to my self-care. I had to be in tune with my body's healing journey, and my healing never really started until my physical trauma ended. My body wouldn't relax until it knew all the surgeries were over. I had a shield of armor around me ready for battle. I had been to hell and back again. Once the surgeries finally ended, I cried alone many times, often over small things. My emotions had been stuffed down for so long, and even I didn't understand what I was going through. Now I do. Our bodies are not machines. I was a broken woman. Our bodies need to heal in wholeness.

I learned to lean on God and to recognize that my heart and brain had to heal just like the scars on my breasts and back. Cancer toughened me up and brought clarity to my life. Cancer is ultimately only a word. We each get one chance, one life in this world. With or without cancer, we all face the same ending: death. Living a life without regrets truly has new meaning for me now.

In a strange sort of way, cancer was OK. It made me dig deeper than I have ever dug. It made me realize that cancer was not just about trying not to die, it was also about making sure to live each and every day.

You will
appreciate family and
friends at a whole new
level. You will appreciate
the simple things
in life.

10 ∾ Making Decisions When Things Go Well and Badly

ONCE YOU'RE DIAGNOSED WITH cancer, your mind is forced to analyze a continuum of questions surrounding the thought, *Could this kill me?* If you are like me, you probably hadn't thought about the possibility of death too often before this.

The thought of death never crossed my mind until I was forty-eight. Sure, I had thought about it before, but only in the context of old age. Because of my profession, I was very familiar with the gradual and rapid decline of seniors. This type of decline was expected, not a surprise. Living to old age is a blessing—it means you have lived a full life with an opportunity for many birthdays.

As a licensed nursing home administrator and CEO of an assisted living company, I have witnessed families managing the progression of diseases such as diabetes, Parkinson's, Alzheimer's and dementia, osteoporosis, arthritis, and various cancers. These are generally journeys toward death in old age, ultimately requiring hospice care.

But once my role changed from caregiver and professional to patient, everything was different. Now it was personal. Now it was all about me and my body. I had to set aside all professional relationships and begin a new process of asking questions and quickly analyzing responses.

For something as serious as a cancer diagnosis, it is nerve-racking to need to make decisions with your caregiver team so quickly. I needed surgery within one month after my diagnosis. For others, "quickly" may mean weeks or even days, depending on the cancer's location, stage, and aggression.

Making these decisions is further complicated because after the diagnosis, your days are consumed with your immediate and future medical needs. Suddenly, you are forced to understand and comprehend an array of medical terms. My diagnosis was invasive ductal carcinoma, left breast, and stage 1. I now belonged by default to a new group, one with many others who have traveled this journey I was now on too.

I approached this chapter of my life much like all others. I knew the problem and simply wanted the cancer removed as soon as possible. This seemed simple enough, because I knew I was among millions of others who faced and survived cancer.

But nothing is that simple. Like most things in life, every decision affects something else. I am a problem solver, so I dealt with cancer like it was a work problem. I based my decision to stay local on my decades-long relationship with the largest health-care provider in northern Minnesota. This provider had information on their website that its

Breast Center was one of only four in Minnesota to be accredited by the National Accreditation Program for Breast Centers.

My surgeon was listed as part of the cancer surgery team, so I assumed her specialty would be breast surgeries. I later learned she also did appendectomies, hernia surgeries, and more. I never thought to ask:

- How many mastectomies had she done before mine?
- How many surgeries like mine resulted in re-hospitalization related to infection?
- How many mastectomies are performed at the hospital?
- How many mastectomies with nipple sparing has the surgeon done?
- Are there patients to speak to for referrals? What are people saying about this surgeon on Facebook and other forum chats, where they can voice their real opinions?

Up to this point in my life, I had made good personal and professional life decisions. Sure, I had made mistakes, but none were life-threatening. I had no past experiences to prepare me for cancer decision-making. After all, what else can you really compare it to? It is not like cramming for a college exam, staying up all night with a crying baby, breaking a bone, losing a job, running out of gas, or working an eighty-hour workweek. This was cancer. This was a new challenge, one I had never met.

Now that it is over, would I have done anything differently? Well, I had tried to make logical decisions based on what I thought was best for my family and business. With all my best intentions, my plan failed. Isn't the road to hell paved with good intentions? So yes, I would do it differently. I would have made sure I was having surgery done by someone who specializes in breast surgery. I would have made sure the plastic surgeon and general surgeon were all part of the same hospital to ensure they coordinated my care in the event of sepsis or a blood clot. I would understand that my real risks may not be the cancer, but rather infection and sepsis.

All too often, patients are unaware of not only the risks when complications occur, but how to document them to share with your medical team for proper treatment. I would also suggest:

· Taking daily photographs of your surgical wound
· Taking your blood pressure reading daily
· Keeping a journal of all changes with your daily sleep, food and water intake, frequency of bowel movements, urine frequency and output, and your overall energy level. It is critical to put your experience and care first at this moment. This is a hard lesson for most women to learn.

Sometimes I wonder why I surrendered my life so willingly, without question, into the hands of a surgeon. But this entire life lesson taught me that not everyone gets ninety-plus birthdays. I have taken life for granted. While the seniors I care for may not all want to reach one hundred years of age, I can guarantee you that not one of them wants to be robbed of life early. Now I know that life can't wait for me to do some things later. It is easy to think, *I'll do that when it is more convenient or better timing.* When tragedy happens, your perspective changes, and you realize life has its own calendar. We just don't know the ending date for any of us. Tragedy stops all our plans and forces us to become a new version of ourselves.

After facing a near-death experience, I will never have blind trust in the medical system again. Before I willingly sign a form that states my surgery risk includes all things up to and including death, I will do the best research I can.

I expected to have a blood clot prevented and I believe my sepsis could have been too. I assumed everyone would read my chart. My disposition is to understand that everyone makes mistakes, so I wanted to grant the same forgiveness as I would desire as a health-care professional. Over and over, I tried to forget and move on. But medical events kept happening that did not match protocol.

After my third hospitalization following my double mastectomy, I ultimately received treatment at Mayo Clinic in Rochester, Minnesota. The vascular surgeon I saw there placed me on a blood thinner, since I had two documented surgically provoked blood clots. So when I fell and hit the back of my head in 2015, I went to my primary internal medicine clinic, since I had a bump on my head. When on a blood thinner, the standard of care is to be seen to ensure no bleeding occurs in the brain. I had a headache, and the doctor ordered an MRI to make sure there was no bleeding. I did not feel sick, I just knew I was told that when on a blood thinner, I should be seen if I had any falls in which I hit my head.

As soon as I went into the magnetic resonance imaging (MRI) machine, I had an intense feeling in my chest. My chest felt hot and like it was burning. It was painful and I knew something was wrong, as I had never had pain like this on prior MRIs. Suddenly, I felt my entire chest wall cave in. I wanted to scream, but I could not. I was inside an enclosed area, and no one would hear me, as the hospital staff were inside another room. So I pushed the call light so the care team could stop the procedure and remove me from the machine to help me. I had a headset on to listen to music, which I used to calm my mind. This procedure makes me and others feel claustrophobic while enclosed in the machine. I started to hyperventilate and panic, as my chest kept hurting from the burning sensation. When I pushed the button, the MRI technician pulled me out as quickly as the machine could go.

The employee was surprised to see me crying and panicked. When I explained the feelings I had in my chest, he quickly stated, "Oh my gosh, do you have expanders?" I responded, "Yes." He stated, "You are not supposed to have an MRI if you have expanders in your chest wall." He stated the MRI would not continue, so he disconnected me from everything and let me get dressed.

My trust in my local medical provider system was eroding even further after this event. Ultimately, it forced me to choose another local medical system in Duluth for primary care. After each in the series of clinic and hospital mishaps, I would ask questions. I never received a follow-up about any of my concerns. Initially, I thought the hospital would call me for an in-depth analysis to find out what went wrong, to ensure this would not happen to another patient. Instead, I received a form letter claiming the hospital had no fault. This wasn't the ending I wanted.

As time went on, so many said, "You need to sue them." I thought about that, and spent some time looking into the laws and met with many people regarding my case. I knew I never intended to sue anyone, but I did want some level of closure with changes made to benefit other women long after me. The real tragedy is the hospital's and surgeon's inability to say they made a mistake. No one wanted to be held accountable. Simply saying "I am sorry" is not enough, as a physician or professional in a higher level of management. These are just empty words that contradict the organization's entire mission.

All my life I had prided myself on being someone who was never "that person" who made a fuss when something goes wrong. Instead, I would slide the trauma of my misfortune to the back of my brain until another event occurred. The events that occurred would often be related to someone else who was diagnosed with cancer, and their treatment involved a series of preventable setbacks too. When women with breast cancer setbacks called me to share their story on the phone, my heart and mind recorded it deep into my memory. When I would try and fall asleep at night, I would find myself thinking of these women and their stories. My mind felt like I was continually hitting a rewind button on an old cassette boom box. It seemed I was becoming the spokesperson for women who were tired, scared, frustrated, and angry when their breast cancer journey became a series of mishaps that never should have happened. Some of these women are nurses and health-care professionals who have a strong internal compass of reasonable expectations. For these women, the feeling of betrayal cuts even deeper.

The hospital professionals team is a critical part of every community. As a citizen and health-care professional, I have had the utmost respect for their services. For trauma cases and tragedies such as car accidents, there is no set course of treatment—many variables determine the outcome. However, as a patient, my brain continued to debate what is reasonable to expect when I am not a trauma patient, not terminal, not on hospice, and in good health. As a low-risk and easy case, with nothing in my lymph nodes, I should live, right? I should not have had to fear death from preventable outcomes, right?

As a patient, there was a large gap between my expectations and my outcome. Having worked for years in health care, I was angry at myself. I felt responsible for my situation, pained that I had naturally trusted and assumed that someone at a higher level was monitoring and managing my case. After spending my life in administration in nursing homes and assisted living, I wondered if the hospital CEO had any idea of my concerns.

Long after my mastectomy, once the wounds had healed, I called the hospital and met with upper management. I remember crying in his office as I described how botched I felt. He said he was sorry, and I said I wanted to know what would be done to prevent this from happening to other women. Then suddenly, I lifted my shirt and showed him my naked, botched, scarred, boobless chest. I asked him if he would want his wife to look like this. I shocked myself when I left his office, but I had made my point, and somehow I had a new level of peace. He would not forget meeting me.

I knew that upper management would likely never run into me at the store like I do with many of my employees, as I live where I work. So since I was likely just a number to him, I wanted to make sure this moment of my emotion would never leave his mind. Since the physicians and hospital exist to serve patients, I felt someone in upper management should see the emotion of a patient when things go wrong. Since I lived with the pain and disappointment from multiple mishaps, I wanted someone to see a patient with bad results from the hands of professionals to whom I had entrusted my care. I wanted someone to see the results of lack of communication and the results when team members within a medical organization do not read a medical record to know the history of the patient they are caring for. Ultimately, I changed hospitals in Duluth, to allow care close to home when Mayo was not necessary or for a partnership for additional care. This gave me the peace of mind I needed.

I am not an attorney for a reason. I am in the business of relationships. When you live in the community of those you serve, you are especially accountable to them. I have always lived in or near the community where I work, so I never forget that principle. Health care is all about people. Health care is all about community, and the CEO is a part of that. When you work where you live, every patient you serve has a face and is known to you.

When I left my meeting with the hospital upper management, I hoped their intentions would be to research best practices and to truly make a difference. There was no guarantee this would happen, so I knew I needed to do my own research so I could try and help women who asked me questions. As the days went on, I found myself drawn to reading articles from the *Journal of Medicine* and many other sources. I found several articles by Johns Hopkins University on the importance of reducing blood clot risks in US hospitals nationwide. My mind was curious to find out what other health-care organizations were doing to prevent sepsis and blood clots. I learned there were numerous articles written by many physicians about this, and several articles about the risks of pulmonary embolisms following a sepsis diagnosis.

Several articles talked about the number of deaths that occur from pulmonary embolisms. I would lie awake at night perplexed. Honestly, I wondered how many women died from preventable blood clots, pulmonary embolisms, and sepsis thirty days or more post-surgery. My guess is there is no data surrounding this. I have learned that sepsis is the cause of one in five deaths worldwide.

While one in eight women may be diagnosed with breast cancer, the survival rate is increasing each year. Since there is no tracking of sepsis deaths related to breast cancer or other medical reasons for those under sixty-five, there is no data to analyze this. We do, however, know that eight million people die annually of sepsis, and many of these are under sixty-five years of age. Therefore, if a sepsis death occurs, it would be listed as related to cancer on the death certificate for a person like me. For a person with a bladder infection that resulted in sepsis, this too could cause heart failure and death. Depending on the patient's diagnosis list, my assumption is the reason for death would likely be one of these even if the patient died of sepsis.

This is not OK. It is not OK for a child to lose their mom

because of something that could be prevented. A spouse should not go through the pain of losing their spouse because of something that could be prevented. Yet I knew one young woman who had died from sepsis at forty-six on her twenty-fifth anniversary, and now I had nearly become a statistic too.

So I had to make a choice about whether to spend months in courtrooms and tens of thousands of dollars to gather physician testimonies in written statements acknowledging that professional standards were not followed in my case. These testimonies would most likely be from physicians in other states. In many professional groups, there is an inherent allegiance to each other, and I don't believe it is any different with physicians. With that being said, I was surprised how many physicians did bother to tell me my situation never should have happened. But a courtroom would have continued to foster the negative emotions that stacked up after years of holding on to the situation. I did not see that route as a way for me to heal or to channel my emotions in a healthy way.

Instead, I opted to write a book. Writing a book was a therapeutic and healing expression for me. Writing allowed me to be me and tell my story, without the interference of attorneys. Writing a book allowed me to reach women and families to let them know that some situations require the ability to ask pointed questions. Writing offered me a healthy way to connect my body-, mind-, and soul-healing process into a unified goal. My goal was to have healing of my whole self. Perhaps, while reaching my goal, I could help others by sharing my journey.

You will
find a sense of
thankfulness through
bad times as well
as *good* times.

11 ∾ Untold Risks beyond Cancer

I T NEVER DAWNED ON me when I was diagnosed with cancer that what I really had to fear was multiple complications related to preventable problems. Cancer was curable, but the complications could kill me. These complications came in the form of sepsis from an infection, followed by not receiving heparin shots when I was hospitalized for days, and then physicians overlooking my resultant blood clot. These things created deadly risks.

My discharge orders talked about fever and signs and symptoms to look for related to my mastectomy. Discharge orders addressed my open wounds following my second hospitalization from infected expanders and a sepsis diagnosis. When an infection is brewing, however, your fever may not appear until it is too late. I had no way of knowing that a severe fever could come on in fifteen minutes.

If you are like me, you might not have any of the symptoms of sepsis listed on your surgical discharge order that warrant a call to your doctor. Remember, I had no fever until I arrived in the ER, and with sepsis your body can crash very fast. Knowing your body's early signs and symptoms is critical.

Here are some early red flags I believe my physicians should have caught:

· Continual pain in my right breast, unlike the left breast.

· Discoloration in my right breast and the physician saying, "I am not sure if your tissue will live or die." (I now know that if the tissue dies, it could likely result in an infection.)

· Days before I landed in the ER, my blood pressure was 80/60 at an oncologist visit.

When admitted to the ER, my blood tests showed a white blood cell count of 12,000. The normal range for a woman my age is 8,000–10,000. I never had any blood levels checked while at my follow-up mastectomy appointments when the items noted above were presented. Maybe blood tests would have been a way to know my white blood cell count was changing before I landed in the ER. High white blood cell counts typically indicate an infection is present. Since physicians know that sepsis is a possibility and there is higher risk during the first thirty days post-surgery, I believe blood tests would have been a reasonable intervention.

Long-term setbacks for those diagnosed with sepsis are concerning. They are at higher risk for future blood clots and pneumonia. The costs that surround sepsis treatment are extremely high, whether Medicare pays, or another form of insurance pays for those under sixty-five. Sepsis puts a strain on all of your organs, and recovery can be a slower process than anticipated, even for those who are young adults.

You may realize you planned for the obvious and were shocked by the non-obvious. The non-obvious will be the moments you find the greatest growth.

12 ❧ Lessons Learned

I AM A VERY loyal person. In the early days of my diagnosis, leaving my community hospital and physician seemed unnecessary. Walking away from what is comfortable is never easy. Even when everything is wrong, there is comfort in your surroundings and knowing you are close to home. When you are in the midst of a personal health crisis, the thought of making a healthcare provider change can feel daunting. I tend to only make changes when I am backed into a corner and have no other choice.

After my series of significant medical setbacks, however, I finally realized I had to leave my local hospital system. I was the only one who could truly look out for myself. I had to go by my gut feeling, my internal compass that was pushing me to pursue treatment elsewhere.

I was disappointed, scared, and tired. The third time I was discharged in Duluth, I waited in my wheelchair at the hospital entrance. When my mom and husband picked me up, we drove straight to the Mayo Clinic in Rochester on June 8, 2015. I was not willing to accept the diagnosis presented to me at the hospital in Duluth. I knew I had stage 1 breast cancer, and I was only forty-eight years old. But now I was in a wheelchair for new reasons unrelated to my breast cancer. I wondered how this could be happening to me, and I needed answers.

On this beautiful June day, tulips were blooming in Rochester. When I saw them, I felt hopeful. I had hope for the first time that the missing puzzle piece related to my health care situation could be found. I had hope that I would not be in a wheelchair for the rest of my life. I arrived at Mayo scared that my second opinion would agree with the initial diagnosis when I was discharged from Duluth of Complex Regional Pain Syndrome (CRPS). I had never heard of this diagnosis, and after researching its symptoms, I did not believe it matched my symptoms.

My love affair with the Mayo Clinic began early on. Everywhere I went, there was someone to greet and help me. I was quickly triaged in the ER upon my arrival from Duluth, and the diagnosis I got at Mayo quickly confirmed my original suspicion that I did have a blood clot in my leg. The teams at Mayo were a godsend. I witnessed multiple members of my medical team communicating on every current and historical medical issue related to my health: the vascular surgeon, cardiologist, plastic surgeon, and internal medicine physician. I was shocked when the physicians actually *called* me.

Finally, after months of frustration, I had gained back trust in a health-care team. But it came with sacrifices: the added time and travel costs of frequently going back and forth to Rochester, and out-of-network costs too. At this point, though, I did not care what it would cost, as I needed peace of mind. I would figure out the financial obligations secondarily. First I needed to feel comfortable and have trust. With trust I could move on with a treatment plan. I had entered Rochester as a broken woman, fragile and afraid. In some ways it was peaceful to have no one know me in the area. I didn't want anyone to come up to me and visit, because I was emotionally exhausted.

I remember my first long outdoor wheelchair ride in Rochester. My mom pushed me, going a mile a minute, and all of a sudden she hit a raised cement curb and nearly launched me out of the wheelchair. Finally, something that was a normal moment of laughter occurred for us both. My mom walks like a runner, and my wheelchair had been going at a great clip. This moment of panic gave way to laughter, a welcome stress reliever for us both.

Later, I was in the dressing room of a clothing store in our hotel. My mom wanted to get me some loose-fitting tops to help me feel better. I tried on a loose, gauzy shirt that would hide my bandages. Outside of the dressing room, I heard a woman call my mom's name. There was no way anyone could know she was here, I thought. Well, there in a small boutique, my mom reconnected with lifelong friends from our hometown of St. Francis, Minnesota, who were there with their mom too. Soon the conversation turned to why we were there. Tears welled in my mom's eyes. I could see it pained her to tell them I had breast cancer. The last time I had seen these people I was a young girl, and in my mom's mind, I was her little girl forever too. She desperately wanted to take all the pain away from me, so sometimes we ended up crying in strange places. That moment, it was a dressing room.

The next time my mom flew back to visit me was a year later, in April 2016, for my second reconstructive surgery. My body needed time, a year of healing, to build back strength before this surgery. It would require me to be in surgery for at least eight hours. This would be my third surgery to follow the original mastectomy surgery, with the second surgery being the one to remove the infected expander due to the sepsis.

This procedure was called latissimus dorsi surgery. My back muscle would be filleted in half like a fish and moved around to the front of my chest wall to cover the area where I now had scar tissue buildup where my right breast used to be. The beauty of this operation was that I would not lose any blood supply as they moved my back muscle to my right chest wall. This would allow a higher success rate for keeping the breast tissue alive. This was my only option to offer hope for a chance for a right breast to exist. In addition, I had lost a lot of skin from the sepsis infection, so this surgery would be complicated for many reasons.

Right before surgery, the surgeon carefully marked my chest and back and sketched me like an artist. She wrote her initials on me and said she would see me after surgery. The artistic sketching is to have an outline marked to ensure the proper areas are surgically altered. I felt her compassion and concern, and her confidence allowed me to relax. I always dread going into the surgery room and seeing the sterile, cold, morgue-like environment. It makes my hands sweat. I hate the feeling of having my arms tied down on the table. It makes me feel beyond claustrophobic. It is a feeling of being completely vulnerable and trapped. Suddenly, everyone is looking at you and you are surrounded by blue masks and blue hats.

Because I couldn't have sedatives before going to the surgery room, I prayed I would not hyperventilate before they put on the mask to get me to sleep. Luckily, I counted to two and was asleep before I could panic.

It was comforting to know that I was not the Mayo Clinic's first challenging case from a mastectomy surgery gone wrong. Driving into the parking ramp and looking at the license plates from around the United States, it was clear this establishment was held in high regard. Each time I sat in a lobby before an appointment, I had amazing conversations with people from around the world. They had traveled there by plane, bus, and car. Many were spending several days at hotels, like I was. Others had rented homes for months, staying miles from their families to try to find answers for their health concerns.

I felt blessed to live in Minnesota, where I did not have to travel across states to have access to this model of care. My hotel stays and long road trips were nothing compared to others' sacrifices, especially parents with younger kids. Still, everyone finds moments to smile in this place of medical miracles. After a while, I knew the community calendar in the Mayo area, and I started to feel like a member of the Rochester community. On Thursdays, my mom and I could sit outside and listen to live music. I knew where to find the shoe store, the café, and all my favorite stores. I felt comfortable there.

Finally, I had a team of confident professionals handling my care, and for the first time I started to let my guard

down and relax. The outcomes confirmed it—the reconstruction of my botched surgery was life-changing. As a
kid, I was told everything happens for a reason. Sometimes
it takes a while to figure out what those reasons are. If you
sit back long enough, you get to watch your life play out.
Many times, we don't get to pick and control the timing of
events. I believe now that it was a blessing that I initially
got treatment in Duluth and had the experience I had. Sure,
things did not go as planned. Sure, I could have avoided a
lot of stress and added expenses from being away from my
business as long as I was. Had this not happened, however,
I would not be able to help other women know what questions to ask and what things they need to know. Now I am
in a position to help others. God puts us where he wants us
to be at every moment in our lives.

Much of my life has felt like being on a potter's wheel.
I have been a piece of clay being molded to learn and
grow, whether I wanted to or not. I am naive and gullible. Sometimes these traits are not the best combination.
Sometimes I have been taken advantage of. But if there is
5 percent good in someone, I am likely the one to find it.
After all, I was a girl from St. Francis who simply wanted to
spend her life caring for the elderly. Owning a business had
never been on my bucket list. Other people saw my passion,
and the train left the station.

My passion never changed when I entered the business
world, but there were many times I felt like a circle in a
square world. The principles of the farm world I grew up
in did not always apply. Where I grew up, your word was
enough. A handshake meant something. To the rest of the

world those standards may not apply, but to me they still do. I had to learn the hard way how to stand up for myself in ways I was not used to.

Now, I have learned how to be the same farm girl I was all my life, gracefully staying true to the principles I value, even when faced with adversity. After all, it is impossible to run a twenty-four-hour business without adversity at times. But I have been blessed with amazing employees who give their best every day. I, too, enjoyed caring for seniors when I started as an aide. Years later, as a CEO, it is still fun to work side by side with staff as we give seniors the best last chapter of their lives possible.

The best advice I ever received came from a business partner who told me that partners are for dancing. He said this as we were starting the business, when I was one of several minority partners for our health-care business. After going through my breast cancer journey, I learned he was right. I was a slow learner, I guess, and maybe that was another one of cancer's silver linings. After my cancer experience, our company went through many changes. Eventually, I would own only the management company, which was appropriately named Full Circle Senior Living, LLC. Full Circle Senior Living would be the corporate office for support services to offer payroll, accounting, and management to several assisted living facilities in northern Minnesota. I jokingly call this the best part of Minnesota—the top half, west to east, from Hinckley up. This has been my traveling path on every rural roadway for the past fifteen years, with miles and miles of windshield time. I have loved it.

I resigned from Full Circle Senior Living and took a new

opportunity as a leader for seniors in MN. I was blessed with a new group of wonderful caregivers, and I was grateful for the opportunity to be creative while also learning myself, side by side with an engaging owner and supportive leadership team.

The Full Circle assisted living facilities were built in 2004 and later were used as an alternative to a nursing home for those who desired a setting with fewer seniors. My passion to serve seniors began with my great-grandparents, who were immigrants from Sweden. They would often come and stay with us at the farm, and at an early age I learned how to lift my frail grandparents in and out of wheelchairs. My first job would be as a certified nursing assistant at the nursing home where they resided. I loved the atmosphere of caring for seniors and learning their life stories.

I grew up very close to my grandparents, Cliff and Hazel. I started writing weekly letters to my Grandma Hazel from 1985 to 2000, first in college, and then continuing when I moved to Duluth and got married. When she moved to Duluth, assisted living was truly a new thing in Minnesota. I was grateful she made the move to the assisted living facility I was running then, as I knew I had a free pass to stop the letter writing.

She resided there for several years until she became bedbound with shingles. She needed to be fed and required a smaller setting, and our family wanted a non–nursing home setting for the last chapter of her life. My parents had cared for my grandpa Cliff at the family farm till his death, and now desired the same quaintness for her. So I helped form something new, a concept of a miniature assisted living facility with the best care principles I learned while working as a certified nursing assistant and nursing home administrator in the nursing homes. Now, thousands of seniors like my grandma, who need a smaller setting for memory loss, higher care needs, medical care, and a secured setting, have more options.

When I was at my sickest point from the sepsis infection, I was relieved my Grandma Hazel had passed away before my diagnosis. She would have worried twenty-four hours a day and felt helpless at her older age. Her inspiration and devoted faith filled me when I was ill.

Grandma Hazel and I shared so much through words in a letter. I loved the anticipation of wondering if a letter would be in the mailbox, and she felt the same. I never knew my early years of letter writing would continue to morph into a love for writing. Over the years, letter writing transformed into multiple monthly newsletters to residents, family, and employees for years to come. In 2021, I wrote my last newsletter for Full Circle Senior Living. I was asked by many why I would resign from something I helped create. The answer was easy—everyone needs to know when it is the time to walk away.

As my Grandma Hazel would so often say, there is a season for everything. I knew it was time for a new chapter in my life. Time for me to grow and learn new things working in a setting I was not part of building. Time for a new season in my life. Change is always hard. But after several surgeries and brushing the edge of death a time or two, it was the easiest decision I ever made. It was easy to decide to choose what was best for me and what was best for my marriage. I was not afraid. For the first time in a long time, I reached a place of peacefulness that allowed me to pursue a new opportunity. I was blessed with the opportunity to work with wonderful caregivers and leaders and continue to serve seniors. I was grateful for the opportunity to be creative while learning myself. Life is good.

You may realize your experiences have prepared you for new opportunities you never planned for, which were blessings in disguise.

13 ～ Color-Blind

ANCER, FOR SOME REASON, is associated with a color. Before I was diagnosed, I never really noticed or cared. Now I cared—I was bombarded with pink symbols everywhere I went. I never liked the color pink before cancer, and I sure didn't like it now.

Early on, I went to an oncology appointment and wished I could pop every pink balloon in the clinic. I realize this decorating is a well-intentioned symbolic gesture, but I hated being reminded of cancer everywhere I went. I was no longer color-blind. Every color now had emotions associated with it, pink especially. When I drove down the road and saw a pink garbage can, I cried. When I went to the grocery store and saw pink ribbons on yogurt containers, I cried.

I did not join this club, I thought. *I am not in a cancer club.* To me, a club is bowling, Bunco, volleyball, or something else fun. Cancer was not fun, and I didn't want pink to label or define me. So I didn't let it. This period would be a time I wanted to forget, to put in the past, so I ignored everything pink so I could cope my own way.

One day, someone sent me a photo of my name on a bag

along a lit pathway. I didn't know what it was for. Finally, it dawned on me it was a cancer benefit. My brain just could not process that I was in this category, but I was touched by family and friends who did cancer walks and events, wore bracelets, and even got tattooed, thinking of me as they did it.

Many fabulous local and national organizations help women dealing with cancer. These incredible programs allow us to donate as we can and give us opportunities to reach out and help our community members. Eventually, I was able to associate the color pink with the various ways people help others with breast cancer, rather than as being only a color symbol for those who have the disease. As I healed as a complete person, in body, mind, and spirit, I was able to re-enter volunteer opportunities in the community to help others. When I am helping others, I forget about my problems and past health issues. Volunteering to help others was a gift, and soon I again appreciated the color pink.

Each time there is a sign-up for cancer walks, motorcycle rallies, and various challenges, I remember that one in eight people are diagnosed with breast cancer in their lifetime. With these statistics, it is likely we all know someone who has been affected by breast cancer.

Fearing the word *cancer* or any other shocking health news sometimes feels like a force that pushes you into your own protective bubble or personal cocoon. Many people asked how I dealt with cancer. Initially, I am not sure I did. Initially, I was living it, and the coping came a few years later. I did quickly learn that rolling into a fetal position would not help me get through anything. Sure I was scared, overwhelmed, tired of all the surgeries, and sad, but everything in me said to fight to not lose myself in my situation. I had things I did not want to miss, like our son's high school graduation party. These events kept me going. I had things in life to look forward to. I kept telling myself, *This is only today and not forever.*

After each surgery, my weeks were consumed with healing. I never had a moment to really process my feelings. It was easier to suppress any emotion, because if I allowed myself to feel sad, I feared I would completely lose my emotional stability. I feared not knowing where my breaking point would be.

When considered as a whole, my medical experiences had been all-consuming and overwhelming during this time. The list of surgeries and hospitalizations would become quite a rap sheet:

- Surgery for double mastectomy, April 2015
- Surgery to remove infected right side breast expander and sepsis, May 2015
- Hospitalized June 2015 for blood clot symptoms, diagnosed with CRPS
- Surgery for reconstruction surgery of right breast, latissimus dorsi flap, for reconstruction of the breast, April 2016
- Surgery for fat harvesting to fill in gap in breast area, and removal of expanders & exchange for permanent silicone implants, September 2016
- Surgery to stop internal bleeding from fat harvesting procedure days earlier and subsequent seven-day hospitalization, September 2016

- Surgery to remove left nipple that was misaligned, June 2017
- Surgery to remove ovaries and tubes due to status as ER+, November 2020

During my fourth surgery in 2017, they removed the nipple from my left breast that was two inches higher than it should have been located, to prepare for tattoos that would match. In addition, they extracted fat from my abdomen to insert in my chest wall where filler was needed. Because of my blood clot risk, my blood needed medication to be thinned for surgery, and that made me higher risk for this surgery. I was grateful the hospital team prevented any further blood clots after this surgery.

In addition, a few days after this surgery, my stomach became very bloated, and I went to the ER and was cared for by my new internal medicine physician. I was bleeding internally and needed a fifth surgery. I didn't even want to tell anyone I was hospitalized. I was so tired and hit a wall for the first time. I walked down the hospital hall with a catheter bag and IV pole, holding a walker and thinking, *Dear God, I am fifty years old and feel like I'm a hundred.* I peeked into the other hospital rooms as I walked at a turtle's pace. I was thinking that every patient looked better than me. My body had become deconditioned and lost so much muscle mass that I had to take baby steps to do basic things. That is the moment that sadness hit me. I had to face how sick I had been for the past two years. My body was black and blue from my chest to my knees from bleeding internally, and I was shocked. I looked like I had been dragged down a freeway for hours. It was a horrifying look.

I had already been hospitalized for seven days, and there was nothing else to do but embrace my feelings, accept my situation, and learn to enjoy the QVC channel. When I placed my first order, I called my niece and asked, "What size are your feet? I am sending you some really cute black boots." Watching QVC served as a great distraction from my emotions. In between QVC shopping, I was relieved to see my internal medicine physician rounding to assess my condition while I was hospitalized. I trusted my care team, and they prevented potential blood clots while I was bedridden. Mission accomplished.

It had taken me nearly two years to break down and cry, and I reached the tipping point not on my own behalf, but on someone else's. My buried emotions were triggered when one of my employees was diagnosed with stage 4 lung cancer. She was thirty-something, with two young boys, and had gone to the doctor for a suspected cold. Her life changed in a moment. I cried more for her than I ever cried for myself. Finally, all the emotion I'd buried was released, whether I liked it or not. Now, years after my diagnosis and initial surgeries, my emotions felt raw. But it wasn't all bad—here was someone I could share my experiences with to help them prepare and cope. Here was an opportunity to volunteer for her fundraiser. Together with friends and family, we decorated the fundraiser with the color white. I learned the color white represented lung cancer, as a cancer ribbon symbol. I was the color pink, and she was the color white. Two different cancers, and two different people. In these moments, you are united by one common cause, to support each other to embrace the journey of treatment and to fight for your life.

You will
realize what you
like and don't like,
including colors.

14 ∾ Embracing Tragedy with Family and Friends, and the Joy of Helping Others

WHEN I WAS FIRST diagnosed, I didn't think about how I would look or feel after I was done with treatment. I figured a double mastectomy would end the cancer, and this chapter of my life would be done and complete once and for all.

My plan seemed straightforward, but it did not account for the emotions that would come from a series of serious setbacks. I never prepared for the day I removed my bandages and looked in the mirror after my second surgery, which removed my infected expander on the side where I never had breast cancer. I sobbed, and as I mentioned, I thought I looked like I should be on the television show *Botched*. I actually considered contacting the show, but I was far too reserved to be on a national television show for breast reconstruction. I'd only ever been on local television, doing commercials for my job.

Although I had researched and opted for nipple sparing to preserve some normalcy, this plan backfired. When the breast on my noncancerous side became infected, everything had to be removed. So now I needed a tattoo on that side. The nipple survived the procedure on the side where my cancer was, but it was now two inches off-center. It was surgically fixable, but I did not want another surgery. How would I ever look normal? No one wants one off-center nipple and one nipple that is tattooed on and creates a non-symmetrical look.

I must have had post-traumatic stress disorder, because for about six months I cried every time I went to the doctor. My scars were not only visually disturbing—I looked like someone had taken a chainsaw to me—but they were also a daily reminder of all that had gone wrong, of what should have never happened. They were a daily reminder of how I had nearly died.

The doctor's office made my regular follow-up photo shoots comical by having trolls mounted on the walls. The photographer would say, "Place your hands on your side and look to the troll on the left. Then the center. Then the right," and so on. This went on for months. The first time I went in the room, I wished I had Kahlúa in my coffee to numb me in this moment. It took me months to feel confident disrobing in front of others, including the photographer. But by my last photo shoot, I nearly left my patient room naked and walked across the hallway because I was so comfortable, and also distracted by multitasking and trying to answer work emails on my phone. This modest woman had come a long way. I just laughed it off as a nurse quickly redirected me.

After my last photo shoot, I realized my scars did not

measure my healing. My healing was just starting—I still needed to heal emotionally too. Once I was strong enough to walk, work, and make it through a day, I realized I had a list of things I could no longer keep putting off. The time was now, and every moment counted at a much deeper level for me. I felt emotions deeply, beyond my typical sentimentality.

As my life went on after my recovery, absorbing every moment became a daily priority at fifty-four years of age. Now, I could hit the pause button and reflect. For the past decade and more, I had pushed hard. I had started an assisted living business from the ground up in my late thirties, had two boys in competitive hockey throughout my thirties and forties, and burned my candle at both ends. God's sense of humor caught my attention in a psalm I now love even more. To me, "makes me lie down" means rest. "Beside the still waters" means peace, and "walking through the valley of death" signals hope. All the words of Psalm 23:1–6 resonate with me:

> The Lord is my shepherd; I shall not want. He makes me to lie down in green pastures; He leads me beside the still waters. He restores my soul; He leads me in the paths of righteousness for His name's sake. Yea, though I walk through the valley of the shadow of death, I will fear no evil; For You are with me; Your rod and Your staff, they comfort me. You prepare a table before me in the presence of my enemies; You anoint my head with oil; my cup runs over. Surely goodness and mercy shall follow me all

the days of my life; and I will dwell in the house of the Lord forever.[3]

The word *makes* here amazes me—God did *make* me lie down. He knew my candle would burn out if I did not change, and perhaps cancer was how he got my attention. I will never know, but my family medical history had never included breast cancer before. There is truth to stress's long-term impact on our bodies, and God does have a plan for us every day of our lives.

Among the things I reprioritized after treatment was keeping my family relationships strong. My siblings and parents live in different states, so time together is something I had to schedule to make sure our memories can continue. After all, I grew up with cousins, aunts, uncles, grandparents, and the joy of all our collective chaos. I realized it took the next generation, which was now me, to keep our traditions going. I just had to get strong enough before I could start putting things on the calendar. Annual family reunions are now a must.

On a smaller family scale, our kids were in their early twenties and in college after my treatment, so I wanted us to treasure our time together all the more. Moving the kids into college was something to look forward to. I vowed not to miss any opportunity to travel to watch a hockey game or meet up for lunch or coffee.

When the boys were young, we went to my husband's family's river retreat nearly every weekend. The boys referred to their time as either school days (weekdays) or

---

3   New King James Version.

cabin days at the river (weekends). We were so lucky to have these years to go four-wheeling and enjoy nature together. Now, I would look forward to making new memories similar to the ones we created years earlier at the river cabin. Now, my husband and I decided to finally act on a longtime dream and purchase a new home on a lake. Now we could enjoy all the things we loved about the river—being in nature and all the activities every season offers. It was time to simplify, downsize, and get ready for the next chapter of life.

Our kids would graduate from college and we would be right back where we started, just the two of us. Now was the perfect time to have a lake adventure—we could kayak, cross-country ski, four-wheel, have bonfires, and enjoy all of Minnesota's seasons. (Sometimes winter occupies six months of the calendar, but I assure you, we do get four seasons here.)

Following treatment, my priorities included finding new ways to help other people too. Volunteering was one of the best ways for me to forget about my years of setbacks and treatment. Helping others takes the focus off ourselves. It is easy to get self-absorbed with our issues, our projects, and our lives. My principles of service always keep me balanced and my perspective focused.

Years ago, I had adopted a military family through the Salvation Army to bring them presents at Christmastime. This was an initiative my business participated in, but when I saw that there was one family left unassigned, I decided to get their presents on behalf of my family. The woman's husband was deployed in the US Army, and she had a baby and a two-year-old and three-year-old at the time. After we brought the gifts to the kids, I held the children. These little kids immediately melted my heart, so I kept in touch with their mom.

As time went by, our relationship grew. The older kids would come to our home to play so the mother could be with the baby or go get groceries. The kids loved coming over and I loved having them. They were great therapy for me, and it was fun to hear children's feet in our home again. I grew up babysitting and loved the joy of young children. They were a great distraction from the daily stresses of management.

Sometimes the kids attended hockey games with me, but most of the time they wanted to just be at our home, eat cheese pizza, and play with toys. One week, when the baby finally got to be a bit older, I got to bring all three kids over. The first time this happened, I looked in my rearview mirror and saw the baby standing in the car seat. The oldest sibling—still a toddler—said, "My mom doesn't let her do this." I quickly pulled over and this toddler instructed me on how to latch the car seat, a new style that was out of my league.

This relationship has continued for years, and as their family has grown, so has the number of car seats in my car. The siblings buckle everyone in, and I simply marvel at how these little kids never forget their routines.

These kids have reminded me how to be as playful as a child. We would hike through the yard or snuggle, as they watched Disney movies I loved too. We sang songs in the car every time I picked them up or drove them home. Because their dad was deployed, the kids even enjoyed seeing our boys or my husband working in the yard. When their dad returned, I realized this was my way of thanking a veteran for their sacrifice.

When I was unable to see the kids, their mom said, "The kids pray for you every night, and they call you Aunt Natalie." They even mailed me sweet pictures they had colored. I was touched by these little souls. Although they are not my direct relatives, I love them as my own.

Whenever I called the kids to let them know I was having surgery so I could not see them for a while, they would say, "Oh no! How long before you are strong again?" They were sad when I said it would be months before I would be strong enough to take them to my house due to lifting restrictions. Even after a year had passed, it was uplifting to know that they never forgot me.

When I finally got to pull up in front of their home again, it was a joy to see their feet scampering down the hill. I'll never forget their smiles and energy, carrying their car seats. They needed me, and I needed them. They thought they were the lucky ones, but I was too.

Not long after I first met them, I began seeing similar number combinations every time I looked at the clock: 1:11, 2:22, 3:33, 4:44, or 5:55. As someone who is always late, I don't look at the clock very often to begin with. This pattern went on for months, and it was very curious. One evening I was at the kids' home so their mom could run errands, and all three of them were sitting on my lap. I glanced up and saw it was 5:55, and suddenly the mystery made sense. I was finally still enough to pay attention. Whenever a long period of time had passed where I had not seen the kids, the numbers always appeared every time I looked at a clock. I knew this meant I was where I was supposed to be—right on time.

So I never questioned that this is where God planted me. I never questioned my role in this family's life again. Now, years later, the family has eight children. Their names all start with M, so I call them my M&M's. The family is still entered in my phone as my Christmas family.

Often I am reminded in life of a motto I learned in Girl Scouts: "Make new friends, but keep the old; one is silver and the other gold." When you are truly present in the moment, you are more in tune to the opportunities that are right before you, with or without cancer. When you have moments to help others, your focus is off your issues, and your mind stays peaceful and healthy.

When I had young children, JoJo, our live-in nanny, entered our lives at seventy-five years of age. She lived with us two days a week. She loved our children as her own and when I would say, "What can I do for you?" her response was always, "Help someone you are *not* related to someday." Well, that someday came.

You will
realize your situation
may feel like a cloud
is hanging over your head,
and then the sun will
shine, and your light
will shine even
brighter.

15 ⌘ Eating Crow

I ALWAYS TOLD MY brother I would never get a tattoo, but the first lesson in life is never to say the word *never*. After completing my surgeries for the breast recon-struction, I decided to fly to Baltimore to meet with an in-credible team that would help me find closure as a woman. I would get not one but two nipple tattoos to complete my breast reconstruction and help me heal. Now I would eat crow, as my brother would say. I would get my first tattoos at age fifty—on my boobs, of all places. I would have tattoos that looked very much like realistic nipples.

My brother researched who would be the best tattoo art-ist for me, and he said the world-renowned Vinnie Myers was the best. When we arrived at the tattoo parlor, it was nothing fancy on the outside, just a neighborhood strip mall. But walking through the doors, the first thing I saw was a world map with tacks all over it, marking where all their clients are from. Their clients are literally from around the world.

After moving to a chair in a private room, I reclined with a towel over my chest. Vinnie came into the room to prep the ink colors to match my skin tones. Suddenly, I heard the door starting to open and I flinched—a remnant of my modesty reflexes. Of course, I had violated rule number one when getting a tattoo: remain still.

As it turned out, the person opening the door was my brother, checking to see if I was OK. He had been in the other room getting a hand tattoo, so I hadn't expected to see him again. It was so sweet—he knew I was nervous, as this was out of my wheelhouse. I assured him I was good and he left, just like our German shepherd at the farm, Sheba, checking that all is well. "Wasn't it odd for your brother to see you?" friends asked me later. Not at all—as a sister with only brothers, I have to say I have been blessed.

On my way out of the tattoo parlor, a nervous-looking woman came in with her husband. I sat next to her and told her I had just had my tattoos done. I assured her it did not hurt. It took thirty minutes, and I was amazed at how they matched my pigmentation. I offered to show her how mine had turned out and she said yes. My wall of modesty lifted, and I raised my shirt to show a complete stranger my nipple tattoos. Afterward, we hugged and wished each other well.

Thankfully, I had put my shirt down just in time, right before my dad walked into the parlor. While my brother and I got our tattoos, Dad did what is normal for him. He went to the nearest gas station to find his three favorite items: a cup of coffee, a donut, and a scratch-off ticket. As my brother would say, Dad is a wuss just like me and hates needles. But Dad was sure happy to be there to bring me a cup of coffee and a donut, just like our farm days.

Nipple tattoos done—another item on the list checked off. I went up to the map in the lobby and put a stick pin on the city of Hermantown, Minnesota, to join many others noting their hometown.

We returned to my brother's house for my niece's graduation party. A few drinks in, several learned I'd just had nipple tattoos done by Vinnie Myers, and soon I was holding nipple tattoo viewings in my brother's living room. I had to laugh—this was so not me, but I did not care.

My brother soon learned of this, and said, "What are you doing? I have teenage boys running around here and we are not at Sturgis." I said, "Relax, no one saw anything." I guess with a body that was no longer mine but rather felt like bocce balls, I was less modest. My brother certainly saw many breasts at Sturgis on his many motorcycle trips with his wife. So I never thought he would get worked up about me showing a chest that was fake with two bocce balls. I was wrong, I was his sister, and he put an end to show-and-tell. I guess he ate crow too.

You may
realize you are
suddenly less opinionated
and less judgmental
of others.

16 ✍ Double Standards

I F I HAD A dollar for every time someone asked me, "Why haven't you sued?" I would be rich. Everywhere I went, people were shocked to hear my story.

As a health-care professional, I understand that accidents can happen to anyone. Everything has inherent risks. But during the worst years of the whole experience, my situation just gnawed at me at many levels, getting deeper with each passing day. I soon realized I was at war with myself. I had invested months of my time researching standards of practice in a field I did not practice in, and this research confirmed and validated my feelings. I was not off base or overreacting. It was not hard to find support across the country for basic, standard practices on early intervention with sepsis post-surgery.

This validation helped me realize how important education is. I wanted to make sure that what happened to me could be prevented for others. After all, if a series of huge mistakes happened to me at a hospital where I had been a patient for more than two decades, I was not convinced others would be spared.

I chose to leave the Duluth hospital system and listen

to my inner voice, which told me I had a blood clot—not CRPS, which the hospitalist stated I had. They told me there was no cure, but I could expect up to level-ten pain. My discharge notes said to go to the pain center for a nerve block in my leg that ended up having an active blood clot.

I wrote a letter to the management of the hospital after I learned I had a blood clot and shared my dismay with my outcomes. I was naïve to hope for a genuine apology or acknowledgment of error. If you choose to ask the hospital to cover your expenses, the hospital or physician will then forward it to their insurance carrier. At some point afterward, you will receive a letter asking you for multiple statements from outside physicians confirming a standard of practice and alleged wrongdoing. From my experience, you will only get supporting physician statements if you are willing to pay thousands of dollars out of pocket up front. Most cancer survivors don't have the endurance and financial means to hire physicians to testify like this. After already paying thousands out of pocket, it seems like a futile attempt to right a wrong.

From my experience, it is difficult for health professionals to question others' judgment when they work collaboratively together, nurse to nurse or physician to physician. What evolves is a professionally understood language to avoid putting each other in this position.

Is it possible that every physician in a system is of equal performance levels? I don't know. I do know that if longterm care and assisted living facilities don't follow standards of practices, they have to answer to a mandated reporting system. In Minnesota, every nurse, social worker, or physician who has reason to believe a vulnerable senior has been abused or neglected must report this to the Office of Health Facility Complaints. This information enters a database and is investigated.

Out in the rest of the world, if I rear-end someone, even if they stopped in a merging lane and I can't avoid hitting them, I can be sued. If someone is hurt on my property, I can be sued. In these cases, the procedures for court cases are much easier for attorneys.

However, if you believe negligence occurred in your surgery or treatment before or after, the process is not simple unless the surgeon removed the wrong limb or something else big happened, leaving you horribly debilitated. Common sense is often dismissed, even when these errors create multiple unnecessary hospitalizations. Even a preexisting diagnosis of cancer should not create an environment in which basic prevention is missed because the cancer can be easily blamed if anything goes wrong.

Who is paying for these errors? For those of you who are under sixty-five and still working, you are. You are paying for it through higher premiums. You are paying your premiums just like your employers are paying their portion. If you don't pay your hospital bill, it goes to collections. The moment one of my bills was one day late, I got calls from the billing department, even when all my re-hospitalizations were related to preventable items.

The rules for car insurance or homeowner's insurance claims are much different—the plaintiff does not have to pay out-of-pocket costs to gather professional testimony. Instead, the plaintiff drafts the charges and both sides typically settle out of court or decide to go to trial. In an assisted living facility or nursing home environment, the expectation is to have no decline for the elderly patient. When someone is on hospice the rules are different. However, when you are a patient who is healthy going into surgery, with a breast cancer diagnosis, if you suffer decline due to routine things that were missed, there is no recourse for the patient. These patients have not had the opportunity to live their life to reach an elderly age yet. It seems there would be standards to ensure no decline from preventable items such as sepsis and blood clots. For whatever reason, there seems to be a strange double standard between hospitals on the one hand and assisted living facilities and nursing homes on the other.

You may experience that money won't buy happiness.

17 ∾ Fighting to Live

FTER MULTIPLE SURGERIES, I couldn't wait to live my life again. What I didn't realize is that I needed to redefine what living meant to me. Beyond your initial surgery and treatment, there are many ways that your body fights to live in your recovery phase.

I was a slow learner when it came to recognizing them. After each surgery, I wanted to resume living with the same energy and doing the same activities that had defined my pre-surgery life. I would eagerly prepare to do the things I had missed, like walking for miles on the treadmill. Then I would overdo it and be laid up for a month to heal with another set of preventable complications—by my own doing this time.

First, I developed shin splints, then lower back pain. My entire body ached. I had to put ice or heat on every part of my body each night. I was so frustrated—how would I ever get stronger? It was hard to think I had to exercise in ten-minute increments in order to not re-injure myself. I felt like I was being lazy if I didn't exercise for my usual thirty minutes, so I would go for the full time, override my body, and suffer the consequences.

I was so eager to put it all in the past and move on, but it took injuring myself several times before I realized my muscles had weakened and I just needed to start off slower. Now I have accepted that walking long distances should not be done fast, rebuilding core strength takes a while, and my new baseline is different than before. I *will* get there, but I need to take baby steps to heal. As I just passed the fifth anniversary of my mastectomy, I am still deconditioned, and I still need to stretch my chest wall muscles daily.

Long after the wounds close, your body is still healing. Prior to surgery, I often went to bed at midnight or later and rose at 7:00 a.m. Now I found myself needing ten or more hours of sleep at times. Post-surgery, I also started taking vitamins. In order to remember all of them, I set up a seven-day vitamin dispenser. I also needed to eat adequate protein and stay hydrated to allow my body to heal. I had trouble sleeping, too, so at bedtime I used lavender oil in a diffuser to prepare my mind to decompress.

I wasn't even premenopausal when I was forty-eight, but my ovaries needed to be shut down because my hormone test showed I was ER+, meaning estrogen positive, with cells that can use estrogen to grow. Therefore, the oncology team wants to ensure you are not producing estrogen. My labs also showed I was not in menopause. I was afraid to have another surgery due to my history of blood clots, so I took Lupron shots to force me into menopause until 2021, when I finally had ovaries and tubes out in my final surgery.

The Lupron shots had major side effects to deal with. I felt like I had been shoved into a 450-degree oven. My body was dripping wet with sweat, and I always needed the fan on high. I was crawling into bed during winter without wearing flannel pajamas and wool socks. For the first time in my life, I was not constantly freezing. What the hell was happening to me? My husband would lie next to me with his teeth chattering as our bedroom was as cold as a walk-in freezer. He wanted as many blankets as possible, and mine were whipped on the floor.

"Don't think I am interested in sex just because I am naked," I'd tell my husband, "because I am not." I am sure he could tell by my snarky voice. Nothing about me felt remotely sexy.

Whenever I wasn't able to sleep, staring at the ceiling, I would think, *Because I am up all night long, I may as well have a baby to rock.* I say that jokingly, but if I had verbalized that to my husband, he would have definitely left for the border. Years ago, following my hysterectomy, I had first said those words with sincerity. My last pregnancy was very hard on my body, but I had always thought I would have four kids. So I researched adoption, and Grandma Hazel sent me newspaper ads saying, "Is your baby waiting for you in China?" Then we started the business, and my husband and I decided it was just not realistic for us to adopt. We ended up with four dogs instead. Eventually, my physician prescribed me medication to help with my hot flashes, and once we tweaked my dosage and I adjusted, I finally began to sleep again. I was put on venlafaxine.

Cancer treatment affected more than just my chest—it uprooted a lot of things I'd taken for granted in my health. It took intentional self-awareness to understand how I was coping, healing, and modifying my lifestyle. Every day was different, and my needs varied. But even as my body and wounds healed, the scars stayed front and center for me every time I looked in the mirror. The scars never really faded, but perhaps as I continue to emotionally heal, the traumatic memories will. I am sure it was hard on my husband, too, as he never knew why I was crying. Many times I did not know why either.

You may need years
to heal, not months.
And that is OK.

18 ∾ Everything Happens for a Reason

AFTER I WAS DIAGNOSED with cancer, everything I had learned in Sunday school rushed to the forefront of my daily thoughts. I would sing a song over and over in my head that I had learned so many years earlier—"This Little Light of Mine." I did not want "my light" to be blown out by Satan, and I would surely be tested at this age in my life.

Cancer tested my faith in ways I could not comprehend, but I had always believed everything happens for a reason. Perhaps the saying is a cliché, but I repeated it to myself every day. I had said that quote when I didn't get something I wanted, like a certain job after college, but cancer was different. It seemed useless to wonder, *Why me?* Choosing to believe that everything happens for a reason was the only path for me to have a sense of peace.

I trusted God up until my diagnosis, but looking back, that was only partial trust. I trusted myself to do my personal best and knew God would do the rest. Then along came cancer, and I had to surrender completely. It wasn't about me at all. It didn't matter if I thought I was a good person. I had to trust in God, whether it meant I would live or die.

My past experiences in business taught me how to persevere during good times and bad. Ultimately, this prepared me for tough battles in my personal life. I am so thankful for those people who believed in me and gave me the opportunities I had. Life is all about taking risks. It's also about continually learning. So when I say everything happens for a reason, I still believe that is true.

When I think back to the situations I lost sleep over in my early twenties, I laugh. I was a new graduate and a nursing home administrator. I would work twelve-hour days and think, *How can I leave? My job here is not done.* I still have to remind myself that there will never be a day when the job is done, because this job runs twenty-four hours a day.

I remember detailing for my dad early in my career how many things I wanted to fix. He laughed, reminding me to be grateful there were things that I could help fix as a leader. "You will learn far more than if you were in a place where everything was already in place and you had no opportunities to be creative," he said. He was right. He often reminded me that leaders exist to find solutions, and to lead the way with a great team. I now had the opportunity to learn how to work with all generations. I was a young woman supervising women and men decades older than me. I had to figure out how to get their respect without using my title and position. I learned fast that expecting people to follow you because of your title or position is not true leadership.

Instead, it is gaining the respect of each individual that creates an atmosphere for accomplishing real change.

The first time state surveyors showed up at the nursing home, I had to quickly learn how to diffuse a tense situation. The surveyors' job was to investigate complaints and check whether standards are being followed. Everyone was afraid of surveyors, and professional nurses and aides were in tears. Then an aide came to me and said, "Try doing your job being while being watched for hours with no one saying a word to you. You feel like you are in a prison or something." I watched and listened to the surveyors' questioning, and I could understand how the staff could feel that way. Even the residents with dementia would ask me why guards with clipboards were standing around. In the end, we were all there for the same reason: to ensure great care for our elderly population. However, perception was reality, and the following years allowed for opportunities to prepare for the awkwardness of being watched continually. Preparing for a process that was not a typical day helped the week flow for every employee while diffusing the stress for residents too.

Often, the surveyors had gone through hours of training but had never worked in a nursing home themselves, and in these situations the expectations were not always realistic. As I have learned, there is textbook, and then there is real life. Sometimes textbook and real life blend perfectly, and other times—especially when you are dealing with people with dementia—they do not.

My career has given me a perspective that is more about realism than expecting total perfection. I believe that accepting this perspective opened the door for many objectives and goals to be met in my personal and professional life. Perfection is not humanly possible twenty-four hours a day. While it is a fabulous goal, staff triage the events of their shifts and make decisions to ensure everyone's best interest is served. Sometimes degrees of flexibility are required to match the event of the moment. Human beings with dementia are not programmable—their brains may follow a different path every day. I learned to trust each caregiver and entrust in them my faith that they would do their best, just like I did as an aide and as a CEO. We work as a team, knowing that we may not be perfect. Together, we create something better than ourselves, as long as we are committed to lifelong learning and growing. Understanding the inner workings of twenty-four-hour operations and working for a collaborative partnership with state and federal agencies has defined for me the saying, "Everything happens for a reason."

Often, the media shares nursing home horror stories. Unfortunately, tragedy seems to make the news rather than the joy of people making a difference daily. I am not sure any other industry is more regulated than long-term care. It often saddened me to see a profession I have given my life to under siege with negative newspaper press. I knew many great providers and they would never tolerate neglect or abuse. Soon, I began to understand that good news does not make the paper, and the news industry thrived when people bought papers to read about bad news. Again, "Everything happens for a reason."

Since I began my career in 1983, nursing homes across

the country have modified how they deliver care. When I first started, the standard of care was to tie everyone to their wheelchair or use bed vest restraints so they did not fall. I was taught as a certified nursing assistant to tie every resident down in bed or in a wheelchair. I was taught by competent and dedicated nurses who wanted to make sure there were zero falls, as the falls would likely cause a fracture and further decline. I was also taught to syringe-feed everyone who had pureed food. If the resident did not willingly open their mouth, the nurse would put the syringe in the side of the resident's mouth, and push the syringe, forcing the resident to swallow the food. The nurses would tell me that we did not want the resident to starve, so we had to ensure they had intake of food and water to prevent decline.

As a certified nursing assistant, I always felt bad hearing residents holler down every hallway and in their rooms. When I would approach them, they wanted to cut the restraint off and would say, "Please help me, I haven't done anything wrong." I never felt comfortable restraining them, as I knew I would hate it myself. However, at that period of time in history, it was normal. Nurses would assure me we were doing what was best for the resident, as they could not look out for their own well-being. As the years went on, many family members began to question the above standards of care. There would be discussion of risks and benefits of restraints and syringe feeding. Today, restraints and syringe feeding are no longer the standard of care. Today, we use minimal restraints of any sort, and seniors are living to record longevity. We have not cured disease diagnoses that often parallel aging, and with a restraint-free world there are also opportunities for more falls. For patients with dementia who are impulsive or have no self-preservation skills left, it is a continual challenge to ensure their constant safety. After years of debate, a new standard of practice evolved. Nurses are still the educators, but their perspective has changed. Facilities are still regulated, but their perspective and rules changed. Again, everything happens for a reason. States and the federal government still regulate, but perspective has changed.

Most providers and caregivers do an amazing job twenty-four hours a day. There will never be a nursing home, or assisted living facility, that provides long-term one-to-one supervision for a senior twenty-four hours a day. The only time one will get one-to-one supervision is if they are home with twenty-four-hour caregivers through a home care agency or assigned family members for each shift of a twenty-four-hour day. For many, this is an excellent route to take. When care needs to advance to where the senior needs higher care, home may not remain the best option. Therefore, it is a constant balance of weighing the pros and cons for every situation. Again, everything happens for a reason.

There are great nursing homes and assisted living facilities across the country, just as there are great hospitals and physicians. Outliers with poor performance should be individually addressed. It should be the same for the hospitals and physicians too. In the business world, a title is never the assurance of successful outcomes. Successful outcomes come from a leader who knows their audience; understands their audience's needs; values the role of collaboration with teams for feedback, ideas, and continuous process improvement; addresses concerns with solutions in a timely way; and gains the respect of those they serve. Prior to the Internet, patients were not able to google everything they wanted to learn about. Now there are scientific briefings, medical journals, and various studies every patient can access, to review any sort of medical questions. While the Internet is not a diagnostic tool, it does allow every person to research items pertaining to their health to allow them to form a list of questions for their physician. I do believe this ability allows patients to research second opinions and various items, which may not have been possible before. This is a whole new level of accountability for everyone, as most can access information twenty-four hours a day. Again, everything happens for a reason.

Your mind remembers every personal skill you used for all previous serious situations, and these become coping mechanisms in your personal health battle. But after using every skill I had learned in my lifetime, I realized my skills were not enough for cancer. I finally had to learn how to completely surrender. This was the first time in my life where I could not fix the problem, and I was scared to death. After years of multiple surgeries, God put me where he knew I should be. He knew my past battles would make me passionate to help others avoid the path I had landed on. I have since helped many people with fundraisers, or just listened as they talked through their fears. Once, while waiting in line to get a glass of wine at a Pink Ribbon Breast Cancer fundraiser, a random person asked how I was feeling. I quickly answered, "Fine." The person looked puzzled and said, "I'm sorry, I thought you were diagnosed with breast cancer?" Oh . . . yes I was. I had attended the event completely blanking out that I ever had breast cancer. It took my brain a few minutes to realize I was one of the women who represented the pink colors and the reason for the benefit. I realized God picked me to be in a position to help others in a different way. I realized I had to experience setbacks in order to truly empathize with the pain others would experience when their setback happened. I was right where God wanted me. Again, everything happens for a reason.

Sometimes I go back and reread my initial diagnosis to see if I really had cancer. I get reminders of it when I look in the mirror. But once I am dressed, my mind wants to put it behind me. If I were driving a convertible and it was filled with pink breast cancer symbols and decorations, I wanted them to fly away for miles behind me and never be seen again.

I had felt so numb during the years I had surgeries, but perhaps that was a blessing in disguise, because it protected me from knowing all the things I could not do. My post-surgery "awakening" period was a time for physical healing and also a time of great anxiety because I knew how much I missed and how much I had to do to protect the business. Sometimes I would ask my husband or sons what we did on certain dates, as I had no memory of what happened.

As luck would have it, I had just gotten out of the hospital when the state health department arrived for an unannounced survey of our assisted living facility business. All the regulations had changed in 2015, at the beginning of my cancer journey, so I knew the process would be different. When the survey ended, my dad drove me to the exit interview. I cried as I listened to the deficiencies cited.

Reviewing our deficiencies and plan of correction, I was flooded with anger. Who monitors the types of deficiencies for items far more serious that happened to me and others in the hospital? I felt as though a non-elderly person had no voice for resolution when surgical issues arise. I felt like I was experiencing a double standard in health care. Even when an aging adult has osteoporosis, for example, care providers are still held to prevent hip fractures or other injuries that may occur from a fall. The senior could be walking down the hallway, and a bone could break first and the fall could be secondary. The fall could create a fracture, which would be a negative outcome. Providers are often sued for negative outcomes that may occur due to normal decline that is part of the aging process. If an aide or nurse doesn't follow the care plan with perfection, deficiencies occur.

With all the media reports of nursing homes rampant with abuse and neglect, I wonder if we are detouring our youth and other great hardworking adults from choosing to work in nursing homes and assisted living facilities. Perhaps job seekers are wondering if they would want to work in a setting that is painted with such negativity. Many job seekers are on social media and the news they read there has few positive and happy stories of a day in an assisted living facility or nursing home. This is very unfortunate, as great things happen every day. Today's youth are who we will

THE SCARS YOU CAN'T SEE

need as future caregivers—no robot could ever replace the love of a human being in your frail senior years.

I have watched countless caregivers across Minnesota give phenomenal care over my career. I wish the media shared these stories too. Staffing nursing homes and assisted living facilities will only become harder as the baby boomers enter these settings. Many settings are already having a difficult time filling positions across the country, as there are far more options for employment than there were in 1983. I truly believe each state must address recruitment methods with a matched commitment by the media. Imaging is very important. If we want to only focus on the select few who make bad choices as a physician, clergy, teacher, principal, coach, health-care worker, police, and other essential service workers, then we are dismissing all the greatness that also occurs in these settings. There is a cause and effect for where people will choose to be educated and employed. Again, everything happens for a reason.

Over the course of my cancer treatment, crucial situations happened that could have resulted in a better outcome for me if they had been handled differently. Still, it all happened the way it did. My grandma often said, "God never gives you more than you can handle." But during my treatment, I often rebutted, "God, you have really tested me this time, because I'm not sure I can do this." But Grandma was right: I did handle it. I did let go of my anger. I did realize this all happened so I could help others know what to look for. I am no longer tormented by my anger, but rather I am peaceful with a mission to help educate others about their cancer, care team, and risks.

As a patient at Mayo Clinic and a second Duluth health care team, I decided health care is like shopping. We all make choices. If we don't get the service we believe we are supposed to get, then we make a decision to change, uproot ourselves, and start over. That is exactly what I did, and it was worth it for the peace of mind it gave me. Each of us has to decide for ourselves. We are all consumers, the ultimate decision makers for our care journeys. Again, everything happens for a reason. And we all must weigh the pros and cons of every decision as we live our lives.

You will realize that perspective is everything.

19 ∾ The Rainbow Comes

MY CANCER JOURNEY WAS full of moments when I had no choice but to laugh, or else I would have cried. One distinct memory was with my husband at the home show. This event was held at the Duluth Entertainment Convention Center for vendors to show their products for homes and various other products. We had been thinking about building a new house and went to see contractors. I showed the contractor photos of our lot on my cell phone, but I inadvertently showed them the wrong photo. The one they saw was of my chest with double mastectomy stitches. I was so embarrassed. "I guess they have the job. They know too much about me," I told my husband later, and we laughed.

Another funny memory happened with my mom at the hotel in Rochester after my reconstructive surgery. My high school friend was coming to visit, so I texted her my room number. A long while later, she still hadn't shown up. Finally, she called my room to confirm the number, and we heard a knock on the door soon after. When we opened it, my friend stood there laughing. "Your attention to detail never ceases to amaze me," she said. "I was knocking on the wrong door on the wrong floor of this hotel. I kept aggressively knocking, thinking you must not feel good. Finally, a woman with bandages all over her face came to the door, and I thought, *Dear God, that is not you.*" Sure enough, I had texted the wrong room number and sent my friend on a wild goose chase. We laughed for hours thinking this poor lady had probably come to Rochester hoping no one would know she had her procedure done.

I had to find silly ways to keep myself entertained during all my long hospital stays too. On one of my most bored days, I was staring at my feet at the end of the bed. My bunions seemed to grow by the minute. So I took a marker and labeled the left bunion MN for Minnesota and the right bunion WI for Wisconsin, and I had border battles in bed. I had been trying not to crack, but on second thought, maybe I did crack and no one told me.

One day, as I drove myself to Mayo, I had to pull over at a gas station to give myself a Lovenox injection for my second blood clot. These shots needed to be twelve hours apart and twice a day. I hate needles, but because I was alone, I had to give myself the injection. My husband typically gave me each shot, and this day he needed to be at work. My hands were wringing wet with sweat—I was full of anxiety, but I *had* to have this shot at the precise time. I took the cap off the needle and kept counting to ten, bringing it closer and closer to my stomach fat. Each time I thought I could do it, I would stop. Eventually, I started crying. I considered asking a stranger at the gas station to inject me, but they would probably think I was a drug addict and call the police. I needed to put on my big girl pants, as my mom would say, and just do it. So, dripping with sweat, I counted to five and stabbed myself with it so hard, then I whipped the needle on the floor. You are not supposed to do this, because the needles are supposed to be capped after use.

With the shot completed, I laughed at myself even more. When I started college, I enrolled in the nursing program. When I toured the nursing department in the first few days of registration, I began to ask questions on how shots were practiced while studying to become a nurse. I was told we practice on each other. Within minutes, I knew that would not be happening, and I transferred to the health-care administration program. As I looked at the needle on the floor of my vehicle, I was reminded how grateful I was that I was rerouted from the nursing program. I knew I did not have what it takes to be a nurse. But my rainbow came when I could be a five-minute nurse when I needed to in order to get that shot in me.

My trips down to Rochester weren't always solo. One of my frequent companions was a seventy-five-year-old retired sheriff who volunteered to drive me weekly for several months. He faithfully cleared his schedule for me without complaint. He was the perfect gentleman—every time, he would drop me off at the curb and load and unload my luggage. When we went on walks together, he would ask if I wanted to stop to look at a clothing store or stop and see the flowers at the flower shop. Whatever I wanted to do, he would never rush me.

One day, while we were walking together on the sidewalk, I ended up on the road side of the sidewalk. He quickly nudged me to the inside and said, "My wife would kill me if you were not protected with me on the road side of the sidewalk." His wife had died years before I met him. I know she and I would have had a great time together, and she was with us in spirit.

When we arrived at the Mayo Clinic for one of my out-patient visits, he asked, "What are we doing today, boss?" I was getting my misplaced nipple cut off. When I told him, all he said was, "OK."

He was the best chauffeur ever. Our road trips became a time to visit or walk to a café for a meal—he eliminated all the stress of traveling. With him, I could take phone calls and answer emails during the drive, which helped a lot. When I was really stressed out, we would go to the pawn store and Dairy Queen. Then we would throw in a trip to the antique stores and look at all the beautiful items. He always calmed me down and reminded me to relax. I was blessed to have his friendship, and it brought me back to my farm days hanging out at the café after doing farm work with my grandpa, dad, and brothers. His generosity allowed my husband to continue working, as my treatment went on for several years. This was a blessing for us both.

During treatment, it takes a village to care for you. If you are ever in the position to help someone else with cancer, just know that whatever you do—chauffeuring, housekeeping, shopping, visiting, or providing money, meals, flowers, childcare, and more—every role matters. When you let your light shine, you shine on someone who feels like their sun is behind a cloud. After the clouds move and the storm rolls through, you will see the rainbow at the end.

My rainbow came and yours will too. In my case, the

rainbow also came literally. In April 2017, I saw a double rainbow over the church where I had married my husband in Duluth. I knew it was another sign of God's double blessings.

My grandpa always said, "When life gives you lemons, make lemonade." I've been making lemonade my whole life. Some kids start out learning about lemonade at lemonade stands. My lemonade stand came in the form of a pickup truck filled with sweet corn. I would drop the tailgate and put my sign out by the truck, saying "Sweet Corn for Sale."

I was selling sweet corn and making deals at a young age. I loved it, except on the days I knew all my sixteen-year-old friends were heading to the beach. On those days, I changed my plan. I quickly learned I could sell an entire truckload to one customer if I lowered the price during customer negotiations. I was thrilled to be done selling the day's sweet corn and couldn't wait to get to the beach with my friends.

I drove home to get my bathing suit with a smile on my face. My dad came out of the barn to see why I was home so early, and when I told him, he asked how I had sold the corn so quickly. I explained that a man wanted to buy the whole truckload if I gave him a discount. I figured it was a win-win for everyone. I sold the sweet corn and then I could go to the beach, and so both my dad and I would be happy. We normally sold it for one dollar a dozen, and I had sold it for fifty cents a dozen. My dad quickly explained that sometimes these trucks take the corn and resell it for higher prices up north. I am not sure it was a win-win that day, and I am quite sure I was reassigned to the tractor after that day of sweet corn negotiations.

I laugh now because all three of my parents' kids ended up selling something in their careers—one a book, one concrete, and one vegetables—and it all started with the sweet corn. The farm was just the beginning of many things for us. While we learned to farm, our minds were cultivated too.

My latest chapter in life is all about writing, but this love affair began long ago. A while ago, I found in my grandma's Bible a story I had written in 1979 about bears lost in the woods. Apparently, I loved writing at a young age. In college, Grandma Hazel and I had our tradition of writing to each other weekly. Grandma Hazel had phenomenal penmanship just like my mom's, unlike mine, but she knew how to decode my writing and understand what I was saying. She would tell me if she cleaned out the refrigerator, for example, and I would tell her if a tooth had come in for one of the boys when they were young. I always cracked up when she wrote, "P.S. I especially like the newsy letters." In other words, do not send a letter that is only half a page long.

Years later, my grandpa told me she would reread the letters over and over. She loved to go to the mailbox in anticipation of a letter. It was a big event in her week, and in mine too. This was really when my love for writing was taking shape. I just did not know it then.

Our love for learning continues as we grow; we are never too old to learn new things. Once, a resident told me she had committed at age fifty to learn one new thing every year until she died. And she did. She learned to paint, sew, crochet, speak many foreign languages—she was a brilliant person.

So I have started my own list, a version of my own personal development plan or bucket list. I want to travel and enjoy as much time with my husband as I can. I want to savor the sunrises and sunsets, explore the lake, and enjoy nature. It is the simple things that matter to me.

I never planned to own a business or have cancer, but that is where my path went. But the things you never planned on can be the things you are the proudest of, the things that push you to grow the most. You never know where your path may go, but these moments push you out of your comfort zone and shape the gifts you have. We all have unique gifts, and as my grandma often told me, it would be a great sin not to use them.

Now that I am five years out from my first surgery, I am still hitting personal growth milestones. Our new chapter in life is one long after cancer, with no more hockey games to attend for the boys, college graduations, our son's wedding, and discovering a new set of hobbies. Before, my only hobby was baking about a hundred dozen Christmas cookies every year. Growing up, my mom and I would bake until 3:00 a.m. on the weekends and then deliver baskets to people all over. My mom was the cookie lady—people still talk about her Christmas cookies.

When my kids started sports, *I* became the cookie lady. It was fun to gather together with moms and bake for hours. As they would say, it was more like a production line. I still distribute cookies to people every year, and from what I can tell, they're just as irresistible as my mom's. Once, after I sent cookies to my kids' hockey coach, he apparently went into the ditch trying to reach for some on the floor of his vehicle on the way home.

It has taken longer than I ever imagined to heal, but I

have also gotten back in the game. I've started cross-country skiing again, and my husband straps on his snowshoes to join me. In the summer, we kayak together. We took ballroom dancing lessons together with friends. Like that wise businessman once told me, partners are for dancing.

I have also started playing the accordion. Yes, the accordion. I have taken a few lessons, and I need hours of practice in my garage. I may have scared the birds. I can't wait until I can play "Roll Out the Barrel." I grew up watching Lawrence Welk on TV weekly, and I hope to someday be able to play all his music. When I practice at work, I have a kind audience. They are all so sweet and encouraging. I love the look of the accordion and learning how to play a keyboard upside down.

When I spend time with my residents, I know I picked the right profession. Even at fifty-something, I am a young girl to all of them. Had I gone into teaching, I would have been old at thirty. But these people think I am a spring chicken. They are all ages eighty to one hundred, and they will say, "I wish I was fifty-something." Everything is relative. If we ever live to have another birthday, we are lucky enough.

Some of my residents have children who are in their seventies. When I've asked them if they ever stop worrying about their children, they all say "never." No matter how old your kids are, you will worry about them. That is just how it is when you are a parent. Then when your kids have kids, you worry about your grandkids, and you have a new list to pray for.

Cancer changes you just like any other tragic life event.

There is no way it couldn't. But if you are open to feeling pain and happiness, then the journey is worth it. At the end of the day, our connections to each other and our thoughtfulness are what make life a joy. I am actively living my life story and enjoying each moment with my husband, sons, daughter-in-law, other family, and friends. So be of good cheer and enjoy those around you. You may need the cheer yourself someday too. Let your light shine!

You may realize you have changed, and that it is taking you where you were meant to be.

∾ Resource List

Here are some resources I recommend to help you in your health-care journey.

Evaluating Your Physician and Hospital

Health Grades (www.healthgrades.com). Look up your physicians and review their experience match value. This value is an aggregated number that reflects whether the physician treats what the patient is looking for; evidence the physician has performed the procedure the patient is looking for; the total number of claims the physician has treated, diagnosed, or performed a procedure on; and the total volume of patients this physician has seen. This data is not specific to any procedure, board certification, specialization, board actions, sanctions, malpractice, education, and degrees obtained.

Visit the website of the hospital you are considering having your surgery at. Review their awards and what you may expect from their service.

Federation of State Medical Boards (www.fsmb.org)
Certification Matters (www.certificationmatters.org)

ProPublica.org Surgeon Scorecard (www.projects.propublica
.org/surgeons)

SurgeonRatings.org (www.checkbook.org/surgeonratings)

Avoiding Surgical Risks as a Patient

Centers for Disease Control and Prevention (www.cdc.gov).
Review surgical infection prevention and blood clot (ve-
nous thromboembolism) prevention. In addition, the CDC
issued the Hospital Toolkit for Adult Sepsis Surveillance in
August 2018: www.cdc.gov/sepsis/pdfs/Sepsis-Surveillance-
Toolkit-Aug-2018_508.pdf

Mayo Clinic (www.mayoclinic.org)

Sepsis Alliance (www.sepsis.org)

Johns Hopkins Medicine (www.hopkinsmedicine.org)

World Sepsis Day is September 13 (www.worldsepsisday.
org/toolkits). This site also has a useful fact sheet.

Open Anesthesia (www.openanesthesia.org/sepsis-
treatment). This site addresses sepsis treatment and blood
clot issues.

World Thrombis Day (www.worldthrombosisday.org)

National Blood Clot Awareness (www.stoptheclot.org)

General Breast Cancer Information

www.komen.org

www.americancancersociety.com, 1-800-227-2345

www.nationalbreastcancer.org

www.lbbc.org

www.breastcancer.org

www.contourne.com

www.youngsurvival.org

www.cdc.gov/cancer/breast/

www.thebreastcancerrecoverycoach.com with Laura Lummer

∾ About the Author

NATALIE ZELEZNIKAR is a writer, CEO, and survivor of breast cancer and sepsis. She is a graduate of the University of Wisconsin–Eau Claire and operated nursing homes and assisted living centers for thirty years. In 2004, she cofounded an alternative option for seniors with higher need care who desired a home-style care community. She currently lives in Duluth, Minnesota, with her husband of twenty-nine years.

THE HOSPITAL IN HISTORY

THE WELLCOME INSTITUTE SERIES IN THE HISTORY OF MEDICINE

Edited by W.F. Bynum and Roy Porter,
The Wellcome Institute

Medical Fringe and Medical Orthodoxy, 1750–1850
W.F. Bynum and Roy Porter

Florence Nightingale and the Nursing Legacy
Monica Baly

Social Hygiene in Twentieth Century Britain
Greta Jones

Problems and Methods in the History of Medicine
Roy Porter and Andrew Wear

Vivisection in Historical Perspective
Nicholaas A. Rupke

Abortion in England, 1900–1967
Barbara Brookes

THE HOSPITAL
IN HISTORY

Edited by Lindsay Granshaw and Roy Porter

ROUTLEDGE
LONDON AND NEW YORK

First published 1989
by Routledge
11 New Fetter Lane, London EC4P 4EE
29 West 35th Street, New York, NY 10001

© 1989 Lindsay Granshaw and Roy Porter

Filmset by Mayhew Typesetting, Bristol
Printed in Great Britain

British Library Cataloguing in Publication Data

The hospital in history. — (The Wellcome
    Institute series in the history of medicine)
    1. Hospitals, to 1987
    I. Granshaw, Lindsay, *1954–* II. Porter, Roy,
    1946–   III. Series
    362.1'1

Library of Congress Cataloging in Publication Data

The hospital in history / edited by Lindsay Granshaw and Roy
    Porter.
    p. cm. – (Wellcome Institute series in the
    history of medicine)
    Bibliography: p.
    Includes index.
    1. Hospitals – History.   I. Granshaw, Lindsay, 1954–
    II. Porter, Roy, 1946–   . III. Series.
    RA964.H67 1988
    362.1'1'09–dc19

88–18285 CIP

ISBN 0-415-00375-X

Contents

Contents

Contributors

Dr Martha Carlin received her PhD in medieval studies from the University of Toronto in 1984. The title of her thesis was *The Urban Development of Southwark, c. 1200 to 1550*. From 1984 to 1987 she was employed by the Institute of Historical Research, University of London, as research assistant to Dr Derek Keene, Director of The Social and Economic Study of Medieval London. Since July 1987 she has been the executive director of the new Medieval and Early Modern Data Bank at Rutgers University. Dr Carlin is one of the joint authors of *The Historic Towns Atlas*, Vol. III (London to 1520), ed. M.D. Lobel (Oxford University Press, 1988).

Sandra Cavallo took a degree at Turin University and then went on to postgraduate research at the universities of Lyon, Essex and the European University Institute. She has published a series of articles on family history and poor relief and is currently completing a comparative doctoral thesis on systems of charity at University College London. Her interest is in the application of social anthropological theory to seventeenth and eighteenth century history.

Dr Lindsay Granshaw is historian of modern medicine at the Wellcome Institute for the History of Medicine, London. Her PhD thesis was on St Thomas's Hospital in the nineteenth century and she is the author of *St Mark's Hospital: A Social History of a Specialist Hospital* (King's Fund Historical Series/Oxford University Press, 1985). She has published articles on the history of hospitals, specialized medicine, surgery, nursing, and nineteenth-century patients.

Dr John Henderson is Fellow of Wolfson College, Cambridge, and Wellcome Trust Fellow at the Wellcome Unit for the History of Medicine, University of Cambridge. He is currently writing a book on plague in sixteenth-century Florence.

Dr Caroline Murphy is currently the Education Officer (Essex) of the RSPCA. This work was carried out while she was a Wellcome Research Fellow at the Wellcome Unit for the History of Medicine, Manchester University. She received support from the Wellcome Trust for the completion of her PhD thesis in Manchester on history of radiotherapy of cancer in Britain.

Dr Roy Porter is senior lecturer in the social history of medicine at the Wellcome Institute, London, having previously been lecturer in European history at Cambridge University and Director of Studies in History at Churchill College, Cambridge. His research into the history of psychiatry was published as *Mind Forg'd Manacles* (Athlone Press, 1987) and *A Social History of Madness* (Weidenfeld & Nicolson, 1987).

Craig Rose graduated at the University of Bristol with a BA in history in 1985 and was awarded the University Prize in History. He has since been a research student at Selwyn College, Cambridge and is now in his third year of research on a PhD thesis entitled *Politics, Religion and Charity in London, 1680–1730*. He is currently a non-stipendiary research fellow of Selwyn College.

Dr Miri Rubin is a research fellow at the History Faculty and Girton College, Cambridge. She is the author of *Charity and Community in Medieval Cambridge* (Cambridge University Press, 1987) and of a number of studies on relief and mutual help in the middle ages. She is currently studying religion and ritual in medieval society.

Professor Dr med. Eduard Seidler studied medicine at Mainz, Paris, Hamburg, Heidelberg. He specialized in pediatrics in 1961, and took additional training in medical history 1963–7 (Heidelberg). He has been chairman and director of the Institut für Geschichte der Medizin der Albert–Ludwigs-Universität, Freiburg i. Br., since 1968. His fields of research are history of childhood, social history of medicine in the eighteenth and nineteenth centuries, history of nursing and hospitals, medical history in Germany 1918–45, and medical ethics.

Professor Morris J. Vogel is Professor of History at Temple University in Philadelphia, Pennsylvania. His work in the social history of American medicine includes *The Invention of the Modern Hospital: Boston, 1870–1930* and *The Therapeutic Revolution: Essays in the Social History of Medicine.* He has also published in American urban and cultural history.

Introduction

Lindsay Granshaw

The sound of ambulances tearing through the streets bearing the very ill to hospital is common enough today. And few would doubt that the best place to be, if seriously ill, is in the hospital. The hospital is recognized as the central institution in medical care, for rich and poor.[1] It is often assumed that this was always the case. Yet until recent times, most people – especially if ill – would have endeavoured to stay out of hospital. Home was where the sick should be treated: hospitals were associated with pauperism and death.[2] How has this change of perception and use come about? Is there any continuity at all between the medieval and modern hospital, or does the very continuity of the name actually mislead? What is the hospital in history?

Hospitals over time have been much more varied than a casual glance at their present-day namesakes might indicate. Accounts of individual institutions have barely scratched the surface of their significance. Some valiant attempts have been made to record hospital histories, usually by those associated with them. Mostly written by doctors, they have tended to focus on the medical staff; it is sometimes difficult to detect that there actually were patients – or any staff besides doctors – in the institutions under scrutiny.[3] After long neglect, however, hospitals are at last receiving serious historical attention.[4] In recent years a general social critique has encouraged investigation of a range of institutions – prisons, schools, factories – and as the critique extended to medicine, the hospital, too, has become a focus of interest.[5] It is coming to be seen as an institution which, though central in modern times, need not necessarily be so, and has not

1

necessarily been so. The hospital's function throughout history has not been constant.

A number of issues of importance are emerging from this new attention, but they are far from fully explored. The older histories tended to assume that hospitals were set up by philanthropic lay or churchmen according to the needs of the sick poor.[6] Patients would receive medical and nursing care before being returned home. In recent times, it is assumed, the hospital came to embody the best that modern medicine could offer – high technology, intensive care, and radical surgery.[7] Such assumptions are now under challenge. Historians are looking beyond the mere act of lay philanthropy and asking who gave, why they gave, and what their relationship to the hospital was. They are also trying, stretching sources as far as they will go, to assess who the patients were, what social class they came from, whether they were young, middle-aged, or old, whether they were friendless and without family, whether they were local or had travelled long distances for special treatment. Historians now want to know what patients suffered from, whether they were acutely ill or suffering from some slow, incurable malady, whether they were bed-ridden or mobile, institutionalized for a long time or a brief spell. Was the hospital simply a place in which to die, or did patients expect to return home either to continue their lives or for their last rites? On a more mundane level, what was the patients' experience of hospital – what did they eat, drink, do in hospital?[8]

The spotlight has also been turned on others associated with the hospital. If doctors were involved with the hospital – and it is no longer assumed that of necessity they were – what did the hospital mean to them? Were they actively and daily involved in care, or did they put in an appearance once a year? Was the hospital always important to the status of doctors – did they seek appointments or were they thrust on them, did they stay long at the hospital or attach themselves only briefly, did they teach or research in the hospital, did they announce proudly to the world that they held hospital positions, even long after they had ceased to practise there?[9] Where doctors are to be found, certainly in the later periods, historians concern themselves with the medicine on offer. Was it considered the best or the worst of the time? How does this reflect either the doctors' view of or use of the hospital? And, for that matter, that of the patient and the wider public? For some historians the clinic was 'born' in the French Revolution as the doctors' 'gaze' shifted from book learning to clinical experience. The hospital, as a result, was fundamentally changed, and later institutions show a total disjunction with their predecessors. Not surprisingly, this view has been challenged.[10]

Besides the doctors, other staff – from nurses to porters, from treasurers to chaplains – are now seen as important in the culture of the hospital.[11] Their social and geographical origins, their remuneration, expectations, length of service, their relationship to the patients and governors, the nature of their work, and the nature of their day, are all seen as part of the legitimate social history of the hospital. Placing hospitals in their social and geographic context, it can no longer be assumed that they were necessarily where the most needy poor were to be found, nor in the largest towns and cities, nor founded in response to epidemics. If their founding purpose was more to serve their endowers than the charity recipients, reasons other than the needs of the sick poor are likely to be paramount in determining such factors. For some historians, social control is a significant feature of hospitals, like other institutions. Were they part of an elaborate system of keeping the poor in their place, sweeping them off the streets and into the hospital, ensuring that they were speedily returned to work, or do other social reasons lie behind their foundation?[12]

In trying to answer some of these questions, wide varieties of sources can be used. Looking away from the published record of doctors – though never forgetting its use – there are the hospital records, the minute books, the records of rents, sales, and purchases, other financial accounts, patient records, from which valuable information can be distilled. Archaeological remains, town and monastic records, court proceedings, crown, state, and papal records, pictures, patients' diaries and letters, other literature, census returns, interviews – all can provide useful material on the history of hospitals. But as the authors here note, all sources, especially propagandist ones, have their difficulties as well as possibilities. Still, for all histories of hospitals, ingenuity in the use of sources is crucially important.

The essays in this volume, we hope, will help to open up

new lines in the history of hospitals – showing it other than dry institutional history, but rather as a microcosm of society. Most of the papers presented here were given at a seminar series at the Wellcome Institute.[13] There are a number of echoes between the papers, although the authors would not always agree with each other. The essays look at the position of the hospital in different societies, from medieval England to seventeenth-century Italy, from eighteenth-century Germany to modern-day America. No monolithic 'hospital' emerges.

A dominant theme that does appear is that hospitals served a major function for those who set them up and supported them, whether church or state, lay or medical; the founders helped to shape what the hospital was to become in each society. Thus, a doctor-centred approach to the history of hospitals is inadequate, but so too would be a patient-centred approach.[14]

The traditional concept of medieval hospitals is that they were founded by the church, more particularly by monasteries, and were outgrowths of hospices which accommodated pilgrims, the monastic sick, and possibly the sick from the surrounding area. It was part of monastic duty, laid down in the gospels, that care should be given to the sick and needy.[15] All these essays challenge accepted beliefs about the pattern of care, and notions of medieval institutions are questioned as much as any. Martha Carlin in 'Medieval English hospitals' (Chapter 1) explains that although medieval English hospitals or hospices certainly cared for the sick poor and for wayfarers, such strict definitions are misleading. There was a wide variety of hospitals, with a number actually finding the care of the sick an unwelcome burden which they later cast off. A point echoed by Miri Rubin (Chapter 2), Carlin argues that even if an institution did care for the ill, this did not mean professional practitioner care; she rarely finds evidence of a doctor giving assistance.

Lay endowment emerges as playing a major part in medieval hospitals, just as it did later. These were not simply monastic foundations. No doubt, as the well-off laity bought indulgences through large gifts to the church, they also saw hospitals as a way of ensuring that their account was in good order in the hereafter. Perhaps as important, they wished to be remembered on earth for their charity, and an institution was a concrete means of ensuring this. As a charitable act, it was the poor who were to be the recipients. Christian teaching dictated as much, and the theme of the rich giving to the poor through hospital endowment runs right through to the twentieth century.[16] Only those deserving of charity should be admitted: the disreputable should be kept out. A hospital gave its charity for the mutual benefit of giver and receiver; recipients therefore must be as deserving of charity as their benefactors were in need of giving it. In different times and different places this meant different things. Rubin argues, for example, that in Britain during the fourteenth-century plague, because the labour market was destabilized, with the poor misbehaving by moving to seek employment, the rich did not feel inclined to assist them through hospitals. Those who had formerly wished to support social order through philanthropy now found new reasons not to be philanthropic; not only were purse strings tighter, there was also a shift in the view of poverty as virtuous to seeing it as a source of disruption. The pursuit of benevolence as part of the social order was undermined and with it, she argues, late medieval hospitals. By contrast, John Henderson (Chapter 3) finds that in Florence during the plague years, more hospitals were set up for the suffering poor.

The close association of benefactor with benefaction is clearly revealed both in Carlin's paper and Rubin's. So dependent were the little institutions on their endowers – rather than, we take it, a more durable monastery – that many were very short-lived. Miri Rubin in 'Development and change in English hospitals: 1100–1500' (Chapter 2) finds instability built into the very foundations of these institutions of supposed 'perpetual memory' – they frequently died not long after their founders. Focusing on Cambridge and its environs, Rubin points out that rural care has received even less attention than urban care.[17] Stressing the varieties of caring institutions, Rubin suggests that the special characteristics of towns – whether they were a port, university town, or commercial centre – were significant in shaping their hospitals. The papers on the medieval and Renaissance hospitals show that those of us who study modern institutions should be wary of portraying earlier hospitals as peripheral to society. They may (or they may not) have been peripheral in overall health care, or they may be seen as peripheral to doctors – who were not that central themselves – but in other ways they were clearly of major importance. Hospitals played a far wider role than simply care of the sick. They provided social and religious rewards for the endower; they no doubt provided a service to those cared for, but they also acted in a variety of other ways. Whether in Cambridge or Florence, for example, hospitals could find themselves as part of a banking system. As Rubin argues, this, too, could be couched in religious terms, since it freed Christians from the hands of Jewish moneylenders.[18]

John Henderson in 'The hospitals of late-medieval and Renaissance Florence: a preliminary survey' (Chapter 3) finds a somewhat different pattern in fifteenth-century Florence, a much more highly-developed mercantile centre than any to be found in contemporary Britain. Not only were more hospitals set up in response to the plague – though Henderson does note, however, that attention turned particularly to orphans and widows, and only secondarily to the sick – but also there was more medical presence. While Carlin found little evidence of doctors in hospitals, Henderson finds active medical care in Florentine hospitals. Such institutions were not for the long-term ill, but for those suffering from acute illnesses, particularly fevers. Patients only remained in hospital on average about a fortnight.[19]

Florentine hospitals were widely admired not only for their practices but also for their architecture. As Henderson points out, the religious intent of such institutions was embodied in their design, which resembled churches, to the extent even of possessing altars and cloisters. The cruciform pattern emerging from Florence then pervaded the rest of the continent.[20] Florentine hospitals were clearly well-funded institutions with extensive property in both city and countryside. As elsewhere, both shady dealings and legitimate banking were to be found in them; widows for example, might receive a pension for life in return for pledging their property to the hospital.

Returning to Italy, but now in the Counter-Reformation period, Sandra Cavallo in 'Charity, power, and patronage in eighteenth-century Italian hospitals: the case of Turin' (Chapter 4) takes for granted that hospitals are more than simply about medical care. Italian historians have seen them, she argues, as pawns in church and state conflict.[21] The expansion of hospital provision in seventeenth- and eighteenth-century Italy has been seen as tied closely to the Counter Reformation, declining as Enlightenment 'anti-Christian' sentiments set in. But Cavallo sees the booming of hospital charity in Turin, for example, reflecting the climax of conflict between the court with its feudal apparatus and the new order of bureaucrats and merchants. The assistance of the poor by the better-off was only partly moral and economic. To a significant extent, she argues, it was to do with privilege among the poor themselves. Charities such as hospitals ensured the defence of the prestige and image of the social group to which the recipient of charity belonged. The emerging classes, as ever, invested in charity as reflections of their position. Hospitals were important to them, and bene-factors endowed beds not for curables, to be pushed through as rapidly as possible, so that hospital statistics looked good, but for incurables – often as an insurance policy for their elderly servants. The power to nominate people for beds was therefore significant.[22]

As seems to have been the case in Florence, doctors were already more involved in the Turin hospitals than in medieval and Renaissance institutions – before the university reforms which were supposed to have changed the scene.[23] Cavallo sees greater continuity in the hospital as a place of research, teaching, and medical practice than previous historians have done. Increase in medical teaching, though, resulted in yet another battle, between state officials and lay governors. Cavallo refutes the idea that change in the Turin hospitals was simply 'progress and rationalization' as the state took over: rather the substitution of an old élite by a new.

The role of the hospital in the wider political scene is the theme of Rose's paper 'Politics and the London Royal Hospitals, 1683–92' (Chapter 5) on late seventeenth-century London hospitals.[24] On the stage of St Thomas's was acted out in miniature all the political struggles of Restoration England. St Thomas's, like the other 'royal' hospitals, owed close allegiance both to its City masters and to its royal founders. In the last few years of Charles II's reign, through James II's, and into William and Mary's, St Thomas's found itself bound up in factional strife between Whigs and Tories. Rose suggests that the hospital, as a major property owner, dispenser of patronage, and a significant influence in South-wark, was not an institution which the Crown felt it could overlook. Charles II, supported by Tories, saw the removal of Whigs from important positions at St Thomas's as part of a wider attempt to remove Whigs from public life. However, from 1686, after James II's accession, it was the Tories who were under attack. Even the surgeons appointed at St Thomas's under Tory dominance eventually found themselves thrown out. It took the Whigs several years before they regained dominance; even then, the Crown, in the shape of William and Mary, sought to intervene again but, interestingly, then thought better of it.

Hospitals are also seen by Roy Porter in 'The gift relation: philanthropy and provincial hospitals in eighteenth-century England' (Chapter 6) as part of a wider pattern in eighteenth-century provincial England. He sees the voluntary hospital as an eighteenth-century invention to absorb charity. Using Braudel's notion of the gift relationship – he who gives, dominates – Porter argues that conspicuous, even self-congratulatory, philanthropy was the reason for so many infirmary creations around the country.[25] Hospitals served to close the rift between rich and poor – and here Porter identifies the chief patrons as being the aristocracy rather than the aspiring middle classes suggested by other authors. Infirmaries became the manifestations of civic pride over which even those of different religious persuasions could unite.[26] The system of annual donations tied in the benefactors closely; the voluntary hospitals did not go under as in medieval times.[27] However, as in earlier foundations, Porter sees the lay desire for a charity outlet rather than medical or patient need, or the professional ambitions of practitioners, as determining their establishment. Doctors offered their skills voluntarily because they too wished to demonstrate gentlemanly status through the gift relationship. In these hospitals, unlike those in Turin, it was beds for curables that were established. And, specifically, it was disapproved that servants of donors should be among the charity recipients. Patients were to be obedient and docile; no money should be taken from them, as that sullied the gift relationship.

In the modern papers several authors look at the relationship of special hospitals to society, as medicine itself became more specialized. Eduard Seidler in 'A historical survey of children's hospitals' (Chapter 7) asks what led to the establishment of sick children's hospitals, and what form and function they took. Unlike Cavallo, Seidler sees a real division between eighteenth-century hospitals and their predecessors. Hospitals change from homes of refuge to the *Krankenhaus* or institution for the sick. In earlier times the complex system of Christian charity was the locus of the hospital; by the eighteenth century the hospital was becoming medicalized, a centre for medical teaching, clinical research, and later the organization of healing for the welfare of all the population.[28] The earliest organized care for sick poor children (as children themselves apparently became the focus of greater attention) was dispensary care in their own homes.[29] Gradually this care was brought into the hospital, first in separate institutions and much later back into the general hospitals. Institutions in different countries seemed to vary and fluctuate (there was no single type) and the hospitals existed in flux between the self-interest of the medical profession and the needs of the sick child. In Seidler's account, therefore, lay philanthropy is already accorded a lesser role.

Picking up on the theme of the importance of hospitals to medical men in the last two centuries, my own paper ' "Fame and fortune by means of bricks and mortar": The medical profession and specialist hospitals, 1800–1948' (Chapter 8) looks at their relevance to medical specialization. Whereas previous foundations had largely been lay in origin, the nineteenth century saw the establishment of large numbers of small hospitals by medical men, as they sought a toe-hold in their profession.[30] Like the medieval hospitals, these hospitals were not firmly based and came and went according to their founders' interests and entrepreneurial abilities. It was the middle classes, not the aristocracy, who underpinned these institutions, as they bolstered their social status.[31] These special hospitals, it is argued, led the way in Britain to the much greater medicalization of all hospitals, with the accompanying breakdown of lay control. Assailed as unnecessary disruptions of the medical *status quo*, the special hospitals had nevertheless by the late nineteenth century become crucial to the medical élite; a large percentage of fellows of the Royal College of Surgeons, for example, had held an appointment with a special hospital by the turn of the century. Special hospitals played their part in the transformation of the image of the specialist from quack to consultant;

of the care for the sick in the home to care in an institution; from the doctor as peripheral in medical care of the majority to the doctor as central.[32]

A sense of coming full circle is gained from Caroline Murphy's 'From Friedenheim to hospice: a century of cancer hospitals' (Chapter 9). Here, in one area of medical care, the process is followed of establishing hospices to care for the sick with little expectation of cure, to the aggressive and interventionist high-technology and radical surgical cancer treatments of the first half of the twentieth century, but thence back to hospice care for the dying.[33] Here are nineteenth-century specialist hospitals along the lines of the others discussed in the previous article, but with a difference. They do not expect cures, good results, or to lure in philanthropic help on such a basis. Until, that is, the twentieth century radical cures – but then the patients for whom nothing can be done suddenly become an embarrassment. Murphy argues that, not surprisingly, given the direction of modern medical care, the cancer charities, the National Health Service, and the general hospitals remain remarkably oblivious to the needs of the dying, and it is again in the voluntary sector that such care is provided.

Morris Vogel in 'Managing medicine: creating a profession of hospital administration in the United States, 1895–1915' (Chapter 10) describes an important feature in the shift of the hospitals to centre stage. In America, as in Britain, the 'modernizing' hospitals, as they became the central institution in medical care, turned to professionalizing managers to run them. In Britain the image was of a civil servant or of an administrator trained in the army or empire, someone from the middle or even lower-middle classes who had risen through hard work and merit. In America the ideas of scientific management associated with Taylorism seem to pervade the hospital just as much as the industrial sector.[34] As ever, the hospital reflected the society which housed it. Many of the issues that the administration faced in the United States would be echoed in Europe: the need to forge a professional identity; the desire to combat the seemingly over-influential doctors; the need to run the institution efficiently. As the middle classes sought care in the hospital, the American administrators worried over curbing charity abuse without damaging potential fund-raising from paying patients.[35]

According to Vogel, it was third-party payment through insurance that shifted the balance of power away from the doctors to the administrators.[36] And in Britain that third-party payment – through the state – possibly had a similar effect. Certainly all blame overweening administrators for hospitals' financial crises. Perhaps hospitals should start their own banking systems once again.

All these papers bring out important themes in the history of hospitals, on a complex, broad scale. What emerges above all is that hospitals are the creation of particular societies. The interests they serve are not necessarily or primarily those of the patients. In many cases, especially before the nineteenth century, they were not those of the doctors either, but of those lay, state, or church leaders who established such institutions. By the time of the nineteenth and twentieth centuries, though, hospitals had become very much the objects of the medical profession, as commentators today usually assume they always were. These papers illustrate how that came to be and why that was not always so.

Notes

1. Any current political debate illustrates the perceived centrality of the hospital. It is seen as the workplace of the élite, and the place that patients increasingly choose to go directly to; see Brian Abel-Smith, 'Foreword', in Frank Honigsbaum, *The Division in British Medicine: A History of the Separation of General Practice From Hospital Care, 1911–1968* (Kogan Page, London, 1979), p. xiv. See W.G. Cannon, 'Hospitals in the UK', and E.C. Atwater, 'Hospitals in the USA', in John Walton, Paul B. Beeson, Ronald Bodley Scott (eds), *The Oxford Companion to Medicine* (Oxford University Press, Oxford, 1986), vol. 1, 551–65.

2. See for example, Florence Nightingale, *Notes on Hospitals*, 3rd edn (Longman, Green & Co., London, 1863); E.M. Sigsworth, 'Gateways to death? Medicine, hospitals and mortality, 1700–1820', in Peter Mathias (ed.), *Science and Society, 1600–1900*, (Cambridge University Press, Cambridge, 1972), 97–110; John Woodward, *To Do The Sick No Harm. A Study of the British Voluntary Hospital System to 1875* (Routledge & Kegan Paul, London, 1974); Henry Burdett, *Hospitals and Asylums of the World*, 4 vols (J. & A. Churchill, London, 1891–3); Morris J. Vogel, *The Invention of the Modern Hospital, Boston, 1870–1930* (Chicago University Press, Chicago, 1980).

3. See for example various histories of British institutions including C.T. Andrews, *The First Cornish Hospital* (pr. Wordens, Penzance, Cornwall, 1975); S.T. Anning, *The General Infirmary at Leeds. Vol. 1: The First Hundred Years 1767–1869* (E. & S. Livingstone, Edinburgh and London, 1963); H.C. Cameron, *Mr Guy's Hospital, 1726–1948* (Longmans, Green & Co., London, 1954); E.W. Dormer (ed.), *The Story of the Royal Berkshire Hospital 1837–1937* (Poynder Press, Reading, 1937); Sir P. Eade, *The Norfolk and Norwich Hospital 1770–1900* (Jarrold & Sons, London, 1900); A.G. Gibson, *The Radcliffe Infirmary* (Oxford University Press, London, 1926); Eric C.O. Jewesbury, *The Royal Northern Hospital 1856–1956* (H.K. Lewis & Co., London, 1956); O.V. Jones, *The Progress of Medicine* (Gomer, Llandysul, 1984); G. Munro Smith, *A History of the Bristol Royal Infirmary* (Arrowsmith, Bristol, 1917); J.B. Penfold, *The History of the Essex County Hospital, Colchester* (John B. Penfold, Colchester, 1984); P. Rhodes, *Doctor John Leake's Hospital* (Davis-Poynter, London, 1977). In P.M.G. Russell, *A History of the Exeter Hospitals 1170–1948* (pr. James Townsend & Sons, Exeter, 1976), Sir Derek Jakeway, Chairman of the Devon Area Health Authority, in the foreword describes the book as 'a disinterested labour of love'. In the same paragraph, this 'disinterested' author is noted to be consultant gynaecologist at the Royal Devon and Exeter Hospital, and in fact the first obstetrician to be appointed to the hospital!

For the United States see, for example, N.T. Bowditch, *A History of the Massachusetts General Hospital*, 2nd edn (The Hospital, Boston, 1872); A.M. Chesney, *The Johns Hopkins Hospital and the Johns Hopkins University School of Medicine*, 3 vols (Johns Hopkins University, Baltimore, 1943, 1958, 1963); J. Hirsch and B. Doherty, *The First Hundred Years of the Mount Sinai Hospital of New York* (Random House, New York, 1952); T.G. Morton, with F. Woodbury, *The History of the Pennsylvania Hospital 1751–1895* (Times Printing House, Philadelphia, 1895).

Many of the histories of hospitals by medical men are very useful, providing much information, even if they may lack a sense of overall context. Perhaps the best history of a British hospital by a medical man is A.E. Clark-Kennedy, *London Pride. The Story of a Voluntary Hospital* (Hutchinson Benham, London, 1979).

Occasionally a history has been written by another member of staff. See for example J. Gooch, *A History of Brighton General Hospital* (Phillimore, London, 1980). Janet Gooch is a nurse at the hospital. One of the histories of St Thomas's Hospital was written by its archivist – E.M. McInnes, *St Thomas' Hospital* (George Allen & Unwin, London, 1963). In the case of E.J.R. Burrough, *Unity in Diversity: The Short Life of the United Oxford Hospitals* (pr. Burgess & Son, for the author, Abingdon, 1978), the hospital administrator seems to have been inspired less by adulation of his institution than revenge against those with whom he worked.

Introduction

Sometimes a local historian has been asked to write a history of a hospital or assist a doctor in doing so; see for example E.R. Frizelle and J.D. Martin, *The Leicester Royal Infirmary 1771–1971* (Leicester no. 1 Hospital Management Committee, Leicester, 1971). And occasionally a journalist has entered the fray. See for example J. Wilds, *Ochsner's. An Informal History of the South's Largest Private Medical Center* (Louisiana State University Press, Baton Rouge, 1985). Wilds has a keen journalistic eye for the wider setting of the hospital, is no great respecter of professional status (although he does regard medicine heroically) and ensures that the politics of the hospital come through clearly.

4. See, for example, M. Vogel, *The Invention of the Modern Hospital* (Chicago University Press, Chicago, 1980). Probably the most influential work in recent years has been by Charles Rosenberg, whose essays on American hospitals are now extended and incorporated into *The Care of Strangers. The Rise of America's Hospital System* (Basic Books, New York, 1987). For many years before the publication of this book, though, Rosenberg has influenced the study of the recent history of British and American hospitals. These influential articles include C.E. Rosenberg, 'The practice of medicine in New York a century ago', *Bulletin of the History of Medicine*, vol. 41 (1967), 223–53; 'Social class and medical care in nineteenth-century America: the rise and fall of the dispensary', *Journal of the History of Medicine*, vol. 29 (1974), 32–54; 'And heal the sick: the hospital and patient in 19th century America', *Journal of Social History*, vol. 10 (1977), 428–47; 'The therapeutic revolution. Medicine, meaning and social change in nineteenth-century America', *Perspectives in Biology and Medicine*, vol. 20 (1977), 485–506; 'Inward vision and outward glance: the shaping of the American hospital, 1880–1914', *Bulletin of the History of Medicine*, vol. 53 (1979), 346–91; 'Florence Nightingale on contagion: the hospital as moral universe', in C.E. Rosenberg (ed.), *Healing and History: Essays for George Rosen* (Science History Publications, New York, 1979), 116–36; 'From almshouse to hospital: the shaping of Philadelphia General Hospital', *Milbank Memorial Fund Quarterly*, vol. 60 (1982), 108–54; 'Disease and social order in America: perceptions and expectations', *Milbank Memorial Fund Quarterly*, vol. 64, supl. no. 1 (1986), 34–55.

Other American historians of hospitals include D. Rosner, *A Once Charitable Enterprise: Hospitals and Health Care in Brooklyn and New York, 1885–1915* (Cambridge University Press, Cambridge, 1982). R. Stevens, '"A poor sort of memory": voluntary hospitals and government before the great depression', *Health and Society*, vol. 60 (1982), 551–84; R. Stevens, 'Sweet charity: state aid to hospitals in Pennsylvania, 1870–1910', *Bulletin of the History of Medicine*, vol. 58 (1984), 287–314, 474–95; V.G. Drachman, *Hospital with a Heart. Women Doctors and the Paradox of Separatism at the New England Hospital, 1862–1969* (Cornell University Press, Ithaca and London, 1984).

In Britain we have B. Abel-Smith's *The Hospitals 1880–1948. A Study in Social Administration in England and Wales* (Heinemann, London, 1964), a very useful overview of the past century and a half, but which explicitly addresses hospitals from an administrative point of view; F.N.L. Poynter (ed.), *The Evolution of Hospitals in Britain* (Pitman, London, 1968); also L. Granshaw, *St Mark's Hospital, London: A Social History of a Specialist Hospital* (King's Fund Historical Series/Oxford University Press, London, 1985); J.V. Pickstone, *Medicine and Industrial Society: A History of Hospital Development in Manchester and its Region, 1752–1946* (Manchester University Press, Manchester, 1985); G.B. Risse, *Hospital Life in Enlightenment Scotland. Care and Teaching at the Royal Infirmary of Edinburgh* (Cambridge University Press, Cambridge, London and New York, 1986). For other information on Scotland see D. Hamilton, *The Healers. A History of Medicine in Scotland* (Canongate, Edinburgh, 1981).

A number of dissertations have also been written; see for example S.G. Cherry, 'The role of the English provincial hospitals in the 18th and 19th Centuries', PhD thesis, University of East Anglia, 1977; L. Granshaw, 'St Thomas's Hospital, London, 1850–1900', PhD thesis, Bryn Mawr College, USA, 1981; J. Lynaugh, 'The community hospitals of Kansas City, Missouri, 1870–1915', PhD thesis, University of Kansas, 1982; J.M. Kingsdale, 'The growth of hospitals: an economic history in Baltimore', PhD thesis, University of Michigan, 1981; Susan Lawrence, 'Science and medicine at the London hospitals: the development of teaching and research, 1750–1815', PhD thesis, University of Toronto, 1985.

5. For critiques of institutions and of medicine, see I. Illich, *Deschooling Society* (Calder & Boyars, London, 1971); M. Foucault, *Discipline and Punish: The Birth of the Prison* (Peregrine, London, 1979); I. Illich, *Limits to Medicine* (Pelican, London, 1977); B. Inglis, *The Diseases of Civilisation* (Hodder & Stoughton, London, 1981); I. Kennedy, *The Unmasking of Medicine* (Allen & Unwin, London, 1981). For examples of essays on a range of Victorian social institutions, see H.J. Dyos and M. Wolff (eds), *The Victorian City: Image and Reality* (Routledge & Kegan Paul, London and Boston, 1973).

6. See for example C. Dainton, *The Story of England's Hospitals* (Museum Press, London, 1961).

7. S.J. Reiser, *Medicine and the Reign of Technology* (Cambridge University Press, Cambridge, London, and New York, 1978).

8. See Vogel, *The Invention of the Modern Hospital*; Granshaw, *St Mark's Hospital*; Rosenberg, *The Care of Strangers*.

9. W.F. Bynum, 'Physicians, hospitals and career structures in eighteenth century London', in W.F. Bynum and R. Porter (eds), *William Hunter and the Eighteenth-Century Medical World* (Cambridge University Press, Cambridge, 1985), 105–28; for professionalization, especially in medicine, see E. Freidson, *Profession of Medicine*

(Dodd, Mead, New York, 1970); E. Freidson, *Professional Powers. A Study of the Institutionalisation of Formal Knowledge* (University of Chicago Press, Chicago and London, 1986); N. Parry and J. Parry, *The Rise of the Medical Profession* (Croom Helm, London, 1976); M. Jeanne Peterson, *The Medical Profession in Mid-Victorian London* (University of California Press, Berkeley, California, 1978); I. Waddington, *The Medical Profession in the Industrial Revolution* (Gill & Macmillan, Dublin, 1984).

10. M. Foucault, *The Birth of the Clinic. An Archaeology of Medical Perception*, trans. A.M. Sheridan (Tavistock, London, 1976); E.H. Ackerknecht, *Medicine at the Paris Hospital, 1794–1848* (Johns Hopkins Press, Baltimore, 1967); Toby Gelfand, *Professionalizing Modern Medicine; Paris Surgeons and Medical Science and Institutions in the 18th century* (Greenwood Press, Westport, Conn., London, 1980).

11. C.E. Rosenberg, 'Inward vision and outward glance: the shaping of the American Hospital, 1880–1914', *Bulletin of the History of Medicine*, vol. 53 (1979), 346–91; Granshaw, 'St Thomas's Hospital'; for changing views on the history of nursing see C. Davies (ed.), *Rewriting Nursing History* (Croom Helm, London, 1980); C. Maggs, *The Origins of General Nursing* (Croom Helm, London, 1983); M.E. Baly, *Nursing and Social Change* (Heinemann, London, 1982); B. Abel-Smith, *A History of the Nursing Profession* (Heinemann, London, 1982); M.E. Baly, *Florence Nightingale and the Nursing Legacy* (Croom Helm, London, 1986).

12. See for example, Andrew Wear, 'Caring for the sick poor in St Bartholomew Exchange: 1580–1676', in W.F. Bynum (ed.), *Living and Dying in London* (Routledge, London, 1989).

13. Academic years 1986–7.

14. In history of medicine, as in social history, recent focus has been on the ordinary person. For history of medicine, that has meant looking at the patient or potential patient. For recent patient-centred history see R. Porter (ed.), *Patients and Practitioners: Lay Perceptions of Medicine in Pre-Industrial Society* (Cambridge University Press, Cambridge, 1985).

15. See for example, Dainton, *The Story of England's Hospitals*; C. Graves, *The Story of St Thomas's, 1106–1947* (pr. St Thomas's, dist. Faber & Faber, London, 1947); D. Knowles and R. Neville Hadcock, *Medieval Religious Houses, England and Wales* (Longman, London, 1971); R.M. Clay, *The Mediaeval Hospitals of England* (Methuen, London, 1909); Walter H. Godfrey, *The English Alms-house* (Faber & Faber, London, 1955); C. Rawcliffe, 'The hospitals of later medieval London', *Medical History*, vol. 28 (1984), 1–21.

16. It is instructive to compare with practice in other cultures; see Lawrence Conrad on medieval middle-eastern hospitals, L.I. Conrad and V. Nutton, *Jundishapur: From Myth to History* (Darwin Press, Princeton, forthcoming). However, Judaic, Christian, and Moslem cultures were closely interlinked, and therefore one system was likely to influence another.

17. In France the Annales school has attempted to tell the history of rural areas; see for example E. Le Roy Ladurie, *Montaillou: village occitan de 1294 à 1324* (Gallimard, Paris, 1976), based on Inquisition reports.

18. So too did other medieval institutions; Knowles and Hadcock, *Medieval Religious Houses*.

19. This was half the average time of at least one London hospital in the nineteenth century; see Granshaw, 'St Thomas's Hospital', p. 78.

20. For further information on the history of hospital architecture see J.D. Thompson and G. Goldin, *The Hospital: A Social and Architectural History* (Yale University Press, New Haven and London, 1975).

21. In much Italian history of church and state, conflict looms large; B.S. Pullan, *Rich and Poor in Renaissance Venice. The Social Institutions of a Catholic State to 1620* (Blackwell, Oxford, 1971).

22. For the nature of philanthropy in Britain see David Owen, *English Philanthropy 1660–1960* (Cambridge, Mass., Belknap Press, 1965). In eighteenth–century Britain it was not seen as appropriate to admit servants.

23. See Foucault, *The Birth of the Clinic*; Risse, *Hospital Life in Enlightenment Scotland*; and Johanna Geyer-Kordesch, 'German medical education in the eighteenth century: the Prussian context and its influence', in W.F. Bynum and R. Porter (eds), *William Hunter and the Eighteenth-Century Medical World* (Cambridge University Press, Cambridge, 1985), 177–206.

24. For further discussion of political dimensions see A. Wilson, 'The early history of the Westminster Hospital', unpublished paper given to the Wellcome Unit for the History of Medicine, University of Cambridge, October 1983.

25. R.H. Titmuss, *The Gift Relationship* (George Allen & Unwin, London, 1970).

26. Museums, parks, and libraries also benefited from this movement; see R.K. Webb, *Modern England From the Eighteenth Century to the Present* (Harper & Row, New York and London, 1968).

27. One of the chief features of the voluntary hospitals was their voluminous annual reports, which recorded lists of names of donors, including the amounts donated.

28. Geyer-Kordesch, 'German medical education'.

29. See Z. Cope, 'The history of the dispensary movement', in Poynter (ed.), *Evolution of Hospitals in Britain*; T. Hunt (ed.), *The Medical Society of London 1773–1973* (Heinemann, London, 1972); G.F. Still, *The History of Paediatrics* (Oxford University Press, London, 1931).

30. For the various methods of covertly 'advertising' see Peterson, *Medical Profession in Mid-Victorian London*.

31. See for example, William Taylor Copeland, Lord Mayor of London in 1835, whose father jointly formed the Copeland Spode

China Works and made a fortune, whereupon W.T. Copeland sought to establish himself in the social hierarchy, successfully in the City of London and less so through Parliament, where he was accused of all the sins of the *nouveau riche*. In his rise, he patronized a number of 'good works', including several hospitals; see Granshaw, *St Mark's Hospital*.

32. On the rise of specialization in medicine, see G. Rosen, *The Specialization of Medicine* (Froben Press, New York, 1944); R. Stevens, *Medical Practice in Modern England: The Impact of Specialisation and State Medicine* (Yale University Press, New Haven, 1966); R. Kershaw, *Special Hospitals* (George Putnam & Sons, London, 1909).

33. S. Stoddard, *The Hospice Movement* (Jonathan Cape, London, 1979).

34. For Taylor's scientific management see F.W. Taylor, 'A piece-work system', *Transactions of the American Society of Mechanical Engineers*, no. 16 (1895), 856–903. For commentary, see D.F. Noble, *America by Design: Science, Technology, and the Rise of Corporate Capitalism* (Knopf, New York, 1979); C.E. Rosenberg, 'Inward vision and outward glance: the shaping of the American Hospital, 1880–1914', *Bulletin of the History of Medicine* no. 53 (1979), 346–91. For Britain see Granshaw, 'St Thomas's Hospital', 48–59.

35. For concern about charity abuse, and the advocacy of paying patients, see Henry Burdett, *Hospitals and Asylums of the World*, 4 vols, 1891–3; Burdett, *Cottage Hospitals, General, Fever, and Convalescent. Their Progress, Management, and Work in Great Britain and Ireland, and the United States of America*, 3rd edn (The Scientific Press, London, 1896) 1; D. Rosner, *A Once Charitable Enterprise: Hospitals and Health Care in Brooklyn and New York, 1885–1915* (Cambridge University Press, Cambridge, 1982).

36. For further information see R. Stevens, *Medical Practice in Modern England: The Impact of Specialisation and State Medicine* (Yale University Press, New Haven, 1966); R. Stevens, *American Medicine and the Public Interest* (Yale University Press, New Haven, 1971); D.M. Fox, *Health Policies, Health Politics: The British and American Experience, 1911–1965* (Princeton University Press, Princeton, 1986); R. Levitt, *The Reorganised National Health Service* (Croom Helm, London, 1979). For Great Britain see R. Hodgkinson, *The Origins of the National Health Service: The Medical Service* (Wellcome Institute, London, 1967); D. Fraser, *The Evolution of the British Welfare State* (Macmillan, London, 1984); J. Pater, *The Origins of the National Health Service* (King's Fund Historical Series, London, 1981); C. Webster, *The Health Services Since the War. Volume 1. Problems of Health Care: The National Health Service Before 1957* (HMSO, London, 1988). On American insurance, see Ronald L. Numbers, 'The third party: health insurance in America', in Vogel and Rosenberg (eds), *The Therapeutic Revolution*, 177–200.

I

Medieval

1

Medieval English hospitals

Martha Carlin

The medieval term 'hospital', *hospitale* in Latin, embraced four main types of institution: leper houses, almshouses, hospices for poor wayfarers and pilgrims, and institutions that cared for the sick poor. There is as yet no satisfactory general study of medieval English hospitals. The most useful work to date is David Knowles' and Neville Hadcock's *Medieval Religious Houses, England and Wales* (2nd edition, 1971), which contains a gazetteer of some 1,103 hospitals, with a brief history of each.[1] These histories were compiled by the authors from printed sources, particularly Dugdale's *Monasticon Anglicanum* (1817–30 edition), Tanner's *Notitia Monastica* (1744 edition), and the *Victoria County Histories*.

Another source frequently cited by Knowles and Hadcock is R.M. Clay's *The Medieval Hospitals of England* (1909). This book, however, is seriously flawed by meagre documentation and by the author's romantic and essentially unscholarly treatment of the subject. Clay's intention was, through this study, 'to secure a fuller recognition of the widespread activity of the Church of England in former days'. She saw the numerous hospital foundations as predominantly ecclesiastical in character, charitable and pious in tone, and stable and effective in activity, from their origins until the Dissolution, when 'charity was crippled for a time by the confiscation of endowments designed for the relief of the destitute, until a new generation of philanthropists arose and endeavored to replace them'.[2]

In contrast was the view of Margaret Seymour in an unpublished King's College, London, MA thesis (1947) on 'The organisation, personnel and functions of the medieval

21

hospital in the later middle ages'. This thesis was handicapped, as the author acknowledged, by the wartime and immediately postwar unavailability of most manuscript sources. Nevertheless, it is a useful study, based on the printed sources then available, and concentrating particularly on the administrative history of medieval English hospitals. Because of this focus, however, the author tended to lump together all types of hospital as being united by their shared administrative characteristics. This enabled her to demonstrate her main thesis, that in all classes of hospital decay and decline were rife in the later medieval period, principally because of financial maladministration. It does, however, make her work rather difficult to use for anyone studying either a particular type of hospital, or individual hospitals, with the exception of St Leonard's, York, to whose history she paid special attention.

Among the most useful primary sources in print are the *Valor Ecclesiasticus* and the *Calendars* of the Patent Rolls, Close Rolls, Inquisitions Miscellaneous, and Papal Letters. Episcopal registers, some of which have been printed, are another important source, particularly of foundation records and visitation reports. For example, the text of the original foundation charter of the hospital of St Thomas the Martyr, Southwark, which is generally assumed to have been lost, survives in a transcript made in the early fourteenth century in the register of John de Stratford, Bishop of Winchester.[3] In the case of hospitals of which the monarch was patron, such records are included among the Chancery Miscellanea, which are partially printed in the *Calendar of Inquisitions Miscellaneous*. Wills, many of which are printed or calendared, also provide much information on hospitals and on the popular support of them.

Of the four classes of hospital described at the beginning of this paper, the first and perhaps the easiest to distinguish is the leper hospital. Of the 1,103 hospitals in England and Wales listed by Knowles and Hadcock, some 345 (31 per cent) were intended wholly or in part for lepers. Leper hospitals generally had the most strictly-defined function among the medieval hospitals. Their inmates were required to be segregated for life from the rest of the population, to wear a distinctive and enveloping form of dress, and to refrain from casual as well as long-term contact with the healthy. Leper hospitals, whose inmates included both religious and lay persons of both sexes, were among the earliest hospitals to be founded in England. Of those leper hospitals whose foundation dates are known, the majority were founded between 1084 and 1224, although there were some later foundations and re-foundations. The later foundations included the hospital at Little Torrington in Devon (1344), and the hospitals of St Leonard, Sudbury (1372), and St John the Evangelist, Thetford (1387), while Holy Innocents, Lincoln, was re-founded in 1461 as an almshouse with accommodation for three lepers.[4] Leper hospitals commonly were placed on the outskirts of towns, to which entry was forbidden to lepers. Most leper hospitals were small, with perhaps fewer than a dozen inmates, although there were some larger houses. The hospital at Sherburn, Durham, for example, was founded *c*. 1181 to house sixty-five leprous monks, nuns, and other religious from monasteries in the north of England.[5] Most leper hospitals were intended to care for lepers only, although a number did accommodate or come to accommodate other inmates as well, usually almspersons.

Most leper hospitals had become redundant by the mid-fifteenth century, and many, particularly the small and poorly endowed, also had become derelict by that time.[6] Those that survived were often re-founded or reconstituted as almshouses, or in some cases as colleges of secular canons, chantry chapels, or grammar schools. The leper hospital at Sherburn, for example, which had been founded for a master, three priests, and sixty-five lepers, had become impoverished by 1429. It was reconstituted in 1434 for a master, four chaplains, four clerks, two boy choristers, two lepers if so many could be found, and thirteen poor brothers, with a woman servant to look after them.[7] The leper hospital of St Giles, Holborn (London), founded in 1101 for forty lepers, was housing nine lepers in 1402, and fourteen paupers in 1535.[8]

Almshouses formed the second and most numerous of the four classes of hospitals. Of Knowles and Hadcock's 1,103 hospitals, some 742 (67 per cent) are listed as almshouses or as having included almspeople among their inmates. Almshouses fell into two broad sub-categories: those intended for the poor in general; and those to which admission was restricted, as, for example, to local residents or to members of the founder's guild or fraternity. Most almshouses received male inmates only, although some were intended solely for women. A number took in poor persons of both sexes, although in such cases the men and women were strictly segregated within the hospital, even if they were married.

Neither leper hospitals nor almshouses provided medical care as such. The inmates were expected to lead a semi-monastic life, typically eating and sleeping in common halls, wearing a distinctive habit, attending daily mass, and offering numerous daily prayers, particularly for the souls of the hospitals' founder and benefactors. Those who fell ill or became infirm were looked after by the lay brothers or sisters or servants who did the cooking and washing; in some houses healthy female inmates were expected to help look after those who were unwell. In the smaller leper houses no provision at all was made for looking after the sick.[9]

No medical or nursing care normally was provided at the third category of medieval hospitals either, those that received poor travellers and pilgrims. Knowles and Hadcock listed 136 hospitals (12 per cent of 1,103) of this type, of which about forty-nine probably were intended solely for this purpose and the remainder included poor wayfarers among their inmates. This category of hospital is the one most likely to have been seriously under-enumerated, because many (perhaps most) monasteries maintained a guest house, but only those hospices that enjoyed an autonomous existence were counted by Knowles and Hadcock.

The fourth category of medieval hospital, that intended wholly or partially for the care of the non-leprous sick poor, seems to have been the least numerous. Of the 112 hospitals (10 per cent of 1,103) of this type mentioned by Knowles and Hadcock, fewer than twenty were devoted solely to the care of the sick, and the remainder included the sick among the inmates they received. At least one hospital, that of St John the Baptist, Oxford, also received casualty cases. In 1305 St John's, which was situated near the east gate of Oxford, treated one Robert Attwyndyate, who lived near the south gate, who had broken his finger, and in 1396 one Roger, who had fallen from the nearby East Bridge into the river.[10] A few hospitals, such as St Bartholomew's, Smithfield (London), specifically included maternity patients among those whom they received, and made special provision for them and for their infants; and a few others, most notably St Mary Bethlehem (later known as 'Bedlam'), London, cared for the distraught and insane. One hospital, St Mary Magdalen in Newcastle-upon-Tyne, originally was founded as a leper hospital. According to its chantry certificate of 1546, however, 'syns that kynde of sickness is abated it is used for the comforte and help of the poore folks of the towne that chaunceth to fall syck in tyme of pestilence'.[11] This is the only English hospital that I know of that was intended solely for victims of pestilence.

For most hospitals, however, and in many cases even for those originally founded to receive the sick, the care of the sick became an unwelcome or impossible burden. For example, the statutes of the hospital of St John, Bridgwater, drawn up in 1219 by Bishop Joscelin of Bath and Wells, and exemplified by a successor in 1457, enjoined that the 'poor, infirm, and needy persons in the infirmary' be ministered to by one of the hospital's brothers and cared for day and night by two or three women servants or lay sisters. In this context, however, 'infirm' evidently meant invalid rather than ill, for the statutes went on to stipulate that:

No lepers, lunatics, or persons having the falling sickness or other contagious disease, and no pregnant women, or sucking infants, and no intolerable persons, even though they be poor and infirm, are to be admitted in the house; and if any such be admitted by mistake, they are to be expelled as soon as possible. And when the other poor and infirm persons have recovered they are to be let out *(licentientur)* without delay.[12]

There are many similar cases of the exclusion of both the sick and the infirm. The hospital of St Bartholomew, Gloucester, became impoverished in the mid to late fourteenth century, and by 1381 it sometimes charged for the admittance of the sick.[13] As early as 1316 the infirm brothers, for whose maintenance the hospital of St Bartholomew, Oxford, had been founded, had been supplanted by the healthy.[14] The hospital of St Nicholas, Salisbury, which in the thirteenth century cared for the poor, the sick, travellers, and the infirm, by 1478 had become an almshouse only.[15] Similarly, the hospital at Kingsthorpe by Northampton was founded in 1200 for the reception of the sick and travellers with a staff of a master, two chaplains, and six lay brothers, but in 1535 it supported only two poor brothers.[16]

The hospitals that cared for the non-leprous sick ranged considerably in size and means. The largest was the great hospital of St Leonard, York, whose infirmary was founded to care for 206 sick.[17] It also was the wealthiest English hospital, with an income in 1369 of £1,369 11s. 2¼d.[18] Also among the largest hospitals were the London hospital of St Mary without Bishopsgate, with 180 beds available for the sick at the time of its dissolution; and St Bartholomew's, Gloucester, which in 1333 cared for ninety sick men and women, although by 1535 it housed only thirty-two poor or sick people.[19]

The middle range included the hospital of St Thomas, Southwark, with forty patients recorded in 1295[20] and the same number in 1535; St Mary, Newark (Leicester), founded in 1331 with beds for thirty sick; and St Giles, Beverley, which in 1279 was ordained to have twenty-one beds for the sick, of whom six were to be priests.[21]

Those hospitals that cared for only a few patients included such institutions as Corpus Christi, York, reconstituted in 1478 with seven beds for the sick poor[22]; and St John the Baptist, Winchester, which apparently cared for no more than six sick persons at a time.[23]

Information on admittance procedures for the sick is very scanty. It is recorded, however, that screening of patients did take place at some hospitals. St Mary's, Newark, for example, was founded in 1330–1 by Henry, Earl of Lancaster and Leicester, for five chaplains and fifty poor and infirm folk, of whom twenty were to be perpetual inmates and thirty were to be poor folk suffering from passing ailments and asking the alms of the hospital in charity. These were to be examined at the hospital gate by the warden, who was required to satisfy himself of the seriousness of their complaint and to hear their confession before admitting them.[24] Following a visitation in 1316 of the hospital of St Bartholomew, Smithfield (London), the Bishop of London enjoined the master to order the brothers or sisters of the hospital who were responsible for admitting the infirm to give preference to those who were most in need and not to send them away until they were restored to health.[25] The statutes of the Savoy Hospital in London, founded by Henry VII and completed in or about 1517, required that applicants be screened by four or five members of the staff of the hospital. This screening was to take place each evening for an hour before sunset at the hospital's great gate in the Strand. Of the 100 poor men to be admitted each night the staff were to give preference to sick persons, but they were forbidden to admit lepers.[26] The doggerel poem *The hye way to the Spyttell house*, written about 1536 by Robert Copland, describes the selection process employed by the porter of a London hospital. He attempts to winnow out the genuinely needy – the aged; poor women in childbed; poor men suffering from injuries, the pox, or the pestilence; wayfaring men and maimed soldiers; and 'honest folk fallen in great poverty' – from among the counterfeit lepers and epileptics, the drunkards, the layabouts, the feigned veterans and scholars, the men who pretended to have been shipwrecked, and those who lived from day to day by rotating amongst the various city hospitals. The porter acknowledges, however, that those admitted unavoidably included disreputable men and women.[27]

The names and particulars of hospital patients normally do not survive, except in accounts of miraculous cures, such as those recorded in the foundation book of the priory of St Bartholomew, Smithfield (London), or in those attributed to Thomas Becket.[28] Surviving financial accounts of the small hospital of St John the Baptist at Winchester do, however, record some information about the patients received. In 1351–2, for example, a poor man from Calais lay sick there for fifteen days and died; a poor man was received for thirty-three days, and a poor chaplain for three weeks; six pilgrims stayed in the hospital for four nights; and one Roger Schorham stayed for thirty days. In 1355–6 a poor man lay sick in the hospital for eight days, and a poor boy for four weeks. In 1367–8 the sick patients were listed as three men and three women for seven weeks, three men and two women for four weeks, and so on, for a total of forty-four weeks. Although the system of enumeration used in these accounts obscures the pattern of admission of patients, it appears that from the mid-fourteenth century to the mid-sixteenth century there were no more than six sick patients in the hospital at any one time.[29]

The physical arrangements of the hospitals are better recorded than are their admissions procedures. Most contained or comprised an enclosed precinct, the access to which was controlled by one or more gates. The infirmary usually was built as a long, rectangular hall, like the nave of a church, which it sometimes was called. Usually there was a chapel or chapels at the eastern end of the infirmary hall, so that the patients could witness the daily celebration of mass from their beds. At the hospital of St Mary, Newark (Leicester), for example, the thirty short-term sick inmates were to be cared for in thirty beds lying in the body of the church, from which they would be able to see the elevation of the host and hear the divine offices.[30] The accommodation for a hospital's staff, religious and lay, was separate from that of the sick or other inmates. Almspeople, if resident, might share the infirmary or a common dormitory or dormitories, or might inhabit individual chambers; travellers seem usually to have been lodged with the sick in the infirmary.

Hospitals of this type included St Thomas's, Southwark, references to which of *c.* 1293, 1380, 1387, and 1415 mention the sick and poor lying in the hospital church. In 1400 Henry Yevele, the royal mason and architect, left a bequest to St Thomas's to aid in rebuilding the old aisle 'where the poor patients lie'.[31] The hospital of Kingsthorpe by Northampton had two chapels, with three rows of beds from which poor or sick travellers could hear mass or prayers.[32] Similar arrangements seem to have pertained at the hospitals of St Mary, Chichester; St James, Lewes; and St Nicholas, Salisbury.[33] Ordinarily there was one large infirmary for all patients, although it might be partitioned if patients of both sexes were received. The hospital of St John the Baptist and St John the Evangelist at Sherborne, Dorset, for example, was built by the inhabitants of the town in 1437 with an upper hall for women and a lower hall for men, each communicating with the two-storeyed chapel at the east end.[34] At the hospital of St John the Baptist, Winchester, excavations have revealed a nave-like infirmary partitioned lengthwise into two aisles with a communicating doorway. At the eastern end were two corresponding chapels, which could be viewed by the patients through traceried openings.[35] In some hospitals, such as the hospital of St John, Canterbury, the infirmary hall stood at right-angles to the chapel.[36]

Little is known about the furnishings of hospitals. At the hospital of St John, Winchester, there seem to have been cupboards in the north wall of the northern infirmary that corresponded to the placement of the beds, allowing patients some private storage accommodation.[37] The hospital furnishings mentioned in documentary sources, however, were beds, bedding, hanging lamps, and little else. The infirmary of the hospital of St Mary without Bishopsgate (London), for example, was said to have consisted of a large open ward containing 180 beds, each with its own lamp.[38] An annuity of 5s. was bequeathed *c*. 1293 to the hospital of St Thomas, Southwark, to maintain certain lamps burning in the hospital church before the sick, and in 1415 a Chichester man gave two lanterns to the same hospital to be hung over the beds of the poor.[39] Other bequests were for bedding. In 1540, for example, Hugh Acton, a citizen and merchant tailor of London, left £2 to St Thomas's, Southwark, to buy 'sheets and coverletts for poor people resorting thereto and harbored'.[40] The beds at the London hospital of St Mary Bethlehem ('Bedlam') were supplied with mattresses, sheets, blankets, and coverlets of red and blue worsted.[41] The amenities of Henry VII's Savoy Hospital were unusually handsome. The 100 beds in the hospital dormitory were furnished with flock mattresses and featherbeds, bolsters and pillows; and each had three pairs of sheets, two pairs of blankets, a linen coverlet, and a green and white tapestry counterpane with a red rose in the centre and other decorations. Each bed also had green and white curtains that could be pulled to screen it. The dormitory was lighted all night by three wheel lamps, and earthenware chamberpots were provided for the use of the inmates.[42]

Although one can thus see a hypothetical patient screened, admitted, and bedded down in a lamplit dormitory, near the comforting presence of the chapel, there is very little record of the actual care provided for the sick poor in medieval English hospitals. What does seem clear, however, is that professional medical and surgical practitioners seldom, if ever, treated hospital patients. Vern Bullough found what he believed was an instance in 1340 of a professional practitioner, Master William de Stafford, receiving payments for treating patients at the hospital of St John the Baptist, Oxford. In fact, however, de Stafford was paid for healing the hand of one of the brothers of the hospital.[43] Margaret

Seymour found only two examples of a hospital retaining its own professional practitioners; both were in London, and both date from the sixteenth century. The first of these was Henry VII's Savoy Hospital. The Savoy, founded with great magnificence in emulation of the contemporary Italian hospitals, retained its own physician and surgeon on a part-time basis.[44] The hospital of St Mary Bethlehem, in a letter circulated in 1519 to solicit contributions, claimed that 'the insane, the frenzied and others . . . are lodged and cared for with great diligence and attention, and treated by the physicians with unceasing solicitude'. It is possible that the Bedlam physicians mentioned in 1519 were identical with its masters; three of the hospital's fifteenth-century wardens, John Arundel, William Hobbys, and Thomas Deynman, were royal physicians (Hobbys was also a surgeon).[45]

A physician's or surgeon's mastership of a hospital is, however, no guarantee that he exercised his professional skills on its patients. An interesting demonstration of this is provided by the case of Master Thomas de Goldington, a surgeon who in 1348 held the wardenship of the hospitals of St Nicholas, Carlisle, and St Leonard, Derby. He also exercised the 'office of the surgery of the commonalty', allegedly to the neglect of his duties as warden. A royal commission was appointed to look into the matter, and the commissioners who visited St Nicholas's found that de Goldington was in fact an able and conscientious warden, and that the only defects in his management of the hospital were that he did not reside there continuously, and that there was not the proper number of brothers and sisters. The commissioners also noted that de Goldington 'sometimes exercises the profession of surgery, not to the damage of the hospital, but rather to its profit, because he acquires friends for it'. This suggests that de Goldington took on wealthy private patients, but there is no reference to his treating any of the sick poor in the hospital.[46]

For the period before the sixteenth century I have seen only one reference, again from London, and dating from the fifteenth century, to an explicit provision of professional care for the sick poor. In 1479 the mercer John Don bequeathed the very substantial sum of £25 so that a surgeon, Thomas Thorneton, could continue for the next five years 'in his daily besynes and comfort of the poure, sore and seke pepele

30

lakkyng helpe and money to pay for their lechecraft in London and the subarbes of the same'. This care was to be provided 'in especiall in the hospitalles of Seint Mary, Saint Bartholomew, Saint Thomas, Newgate, Ludgate [both prisons] and in other places, whereas peple shal have nede'. Should Thorneton prove 'slouthfull and nott diligent to attende the pour peple', Don directed that he be replaced by a practitioner willing to observe those conditions.[47]

Outside London I have found no evidence of professional medical or surgical treatment of the sick poor in hospitals. Even St Leonard's, York, with its considerable income and its upwards of 200 sick patients, seems never to have called upon professional practitioners.[48] Similarly, evidence for the purchase by hospitals of medicines or apothecary assistance is virtually nonexistent. The infirmary expenditures of St Leonard's, York, for example, included payments for oil for lamps and lanterns in the infirmary, for candles, and for clothes-washing, but apparently nothing for medicine. The only concrete evidence that Margaret Seymour was able to find that medicine was ever provided for the sick poor comes again from the sixteenth-century royal hospital, the Savoy, the second wealthiest foundation in the country. Among the expenses listed for the poor in the *Valor Ecclesiasticus* return for the Savoy were a number of payments to apothecaries for medicine. The Savoy was the only hospital to list such payments in the *Valor*.[49]

The treatment most likely to have been available to the sick in hospitals was bed rest, warmth, cleanliness, and an adequate diet. It is these provisions that occur time and again in hospital statutes, visitation injunctions, and charitable gifts and bequests. This kind of treatment is exemplified, for example, in the arrangements at Henry VII's Savoy Hospital, where all incoming patients were given a hot bath and a clean suit of clothes to wear while their own clothing was being deloused in two special ovens, and where two fires were provided in the dormitory in winter evenings for the inmates.[50] Ela, countess of Warwick (d. *ante* 1303), left bequests to the hospital of St Mary without Bishopsgate, London, that included perpetual annual payments for the poor in the hospital of £1 for milk, £1 for sheets, and £1 for firewood.[51] In 1458 Stephen Forster, a former mayor of London, left £10, and in 1479 the London mercer John Don bequeathed £13 6s. 8d., to St Mary Bethlehem to be spent on food, drink, linen, and woollen clothing for the sick poor detained there,[52] while two benefactors of the hospital of St Bartholomew, Smithfield, made possible the occasional provision of white bread for the inmates.[53] The foodstuffs purchased in 1363 by the hospital of St Leonard, York, for the poor in the infirmary consisted of wheat, rye, oaten malt, beef, pork, mutton, butter, cheese, and fish.[54]

The actual care of the sick poor in hospitals was the responsibility of the sisters or women servants. At St Thomas's, Southwark, for example, a donation made in 1379 for drink for the paupers and the sick in the hospital was to be distributed by the sisters to whom the care of the sick poor was assigned (*per manus sororum ad custodiam infirmorum pauperum deputarum*).[55] At the hospital of St John the Baptist, Oxford, re-founded in 1234 by Henry III to aid *infirmi* and pilgrims, and 'for the relief of poor scholars and other miserable persons', six sisters were to be maintained to tend the infirm and the paupers of the hospital. The sisters of St John's were replaced in the 1380s, however, by lay servants, two of whom (both women) deposed in 1390 that they served the infirm in the hospital and worked very hard at this (*serviunt infirmis in dicto hospitali existentibus et multum circa eos vigilant et laborant*).[56]

The function of a hospital's brothers, on the other hand, was purely religious. This separation of duties is reflected in the episcopal injunctions sent to the hospital of St Thomas the Martyr, Southwark, following a visitation in 1387. The brothers, for example, were enjoined to conform to the rule of St Augustine, in which they were professed; they were to study the scriptures, the chant, grammar, and the observance of the rule; they were to observe the canonical hours; and, except when saying the divine office or engaged on the business of their house, they were to occupy themselves in the cloister with reading and studying the scriptures. In contrast the sisters, who also were professed in the Augustinian rule, were ordered to supervise the sick paupers daily and visit them personally, which work of piety they were bound to do 'solicitously'. The master of St Thomas's was ordered to check as often as possible on how well the sisters supervised and visited the sick, and how well they ministered to them and fed them.[57]

A few hospitals catered to special classes of patients, and had special facilities for them. The hospitals of St John the Baptist, Bath, and St Michael at Welton, Northumberland, for example, were established for the reception of the sick poor who came to have the benefit of the medicinal waters.[58] At least four hospitals made special provision for maternity patients: the hospital of St John the Evangelist at Blyth in Nottinghamshire, formerly a leper hospital, was re-founded in 1446 for poor strangers and pregnant women[59]; and the three London hospitals of St Thomas, Southwark, St Bartholomew, Smithfield, and St Mary without Bishopsgate also received pregnant women. A taxation survey of St Thomas's carried out in 1295 reported that £1 4s. 0d. a year were spent on coals and fuel for women lying in childbed in the hospital.[60] A fifteenth-century London chronicler mentioned that both St Bartholomew's and St Thomas's had especial care for unwed mothers, and asserted that the wealthy mercer and mayor of London, Richard Whittington, had built an eight-bed chamber at St Thomas's to be used as a maternity ward for unwed mothers, and that everyone in that chamber was strictly enjoined to discretion so as not to hinder the women's chances of marrying.[61] In 1445 the hospital of St Mary without Bishopsgate was described in a papal indulgence as caring for the poor, sick, and miserable in general, and children and pregnant women in particular.[62] A few years earlier, in 1437, St Bartholomew's was given a royal licence to acquire lands and rents in mortmain in consideration of the hospital's 'great charges in receiving the poor, feeble and infirm, keeping women in childbirth until their purification and sometimes feeding their infants until weaned'.[63] In addition, St Bartholomew's tried to rescue babies from the nearby Newgate prison.[64]

Knowles and Hadcock list four other hospitals that cared for special classes of patients. One of these was the hospital of St Leger, Stamford, which was said to have been for the blind, the deaf, the mute, or other infirm.[65] The remaining three hospitals specialized in the care of mentally handicapped, insane, or frenzied patients. These were the hospital of St John the Baptist, Chester, founded in 1232 'for the sustentation of poor and silly persons'[66]; a nameless hospital at Charing Cross, near London, said to have been founded at an unknown date for distraught and lunatic people, whose inmates were unwelcome to the king, who removed them thence to the third hospital, St Mary Bethlehem.[67] Another such hospital evidently was planned for London, for in July 1370 Robert de Denton, a chaplain, obtained a royal licence to found a hospital near the Tower of London for poor priests and other men and women, who had suddenly fallen into a frenzy and lost their memories, until such time as they should recover. Denton changed his mind, however, and in 1378 he obtained another licence to found a perpetual chantry in St Katharine's Hospital instead.[68]

Of these special hospitals, the only one for which detailed information survives is St Mary Bethlehem. In 1403 a royal commission was called to investigate reported abuses there by the porter and acting deputy warden, Peter Taverner. Some eighteen witnesses were examined, including several of the patients, who at that time numbered six insane and three infirm. The commissioners found that Taverner, aided by his wife, had ruthlessly exploited his position in every way possible, and had stolen the entire revenues of the hospital for the preceding four years, and portions of them for the preceding fourteen years. Taverner stole not only money from the almsboxes and food given as charity to the patients, but also everything from bedding to cooking utensils, gardening tools, two keys to the garden gate, a bier, and a complement of four pairs of iron manacles, five other chains of iron, and six iron chains with locks.[69] These presumably had been used as restraints for the patients; an indulgence of 1446 asked for donations to the hospital to support 'the multitude of miserable persons of both sexes dwelling there, who are so alienated in mind and so possessed of unclean spirits that they must be restrained with chains and fetters'.[70]

The kind of corrupt and crippling maladministration revealed by the inquiry into the dealings of Peter Taverner seems to have become a common feature of medieval hospitals, and to have been responsible for the decay and disappearance of many, and the conversion of many more from hospitals offering free care to the sick and needy to fee-demanding almshouses, secular colleges, or schools. Large and wealthy hospitals as well as small and poor ones suffered under this kind of regime. For example, St Leonard's, York, the largest and wealthiest hospital in England, intended in 1364 to care for 206 sick poor in its large dormitory, and to maintain orphans in a hall below, fell victim to the cupidity of its masters, who excluded the poor in favour of those who could pay large sums for places, much of which payments were appropriated by the master.[71] At the large London hospital of St Mary without Bishopsgate, an episcopal visitor found in 1303 that legacies intended for the sick poor were not being paid, that the poor were stinted of their allowances of food and drink, and that the lamps that formerly had hung among the infirm 'for their solace' had been removed. The bishop ordered the hospital to restore the legacies, allowances, and lamps, and added that the lamps were to be provided at the hospital's own charge, and not by selling the clothing of the poor.[72] The hospital of St Thomas the Martyr, Southwark, suffered a number of incompetent and larcenous masters in the fourteenth and fifteenth centuries, culminating in the sixteenth century with the infamous Richard Mabott, a man who abused his position as thoroughly and disastrously as had Bedlam's Peter Taverner.[73] Mabott's contemporary, the master of the leper hospital of St Giles, Norwich, was found in 1541 to have turned that hospital into a sort of Fagin establishment, enticing 'pour lame and diseased personz' into his charge by promising them board and lodging, and then 'when he hath them he compellith them to begge for thir lyuyng or elles they shall have nothing of hym'.[74]

There were genuine exceptions to this very dismal picture. A number of hospitals, of which St Bartholomew, Smithfield, was perhaps the most outstanding, did not succumb to the prevailing pattern of decay and conversion. In general, however, hospitals that cared for the sick poor suffered an extremely high attrition rate, and this process was not effectively counterbalanced in the later medieval period by new foundations or endowments. In fact, the provision of free medical care for the poor evidently was extremely low on the list of charitable priorities in later medieval England. This low priority is reflected in the scarcity of such provision in contemporary bequests, and in the apparent absence of professional care for hospital patients before the sixteenth century, as well as in the falling numbers of the hospitals themselves. Of Knowles and Hadcock's total of 112 hospitals in England and Wales that cared for the sick poor, twenty-four had disappeared altogether by 1535, forty-nine had ceased to provide that kind of care, and in 1535 only thirty-nine hospitals were still providing it.[75]

Notes

1. David Knowles and R. Neville Hadcock, *Medieval Religious Houses, England and Wales*, 2nd edn (Longman, London, 1971) (hereafter K & H), 313–410.

2. Rotha Mary Clay, *The Mediaeval Hospitals of England* (Methuen, London, 1909) xvii, xx.

3. Hampshire Record Office (Winchester), Reg. Stratford, fo. 170.

4. Clay, *Mediaeval Hospitals*, 210; K & H, 325, 334, 335, 371, 396, 398.

5. K & H, 391.

6. Margaret A. Seymour, 'The organisation, personnel and functions of the medieval hospital in the later middle ages', unpublished MA thesis, University of London, 1947, 73.

7. K & H, 391.

8. K & H, 365.

9. Seymour, 'Medieval hospital', 41.

10. H.E. Salter (ed.), *A Cartulary of the Hospital of St. John the Baptist*, vol. 3 (Oxford Historical Society, vol. 69, 1917), xlvi.

11. John Brand, *History and Antiquities . . . of Newcastle upon Tyne*, vol. 1 (London, 1789), 425–7.

12. H.C. Maxwell-Lyte (ed.), *The Register of Thomas Bekynton, Bishop of Bath and Wells 1443–1465* (Somerset Record Society, vol. 49, 1934), p. 289.

13. K & H, 360.

14. *Calendar of Close Rolls, 1313–18*, 323–4.

15. K & H, 389; Seymour, 'Medieval hospital', 60.

16. K & H, 367.

17. K & H, 407; Seymour, 'Medieval hospital', p. 316, citing *Calendar of Inquisitions Miscellaneous, 1348–77*, 202.

18. Seymour, 'Medieval hospital', xxii; *Victoria County History, Yorkshire*, vol. 3, 336–7.

19. K & H, 360, 373.

20. Cecil Deedes (ed.), *Registrum Johannis de Pontissara Episcopi Wintoniensis*, vol. 2, Canterbury and York Society, Canterbury and York Series, vol. 30 (London and Oxford, 1924), 508–9.

21. K & H, 342, 369, 393.

22. K & H, 407.

23. Derek J. Keene, *Winchester Studies. II. Survey of Medieval Winchester*, ii (Oxford University Press, 1985), 815.

24. A.H. Thompson, *History of the Hospital and the New College of St Mary in the Newarke, Leicester* (Leicester Archaeological Society, 1937), 11, 13–19.

25. R.C. Fowler (ed.), *Registrum Radulphi Baldock, Gilberti Segrave,*

Ricardi Newport, et Stephani Gravesend, Episcoporum Londoniensium,
Canterbury and York Society, Canterbury and York Series, vol. 7,
Diocese of London, vol. 1 (1911), 191.

26. Robert Somerville, *The Savoy* (Savoy, London, 1960), 9, 30.

27. Arthur Valentine Judges (ed.), *The Elizabethan Underworld*
(George Routledge & Sons, London, 1930), 1–25.

28. Norman Moore (ed.), *The Book of the Foundation of St.
Bartholomew's Church in London* (Early English Text Society, London,
original series, vol. 163, 1923), 18, 20, 22–4, 26–30, 35–6, 45–7,
51, 52, 57–60; Frank Barlow, *Thomas Becket* (University of California Press, Berkeley and Los Angeles, California, 1986) 265–7.

29. Keene, *Winchester Studies. II*, ii, 815–16.

30. Thompson, *St Mary in the Newarke*, 13–19.

31. New College, Oxford, New College Archives, MS 3,691, fos
90^r–93^r; John H. Harvey, 'Henry Yevele reconsidered', *The Archaeological Journal*, vol. 108 (1951), 107.

32. K & H, p. 367; Clay, *Mediaeval Hospitals*, 112.

33. Clay, *Mediaeval Hospitals*, 112–13.

34. Walter H. Godfrey, *The English Almshouse* (Faber & Faber,
London, 1955), 39–40.

35. Keene, *Winchester Studies. II*, ii, 810–20; Clay, *Mediaeval
Hospitals*, 112–14.

36. Godfrey, *English Almshouse*, 33.

37. Pers. comm. Dr Derek Keene.

38. Carole Rawcliffe, 'The hospitals of later medieval London',
Medical History, vol. 28 (1984), 12.

39. ibid.

40. Hilda J. Hooper, 'Some Surrey wills in the Prerogative
Court of Canterbury, 1383–1570', *Surrey Archaeological Collections*,
vol. 52 (1952), 37 (calendaring PCC 26 Hankyn, dated 17 June
1534).

41. E.G. O'Donoghue, *The Story of Bethlehem Hospital* (T. Fisher-
Unwin, London and Leipsic, 1914), 79.

42. Somerville, *The Savoy*, 31–2.

43. Vern L. Bullough, 'A note on the medical care in medieval
English hospitals', *Bulletin of the History of Medicine*, vol. 35 (1961),
76; Salter (ed.), *Cartulary of the Hospital of St. John the Baptist*, vol. 3,
24–5.

44. Seymour, 'Medieval hospital', 48.

45. O'Donoghue, *Bethlehem Hospital*, 100; C.H. Talbot and E.A.
Hammond, *The Medical Practitioners in Medieval England, a Biographical
Register* (Wellcome Historical Medical Library, London, 1965), 339,
402; A.B. Emden, *Biographical Register of the University of Oxford to
A.D. 1500*, vol. 1 (Oxford, 1957), 50.

46. *Calendar of Patent Rolls, 1348–50*, 175–6; *Calendar of Inquisitions
Miscellaneous*, vol. 3, no. 6, p. 2; see also vol. 2, no. 1,456, 354–5.

47. Rawcliffe, 'Hospitals', 8 (citing PCC Logge 2).

48. Seymour, 'Medieval hospital', 48.

49. Seymour, 'Medieval hospital', 46–7.

50. Somerville, *The Savoy*, 31.

51. Fowler (ed.), *Reg. Baldock*, 32.

52. Frederic W. Weaver (ed.), *Somerset Medieval Wills 1383–1500* (Somerset Record Society, vol. 16, 1901), 181–2.

53. Nellie J. Kerling (ed.), *The Cartulary of St Bartholomew's Hospital* (St Bartholomew's Hospital, London, 1973), nos. 446, 772 (*c.* 1200 and 1325, respectively).

54. *Calendar of Inquisitions Miscellaneous*, vol. 3, no. 550, 202–4.

55. British Library, Stowe MS 942, fo. 74ʳ (calendared in *Cartulary of the Hospital of St. Thomas the Martyr, Southwark*, Lucy Drucker (trans.) and F.G. Parson (ed.) (privately printed, 1932), no. 231.

56. Salter (ed.), *Cartulary of the Hospital of St. John the Baptist*, vol. 3, xiv, xvi–xvii, xxxi, 7.

57. New College, Oxford, New College Archives, MS 3,691, fos 90ʳ–93ʳ.

58. K & H, 341, 401.

59. K & H, 344.

60. Deedes (ed.), *Reg. Pontissara*, 508–9.

61. James Gairdner (ed.), *The Historical Collections of a Citizen of London in the Fifteenth Century*, Camden new series, vol. 17 (1876), viii–ix.

62. *Calendar of Papal Letters*, vol. 9, 489–90.

63. *Calendar of Patent Rolls, 1436–41*, 48.

64. Nellie J. Kerling, note on Newgate Prison, *Transactions of the London and Middlesex Archaeological Society*, vol. 22, part 1 (1968), 21–2.

65. K & H, 394, citing pers. comm. from Rotha Mary Clay.

66. K & H, 351.

67. K & H, 402.

68. *Calendar of Patent Rolls, 1367–70*, 449; *Calendar of Patent Rolls, 1377–81*, 266; John Stow, *Survey of London* (1603 edn), C.L. Kingsford (ed.) (Oxford University Press, 1908), vol. 1, 137.

69. O'Donoghue, *Bethlehem Hospital*, 76–83; Seymour, 'Medieval hospital', pp. 90, 139–40.

70. Maxwell-Lyte (ed.), *Reg. Bekynton*, 59.

71. Seymour, 'Medieval hospital', 66, 68, 86–7.

72. Fowler (ed.), *Reg. Baldock*, 32–3.

73. Martha Carlin, 'The urban development of Southwark, *c.* 1200 to 1550', unpublished PhD dissertation, University of Toronto, 1983, 405–11; J.S. Brewer, James Gairdner, R.H. Brodie (eds) *Letters and Papers, Foreign and Domestic, of the Reign of Henry VIII, 1536*, 73–4; *1538* (vol. 13, part 1), 494; *1539* (vol. 14, part 2), 301.

74. John Cottingham Tingey (ed.), *The Records of the City of Norwich* vol. 2 (by authority of the Corporation of Norwich, Norwich and London, 1910), 169.

75. These figures are subject to slight revision, because the hospital histories in K & H are abbreviated, and are not always

clear as to the status of individual hospitals at the time of the Dissolution. In some cases, therefore, I have had to make arbitrary decisions in these attributions.

2

Development and change
in English hospitals, 1100 – 1500

Miri Rubin

A pioneering scholar in the study of charitable institutions, Paul Bonenfant, expressed his view of the state of research in these words: 'Despite its multiple interests the study of medieval hospitals has not yet given rise to works of general synthesis.'[1] This was in 1965. Two years earlier he had founded the Belgian Society for the Study of the History of Hospitals and had launched its bulletin. Independently and concurrently Michel Mollat of the Sorbonne initiated the Parisian seminar on the History of Poverty, a forum which inspired pioneering works on the concepts, reality, and relief of poverty.[2] These early studies tended to use medieval source material such as theological tracts, literature, civil legislation, canon law, and art, in an attempt to understand medieval poverty. The methodological difficulties inherent in the study of the poor through material emanating primarily from government and from the church soon unfolded, and underlies some of the weaknesses of the early works. An alternative approach emerged in the 1970s, one which used charitable institutions as bridges to the study of poverty. Applied by a number of continental scholars, it focused on asylums, the institutions which harboured, fed, and clothed the needy. These were deemed to be important indicators of some of the options and conditions experienced by the poor. An important attraction was the fact that not only have many charitable institutions left rich archives, cartularies, rentals, and accounts, full of details on every facet of medieval life, but also that institutions of relief, placed as they were at the convergence of religious and social sensibilities of contemporaries, are an important area for a focused yet total view of society. At their best, studies of medieval hospitals can lead us to an improved and indeed new understanding of social commitment, of attitudes towards the poor and towards the clergy, and to an appreciation of the ways in which a resonant message of charity interacted with prevailing and developing economic factors to produce the changing forms of relief. Historians drawn to the study of hospitals, especially in England, could also benefit from a long tradition of local history and of archaeological examination of hospital structures.[3] But there is an urgent need to formulate new concepts and questions and to devise subtle approaches which can do justice both to the complexity of contexts in which hospitals existed and to the diversity of sources relevant to their study.

The rise of interest in hospitals and the poor also coincided with the rise in urban history. The awareness of structural problems of urban life, the peculiarities of its complex social structure, and the importance of towns as venues for experimentation in social and political ideas, as well as in bureaucratic and administrative procedures, underlay an understanding of the ways in which new solutions to old problems were sought. As to the study of poverty and relief, towns possessed a concentration of excess wealth and a close mingling of the haves and have-nots, producing greater need and greater awareness alike. Thus, the urban study suggested itself, with the concentration of institutions and their remaining archives, but, more importantly, as a meaningful conceptual framework for the treatment of what was a network of redistribution determined by a multitude of social, economic, religious, and political circumstances. First among these is Brian Pullan's monumental *Rich and Poor in Renaissance Venice* which demonstrated that the intimate understanding of all aspects of town life – its economy, traditions, social structure, and topography – is vital in any serious attempt to assess its system of relief.[4] Be it a greater commercial centre, a port, an episcopal see, or a university town, its special characteristics affected a town's needs for relief, its ability to give it, as well as the institutional forms in which it could be provided. Thus, studies of poor relief in Lyon, in Narbonne, in Bruges, followed the wake of medieval urban history.[5] And a parallel development occurred in the field of early modern history; we now know much about relief in Lyon,

Aix, Toledo, and Warwick.[6] As urban studies developed a better understanding of the interdependence between town and countryside, and integrated the flow of labour, administrative models, wares, raw materials, ideas, and power between them, into models of urban life, a more complex approach was signalled for the treatment of poverty and relief in towns and their surroundings. Thus, in addition to its local aspects, the study of urban relief should consider several characteristics of the rural neighbourhood; fluctuations in rural prosperity and the charitable solutions which it offered could have immediate bearing on urban needs for relief. The concentration on towns, understandable and necessary as it is, has left the study of non-institutional forms of relief devised by the rural community and enshrined in its customs, awaiting rigorous examination; Richard Smith's interest in life-cycle effects on poverty,[7] as well as Christopher Dyer's contribution to the understanding of medieval nutrition, promise to enlighten us on the structural poverty and morbidity traps which threatened medieval folk.[8]

This paper will trace some of the trends in the foundation and development of charitable institutions in Cambridge and its surroundings. The great wave of hospital foundation in the second half of the twelfth and the early thirteenth century occurred in a period of demographic and economic growth, of urban development, of acceleration of exchange, and the proliferation of markets. All in all it was a period of diversification in economic and social activities. Communal initiatives were taken in new boroughs, in the increasingly effective parish framework, in new village communities, and in old ones where management and exploitation of resources increased in sophistication.[9] These years saw the development of urban institutions promoting and accommodating trade and crafts, and witnessed collective efforts to address their problems of communications, hygiene, and security. In this world of change and prosperity, substantial peasant-holders, manor administrators, master craftsmen, and traders were organizing and improving the environment of their respective towns and villages. Charitable institutions were the result of some of these efforts.

As the community of the borough defined and extended its areas of activity, members explored opportunities in patronage of religious and charitable houses. At least 110 hospitals are known to have been founded in England in towns of differing sizes and characters[10] – in monastic boroughs, in episcopal towns, and in royal boroughs. As the particular, and new, needs and opportunities for urban relief manifested themselves, substantial members of towns and their hinterlands recognized the political advantage, the chance to participate in public activity deemed worthy and rich with social and religious rewards. The earliest attempts at relief looked to existing religious institutions as both recipients and dispensers of charitable funds and as models for organization. Autonomous leper and hospital communities often followed existing guidelines such as parish boundaries, the secular religious framework, or the life of the cloistered religious. The first stage of hospital foundation was a period of experimentation in towns and countryside; and its flexible tentative results provide our earliest examples of charitable institutions.

In Cambridgeshire – and the medieval county boundaries were conveniently almost identical to the diocesan ones – the earliest institutions are two twelfth-century leper-houses, St Mary Magdalene's in Ely and St Mary Magdalene's at Stourbridge, near Cambridge, both mentioned in Pipe Rolls for the 1160s and 1170s as recipients of royal and episcopal alms.[11] The hospital in Cambridge was situated some two miles out of the town centre and boasted a lovely Norman chapel, which is one of the earliest remains of medieval Cambridge. As the need for leper houses probably declined by the mid-thirteenth century, we witness the transformation of these institutions. The hospital at Ely was united to another hospital, St John's, to create a new house living by an Augustinian rule and under episcopal patronage. The leper hospital at Stourbridge had become a free chapel by 1279 and remained in episcopal gift well into the fifteenth century, maintaining no pastoral or charitable duties whatsoever. That England was dotted with such small self-regulating communities of lepers living outside towns, along roads, by streams, and by town-gates, is borne out by stories of houses such as Stourbridge, and by the silent evidence of place names. These typical twelfth-century foundations evolved from a need for segregation tended to by communities of the vills and by burgesses. The treatment of lepers, with its biblical associations, also captured the imagination and largesse of kings and queens, who founded and endowed tens of *leprosaria*.[12] Throughout the thirteenth century, leprosy was in decline and the need for such houses was less pressing: they were then manipulated and transformed by powerful groups and individuals within whose jurisdiction and patronage they fell. In Ely and Cambridge they entered the gift of the Bishop and Priory of Ely. For this the burgess community of Cambridge harboured a grievance and complained bitterly in the Hundred Rolls of 1279; they saw in Stourbridge's demise the loss of an institution which had benefited their town.[13]

The rural institution closest to Cambridge was the hospital at Stow, some 7 miles from Cambridge, founded by the vicar of Stow, and endowed by Sir Aubrey, who appears in the Book of Fee in 1250.[14] This group of maidens, 'the sisters of Stow', wore red habits and possessed a chapel. Similar female communities living outside established religious orders and engaged in charitable works were a common phenomenon in England and the continent in the twelfth and thirteenth centuries. In more formal groupings, layfolk devoted their lives to charity in the third orders related to Franciscan and Dominican friaries. The sisters of Stow are still mentioned in the second half of the thirteenth century and as late as 1338, but seem to have disappeared after the Black Death. This short-lived community was clearly an attempt to provide relief and comfort within the framework of the rural parish.

Another type of charitable provision grafted a group of recipients on to an existing religious house. Some time around 1200 the Gilbertine priory at Fordham was given a messuage, 60 acres of arable and 5 acres of meadow, by a substantial tenant in the parish of Wicken, and in return the house was to keep thirteen poor men in food, clothes, and cover.[15] Such an obligation would have weighed heavily on the purses of small religious houses after a while, and charitable duties were often put aside as memories of patronage and the value of the endowment declined. We encounter numerous papal and episcopal dispensations of the thirteenth and fourteenth centuries freeing religious houses from earlier commitments to relief and hospitality. In some charitable communities the religious element came to dominate and, especially where a rule was observed, there was a good

chance that the hospital would be turned into a full Augustinian priory, as occurred in several places.[16] Charitable experiments were thus conducted in a variety of forms in which
benefactors and founders wished to achieve the greatest possible stability and continuity of endowment, reliable management and maintenance of a religious framework ensuring
perpetual intercession, display, and accumulation of merit.
The instability of many early houses bears witness to the
failure of existing religious houses to provide institutional
forms for charitable foundation which were compatible with
the wish of benefactors for meritorious and perpetual functioning.

With the development of urban institutions, charitable
activity seems to have been naturally drawn into the urban
environment where clearer and more rigorous ideas about
organization of corporate projects, and thus on the management of charitable endowments, were evolving. Thus, in the
second phase of charitable initiatives, in the late thirteenth
century, we witness the rise of a new type of charitable
religious house – an endowed institution which combined the
relief of poverty with a religious and liturgical regime maintained by a regular group of secular clergy and assisted by a
group of lay brethren or sisters. These hospitals were founded
by leading burgesses and supported by a stream of donations
from humbler townsmen and substantial villagers. They were
founded at the entrances to towns, in areas unsuitable for
settlement, on the sidelines of a town's business and social
centre. The permanent community of such a hospital usually
followed a religious rule, maintained a chapel, and soon
needed and procured the ecclesiastical privileges of burial,
bell-ringing, and cure of souls.[17] The evident need for relief,
which was ever growing in the thirteenth century with the
gradual pauperization of a teeming countryside and migra-
tion of workers to towns, was largely answered in such
institutions whose forms were determined by the current
understanding of the organization of religious life. Groups of
canons, or semi-religious layfolk, maintained centres of relief
which offered succour to the poor as well as spiritual benefits
to founders and adherents.

Such foundations were ubiquitous – St John the Baptist,
Oxford, St John's, Bath, St Mark's, Bristol. A leading burgess or group of burgesses would found the house, keeping

its patronage and the right to nominate its master. But the need for ecclesiastical protection and privilege would soon turn it into a full religious existence made formal by the assumption of a rule granted by the diocesan. In Cambridge, it was one Henry Frost, who by 1204 had given the community of Cambridge what the Hundred Rolls call 'locus pauperrimus', a bit of poor waste land beyond the parish of All Saints, a marshy tract east of the river Cam, which was dried and filled only decades later to allow the early Cambridge colleges to be built there.[18] The tradition maintained in the Hundred Rolls described the subsequent usurpation of patronage by the Bishop of Ely. Similar complaints about the loss of control over their hospitals were made in the Hundred Rolls by the burgesses of Nottingham and Norwich.

Occurring first in 1204, by 1215 the hospital at Cambridge had become an Augustinian house in the parish of All Saints; an addition not only to the religious map of thirteenth-century Cambridge, but also to its business and proprietorial scene, as an enterprise which people from near and far wished to join. A period of abundant donation followed the foundation and the assumption of religious status. Benefactors were not only the leading burgesses but also a multitude of tradesmen and artisans who gave the new institution shops, rents, strips in the Cambridge fields, tenements, bits of gardens, and crofts. They were joined by villagers from the neighbourhood, the majority of whom resided in villages within a distance of ten miles from the town, who contributed acres and half-acres, a piecemeal endowment reflecting the pattern of their own tenure in the village fields. After a generation of donation the hospital possessed a considerable amount of urban property, mainly in the market and in its own parish of All Saints. Its estate brought the hospital into contact with other owners, and a sequence of exchanges of properties allowed it to participate in the active land market and to consolidate its holdings. In the surrounding villages it had a fragmented presence, and only in those closest to Cambridge did it hold more than a scattering of half-acres and roods. In its dealings and exchange transactions the hospital aimed at simplification and commutation into annual rents as far as was possible. Once this was achieved, a striking stability seems to have come over the estate. In the rentals for the late thirteenth and the fourteenth century most properties can be traced back to an origin in the first enthusiastic phase of donation in the prosperous years of the early thirteenth century.

The hospital also engaged in a modest moneylending activity. Some loans were forwarded to great men, squire-burgesses, such as the Dunnings of Cambridge, who found that the maintenance of their urban and rural obligations exceeded their income. In such cases the hospital stepped in and provided a breathing space, by freeing them from debts to the Jews and receiving the pledged land thus released as a security. Many such loans turned, in the long run, into dona-tions to the hospital, upon default of payment. When a borrower lost land to his creditor, the hospital, this none the less resulted in procuring the status of benefactor and the spiritual rewards attached to it. Through another instrument the hospital provided credit on a smaller scale; these were in fact mortgages for short terms (between four and six years). Villagers would pledge a few acres, promising to pay a so-called rent for it in a lump sum at the end of the period. The hospital forwarded the sum, usually under 10s. for a number of years, and enjoyed the usufruct during the term of the agreement. These credit agreements were primarily enacted between the hospital and the parishioners of Horningsea, a parish which was appropriated to the hospital at the time of its religious foundation. It is interesting to speculate on the ways in which this lending activity fits into the view of the hospital as a primarily charitable institution. Provision of low-interest loans was often interpreted by contemporaries as an aspect of charitable aid, and the freeing of Christians from Jewish moneylenders was presented in popular preaching as an act of charity and brotherhood. Such activities beyond the purely charitable and religious illustrate the degree to which medieval hospitals responded to the needs of their environment, and in particular to those of existing or potential benefactors.

The foundation and life of hospitals were couched with a terminology and imagery of charity, and those living and working in them were expected to undertake a rigorous religious routine. In the Hospital of St John, Cambridge, a male community was founded following what had become the model of communal charitable life – the hospital statutes based on the Augustinian rule. Augustine's fourth-century set of instructions for communal clerical living was revived in the eleventh century for the reform of clerical living and provided a way of life for a group of priests in proximity to lay society; it was essentially a secular rule, which allowed priests to fulfil functions such as pastoral care, teaching, and charity, and yet to live purely and modestly, to escape temptations, and to observe a full liturgical life. The first to adopt the Augustinian precepts to charitable institutions was the Hospitaller order in the Crusader state.[19] Throughout the twelfth and thirteenth centuries single hospitals took up a modified version which allowed for the coexistence of a religious community with lay inmates and servants, and for flexibility in the routine of those members tending the sick. Hospital rules refer to the life of inmates in varying degrees of detail, and they provide much of our scanty knowledge of the life of the poor and sick. The clauses usually laid down the principles of admission; in the Hospital of St John, Cambridge, these criteria excluded the chronically ill and the permanently maimed: 'We strictly ordain . . . that sick and weak people should be admitted kindly and mercifully, except for pregnant women, lepers, the wounded, cripples and the insane.'[20] Like most hospitals, it assisted the passing sick and poor, those who could benefit and grow stronger and healthier during a limited stay in the hospital, or else die there and be properly buried by the community. Thus, lepers, paralytics, the insane, and those suffering from falling sickness were not admitted, nor were wounded people, and, for other reasons, pregnant women. The rule of the Hospital of St John the Baptist in Oxford explicitly states the rationale behind these stipulations: 'those suffering from falling sickness, ulcers or incurable diseases will not be accepted . . . nor will lewd pregnant women be admitted'.[21]

The incomplete fourteenth-century copy of the rule of the Hospital of St John, Cambridge, does not mention the number of inmates, brethren, or lay brethren.[22] However, the Hospital of St John in Ely, which was given a very similar rule by the same bishop, was a community of thirteen brethren, a master and a mixed lay and clerical community of twelve. In a fourteenth-century list of stipends and later in the clerical poll tax of 1379, both hospitals were said to have a master and five chaplains, which, combined with an equal number of lay brethren, would fit in with an assessment of twelve or thirteen. No surviving material allows us to assess the bed capacity of the Cambridge hospital, but since the inmates were treated in the nave of a chapel divided into four bays, it is reasonable to assume that some eight to ten people were lodged in it, in what is known as the wide-hall form.[23] The rule ordered that inmates be confessed and given communion upon arrival, and like many rules it insisted that they be treated kindly. The strict diet observed by the chaplains, which allowed the eating of meat only twice a week, was to be relaxed in cases where fine and rich meats could fortify the ailing. Unfortunately, only one set of kitchen accounts for the Hospital of St John of Cambridge survives, describing some forty weeks in the year 1343–4; the hospital received grain from its land, and maintained fish-ponds across the Cam, as well as a sheep-fold, but the accounts record regular purchases of butter, eggs, cheese, veal, chickens, and a variety of fish brought up the river. Occasionally purchases of spices are recorded – saffron, pepper, and cumin from the Stourbridge fair.[24]

Gifts to the hospital sometimes stated particular needs: the income from Hugh of Barton's messuage in Newnham was to provide lighting in the inmates' quarters during the night; an episcopal gift granted peat and reeds from the marshes of Ely annually; Harvey Dunning's charter granting arable in Chesterton instructed the hospital to use its income for the maintenance of two sets of bedding. From its fourteenth-century accounts we learn that the hospital employed a cook, a malt-maker, a baker, and a servant. By the fifteenth century a barber, a laundress, and an organ-player were on the payroll. The rule exhorted brethren to keep themselves clean, a clause reminiscent of the rule of St Laurence's, Canterbury, which instructed them to wash their heads at least once a month lest their smell disturb the inmates.[25]

The religious community of the Hospital of St John also maintained liturgical offices and prayers for benefactors, and tended to the pastoral needs of its members and of the parish of Horningsea, of which it was the communal rector. A copy of a fourteenth-century list of benefactors minutely recorded those for whom the brethren were to intercede, a list of names spanning over a century and a half. The hospital was also connected with the Hospital of St John in Ely by a mutual agreement ensuring commemoration for the dead brethren of either community.[26] The non-liturgical nursing duties were filled by lay brethren who were in charge of maintenance, catering, and cleaning, while the more responsible jobs of cellarer and sacrist were filled by the chaplain brothers. The whole community was led by the master, a priest to whom all confessed and all owed strict obedience. Recurrent readings of statutes and weekly chapter gatherings provided the occasion for enforcement of discipline and mutual correction.

The question of medical practices in medieval hospitals is a difficult and puzzling one. One often deals with quite a full hospital archive covering hundreds of years and yet encounters not one mention of purchases of drugs or payments to physicians or surgeons. At the basis of hospital foundation lay the understanding that separation of the sick from everyday life and from neighbours and family was necessary, both for the welfare of the community and to effect their cure. Indeed, the provision of food, cover, a cleaner surrounding, and warmth could go a long way to increase chances of recovery from common illnesses. Little more can be said. In one of the charters of donation to the hospital *c.*1230 one Robertus *medicus* appears as a witness. He may be the same as Robert *le surgien* who held a house in the parish of All Saints near the hospital around 1200. Was he a friend of the donor, or a medical practitioner connected with the hospital? It is impossible to say. In 1279 a university master, Nigel de Thornton, physician, is mentioned as a householder in Cambridge, though he has no explicit connection with the hospital. In 1314 some land in Cambridge was sold to Master Hugo *medicus*; later, in the fifteenth century a doctor of medicine at Peterhouse was paying tithes on his earnings to the parish of Little St Mary. Were these earnings gained from dispensing medical care?[27] The yearly payments of 8s. to a *barbitonsor* in the fifteenth century must be seen as a service to the religious community since by then there were no longer sick folk in the hospital.

The pattern of foundation and development of the Hospital of St John, Cambridge, is characteristic of the initiatives undertaken by burgess communities in the late twelfth and early thirteenth centuries, when urban hospitals were founded in Cambridge, Wisbech, and Ely. It started as a concerted attempt on the part of leading burgesses and substantial landholders to meet problems which were becoming a pronounced aspect of town life such as industrial accidents, sickness among destitute people, and unemployable folk who could not be tended by an extended family or supported by customary mutual help maintained by rural communities. These activities were also couched with religious imagery and promise of salvation, by a spirituality preached and disseminated more frequently and more effectively throughout the thirteenth century. But the efforts for co-operative action and the willingness to apportion a part of one's income and security for the general weal and for spiritual benefits was bound to change once economic fortunes changed and social relations were realigned. By the early or mid fourteenth century the once pauperized countryside was experiencing demographic decline which caused prices to fall, wages to rise, and income from land and trade to fall. The demand for goods and services provided by the towns was slackening, which effected a decrease in the incomes of burgesses. As burgess communities realized that they could no longer easily allocate charitable funds, and that their bounty would be better used in other endeavours, hospitals were left with their declining endowments and, as burgess interest and control waned, with their lax and inefficient administrations. Neither papal directives for reform such as the injunctions published in the collection of canon law, the Clementines, in 1317,[28] nor the episcopal ordinances following visitations, of which there are three sets for the Hospital of St John,[29] could alter the fact that those who had nurtured hospitals were developing different views of their welfare and altered expectations from social and religious action.

The fourteenth century saw the reversal of the process of expansion and population growth and the gradual decline of population by a combination of internal demographic checks, recurrent famines, and finally by the Black Death in mid-century.[30] These changes fundamentally altered the relations between employers and employees, landlords and tenants, and allowed the standard of living of workers to rise while the income of landlords and substantial burgesses was declining. A virulent legislation in an acerbic rhetoric attempted to keep poor labourers in a stable abode and in full employment. In France hospitals came to be used as tools of labour legislation and as locations for punishment and recruitment of able-bodied beggars to work.[31] This interpretation of economic ills as being the outcome of wilful withdrawal of labour by workers inspired a highly suspicious attitude towards all forms of charitable benefaction, which were not closely scrutinized. Thus, hospitals were criticized as assisting the lazy shirkers, and at the same time charitable funds were more discriminately deployed.[32]

In this climate hospitals were obliged to adapt or perish. They were transformed in a variety of ways in order to survive and to suit current patronage choices of potential benefactors. In this process, a burgess foundation of around 1250 such as St John's Hospital, Wisbech, became a royal sinecure by 1352.[33] Many, like St Mary's Bootham, York, turned into chantries for the commemoration of the original founder or of a later re-founder and his family.[34] Some developed educational functions, and many simply disappeared as income from land endowments diminished dramatically in the fourteenth century. Those houses which adapted did so through a total reorganization and redefinition of aims. In the Hospital of St John, Cambridge, inmates are not mentioned after the mid-fourteenth century. The hospital now fulfilled different tasks; its brethren supplied chantry services to burgesses, and served in chantries established in Cambridge parish churches. It continued to provide the cure of souls in the parish of Horningsea, and one of the brethren moved to the rectory permanently. St John's Hospital also accommodated numerous corrodarians, even women, and became the *pied à terre* of the Archdeacon of Ely on his rounds in Cambridge. In 1280 the hospital was the subject of an experiment in academic charity on the part of the Bishop of Ely; Hugh of Balsham installed a group of his favoured students there, only to remove them three years later due to conflict rife between the communities, re-founding the group as the first Cambridge college, Peterhouse. The hospital provided lodging for four university masters during term, and, finally, in 1470 it came to receive full university privileges, allegedly for protection from the harassment of townsmen.[35]

A long road away from the original communal and charitable objectives had been travelled; at its end, and in the particular setting of Cambridge, a group of Augustinian canons observing canonical hours and engaged in commemoration seemed little different from the academic colleges surrounding it. The hospital was assimilated into the liturgical and academic milieu to such a degree that, when it was re-founded as St John's College in 1511, few murmured at what seemed like a natural progression.[36]

While the old institutions, devised in a period of growth and prosperity, combined religion with relief for the poor and sick and were developing away from their original purposes, new foundations were springing up in the late fourteenth and fifteenth centuries which signalled a new understanding of the task and scope of relief. The hospital of Sts Anthony and Eligius of Cambridge was founded in 1361 by the will of a leading burgess and financier Henry Tangmere. His will was to be executed by Corpus Christi College, with which he was associated in his lifetime, and among numerous provisions one was made for the creation of a hospital in two tenements in Trumpington Street.[37] This was to be a leper house, a curious foundation for the fourteenth century when leprosy had all but disappeared, but not one without parallel. The house came to assist all types of disorder, and by the sixteenth century was primarily a small insane asylum. Henry Tang-mere's was a lay foundation which did not support a religious community, although it received some episcopal favour in the form of indulgences for its helpers, and had a chapel decorated with paintings and hangings. This clear choice on the part of an astute burgess, to administer his relief programme outside a religious house and without the help of a religious commun-ity, falls in with the general trend of distancing from religious houses and employment of the clergy as direct intercessors. The model of St John's Hospital, Cambridge, stood clear before the founder's eyes and could teach a lesson. He chose to entrust the supervision of relief to a perpetual institution such as Corpus Christi, which administered the endowment. Similar appreciation of the power of municipal authorities as brokers in the charitable game is attested by the growing number of charitable and commemoration trusts left to the execution of the Cambridge Town Corporation in the fifteenth century. This movement away from organized religion and towards more discrete and controlled forms of secular relief are expressions of the self-help in religious life, so characteristic of the late middle ages.

A fifteenth-century foundation, the hospital at Newton-in-the-Wash, is yet another form of organization of piety and relief which bore the name *hospitale*. The hospital at Newton was founded in 1403 by Sir John Colvylle as a college of priests and clerics together with some poor men.[38] By 1405 it had received papal protection and in 1411 the parish church of Newton was appropriated to it. In 1452 it was reorganized by the Bishop of Ely, who provided it with a set of statutes; it was to continue as a group of chaplains under a priest as master and to be engaged in the commemoration of the King, the founder, and his family. The master, three chaplains, and four clerks lived in a house attached to the chapel and received generous stipends. The house also accommodated three poor men and a poor woman in charge of all cleaning and cooking for the almsmen.[39] These bedesmen, as the statutes called them, were to live chastely and provide grateful prayers for the founder. They wore habits made of white heavy cloth and were given two pairs of shoes a year. Their weekly stipend of sixpence was paid on Fridays and was supplemented by pittances on feast-days. This house is an extreme example of an institution which offered poor relief as part of a planned and concerted effort to benefit the founder's soul. A lay fraternity was created in connection with the house for those wishing to share the spiritual merit generated by the pious charitable hospital-chantry. No scheme of intercession seemed quite complete, just as no funeral appeared to be well provided, without the presence of the statutory poor, the meek who owed their survival to charitable giving. These poor were not the *raison d'être*; rather they were grafted on to the foundation, and supported by it, just as a single almsman was maintained by the Hospital of St John, Cambridge, throughout the fifteenth century.

Forms of charity and relief were thus re-evaluated and refashioned as the perception of the community's economic well-being and its religious and social aims changed. The shift in attitudes towards poverty in the later middle ages, away from the traditional view of it as virtuous to viewing it as a social menace and a source of disruption, altered the forms in which charity was dispensed. It was no longer through reliance on the good working of religious charitable communities, but rather in more discriminating and controlled frameworks. A multitude of urban almshouses of the late fifteenth century attest to such choices, which were already signalled by a foundation such as Sts Anthony and

Eligius in Cambridge. These almshouses were modest affairs, often located in a house left by the founder, which did not attempt to create a charitable religious unit observing a liturgical routine. It was the bare act of relief, of clearing the streets, of helping the deserving parish poor, that seems to have guided their founders. These almshouses – Daniel's, Lyon's, Jakennet's – offered limited but direct relief, as did their testamentary bequests. In Cambridge, where colleges had emerged as reliable and perpetual corporations, four almshouses were founded between 1463 and 1484; three were supervised by colleges, by King's, Queens', and Gonville and Caius.[40] These foundations survived throughout the sixteenth century and are occasionally mentioned in church-wardens' accounts of the parishes in which they were situated. Such almhouses which carried the names of founders and were managed by layfolk or parish priests under the supervision of executors, guilds, colleges, or town authorities are typical fifteenth-century foundations; they were often conceived as an economic and moral remedy for the homeless poor, for vagrants, migrants, and to the dangers they posed.[41] These almshouses which were founded and controlled by individual layfolk, by gilds, and by town authorities were independent from episcopal supervision and from the intermediation of a religious community. They never developed into the large-scale municipal hospitals and shelters that were maintained by Italian, Flemish, and French towns,[42] but in the English towns they expressed a re-evaluation of charitable aims and means. The choice of the parish framework reflects the preference of an organizational framework based on social ties, co-operation, and responsibility between neighbours; it represented a task of relief which could be controlled and checked by parishioners, family, and friends.

In search of personal and collective gratification and in the attempt to promote the stability and order of their communities, medieval men and women of property and substance allocated excess funds and savings to public charitable institutions. That their willingness to give fluctuated with their prosperity and sense of economic security is abundantly clear. This chapter has shown the resulting changes in the forms assumed by acts of giving and in availability of relief. The study of medieval hospitals and relief agencies has led us on a journey of discovery about the responsiveness of institutions to the values and expectations of those supporting them. It has shown us that a system of relief is little more than the succour which the 'haves' are agreed and willing to provide to the 'have nots'. Institutions relying on co-operation are hit hard when consensus and trust diminish; this was as true in the medieval community as it is in the welfare states of the 1980s.

Notes

1. P. Bonenfant, *Hôpitaux et bienfaisance publiques dans les anciens Pays-Bas des origines à la fin du XVIIIe siècle* (Société Belge d'Histoire des Hôpitaux, Brussels, 1965), 5.

2. M. Mollat (ed.), *Etudes sur l'histoire de la pauvreté*, 2 vols (Publications de la Sorbonne, Paris, 1974).

3. R.M. Clay, *The Medieval Hospitals of England* (Antiquary's Books, London, 1909).

4. B.S. Pullan, *Rich and Poor in Renaissance Venice. The Social Institutions of a Catholic State, to 1620* (Blackwell, Oxford, 1971).

5. N. Gonthier, *Lyon et ses pauvres au moyen-âge (1350–1500)* (Hermes, Lyon, 1978); J. Caille, *Hôpitaux et charité publique à Narbonne au moyen-âge de la fin du XIe siècle à la fin du XVe siècle* (Privat, Toulouse, 1978); G. Maréchal, *De sociale en politieke gebundenheid van het Brugse hospitalwezen in de Middeleeuwen*, Anciens Pays et Assemblés d'états, 73 (UGA, Heule, 1978).

6. J.-P. Gutton, *La société et les pauvres: l'exemple de la généralité de Lyon, 1534–1789*, Bibliothèque de la Faculté des Lettres et Sciences Humaines de Lyon 2 (Les Belles Lettres, Paris, 1971); C.C. Fairchilds, *Poverty and Charity in Aix-en-Provence 1640–1789*, Johns Hopkins University Studies in Historical and Political Science, 94i (Johns Hopkins University Press, Baltimore, 1976); L. Martz, *Poverty and Welfare in Habsburg Spain. The Example of Toledo* (Cambridge University Press, Cambridge, 1983); A.L. Beier, 'The social problems of an Elizabethan country town: Warwick 1580–1590', in P. Clark (ed.), *Country Towns in Pre-Industrial England* (Leicester University Press, Leicester, 1981), 46–85.

7. R. Smith, 'The manor court and the elderly tenant in late medieval England', in Z. Razi and R. Smith (eds), *The Manor Court and Medieval English Society* (Oxford University Press, Oxford, forthcoming, 1990).

8. C. Dyer, 'English diet in the later middle ages', in T.H. Aston, P.R. Coss, C. Dyer, and J. Thirsk (eds), *Social Relations and Ideas: Essays in Honour of R.H. Hilton* (Cambridge University Press, Cambridge, 1983), 191–216.

9. For a study of urbanization in this period see D. Keene (with

A.R. Rumble), *Survey of Medieval Winchester*, Winchester Studies, 2 (2 vols, Clarendon Press, Oxford, 1985).

10. Aggregate figures on hospital foundation are based on the listings in D. Knowles and R.N. Hadcock, *Medieval Religious Houses: England and Wales* (Longman, London, 1971).

11. On the former see M. Rubin, *Charity and Community in Medieval Cambridge*, Cambridge Studies in Medieval Life and Thought, fourth ser., 4 (Cambridge University Press, Cambridge, 1987), 129–35, and the latter, *ibid.*, 111–18.

12. P. Richards, *The Medieval Leper and his Northern Heirs* (D.Brewer and Rowman & Littlefield, Cambridge and Totowa, NJ, 1977).

13. For other instances of patronage losses and disputes see Rubin, *Charity and Community*, 99–103.

14. Op. cit., 135–7.

15. Op. cit. 137.

16. Like Anglesey in Cambridgeshire by 1220, and North Creake in Norfolk by 1208.

17. On the development of pastoral care in the twelfth and thirteenth centuries, see J. Avril, 'La Pastorale des malades et des mourants aux XIIe et XIIIe siècles', in H. Braet and W. Verbeke (eds), *Death in the Middle Ages*, Mediaevalia Lovaniensia, ser. 1, studia 9 (Louvain University Press, Louvain, 1983), 88–106.

18. On hospital locations in general, Rubin, *Charity and Community*, 99–109, 114–16.

19. On the Hospitaller rules see E.J. King, *The Rule, Statutes and Customs of the Hospitallers, 1099–1310* (Methuen, London, 1934); L.Le Grand (ed.), *Statuts d'hôtels-dieu et de léproseries* (L.Le Grand, Paris, 1901).

20. Rubin, *Charity and Community*, 300–1.

21. H.E. Salter (ed.), *A Cartulary of the Hospital of St John the Baptist, Oxford, III*, Oxford Historical Society, 69 (Clarendon Press, Oxford, 1920), 3–5.

22. Printed in Rubin, *Charity and Community*, 300-301.

23. On hospital architecture see D. Leistikow, *Ten Centuries of European Hospital Architecture* (Boehringer, Ingelheim, 1967).

24. Cambridge, St John's College Archive C7.1 (Cartulary of the Hospital of St John), fos 89-90.

25. See the rule of Sr. Laurence's, Cambridge University Library, Add. 6845, fo. 6ᵛ.

26. Rubin, *Charity and Community*, 181.

27. On physicians in medieval English hospitals see R.S. Gottfried, *Doctors and Medicine in Medieval England, 1340–1530* (Princeton University Press, Princeton, NJ, 1986), 259–60.

28. E. Friedberg (ed.), *Corpus iuris canonici*, (B. Tauchnitz, Leipzig, 1879), vol. 2, Constitutiones Clementinae lib. III, 11, cols. 1170–71.

29. Rubin, *Charity and Community*, 171, 190.

30. J. Hatcher, *Plague, Population and the English Economy 1348–1530* (Macmillan, London, 1977), 31–5; E. Miller and J. Hatcher, *Medieval England: Rural Society and Economic Change 1086–1348* (Longman, London, 1978), 53–63; Z. Razi, *Life, Marriage and Death in a Medieval parish. Economy, Society and Demography in Halesowen, 1270–1400* (Cambridge University Press, Cambridge, 1980), 27–32, 114–31.

31. B. Geremek, 'Le Renfermement des pauvres en Italie (XIVe–XVIIe siècle): remarques préliminaires', in *Mélanges en l'honneur de Fernand Braudel. Histoire économique du monde méditeranéen 1450–1650*, II (Privat, Toulouse, 1973), 205–17; idem, 'Criminalité, vagabondage, paupérisme: la marginalité à l'aube des temps modernes', *Revue d'histoire moderne et contemporaine*, vol. 21 (1974), 337–75, esp. 372.

32. On perceptions of poverty in the late fourteenth century see D. Aers, '*Piers Plowman* and problems in the perception of poverty: a culture in transition', *Leeds Studies in English*, new ser., vol. 14 (1983), 5–25.

33. Rubin, *Charity and Community*, 138–9.

34. A.F. Leach (ed.), *Early Yorkshire Schools*, Yorkshire Archaeological Society, record ser. 27 (1898), 33–8.

35. Rubin, *Charity and Community*, 182.

36. E. Miller, *Portrait of a College. A History of the College of St John the Evangelist, Cambridge* (Cambridge University Press, Cambridge, 1961), 1–8.

37. Rubin, *Charity and Community*, 119-22

38. ibid., 142–6.

39. For a similar arrangement at St Katherine's Hospital, Heytesbury, see M. Hicks, 'St Katherine's hospital, Heytesbury: prehistory, foundation, and refoundation 1408–1472', *Wiltshire Archaeological and Natural History Magazine*, vol. 78 (1984), 62–9, 66.

40. Rubin, *Charity and Community*, 127–9.

41. M. McIntosh, *Autonomy and Community: The Royal Manor of Havering 1200–1500*, Cambridge Studies in Medieval Life and Thought, fourth ser., 5 (Cambridge University Press, Cambridge, 1986), 238–9.

42. Pullan, *Rich and Poor*, 202–15; Gonthier, *Lyon et ses pauvres*, 212–23; Bonenfant, *Hôpitaux et bienfaisance publiques*, 39–44.

II

Early Modern

3

The hospitals of late-medieval and Renaissance Florence: a preliminary survey

John Henderson

There have been few comprehensive studies of the hospitals of Italian cities in the later middle ages.[1] This is despite the fact that Italy was one of the few countries in Europe to have experienced a precocious urban development. Cities such as Florence, Venice, Milan, and Genoa, are all supposed to have had populations approaching or in excess of 100,000 before the Black Death, while north of the Alps only Paris was of this size and the large conurbations such as Ghent and Bruges contained no more than 50,000 souls.[2] The relevance to our subject hardly needs pointing out; that it was in these cities that there was the greatest concentration of poor people needing alms, food, and medical treatment. Thus in the later middle ages these centres also saw the growth of poor relief facilities, an important element of which were hospitals.

The term 'hospital' covered a wide variety of institutions, and only some of these were intended to cater exclusively for the sick. The role of late-medieval hospitals should be set squarely within the context of other charitable institutions, including the soup kitchens of monasteries and convents, the social assurance schemes of religious fraternities (either independent or associated with a professional guild), and the more informal systems of parish, neighbourhood, and family.[3] Thus although we shall concentrate on institutions providing medical services, it should not be forgotten that many of the so-called 'hospitals' of medieval Europe were little more than almshouses for the elderly or centres for the reception of travellers and the poor.

Contemporaries and historians have seen the hospitals of Renaissance Florence[4] as in some ways exceptional. The

grounds for this are made clear in the prologue to a Florentine law of 1464[5]:

> Considering it is said that your city is above all others
> copiously [provided] with hospitals which are beautiful,
> and sufficient, and suitable and ordered to receive any
> sick or well person who is miserable and has need of
> being given shelter for any reason. . . .

This eulogistic passage was not merely self-conscious human-
istic window-dressing. Individual rulers as far apart as
Francesco Sforza of Milan in 1456, Henry VII of England in
the early sixteenth century, and Emperor Ferdinand in 1546,
all looked to Florence when remodelling hospitals.[6] Even
Martin Luther, that arch-critic of Roman Catholic institutions, praised Florentine hospitals as 'Regal buildings, with
the finest food and drink, attentive service, very learned
physicians and clean beds' when he visited the city on his
journey to Rome in 1510–11.[7]

If the hospitals of Florence so much impressed the rulers of
states in Italy and abroad, was there anything unusual about
their evolution or the character of individual institutions?
This essay will examine the basis of this reputation. We shall
look at the development and functions of hospitals in Florence
in the period 1000 to 1500 and also consider the extent to
which they may have differed from the hospitals of other
Italian states. It will be obvious that we can do little more
than scratch the surface of an important subject, which
despite the survival of very detailed documentation has, until
very recently, remained almost untouched by Florentine
historians.

The development of Florence and its hospitals, 1250–1500

An overall picture of the chronological development of
Florentine hospitals is provided by Figure 3.1.[8] This is
based on a provisional list of either the year of foundation or,
when this is not known, the date when a particular institution
was first documented.

The dramatic contrast between the period 1000–1200 and
the subsequent 300 years may partly reflect lack of surviving

Figure 3.1 Hospitals in Florence, 1000–1500 (by date of foundation or first mention).

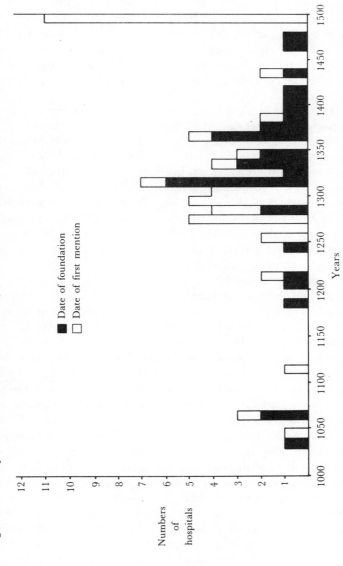

Source: see note 8.

65

documentation in the earlier period. But this does not mask the considerable increase in the number of new hospitals in Florence between *c*. 1280 and 1350. These foundations coincided with the period of maximum pressure on existing resources. The demographic expansion of the thirteenth century peaked around 1300 and during the succeeding half-century the population of the city was faced with a steady drop in the real value of wages. The foundation of these hospitals reflects one of the ways in which Florentines sought to alleviate worsening conditions among the lower levels of society.[9]

After the Black Death the standard of living improved considerably for the majority of survivors. Florence, like other places, lost at least a third of its population, which fell from about 100,000–120,000 in 1338 to *c*. 70,000 in 1360, and then subsequently dropped to *c*. 37,000–40,000 in the 1420s, as a result of epidemics which occurred at almost ten-year intervals.[10] While lower levels of population may have reduced the scale of poverty, it did not eliminate the poor. As Figure 3.1 shows, other hospitals continued to be founded after the Black Death, partly reflecting the greater availability of cash to finance new institutions.

A graphic presentation of foundations masks a series of important factors, especially the number and size of hospitals in particular periods. A preliminary investigation of contemporary sources reveals that fifty-eight different hospitals were active at some time during the period 1000 to 1500. This does not mean that all these existed at the same time. Like other small associations of laymen, such as religious confraternities, these institutions were often very volatile and may have had rather limited lifespans in the thirteenth and fourteenth centuries.[11]

An idea of how many hospitals were simultaneously in operation can be gained from contemporaries, who also calculated the number of hospitals in their day. The chronicler Giovanni Villani, for example, records the presence of thirty hospitals in Florence in 1338, and the humanist Cristoforo Landini mentions thirty-six in 1480.[12] Fiscal records also give some idea of the number of hospitals in the city, since even exempt institutions had to submit tax returns. Thus the *Catasto* of 1427–8 includes the returns of thirty-five religious corporations termed 'hospital'; the *Decima* of 1495 records thirty-two and the 1527 census of the male population of the city records twenty-nine.[13] It is difficult to judge which figures are more accurate, since chroniclers may have rounded up their calculations, while tax records may have omitted the returns of small institutions. At least it is possible to say that from the early fifteenth century there were at any one time thirty to thirty-five institutions in Florence which called themselves *ospedale*.

This general sketch of the evolution of Florentine hospitals has not yet revealed any feature which makes it markedly different from other cities. The pattern of foundations coincides with that established by studies of other Italian urban and rural areas, and also of other European centres.[14] Nor does the number of hospitals in Florence seem particularly unusual. Florence, like many cities in the fourteenth century, had a ratio of about one hospital for every 1,000 inhabitants.[15]

If Florence was not exceptional in the period of foundation or the number of its hospitals, we should therefore look in more detail at individual institutions to find out whether they had features which differentiated them from hospitals in other cities. This study will be divided into two chronological sections; the first will deal with the period 1000–1348 and the second from 1348 to *c*. 1500.

Hospitals in medieval Florence, 1000–1348

Little detail is recorded about the hospitals founded in the period 1000-1200. A majority of hospitals in this period appears to have been established by churches and monasteries to care for their own personnel, providing infirmaries and sanatoria for sick and elderly monks and nuns.[16] One example was the hospice belonging to the convent of S. Pier Maggiore, which was constructed in 1065 and known as the Spedale de' Pinti. It is typical of the majority of hospices founded before 1300 that we know of its existence through judicial records. The Spedale de' Pinti came to the attention of the court in 1300. The director of the hospice, Giunta Bencivenni, had decided to travel to Rome to attend the Jubilee, and was later discovered to have funded his journey with an unauthorized sale of property, the income of which was intended for the maintenance of the old and sick.[17]

Thus institutions not associated with any offence recorded by the judicial authorities may escape our knowledge.

The largest of these early foundations was the Ospedale di S. Giovanni Battista, which was established in the very centre of the city, between the baptistry and the cathedral, some time before 1040 for pilgrims and the poor.[18] The conditions there in about 1230 were recounted by Boncompagn da Signa, who described the somewhat depressing ambience full of impoverished old men who were given disgusting food and vinegary wine, and were kept awake at night in their foetid beds by the sighs and laments of the sick.[19] Thus although the Ospedale di S. Giovanni Battista, in common with many other institutions of this period, did serve the needs of those suffering from illnesses, this was only one among a number of its functions. It is in this context that one can appreciate the significance of the wording of the statement by the chronicler Giovanni Villani that 'in Florence there are [in 1338] thirty hospitals for the poor and sick'.[20] The poor are placed before the sick in this statement because tending to the sick was seen as only one of the Seven Works of Mercy.

Shelter was the traditional function of a hospital and many of these early foundations provided temporary accommodation for travellers and pilgrims. This is reflected in the location of hospitals throughout the city.[21] In common with the geographical distribution of hospitals studied in places such as Valencia, Arles, Lyon, and Paris, many were founded along the main roads leading into the city.[22] Especially popular locations in Florence included Via S. Gallo, the main entry from the north, and Via Romana and Via S. Pier Gattolino, the two streets leading up to the point of entry for travellers coming from the south.[23] Moreover, virtually all hospitals were established in the suburban area within the city walls constructed between 1284 and 1333.[24] The most obvious reason for this choice of location was that outside the crowded city centre there was space to build. But also of importance was the fact that it was in this area that the poorer inhabitants of the countryside had tended to settle when they came into the city in search of work.[25]

Many of the institutions appearing in Figure 3.1 for the late thirteenth and early fourteenth centuries were founded by small groups of artisans to provide sickness benefit and almshouses for themselves rather than for outsiders. This reflected the policy of most professional guilds and religious confraternities,[26] whose membership among them probably accounted for a majority of the male population above the level of the very poor. Thus in 1317 the porters of Norcia decided to found a fraternity, one of whose aims was to institute a *spedaletto* to be put at 'the service of the poor of Christ', who in practice were their own old and infirm members.[27]

There were two larger hospitals founded in this period which stand out from the mass of smaller institutions – S. Paolo and S. Maria Nuova.[28] The way in which both developed reflects one of the main trends in charity in the first half of the fourteenth century, a movement towards catering for the poor in general. When S. Maria Nuova was founded in 1288 by Folco Portinari there was little to distinguish it from the many other new hospices of the city. The act of foundation stipulated that a house was to be built to give 'hospitality and sustenance to the poor and needy', for whom twelve beds were to be made available.[29] Although treatment of the sick may have been part of Portinari's original aim, the emphasis in practice was to help the poor in general, largely by distributing sums of money to the needy living in their own houses.[30]

Thus by the time of the Black Death, Florence, in common with cities elsewhere, had a series of small institutions which aimed to provide accommodation to travellers and sickness and unemployment benefits to members of those trades and professions represented within the guild structure. Also, like other Italian states, Florence had a number of larger charities which aimed to reach a much wider clientele; the most important were the two hospitals mentioned above and the Fraternity of Orsanmichele.[31] Each one of these institutions expanded its services from the second decade of the fourteenth century, when conditions began to worsen for the poorer members of society.

Hospitals in early Renaissance Florence, 1350–c.1500

The demographic and economic crisis of the 1340s has been seen as having a significant effect on charitable institutions in both the short and long term. The immediate effect of the famines and epidemics of the 1340s was a reduction in the scale of poverty. This led to the acceleration of a process which had been begun before the Black Death, a greater specialization in the type of person who was chosen to be subsidized by governments, charitable institutions, and testators.

Even though there were three categories of people who were regarded as equally deserving of charity – orphans, widows, and the sick – there is a common assumption among historians that the Black Death led to the immediate diversion of all charitable funds to medical hospitals. This assumption has to be qualified considerably when one looks more closely at the local level, for the main concern of the governments of a number of Italian cities was the plight of widows and orphans.[32] Many of these people, who had little standing in law, had found themselves in dire financial straits following the Great Plague owing to the death of the main wage-earner of a household and the difficulties in obtaining inheritance. It is significant of the priorities of testators in Florence that the largest charity which distributed alms to the poor in general, the Fraternity of Orsanmichele, should have received bequests worth over ten times the amount left to S. Maria Nuova, the main hospital for the sick – 350,000 florins as opposed to 25,000 florins.[33] It is equally significant that the Florentine government should have passed a law in August 1348 ordering the captains of Orsanmichele to pay the bulk of their alms to widows and orphans.[34]

These two categories of paupers continued to be important recipients of charity in late-medieval and Renaissance Florence. In 1372 the Ospizio of the Orbatello opened with room to accommodate 200 poor women, the foundling hospital of the Innocenti was established in 1419, and then in 1425 the Monte delle Doti was set up to allow fathers to invest a capital sum to provide a dowry for their daughters when they came of age.[35]

Interest in widows and orphans did not preclude interest in the sick, and indeed it has been argued that the Black Death led to an increased 'medicalization' of hospitals.[36] This process can be seen clearly in the case of S. Maria Nuova, the largest and most important medical hospital in Florence. Already by 1348 it had gained the reputation as 'always full of sick men and women, who are cared for and treated with much diligence and abundance of good food and medicines'.[37]

As has been seen, its founder Folco Portinari envisaged its function as providing for all the poor of Christ, but by the late 1320s the hospital was beginning to concentrate on helping the sick.[38] This process was accelerated during the decades following the Black Death, so that by 1374, when the hospital recodified its practices in a new set of statutes, paupers who had no physical disability were not allowed to stay for longer than three days.[39]

The same process can be seen at work in other charitable institutions in Florence. The Ospedale di S. Paolo, for example, gradually moved away from concentration on the poor in general to the sick in particular.[40] Then in the 1380s construction work on two substantial new medical hospitals was begun, S. Matteo in 1385 and that of Messer Bonifazio in 1386.[41]

The period between the Black Death and the third decade of the fifteenth century saw some striking changes in the facilities offered by the hospitals of Florence. Although she shared with other cities the development towards greater specialization of charity, what served to distinguish Florence was the foundation of a series of large hospitals for orphans, widows, and the sick. In order to understand better how these new foundations contributed to the charity available to the poor in this period, we shall turn to their tax returns in 1427–8. Tables 3.1 and 3.2 summarize details about the function and bed capacity of those hospitals represented in the *Catasto*, and include details about other hospitals known to have been active in the early fifteenth century but which cannot be traced in the tax records.

As might be expected, the largest number of hospitals fell into the catch-all category, for the 'poor of Christ'. Three provided beds for between ten and nineteen people, though the majority – for which there is no information – were probably smaller.

The next largest category, hospitals for the sick (21.2 per cent), varied greatly in size, from those with only eight beds to S. Maria Nuova with 230. The smallest was S. Jacopo a S. Eusebio which had been founded in the late twelfth century as a leprosarium.[42] However, with the declining incidence of leprosy, by 1428 this *ospedale* catered only for eight lepers and 100 years later for only two.[43] Most of the earlier large hospitals for the sick were, however, for illness

Table 3.1 Hospitals in early fifteenth-century Florence –
typology

Type	Nos.	%
'Poor of Christ'	8	24.2
Sick	7	21.2
Professional groups	6	18.2
Women	5	15.1
Orphans	3	9.1
Pilgrims	2	6.1
Priests	2	6.1
Total	33	100.0

Table 3.2 Hospitals in early fifteenth-century Florence – number
of beds

Type	Number of beds							
	1–9	10–19	20–29	30–39	40–49	50 +	n/a*	Total
Poor in general	0	3	0	0	0	0	5	8
Sick	1	0	1	2	1	1	1	7
Professional groups	3	3	0	0	0	0	0	6
Women	2	0	0	0	0	1	2	5
Orphans	0	0	0	0	0	3	0	3
Pilgrims	0	1	0	0	0	0	1	2
Priests	0	0	0	0	0	0	2	2
Total	6	7	1	2	1	5	11	33

*n/a = not available
Source: see note 8

in general rather than for a particular disease. This can be
seen from the description of Florentine patients from an early
fourteenth-century sermon by the Dominican Fra Giordano
da Pisa[44]:

> Go also to the hospitals . . . you will see the sick, of
> whom one lacks a nose, another a hand or a foot;
> another who is deaf or blind; another has cancer or a
> fever; while another is in severe pain or is mad; you will
> find a 1,000 miseries and a 1,000 infirmities.

This picture is modified by two recent studies of hospital
patients in Renaissance Florence. These scholars emphasize

that by the sixteenth century these hospitals treated a wide range of diseases, but were designed increasingly for acute illnesses rather than chronic conditions. Of the patients of the Ospedale di S. Paolo, 64 per cent were described as suffering from fevers, and the next largest number (14 per cent) from skin diseases such as scabies.[45]

According to Table 3.1, the third largest group of hospitals in Florence were those run by artisans. The majority were, as has been suggested, on a much smaller scale than both the newer institutions for the sick and the orphanages. Orphanages also tended to cater for a substantial number of children. In 1428 S. Maria della Scala had 151 children in its care, in 1448 S. Gallo had 150, and the Innocenti 700 by 1469.[46] The fifth category of hospital, those for widowed women, were, on the other hand, on a very small scale, with the notable exception of the Orbatello.

Table 3.1 also shows that what are regarded usually as more 'medieval' preoccupations − such as giving shelter to pilgrims − did remain a prominent feature of even later foundations. The Ospedale di S. Lò, for example, was founded in 1435 to provide six beds for pilgrims, each of whom was only allowed to stay for a maximum of three days.[47]

Inevitably categorization of this kind, even if divisions follow contemporary descriptions, are artificial because there was a considerable overlap of function. This can be seen in the 1427 tax return of the small hospice for widows in Piazza di S. Maria del Carmine. Of the seven women present, nearly half were ill and required medical attention. One woman who was aged 80 was described as 'ill and does not leave bed', while another of only 25 was obviously beyond redemption: '[she] has been sick for a year or more and from this illness will not ever recover except when she dies from it (sic)'.[48]

Hospitals in Florence by the mid-fifteenth century were therefore able to provide considerably more accommodation than 100 years earlier. Villani notes that in 1338 there were thirty hospitals with 1,000 beds, which with his population estimate of roughly 90,000 would have provided a bed for every ninety inhabitants.[49] The population of the city probably stood at about 60,000 in the early 1370s, which would have increased the ratio of beds to inhabitants of the city to 60:1. Then by the fifteenth century the facilities for the poor had improved considerably and the per capita:bed ratio would probably have been in the region of 40:1.[50] This was partly because there were fewer people, but also because the city was now served by a series of large hospitals for the sick, orphans, and widows.

It was probably these large charitable institutions rather than the myriad of small hospices which formed the basis for the self-congratulatory statement in 1464 that Florence was a city which was 'above all others copiously [provided] with hospitals, which are beautiful, and sufficient and suitable'.[51] In what follows we shall examine the comments of contemporaries from outside Florence to discover which particular features of the Florentine hospital system they singled out for praise.

The reputation of Florentine hospitals

According to *L'architettura* of the humanist architect Leon Battista Alberti, not only Florence but the whole of Tuscany had the reputation of being 'a land of the oldest tradition of religious piety'. What typified the exercise of this 'religious piety' were the 'splendid houses of treatment built at vast expense'.[52] This suggests that Tuscany's reputation was based on the largest hospitals, which at the time he was writing in the 1440s meant S. Maria Nuova in Florence and S. Maria della Scala in Siena.[53] Other contemporary evidence confirms this assumption. For example, a Bull of 1449 gave the confraternity of S. Matteo in Pavia papal approval to erect a hospital in the city which was to be designed 'with a chapel, bells and cemetery for the poor . . . in the likeness of the hospitals of Florence and Siena'.[54]

Again in 1456, during the planning of the Ospedale Maggiore in Milan, the Duke, Francesco Sforza, asked his ambassadors for details of the hospitals of Siena and Florence.[55] He was clearly interested in every aspect of their organization and appearance. The report of the Sienese ambassador included details of the personnel, the income, and the layout of S. Maria della Scala.[56] Sforza then wrote to Giovanni de' Medici in Florence to explain that because 'in this our city of Milan a large hospital has been begun' he was sending to Florence the architect of the

Ospedale Maggiore, Filarete, together with Giovanni di Sant'Ambrogio, 'so that they might see in its entirety all that hospital of that your city [presumably S. Maria Nuova], and in order to examine it and to obtain [a copy of] the design'.[57] In this way it was hoped 'we may produce the best design that will be possible'.[58]

There appear to be conflicting views among architectural historians concerning the exact nature of the influence of these two great Tuscan hospitals. Traditionally it has been assumed that S. Maria Nuova's cruciform groundplan inspired Filarete's design of the Ospedale Maggiore in Milan.[59] However, it has been pointed out that S. Maria Nuova did not have a completed cruciform groundplan for twenty-three years after the planning of the Ospedale Maggiore.[60] Even so, the two Tuscan hospitals may have been more influential than this suggests. First, the design of S. Maria Nuova, which was so carefully inspected by Filarete, probably already included a plan to extend the existing structure – an inverted L-shape – to form a cross.[61] Secondly, the 1456 description of S. Maria della Scala indicates that it definitely did have two wards connected by a corridor to form the shape of a cross.[62] These two hospitals were, however, not the most immediately obvious models for the Ospedale Maggiore; by 1456 there were two cruciform hospitals being built much closer than Florence, in Pavia and Mantua.[63] At the present state of research, however, it is difficult to make a definitive statement about the possible influence of any Tuscan cruciform designs on the hospitals of northern Italy.

Hospital designers of northern Italy of the mid-fifteenth century evidently did see themselves as indebted to the models provided by Tuscany. It was above all the scale of these institutions which impressed them. S. Maria Nuova and S. Maria della Scala were dominated by two long wards for the male and female patients respectively. By the middle of the fifteenth century S. Maria della Scala catered in just one of these *corsie* for 130 male patients and pilgrims, and S. Maria Nuova treated each month more than 300 patients.[64] Further important parts of these large hospital complexes included service areas such as the kitchens, laundries, and pharmacies, and accommodation for the resident staff, many of whom were members of a religious order.

Finally another characteristic of Florentine hospitals which was imitated elsewhere was their porticoed facades. The most well-known example was that of the Ospedale degli Innocenti, where the *loggia* acted as the intermediary space between the public street and the private world of the residents.[65]

However innovative the scale and design of these new Renaissance hospitals, it should not be forgotten that all were based on a medieval ecclesiastical model. The wards were based on the plan of a church, emphasized by placing an altar at the head of the nave or, in the case of a cruciform design, at the meeting-point of the four arms of the cross. This was to have both a practical and spiritual purpose, in order that the medical staff could have a clear view of all the patients and that the latter could always be able to see Mass being celebrated. The ecclesiastical model was further emphasized by the invariable inclusion of a cloister, which often separated the two main wards and was designed for the use of the members of the order who ran the hospital.[66]

But it was not just the design of the hospitals which interested people from outside Tuscany. Both the report on S. Maria della Scala for Francesco Sforza and the copy of the ordinances of S. Maria Nuova prepared for Henry VII of England include detailed information about administration and finance.[67] These two subjects will form the basis of the final section.

The finance and administration of Florentine hospitals

The finances of many religious corporations in early fifteenth-century Florence appear in their tax returns of 1427–8. Even though exempt as a 'luogo pio', each hospital had to submit a detailed account of all its assets and main financial obligations. Using these returns to assess the relative wealth of hospitals in Pistoia, one historian concluded that they were by far the richest corporations in the city. The budget of the large Ospedale del Ceppo, for example, was nearly twice that of the very considerable budget of the Bishop.[68] The same is true of Florence. Although the complete *Catasto* return for the city's largest hospital, S. Maria Nuova, does not survive, a century later it was estimated that its annual income from its possessions was 25,000 florins.[69] Even if its income had been only half as large in 1428, its capital would still have amounted to 178,571 florins or five times the total capital of the largest ecclesiastical entity in the city, the archbishopric and cathedral canons.[70]

Although the capital of other Florentine hospitals did not approach that of S. Maria Nuova, both S. Gallo and S. Bonifazio, at 13,557 and 15,527 florins respectively, held substantial assets.[71] It is instructive that this placed these hospitals at about the same level of wealth as the largest charitable confraternity of the city, Orsanmichele with 14,947 florins, and not much less than the combined assets of the two companies of the Misericordia and Bigallo with 18,085 florins.[72] Another of the new hospitals, that of S. Matteo, had capital worth 8,186 florins, only just lower than the largest and most affluent canonical church, S. Lorenzo (9,359 florins), patronized heavily by the Medici family.[73] However, as with most Florentine parishes and confraternities, many of the city's hospitals had assets valued at well below 300 florins. These ranged from the Ospedale di SS. Jacopo e Filippo in Via Porcellana with assets of 249 florins and S. Salvadore with 225 florins, down to S. Lucia with only 64 florins.[74]

The main assets of most hospitals consisted of property in the city and countryside, although the larger institutions tended to diversify their financial investments. Property consisted of private houses, commercial shops and stalls in the marketplace, and farms, fields, and vineyards in the Florentine *contado*.[75] The more enterprising directors of the larger hospitals managed their assets with a view to maximizing their output. Research on the records of the orphanage of S. Gallo, for example, reveals a deliberate policy of rationalizing landholdings over a number of years, mostly by selling off far-flung parcels of land and buying up farms in an area just north of the city. In this way the land could be farmed more efficiently and fresh produce for patients procured at a shorter distance.[76]

Larger institutions, such as S. Maria Nuova, also became involved in a whole series of investment strategies, partly through inheritance and partly through deliberate policies of individual directors. Hospitals, in common with large charities such as Orsanmichele, were left not just property, but also shares in the *Monte Comune* or the city's communal debt.[77] And from 1464 S. Maria Nuova itself offered a service to investors; interest of 5 per cent was paid to anybody who deposited money with the hospital.[78] Evidently the handling of such large sums could lead to abuses, for in 1527 the director of S. Maria Nuova was dismissed for allowing his Medicean friends access to the funds which they then proceeded to lend to the commune for a return of 14 per cent.[79]

Although the contemporary chronicler, Giovanni Cambi, remarked dismissively of this affair 'and this was the charity and love they bore their country',[80] hospitals did not view financial dealings as inconsistent with charity, and often combined them. Most important were the retirement contracts it offered to the elderly. Frequently widows, short of cash to meet their everyday living expenses, made over their property to a hospital in return for a guaranteed income for the rest of their lives.[81]

Although the surviving financial records of a hospital such as the Ceppo or S. Maria Nuova suggest that large sums passed through their treasurers' hands, this does not necessarily mean that the hospital itself was thereby enriched.[82] As in the case of S. Maria della Scala in Siena, it was quite possible for an institution to be appointed as executor of substantial legacies, the proceeds of which then had to be distributed to the relatives of the deceased or even to other pious institutions. In this way little might be left for the executing institution, the hospital, or religious confraternity.[83] This becomes clear when examining the expenses and obligations of hospitals represented in the *Catasto*, as can be seen in the case of the Ospedale di S. Matteo (see Table 3.3).

S. Matteo was very much in debt, which is somewhat surprising considering that it had been founded only forty-two years before. Although it had substantial holdings – twelve houses of various sizes, nineteen farms, four vineyards, and three shops – a large number of people owed money to it. At the end of its tax return was written 'From all the above listed debtors it is impossible to collect one penny either because he is dead or has gone away or has gone bankrupt . . . so we have to conclude that these debts are lost.'[84] While it would be easy to conclude from this lament that the hospital was exaggerating the parlous state of its finances in order to protect itself against the depredations of

Table 3.3   Income and expenditure of the Ospedale di S. Matteo
in 1428 (all amounts are in florins)

	Amount	%
Income		
Total annual income	573	100
Expenditure		
1. *Salaries*		
4 priests	41	2.8
2 doctors	15	1.0
1 factor	24	1.6
	80	5.4
2. *Expenses for attendants and servants*		
Food	432	29.5
Clothes	125	8.5
	557	38.1
3. *Expenses for patients*		
Food at 15 florins p.a. for 45 patients	675	46.2
Bed repairs and medicine	70	4.8
	745	51.0
4. *Maintenance*		
Building repairs	40	2.7
Repairs to household objects	10	0.7
	50	3.4
5. *Church services*	11	0.8
6. *Legatees*	19	1.3
Total annual expenditure	1,462	100.0
Balance	– 889	

Source: Catasto 185.2, ff. 601ʳ, 607ʳ; see note 8

future tax officials, this picture is confirmed by the returns of
other hospitals. The Ceppo in Pistoia, for example, had a
deficit of roughly 525 florins, the Innocenti complained that
it had incurred a debt of more than 100 florins because of the
expenses of building, and the Spedale de' Preti told the tax
officials 'Do not marvel' that expenditure on its hospital
exceeded its income.[85]

S. Matteo's largest single item of expenditure was the
maintenance of the patients, although food (at 46.2 per cent
of total expenditure) far exceeded medicine (at 4.8 per cent,
which included repairs to beds). While the daily fare listed in
these hospitals account books does not seem very different

from that of a typical trattoria today, it was a considerable improvement over the diet of the average Florentine; it included meat, poultry, fish, grain, fresh fruit, and vegetables, as well as a substantial amount of wine.[86] It is usually difficult to distinguish the food provided for employees from that for patients, but the records of S. Maria Nuova suggest that a major medical hospital tended to feed its patients mainly on a diet in which chicken broth and eggs predominated; in the early sixteenth century the hospital purchased each year 40,000 chickens and 80,000 eggs.[87]

The rest of the expenditure was concerned with running the hospital, an important part of which was paying salaries and the maintenance of the live-in staff. Information from the *Catasto* concerning the hospital personnel reveals a similar administrative structure for all Florentine hospitals. Each was headed by a *spedalingo* or director. He was helped by assistants, varying in number according to the size of the institution; these included staff to help with the administration of the hospital, as well as clergy to perform the holy office, gardeners to till the soil, and a medical staff of doctors and nurses to tend to the inmates.[88]

The *spedalingo* established the reputation of a hospital and dictated its fortunes. Most remain fairly shadowy figures, but some particularly active *spedalinghi* do stand out. Two especially well-known figures of the late fifteenth and early sixteenth centuries are the priest Benino de' Benini and Lionardo Buonafe, a monk and later Bishop of Cortona. Benini has emerged from a recent study of S. Paolo as the driving force behind the development of the hospital and the redesign of the whole building complex, while Buonafe has traditionally been portrayed as the man who restored the flagging finances of S. Maria Nuova, increased considerably its revenues, and extended the facilities available for the sick.[89] One characteristic both men shared with the directors of the smaller hospitals was that they stayed in office until they were elderly. The average age of the *spedalinghi* of seven smaller Florentine hospices was 65, with two of them over 80; each was a layman who was married to a woman on average eight years his junior.[90] It may well be that these posts were seen as most suitable for the retired, a way of providing free board and lodging for one more elderly couple.

Just as hospital directors were professional religious or

laymen without any medical training, so were the nursing staff. This is not surprising, given that looking after the sick was seen in this period as only one of an number of ways in which a layman could help the poor. Their role was to 'give shelter . . . to the sick poor who come to the hospital, as they would to Christ himself'.[91] The main qualification for those who chose to work full-time as nurses in a hospital was therefore complete dedication. Many of the nurses at the larger hospitals lived on the premises and were members of a religious order, such as the Franciscan Tertiaries of S. Paolo or the male *conversi* and female oblates of S. Maria Nuova.[92]

Many of the larger Florentine hospitals seem to have had a substantial number of live-in nurses: Messer Bonifazio had a patient population of thirty-one who were tended by six male and twenty female nurses; S. Matteo's forty-five patients were looked after by thirty-six men and women; and S. Maria Nuova, without counting male staff and with a bed capacity of 230, had 100 female nurses.[93] While this ratio may seem high even by modern standards, one should not forget that hospitals were also providing a charitable service to those whom they employed. Single women, and in particular widows, found themselves frequently on a very low income; the fact that they received free board and lodging may have been as great an incentive to dedicate themselves to serve the sick poor as the possibility that later they too might receive support in old age.

In addition to nurses, medical staff included doctors; indeed, their presence in a hospital can be taken to distinguish them as institutions which treated the sick from the more general almshouses. Most doctors appear to have been paid on a retainer and therefore received low salaries. For example, S. Maria della Scala paid its Maestro Benedetto *medicho* 16 bushels of wheat, which was equivalent to about 3 florins, while the hospital's barber-surgeon, Antonio di Giuliano, received 2.5 florins.[94] These sums would have represented probably no more than 3 per cent of the annual income of what has been described as a 'medium level physician',[95] which also suggests that many doctors may have charged less for their professional services, seeing their work in hospitals as an act of charity.

One hundred years later doctors in S. Maria Nuova received higher salaries; physicians were paid 24 florins a year and barber-surgeons 14 florins.[96] Judging from the hospital's early sixteenth-century ordinances, this was partly because the large number of patients made these doctors' duties more onerous, and partly because they were chosen from among the six 'most excellent in all the city'.[97] These men visited the hospital on a daily basis and prescribed the relevant treatment and medication, which was then administered by the nurses and supervised by three junior doctors, who provided their services free of charge in exchange for board and lodging and the opportunity to gain direct clinical experience. Finally, a surgeon came daily to the hospital to treat 'those with sores [i.e. skin lesions]' and the wounded.[98]

As in most large hospitals, female patients were housed in a separate ward and looked after by women rather than men. In addition to nurses, a female 'magistra' was employed who 'has experience in these things', as well as a woman who was 'well skilled in surgery'.[99] Little is known about these medical women, although it is possible that they had gained experience through living in the hospital and in this way, as the compiler of the ordinances somewhat incredulously remarks, they achieved 'many cures [which] are remarkable and indeed incredible'.[100]

Towards a conclusion

It is hard not to come away from examining the ordinances of S. Maria Nuova without an optimistic view of patient care in Renaissance Florence. This picture would seem to be confirmed by recent studies of the Ospedale di S. Paolo and S. Maria Nuova, which show that patients stayed on average only eleven to fifteen days and that 80 to 90 per cent were cured and returned home.[101] Furthermore, the overall picture which has emerged from this brief survey of the various stages in the development of Florentine hospitals points to the gradual improvement and expansion in the facilities available to the poor and sick. In particular, after the mid-fourteenth century, with the reduction in the scale of poverty, there was an increased opportunity for greater specialization in the distribution of poor relief. Charitable institutions, including fraternities and hospitals, began to concentrate on helping not just the traditional biblical categories of orphans and widows, but also the sick. In addition to the expansion of existing hospitals, new ones emerged which impressed contemporaries by the scale of their operation and design. It was these large hospitals which formed the basis of Florence's reputation abroad.

However, it must be borne in mind that many of the sources which have so far been used by historians when assessing the services provided by Florentine hospitals tend to have been literary or even oratorical in origin.[102] They include comments by chroniclers like Villani, or by a chancellor of the Florentine state like Leonardo Bruni,[103] or humanists such as Alberti or Landini. Other sources are more overtly propagandist in intention, such as the prologues of contemporary laws. Even Luther's eulogistic description of the treatment he is presumed to have received in S. Maria Nuova would hardly have been representative of the experience of the patients of all Florentine hospitals. The features he described included the 'finest food and drink', 'beautifully painted beds', and 'gentlewomen in veils' who nursed the patients. But it is possible that these services may have been only available to the inmates of the *Sapientia*, the room especially reserved for the clergy, rather than to the average sick pauper.[104] Indeed when discussing the ordinances of S. Maria Nuova, one should not forget that they were probably prepared to impress a foreign monarch, Henry VII of England.

This study has also shown that other types of documents can reveal rather different and less optimistic aspects of the same picture. The *Catasto* returns of, for example, even a relatively new hospital such as S. Matteo show a charitable institution struggling to meet mounting debts. Further work on the very rich financial records of other hospitals may well indicate more widespread indebtedness than we are aware of at the present state of research. These institutions, which often relied for the bulk of their income on fixed assets, could easily go through periods of decline, especially as a result of maladministration or the inability to collect rent. Thus in 1444 a letter from the Florentine government stated that the finances of some of the main hospitals of the city were strained: 'because of the quantity of miserable people, and the [abandoned] male and female children to feed, they [the hospitals] are only able to meet their needs and necessities with the greatest difficulty'.[105]

Their resources were stretched even further during famines and epidemics. During the 150 years following the Black Death, epidemics recurred at almost ten-year intervals.[106] On each of these occasions existing hospitals bore the initial brunt of the problems caused by the sudden proliferation of sick people.[107] Although governments provided subsidies for hospitals, their facilities proved very inadequate and by 1464 the Florentine regime recognized that by placing plague victims in S. Maria Nuova 'it harms the others who are sick from another infirmity'.[108] However, when the much trumpeted solution of building a separate *Lazzaretto* for plague victims was finally realized some time after 1479, its capacity was so minimal that existing charitable institutions continued to be the principal agencies to cater for the sick during epidemics.[109]

The lack of a *Lazzaretto* in 1464 was regarded at that time as the major flaw in the facilities offered by hospitals in Florence. But while their hospitals continued to be admired as 'more beautiful and sufficient and suitable' than those of other cities,[110] by the second half of the fifteenth century many Italian city-states were founding their own large institutions which could rival the facilities available in Florence. The famous cruciform design soon became a standard feature of many institutions in northern Italy and it was the Ospedale Maggiore of Milan rather than S. Maria Nuova or S. Maria della Scala which architectural historians see as being 'among the six most influential hospital designs in the world'.[111] Moreover elsewhere, and particularly in Lombardy, there was a move towards rethinking the way in which hospitals were organized. Instead of the myriad of small institutions so familiar to many late-medieval towns, city-states began to establish more centralized systems by uniting the smaller hospitals into a coherent framework controlled from the centre.[112] However, despite Tuscany's reputation for charity, it was not until the middle of the sixteenth century that the grand-dukes began to follow the lead of other states and centralize their poor-relief facilities.[113] Whether this really did lead to an improvement in the facilities available to the poor and sick must remain open to debate when the basic research on so many aspects of the history of Florentine hospitals still needs to be completed.

Notes

1. I am grateful to Richard Goldthwaite, Katharine Park, and Patrick Sweeney for their comments on an earlier version of this paper, which was written while the author was a Wellcome Trust Fellow at the Wellcome Unit for the History of Medicine, University of Cambridge.

All manuscripts, unless otherwise stated, are in the Archivio di Stato di Firenze.

Until very recently the best studies of hospitals in southern Europe have tended to have been sections of books on wider issues, such as: B. Pullan, *Rich and Poor in Renaissance Venice. The Social Institutions of a Catholic State to 1620* (Oxford, 1971); I. Naso, *Medici e strutture sanitarie nella società tardo-medievale. Il Piemonte dei secoli XIV e XV* (Milan, 1982); L. Martz, *Poverty and Welfare in Habsburg Spain. The Example of Toledo* (Cambridge, 1983). For Spain see now: D. Jetter, *Spanien von den Anfangen bis um 1500. Geschichte des Hospitals*, IV (Stuttgart, 1980); and *Drei spanische Kreuzhallenspitäler und Ihr Nachhall in aller Welt* (Stuttgart, 1987). See also U. Lindgren, *Bedürftigkeit, Armut, Not: Studien zur Spätmittelalterlichen sozialgeschichte Barcelonas* (Munster, 1980); and A. Rubio Vela, *Pobreza, enfermedad y asistencia hospitaria en la Valencia del siglo XIV* (Valencia, 1984).

Although in the past most studies of Italian hospitals have been merely descriptive, recently more analytical monographs of individual hospitals have begun to appear, based on careful archival research. For example: L. Grassi, *Lo 'spedale di poveri' del Filarete* (Milan, 1972); M.O. Banzola, *L'ospedale vecchio di Parma* (Parma, 1980); *Lo spedale Serristori di Figline. Documenti e arredi* (Figline, 1982); S. Lunerdon (ed.), *Hospitale S. Marie Cruciferorum. L'ospizio dei crociferi a Venezia* (Venice, 1985); L. Sandri, *L'Ospedale di S. Maria della Scala di S. Gimignano nel Quattrocento. Contributo alla storia dell'infanzia abbandonata* (Florence, 1982); S.R. Epstein, *Alle origini della fattoria toscana. L'ospedale della Scala di Siena e le sue terre (metà '200- metà '400)* (Florence, 1986); M. Heinz, 'San Giacomo in Augusta in Rom und der Hospitalbau der Renaissance' (PhD diss., Rheinischen Friedrich-Wilhelms-Universität zu Bonn, 1977).

2. N.J.G. Pounds, *An Economic History of Medieval Europe* (London, 1974), 258–9.

3. For a valuable general introduction to charity in Italy see B. Pullan, 'Poveri, mendicanti e vagabondi (secoli XIV–XVII)', *Storia d'Italia. Annali 1. Dal feudalesimo al capitalismo.* (Turin, 1978), 981–1,047. See also the following collections of essays on the subject: T. Riis (ed.), *Aspects of Poverty in Early Modern Europe* (Stuttgart, 1981); G. Politi, M. Rosa, F. della Peruta (eds) *Timore e carità. I poveri nell'Italia moderna* (Cremona, 1982); and 'Charity and the poor in Medieval and Renaissance Europe', in J. Henderson (ed.), *Continuity and Change*, 3 (2) (1988).

4. The only comprehensive survey of hospitals in Florence is still L. Passerini, *Storia degli stabilmenti di beneficenza e d'istruzione elementare gratuita della città di Firenze* (Florence, 1853). A few useful studies have appeared recently of individual hospitals: the general book by G. Pampaloni, *Lo spedale di Santa Maria Nuova* (Florence, 1961); R.A. Goldthwaite and W.R. Rearick, 'Michelozzo and the Ospedale di San Paolo in Florence', *Mitteilungen des Kunsthistorischen Institutes in Florenz*, XXI (1977), 221–306; R.C. Trexler, 'Infanticide in Florence: new sources and first results', *History of Childhood Quarterly. The Journal of Psychohistory*, 1 (1973–74), 96–116, and 'The foundlings of Florence, 1395–1455', op. cit., 259–84; B.J. Trexler, 'Hospital patients in Florence: San Paolo, 1567–68', *Bulletin of the History of Medicine*, XLVIII (1974), 41–59. Other recent works tend to be of short descriptive articles: M.A. Mannelli, 'Istituzione e soppressione degli ospedali minori in Firenze', *Ospedali d'Italia. Chirurgia*, 12 (1965), *Studi di storia ospitaliera*, 111 (1965), 171–82; Mannelli, 'L'Ospedale di Sant'Antonio in Firenze', 505–8; Mannelli, 'Lo spedale di San Paolo dei convalescenti in Firenze, *Ospedali d'Italia. Chirurgia*, 12 (1965), 241–5; E. Coturri, 'L'Ospedale così detto "di Bonifazio" in Firenze', *Pagine di storia della medicina*, 3 (1959), 15–33; Mannelli, 'L'ospedale di San Matteo in Firenze', *Ospedali d'Italia. Chirurgia*, 11 (1964), 730–2.

5. A. Corsini, *La morìa del 1464 in Toscana e l'institituzione dei primi lazzaretti in Firenze ed in Pisa* (Florence, 1911), 34: 12 June 1464.

6. P. Foster, 'Per il disegno dell'Ospedale di Milano', *Arte Lombarda*, 38–9 (1973), 9–10; Passerini, pp. 851, 867. Passerini mistakenly suggests that the description of S. Maria Nuova was prepared for Henry VIII.

7. Quoted in R. Friedenthal, *Luther* (London, 1967), 78.

8. The sources consulted to compile Figure 3.1 and Tables 3.1, 3.2 and 3.3 are partly published and partly unpublished. See the references in R. Davidsohn, *Storia di Firenze*, trans. G.B. Klein (Florence, 1972), VII, 87–104 and G. Fanelli, *Firenze, architettura e città. Atlante* (Florence, 1973), 154: Passerini, *Storia*; W. and E. Paatz, *Die Kirchen von Florenz* (Frankfurt-am-Main, 1954), 6 vols; and M. Giusti and P. Guidi (eds), *Rationes decimarum Italiae: Tuscia. Le decime degli anni 1295–1304* (Città del Vaticano, 1942), 2 vols. Unpublished sources include the 1427–28 tax returns of hospitals in the *Catasto* 185.11, 190, 194, 195, 291, 292, 293, and the 1495 tax returns in *Decima della Repubblica*, 66–70.

9. For population estimates of Florence see D. Herlihy and C. Klapisch-Zuber, *Les toscans et leurs familles. Une étude du catasto florentin de 1427* (Paris, 1978), 165–77, and wage rates R.A. Goldthwaite, *The Building of Renaissance Florence. An Economic and Social History* (Baltimore, London, 1980), 436–9.

10. See Herlihy and Klapisch, *Les toscans*, 176–7.

11. On the numbers of confraternities in Florence of this period

see J. Henderson, *Piety and Charity in Late-Medieval Florence*, Ch. 1 (forthcoming).

12. *Cronaca di Giovanni Villani a miglior lezione ridotta* (Florence, 1825), vol. 5, XI, xciv; C. Landino, *Scritti critici et teoretici*, ed. R. Cardini (Rome, 1974), vol. 1, 115.

13. Hospital returns appear in the following volumes of the *Catasto*: 185. 1–11; 190; 194.11; 195; 291; 292; 293; *Decima della repubblica* 66–70; for the 1527 census see Biblioteca Nazionale Centrale di Firenze (cited as BNF), NA 987.

14. On France see Michel Mollat's chapters in J. Imbert (ed.), *Histoire des hôpitaux en France* (Toulouse, 1982), and especially 35–47, 78–9; for Avignon see J. Chiffoleau, *La compatibilité de l'au-delà. Les hommes, la mort et la religion dans la région d'Avignon à la fin du moyen-age (vers 1320–vers 1480)* (Rome, 1980), 314–21; Genoa, C. Marchesini and G. Sperati, *Ospedali Genovesi nel medioevo. Atti della società Ligure di storia patria*, n.s. XXI (1981), 60–2; *contado* of Florence, C.M. de La Roncière, *Florence, centre économique regional au XIVe siècle* (Aix-en-Provence, 1976), 921–36; Milan, G. Albini, *Guerra, fame, peste. Crisi di mortalità e sistema sanitario nella Lombardia tardomedioevale* (Milan, 1982), 63–78.

15. This was also the case for Genoa (Marchesini and Sperati, 60–63), Lyon (N. Gonthier, *Lyon et ses pauvres au moyen-age (1350–1500)* (Lyon, 1978), 142), Toulouse (Imbert (ed.), *Histoire des hôpitaux*, p. 107), and London (C. Rawcliffe, 'The hospitals of late medieval London', *Medical History*, 28 (1984), 4–5). Pistoia, however, seems to have been somewhat exceptional with eleven hospitals for 4,500 inhabitants (D. Herlihy, *Medieval and Renaissance Pistoia. The Social History of an Italian Town* (New Haven, 1967), 247–8).

16. Their development is surveyed by Davidsohn, *Storia di Firenze* VII, 87–104, esp. 87–91.

17. Op. cit., 87–8.

18. Op. cit., 89.

19. ibid.

20. Villani, *Cronaca* XI, 94.

21. See the map showing the locations of the 'Principali ospedali dei secoli XIII e XIV' in the city of Florence in G. Fanelli, *Firenze. Le città nella storia d'Italia* (Rome-Bari, 1981 ed.), 49. See also the maps of Florence at the end of the last volume of W. and E. Paatz, *Die Kirchen von Florenz*.

22. Rubio Vela, *Podreza, enfermedad*, 26: Mollat, in Imbert (ed.), *Histoire des hôpitaux*, 100: G. Giordanego, 'Les hôpitaux arlésiens du XIIe au XIVe siècle', *Assistance et charité*, Cahiers de Fanjeaux, 13 (Toulouse,1978), 190–3.

23. Cf. also the discussion of the position of the Ospedale di S. Paolo in Goldthwaite and Rearick, 'Michelozzo and the Ospedale di San Paolo in Florence', 222–3.

24. On the building of the walls see G. Fanelli, *Firenze*, 35–7.

25. See de La Roncière, *Florence, centre économique*, 679–91.

26. See J. Henderson, 'Charity in late-medieval Florence: the role of religious confraternities', in *Florence and Milan. Acts of two conferences at Villa I Tatti in Florence*, 11 (Florence, 1988), 147–63.

27. P. Fanfani (ed.), *Capitoli della Compagnia dei Portatori o S. Giovanni Decollato* (Bologna, 1858), 9–10, 6–7.

28. On S. Paolo see Passerini, 163–88, Goldthwaite and Rearick, 'Michelozzo', and B.J. Trexler, 'Hospital patients'; S. Maria Nuova see Passerini, 284–395 and Pampaloni, *Lo spedale di Santa Maria Nuova*. Another substantial hospital, that of S. Gallo, had been founded in 1218: Passerini, 659–75 and R.C. Trexler, 'The foundlings of Florence, 1395–1455'.

29. Passerini, 835–6.

30. See J. Newton, 'Poverty and charity in late-medieval Florence' PhD dissertation (Brown University, Rhode Island, forthcoming). I am grateful to Jeffrey Newton for having given me the opportunity to read a draft version of his thesis.

31. On Orsanmichele see S. La Sorsa, *La compagnia d'Or S. Michele ovvero una pagina della beneficenza in Toscana nel secolo XIV* (Trani, 1955) and Henderson, *Piety and Charity*, Part 2.

32. In Florence the legal position of women is discussed by T. Kuehn, *Emancipation in Late-Medieval Florence* (New Brunswick, 1982) and 'Some ambiguities of female inheritance ideology in the Renaissance', *Continuity and Change*, 2 (1987), 11–36, as well as C. Klapisch-Zuber, *Women, Family and Ritual in Renaissance Italy* (Chicago and London, 1985), Ch. 6, 10. A number of Italian communes passed legislation protecting the rights of orphans and widows: for Florence see *Provvisioni registri* 36, f. 3r: 29 August 1348; for Milan, G.C. Bascapé, 'L'assistenza e la beneficenza a Milano dall'alto medioevo alla fine della dinastia sforzesca', *Storia di Milano* (Milan, 1957), VIII, 394; and for Orvieto, E. Carpentier, *Une ville devant la peste. Orvieto et la peste noire de 1348* (Paris, 1962), 146.

33. M. Villani, *Cronaca di Matteo Villani a miglior lezione ridotta* (Florence, 1825), 1, 1, vii.

34. *Provvisioni Registri* 36, f. 3r: 29 August 1348.

35. On the Orbatello see Passerini, 641, and R.C. Trexler, 'A widow's asylum of the Renaissance: the Orbatello of Florence', in P.N. Stearns (ed.), *Old Age in Pre-Industrial Society* (New York, 1982), 119–49; on the Innocenti see Passerini, 685, 704; on the Monte delle Doti see J. Kirschner and A. Molho, 'The dowry fund and the marriage market in early Quattrocento Florence', *Journal of Modern History*, 50 (1978), 403–38.

36. This is a theme of Mollat in Imbert (ed.), *Histoire des hôpitaux*, 130, and K. Park, 'Healing the poor: hospitals and medicine in renaissance Florence', an article which is forthcoming and conceived as complementary to the present paper.

37. M. Villani, *Cronaca*, 1, vii.

38. See S. Maria Nuova 1, f. 1r.

39. Passerini, 843.

40. Goldthwaite and Rearick, 'Michelozzo', 222–4.

41. Passerini, 150 and 223.

42. Passerini, 125–33.

43. *Catasto* 291, ff. 23^{r-v}; BNF, N.A. 987, f. 23^v.

44. D. Moreni (ed.), *Prediche del Beato Fra Giordano da Pisa dell'ordine dei predicatori recitati in Firenze dal MCCCIII al MCCCVI* (Florence, 1831), 1, 55. It is unclear from the first sentence ('Va' pure agli spedali, o cola a San Gallo') whether he is suggesting that these patients were from the Ospedale di S. Gallo or from other hospitals in Via S. Gallo. Although the Ospedale di S. Gallo is best known as an institution for foundlings, in the late thirteenth century it also catered for more general categories of poor people, as can be seen from a law of 19 May 1294, which refers to both paupers and infants: Passerini, 936.

45. B.J. Trexler, 'Hospital patients', 45–6, 53, and Park, 'Hospitals and medical welfare'.

46. For S. Maria della Scala see *Catasto* 185, ff. 584^r–585^v; S. Gallo, Passerini, 669; the Innocenti, Passerini, 704. For more details about the foundling hospitals see Trexler, 'The foundlings of Florence'.

47. Passerini, *Storia*, 106.

48. *Catasto* 185, f. 626^r: 'una vedova d'anni 80 ed è inferma e non escie di letto; una donna d'anni 25 è stata inferma un' anno o più e da infermità da non ghuarire mai sennone quando si morra di quello'.

49. *Cronaca di Giovanni Villani*, XI, 94.

50. Population estimates in Herlihy and Klapisch, *Les toscans* 177, 183.

51. Corsini, *La 'morìa'*, 34.

52. L.B. Alberti, *L'architettura* [De Re Aedificatoria], ed. G. Orlandi and P. Portoghesi (Milan, 1966), 1, 367–8.

53. On S. Maria della Scala see D. Gallavotti Cavallaro, *L'ospedale di S. Maria della Scala in Siena. Vicende di una committenza artistica* (Pisa, 1985); O. Redon, 'Autour de l'Hôpital Santa Maria della Scala à Sienne au XIIIe siècle', *Ricerche storiche*, XV (1985), 17–34; and S.R. Epstein, *Alle origini della fattoria toscana. L'ospedale della Scala di Siena e le sue terre (metà-'200-metà-'400)*, (Florence, 1987).

54. Foster, 'Per il disegno', 7.

55. F. Leverotti, 'L'ospedale senese di S. Maria della Scala in una relazione del 1456', *Bullettino senese di storia patria*, XCI (1984), 276–92.

56. Leverotti, 'L'ospedale senese', 278–83.

57. Antonio Averlino detto il Filarete, *Trattato di architettura*, eds A.M. Finoli and L. Grassi (Milan, 1972), 299 n. 1.

58. M. Lazzarini and A. Munoz, *Filarete, sculture e architetto del XV* (Rome, 1968), 186.

59. Recent formulations of this idea are in H.M. Colvin, D.R.

Ransome, and J. Summerson (eds), *The History of the King's Works* (London, 1975), 199, and M.O. Banzola, *L'Ospedale vecchio di Parma* (Parma, 1980), 45.

60. See Foster, 'Per il disegno', 4–7.

61. ibid. I am grateful for this suggestion to Patrick Sweeney, who is at present preparing a history of the architectural development of S. Maria Nuova.

62. Leverotti, 'L'ospedale senese', 280, n. 22.

63. Foster, 'Per il disegno', 7–8.

64. Leverotti, 'L'ospedale senese', 301; C. Landino's Commentary on Dante's *Divine Comedy*, quoted in Passerini, 301.

65. See Goldthwaite and Rearick, 'Michelozzo', 279–80.

66. The cloisters for the Florentine hospitals of S. Paolo, S. Maria Nuova, Messer Bonifazio, and S. Matteo are visible in their ground plans, which are reproduced in Goldthwaite and Rearick, 'Michelozzo', 228, 274, 276, and 277. The cloisters of S. Maria Maggiore of Milan can be seen clearly in Filarete's designs: Foster, 'Per il disegno', 1–22.

67. Leverotti, 'L'ospedale senese', 281–3; Passerini, 851-73.

68. Herlihy, *Medieval and Renaissance Pistoia*, pp. 247–8.

69. L. Arbib (ed.), *Storia fiorentina di Benedetto Varchi* (Florence, 1838–41), 2, 101. S. Maria Nuova's property is listed in *Catasto* 185.11, ff. 640^r–699^r.

70. G. Brucker , 'Urban parishes and their clergy in Quattrocento Florence: a preliminary "sondage"', *Renaissance Studies in Honor of Craig Hugh Smyth* (Florence, 1985), 1, 27, n. 21.

71. *Catasto* 194.11, f. 380^r; *Catasto* 292, ff. 230^v–232^v.

72. *Catasto* 291, ff. 72^r, 68^r.

73. *Catasto* 185.11, ff. 601^r–606^r; Brucker, 'Urban parishes', 27 n. 21.

74. *Catasto* 194.11, ff. 172^v, 646^v, and 610^{r-v}; on confraternities see Henderson, *Piety and Charity*, Ch. 2, Table 3.

75. See, for example, the property belonging to S. Maria Nuova in *Catasto* 185.11, ff. 640^r–699^r, and below for a discussion of S. Matteo's assets.

76. See G. Pinto, *La Toscana nel tardo medioevo. Ambiente, economia rurale, società* (Firenze, 1982), 247–329.

77. The shares of Florentine hospitals in the communal debt are listed among their assets in their *Catasto* returns, as for S. Matteo (*Catasto* 185.11, ff. 601^r–606^r), and the Ospedale degli Innocenti (*Catasto* 190, ff. 80^r–82^v).

78. Passerini, 335, and R.A. Goldthwaite, 'Local banking in Renaissance Florence', *Journal of European Economic History*, 14 (1985), 44–5.

79. Passerini, 335.

80. ibid.

81. See I. Chabot, 'Poverty and the widow in late medieval Florence', in J. Henderson (ed.), *Charity and the Poor in Medieval and*

Renaissance Europe, Continuity and Change, 3 (2) (1988), 291–311. This process may be seen, for example, in the *Catasto* return of the Ospedale di S. Maria della Scala in *Catasto* 185, ff. 528[r]–575[v], where a number of houses were listed as not providing any income because they were occupied for life by the inhabitant.

82. Some idea of, for example, S. Maria Nuova's finances after the Black Death can be gained from the hospital's account books: S. Maria Nuova 4,397–4,400 (Uscita, 1348–1353) and 4,401–4,403 (Entrata e Uscita, 1349–1352). The records of testaments, though not complete, are in S. Maria Nuova 59 for 1300–1500 and S. Maria Nuova 60 for 1340–1379. The history of S. Maria Nuova from its foundation up to the Black Death is dealt with by J. Newton in 'Poverty and charity'.

83. On S. Maria della Scala see Epstein, *Alle origini*.

84. *Catasto* 185.11, ff. 604[v]–605[r]: 'Di tutti i sopra ditti debitori mai non se ne chavera uno denaio però chi è morto e chi se ne ito e chi fallito e di loro niente si truova . . . sichè anchora i sopradetti debitori si può dire siamo perduti.'

85. Herlihy, *Medieval and Renaissance Pistoia*, 247–8; *Catasto* 190, f. 83[r]; 185, f. 619[r].

86. See the purchases of the Ospedale di S. Jacopo a S. Eusebio in *Catasto* 291, f. 23[r]; S. Bonifazio, op. cit., ff. 33[v]–34[r]. Examples of food purchases by S. Maria Nuova are contained in the Libri dell'Uscita for 1440–1 and 1456–8 (S. Maria Nuova 4,489 and 4,499).

87. Passerini, 305.

88. The duties of the staff of S. Maria Nuova are outlined in its early sixteenth-century ordinances: Passerini, 851–67. The accounts of S. Maria Nuova have been used by two economic historians to calculate wage-rates for skilled and unskilled labourers: de La Roncière, *Florence, centre économique*, and Goldthwaite, *The Building of Renaissance Florence*.

89. See Goldthwaite and Rearick; 'Michelozzo'; and Passerini 304–6.

90. *Catasto* 185.11, f. 613[r], Spedale di S. Antonio e S. Niccholo; f. 615[r], Spedale di San Giuliano; f. 617[r], Spedale di Sancto Lò; f. 629[r], Spedale di S. Maria al Merchatale della Scarperia. *Catasto* 293, f. 35[v], Spedale di S. Maria dell'Umiltà; ibid., Spedale di San Lorenzo a San Piero Ghattolino; f. 56[r], Spedale di San Nicholò a San Felice in Piazza.

91. Passerini, 304–6.

92. Goldthwaite and Rearick; 'Michelozzo', 223; Passerini, 305.

93. *Catasto* 291, f. 34[r]; 185.11, f. 606[v]; Passerini, 302, 305.

94. *Catasto* 185, f. 58[r].

95. K. Park, *Doctors and Medicine in Early Renaissance Florence* (Princeton, 1985), 157.

96. Passerini, 859.

97. Passerini, 859.

98. For more details see the ordinances themselves in Passerini, 858–61 and a fuller discussion of the medical aspects see the forthcoming article by Park, 'Healing the Poor: hospitals and medicine in renaissance Florence'.

99. Passerini, 865.

100. ibid.

101. B. Trexler, 'Hospital patients', 41–59, and Park, *Doctors and Medicine*, 106 and expanded in her forthcoming article 'Healing the poor: hospitals and medicine in renaissance Florence'.

102. The exceptions are the articles mentioned above by Goldthwaite and Rearick, Park, B.J. Trexler and R.C. Trexler.

103. See the speech delivered by Leonardo Bruni in favour of providing finance for the building of the Ospedale degli Innocenti in 1421: F. del Migliore, *Firenze, città nobilissima illustrata* (Florence, 1694), 307–9.

104. Friedenthal, *Luther*, p. 78.

105. Quoted in Passerini, 333.

106. On plague in Florence see M.S. Mazzi, 'La peste a Firenze nel quattrocento', in R. Comba, G. Piccini, and G. Pinto (eds), *Strutture familiari, epidemie e migrazioni nell'Italia medievale* (Naples, 1984), 91–115, and A.G. Carmichael, *Plague and the Poor in Renaissance Florence* (Cambridge, 1986).

107. On S. Maria Nuova, for example, see Passerini, 296–8, 300.

108. Corsini, *La 'moria'*, 34.

109. ibid., and on the role of charitable institutions in Florence during subsequent epidemics see J. Henderson, 'Plague in Renaissance Florence: medical theory and government response', in N. Bulst, R. Delort (eds) *Maladies et Société* (XIIe–XVIIIe siècles) (Paris, 1988).

110. Corsini, *La 'moria'*, p.34.

111. J.D. Thompson and G. Goldin, *The Hospital: A Social and Architectural History* (New Haven, London, 1975), 31.

112. Examples include Brescia, Bergamo, and Cremona: *Storia di Brescia* (Brescia, 1961), 1, 1,117–1,119; B. Pullan, *Rich and Poor*, 203–5; Foster, 'Per il Disegno', 8.

113. See A. d'Addario, *La formazione dello stato moderno in Toscana dal Cosimo il Vecchio a Cosimo I de'Medici* (Lecce, 1976), 243–5, and Passerini, 307–8.

4

Charity, power, and patronage in eighteenth-century Italian hospitals: the case of Turin

Sandra Cavallo

1

Recent research on the system of poor relief in Italy has largely overlooked the question of philanthropy, that is the involvement of the laity in managing and financing charitable institutions. Research on the English case has paid considerable attention to the role of private benefactors, prestige, social influence, and competition between individuals and groups via charitable actions. However, studies in the field in Italy, which emerged above all from the 1970s onwards, have tended to explain the evolution of the poor relief system almost entirely in terms of religious ideology and state policy. The church and state are held responsible for the transformation in the patterns of relief and care for the poor and sick from the fifteenth to the eighteenth century.

According to the standard chronology and interpretation, the religious and moral climate of the Catholic Reformation, and then Counter Reformation, brought about the boom in charitable initiatives designed for different categories of the needy from the late sixteenth to the early seventeenth century (these initiatives included provision for incurables, beggars, young women, prisoners, and prisoners condemned to the gallows). Although groups of lay people were the real creators of the dense network of charities set up over some 200 years, their activity is usually seen as driven by religious motivations; they are pictured as little more than the executors of the will of the Counter Reformation Church, and their behaviour is regarded as prompted by the preaching of the religious orders and the voice of the confessor.

The lack of interest amongst historians in the role of private charity is even clearer in the studies dealing with the period of absolutism. The control of the relief system is said to have been taken over by the state from the seventeenth century. The central authority is thought to have engaged in a comprehensive restructuring of the poor relief system in an effort to distinguish the deserving from the undeserving poor, and then to separate them through a series of measures, such as banishment and segregation. It is forgotten, however, that, even while the state's control over institutions was strengthened, private charity often remained the main source of finance for charitable provision.[1] Finally, the evolution of hospitals for the sick is seen as separate. The hospital's transformation from a 'general refuge' into a place devoted to sick care, with clinical and experimental functions, is usually linked to the Enlightenment reforms, which took place in a few Italian states in the late eighteenth century. In fact, the phenomenon is seen as restricted to those areas most affected by Enlightenment thought. Meanwhile, the persistence of the idea of the charitable vocation is seen as retarding the 'medicalization' of the Italian hospital well into the late nineteenth century.[2]

The scant attention given to lay involvement in charity, in my opinion, largely reflects shortcomings in methodology and approach rather than any peculiarity of the Italian model, i.e. the hypothesis of the predominance of centralization over charitable activities. Indeed, the tendency to attribute the development of the charity system to impersonal forces seeking ideological and social control has meant ignoring the actions of real social subjects and neglecting their motivations. It is not, therefore, by chance that the most valuable sources for documenting the aims and functions of charitable provision, the social groups involved, and the systems of power at work have been largely disregarded by recent histories; the minute books, the records of recipients and patients, budgets, donations, and wills have largely gone unconsulted.

My research has pursued a different approach in seeking to identify *who* managed the provision for the poor and sick, and to analyse the social characteristics of benefactors, governors, and recipients. It has aimed to throw light on the motivations guiding philanthropy and the social meaning of various forms of poor relief. Charitable activity has therefore been examined in the wider context: first, of relationships within the local elites, connecting different influence groups; and, second, the vertical ties joining the ruling social groups and the labouring classes. The picture which emerges from this reconstruction differs at important points from the normal representation of the poor and sick relief systems. Above all, explanations based on the concepts of social control and religious sentiment are shown to be inadequate, while the part played by private initiative turns out to be crucial. Moreover, the trends in development and characteristics of charity appear deeply rooted in the local dynamics of protection, patronage, and social conflict.

My argument will be mostly grounded in the findings of research on the operation of the charity system in Turin, the capital of the Savoy Kingdom, during the eighteenth century. This case is especially interesting in that the Savoyard state has frequently been described as an example of absolutism and marked centralization, from the time of the reforms of Victor Amadeus II from 1680 to 1730, later consolidated by his successor. The poor relief system is usually regarded as a 'creation' of the absolute monarchy, as embodied by the celebrated measures of 1717 designed to eradicate begging and pauperism by setting up a network of hospitals and charities in every part of the kingdom.[3]

Turin, which was the centre of court life and state administration, also became the principal manufacturing centre of the kingdom in the last quarter of the seventeenth century. Its industrial structure, hingeing mainly on silk manufacture, was further reinforced in the following century. A consequence of this (together with demographic growth and the concentration of landed property) was that the city attracted more and more people from the countryside, doubling its size during the eighteenth century, from 45,000 to 90,000 inhabitants.

I will begin this article by broadly outlining the structure of charitable provision in the capital in the eighteenth century, underlining some of the features common to the systems of relief in Italy under the *ancien régime*. I will then focus on the main hospital for the sick in Turin, and follow its development from the late seventeenth century, dealing in particular with the consequences for the hospital's functioning arising from the shift to state control and to closer links with the medical faculty established during the eighteenth century.

2

By the eighteenth century, charitable aid to the sick was concentrated in just two hospitals: the Hospital of San Giovanni, which was very old and had from 1440 been the city's principal hospital following the incorporation of twelve small medieval hospitals that were located near the main access roads into Turin; and, second, the Hospital of San Maurizio and Lazzaro, which was established in 1575 at the initiative of the knightly order of that name.[4] The Hospital of San Giovanni, originally administered by the Metropolitan Chapter and put under the jurisdiction of the bishop, passed into the hands of a mixed administration in 1541. The city council saved the hospital from a crisis following a long period of invasions, plague, and famine, and, in exchange, took a role in the hospital's administration. From then on, the board of governors was always made up of four city councillors and four canons from the Metropolitan Church. So, here we have an authority with a strong civic identity, the expression of the local oligarchy, and independent of central control. The case of the Hospital of San Maurizio and Lazzaro was different. While under the administration of a military order subject to the sovereign, it was within the sphere of influence of an aristocracy whose powers extended beyond the confines of the city, as well as being tied to the court and military authority. It was no coincidence that the Hospital of San Maurizio and Lazzaro received handsome endowments from the sovereign, while that of San Giovanni was economically self-reliant.

The way in which the particular institutions belonged to different social contexts and areas of influence is clear at first glance, and this seems to have been a characteristic of the organization of relief until the late eighteenth century; that is, until these spheres of influence were swept away and the management of the institutions passed into the hands of state officials. Even the governing body of the Ospedale di Carità, Turin's large centre for poor relief, strongly reflected a particular social milieu – that of the mercantile and industrial elites. If we bear in mind that the majority (over 40 per cent) of those helped by the hospital were artisans, it is evident that the governor's post was a highly influential one, and enabled bankers, merchants, and masters to control the distribution of relief to the urban working population and industrial sectors in crisis, correcting imbalances in the labour market.

The charitable institutions in Turin seem to have had a defined function from the time of their origin. For example, the Hospitals of San Maurizio and San Giovanni were designed for the sick from the time of their foundation. In consequence, we have not come across cases which evoke the image of the 'refuge for all' often referred to. Previously, the Hospital of San Giovanni had also occasionally played the role of assisting the poor, above all by distributing bread and money rather than by providing shelter.[5] However, such functions were soon assumed by the Ospedale di Carità, a poorhouse founded in 1627 by a private benefactor, though not properly operational until 1649 (due to plague and war interrupting), and not so large until the move to a new site in 1682.

The Ospedale di Carità is one of the number of hospitals for the poor and for beggars set up during two bouts of hospital founding in several Italian cities at the end of the sixteenth and at the end of the seventeenth centuries. Historians have usually pointed to the common set of factors behind the initiatives, through which a new model of relief provision was supposed to have taken shape on the basis of separating 'genuine' and 'false' beggars, and subjecting the latter through repression and segregation. Within an Italian context, the Ospedale di Carità in Turin is often considered to exemplify the procedure of *renfermement*, following the 1717 edicts outlawing begging in the kingdom. However, the hospital's records of recipients and registers of admission, along with other documents, throw a different light on the matter. The violent repression of begging via arrest and punishment seem, instead, to have been of marginal significance in the hospital's overall activities, and was resorted to only in moments of acute crisis, serving as a deterrent against the immigrants who used then to flock into the city. However, the majority of the inmates were admitted on a voluntary basis – up to 2,000 of them in crises. They included the single old people unable to work, and the legitimate children of large families who were left in the hospital's care for a limited period. Moreover, the inmates did not belong to marginal groups, but to the productive and established sections of the city economy. In fact, relief was restricted to those born or long resident in the city. Rather than being a place for the detention of beggars, the Ospedale di Carità seems to have been a centre for relief on which the working population depended for its subsistence strategies.[6]

The system for selection of supplicants judged worthy to receive relief was rigorous. The poor were examined in person by a delegation of governors who required the presence of the whole family of supplicants. They checked not only their citizenship qualifications, but whether they were able to work, whether they were genuinely sick (as certified by a physician or surgeon), and the proportion of bread-winners to the number of mouths to be fed in a family unit. The relief given was often a combination of different kinds, ranging from the admittance of old people and children aged 7 to 14 to payment for wet-nursing newborn infants and the weekly distribution of a fixed quantity of bread.

The selection of supplicants was, therefore, carried out on the basis of criteria designed to differentiate the poor according to their degree of need. Nevertheless, it is clear that other factors entered into the decision as to who was eligible for relief – factors like status, protection, and the capacity certain groups had to bring pressure to bear. An obvious case in point is the favour that was invariably extended to the domestics of the more distinguished families. As for artisans, some trades were better protected because of the power of parts of the merchant and industrial elites, who, of course, were often represented on the board of governors of the hospital. Relief was only to a limited extent given on an equitable basis. Historians have generally held up the distinction made between the 'deserving' and 'undeserving' poor as an important step in the development of more rational forms of relief – that is, when it ceased to be given universally and indiscriminately as required by the Christian ideal, and became a social action. However, we should not forget that the category of 'deserving' poor was only partly moral and economic. Apart from degree of need, this category amply reflected the configurations of privilege and protection that were found among the poor.

The link between relief and privilege is, of course, a characteristic of charity in an *ancien régime* type of society. This becomes especially clear if we examine several forms of relief found in pre-industrial European societies. Take, for example, the secret relief given to the 'shamefaced poor' (*poveri vergognosi*), who did not dare to beg since they had fallen from a higher social station; or the dowry funds and institutions created for girls of respectable family origins; or the relief reserved for specific professional groups. These appear to be initiatives that helped relieve a kind of poverty that we can call 'relative' – relative, that is, to status, family of origin, to the style of living considered appropriate to the social or professional group to which the needy person belonged. These initiatives were found in Spain, France, and in many Italian states, though in seventeenth and eighteenth century England they survived only in the form of relief reserved for members of craft companies or specific national groups.[7]

Recent historical research inspired by Foucault's work has tended to deal with large institutions, overlooking these activities, and considering them obsolete remnants of Counter-Reformation forms of charity.[8] Yet their scale was anything but insignificant, and often accounted for a high percentage of money paid out in charity. In Turin, the Compagnia di San Paolo had, in the eighteenth century, a budget equivalent to that of the Hospital of San Giovanni or the Ospedale di Carità, for three purposes: the administration of dowry funds; for the shamefaced poor; and for the women's institutions. In Naples, lay groups distributed 655 dowries and helped approximately 5,000 persons in thirty-nine institutions in one year alone in the seventeenth century. These included *conservatori* for young women, institutions for the young and aged, and hospitals reserved for the 'relative poor' (those belonging to specific social or professional groups, such as craft companies, employees in public administration, the army). Furthermore, these practices did not die out, but continued to thrive in the next century. The institutions for women went on sprouting in the eighteenth century, so that by the 1800s there were at least eighty of them. Likewise, in Rome and Turin four new institutions were added to the existing three.[9] Although these *conservatori* or *ricoveri* for women have been described as typical expressions of Counter-Reformation thinking designed to defend female honour and prevent sinfulness, the timing of their development seems to contradict this interpretation. Even relief for the shamefaced poor, usually considered a sixteenth-century phenomenon, develops at different times in different situations. This form of relief developed in Venice in the sixteenth century, in Bologna in the following century, and became particularly important in Turin in the mid eighteenth century.[10]

What then was the significance of these initiatives? Despite the variations in chronology, these different forms of charity seem to have shared a common goal; namely, the defence of the prestige and image of the social group to which the recipient of charity belonged via measures to arrest the decline of individuals and families. For instance, the dowry subsidy, one of the most widespread forms of relief, allowed respectable families in economic difficulties to marry off their daughters to a person of similar rank. The dowry allowed them to maintain the name and honour of the family, and, at the same time, reaffirmed the dignity of the social group and lines of demarcation between the social classes.

The measures for the relief of 'relative' poverty, which were common in *ancien-régime* societies, appear, therefore, to have corresponded to the need to reaffirm or redefine the hierarchical social order. It did so by upholding the prestige of an old or new elite – an acutely felt need when new social groups were emerging. Hence, the unevenness of developments, even within the Italian context. It could be suggested that, as a general rule, the importance of these forms of charity was strictly related to whether a period was stable or marked by major upheavals in the social order. We can see in the Turin case that a visible increase in measures to help the shamefaced poor (together with dowry funds and the creation of new institutions for women) correlates with a phase of conflict and social change in which the hereditary and court nobility's loss of status coincided with the emergence of a new class of officials who pressed for public recognition and marks of prestige. In 1734 the latter obtained a revision of the category 'shamefaced' poor; it was redefined so that it included not only 'nobles by birth' and 'those nobles so declared by the royal sovereign', but also 'all those rendered noble by their profession'. In effect, this encompassed almost the entire state bureaucratic class, right down to the lowest rungs of the professional and military ladder.[11] Even the merchant classes in this period managed to have the privilege extended to its members with the establishment of a fund for the 'shamefaced poor of the second class'; a fund, that is, for merchants, shopkeepers, and bankers, 'to the exclusion of the nobility'.[12] So, the investment on behalf of the 'relative' poor was not limited to a purely defensive need to conserve social status pursued by social groups threatened by the rise of new elites. It also represented a means of achieving upward mobility. In mid-eighteenth century Turin a desire for symbolic recognition of gains made pushed the emerging classes to invest in these forms of 'privileged' charity. Redefining who was deemed worthy of receiving special types of relief entailed reflecting and sanctioning changes that had taken place in the assignation of prestige.

There is not space here to provide a detailed reconstruction of the transformations affecting the make-up of the elites in Turin at the time. Yet it is worth noting how the re-ordering of the configurations of power at the top of the social hierarchy was also reflected in the criteria regulating the provision of charity. In the second half of the eighteenth century, if a family included a state employee among its members, it had a far better chance of gaining access to relief provision. As we have already mentioned in relation to the relief provided by the Ospedale di Carità, the category of the 'deserving poor' was fluid and ill-defined, and acquired different meanings depending on the model of protection in a particular social context.

3

The extent and significance of the laity's role in the poor relief institutions can best be appreciated if we examine a particular example. For Turin, a good case to take is the Hospital of San Giovanni, the largest hospital for the sick in the city. For a long time, the Hospital of San Giovanni remained a modest institution with only thirty-six beds (half for men and half for women), in the middle of the seventeenth

Table 4.1 Endowments of beds for incurables and curables from private benefactors at the Hospital of San Giovanni, 1668–1790.

Year	No. of beds Inc.	Cur.	Year	No. of beds Inc.	Cur.	Year	No. of beds Inc.	Cur.	Year	No. of beds Inc.	Cur.
1668	2	–	1700	2	–	1732	4	–	1764	1	–
1669	–	–	1701	3	–	1733	–	–	1765	1	2
1670	2	–	1702	–	–	1734	4	–	1766	–	–
1671	1	–	1703	2 + u	–	1735	8	2 + u	1767	–	–
1672	–	–	1704	1	1	1736	2	–	1768	1	–
1673	–	–	1705	1	1	1737	1	–	1769	–	–
1674	–	–	1706	–	–	1738	2	–	1770	–	–
1675	–	–	1707	–	–	1739	5	–	1771	3	–
1676	1	–	1708	–	1	1740	4	–	1772	–	–
1677	2	–	1709	3	2	1741	4	–	1773	2	–
1678	7	–	1710	1	–	1742	–	–	1774	1*	–
1679	1	–	1711	12	–	1743	3 + u	–	1775	1	–
1680	4	–	1712	9	–	1744	1	–	1776	–	14
1681	u	–	1713	4	–	1745	1	–	1777	1	–
1682	3	20	1714	4	1	1746	3	–	1778	–	–
1683	2	–	1715	2	–	1747	5	–	1779	–	–
1684	2	–	1716	1	–	1748	2	–	1780	–	3
1685	2	–	1717	2	1	1749	1	–	1781	–	–
1686	–	–	1718	1	2	1750	4	–	1782	–	1
1687	2	–	1719	2	–	1751	1	–	1783	1	–
1688	2	–	1720	2	1	1752	3	40	1784	2	2
1689	1	–	1721	1	–	1753	–	–	1785	–	1
1690	–	2	1722	–	–	1754	4	1	1786	–	1 + u
1691	3	–	1723	1	–	1755	7	–	1787	–	7
1692	–	–	1724	–	–	1756	2	1	1788	–	–
1693	2	–	1725	2	–	1757	3	–	1789	–	2 + u
1694	1	–	1726	–	–	1758	4	–	1790	–	1
1695	3	–	1727	–	–	1759	2	–			
1696	–	–	1728	2	–	1760	21*				
1697	1	–	1729	1	–	1761	–	–			
1698	1	–	1730	5	–	1762	1	2			
1699	–	–	1731	6	1	1763	2*	–			

Inc. = incurables   Cur. = curables

The dates refer to the moment of the disposition, which does not always coincide with that of the setting up of beds (see note 14 at end of chapter). Sometimes the testator did not indicate the exact number of beds but stated that as many as the estate permitted be established (usually the choice was between one or two), once the debts and other dispositions had been taken care of. In this case the letter 'u' (undetermined) appears in the table. The asterisk indicates the acquisitions of rights of nomination for beds existing already (see note 19 at end of chapter).

century. Its expansion began in 1668 when a new ward for the chronically ill was opened, the Opera Incurabili. The need for this ward had been discussed for a couple of years by the civic authorities and representatives of the various charities.[13] Unfortunately, the records of these discussions have not survived, but perhaps one of the factors that motivated the hospital's decision was that a ward for incurables would attract private donors. This, in any case, was the effect.

The endowment of a bed for incurables (via the payment of 5,200 lire until 1752, when the sum was increased to 6,250 lire) gave the benefactor and the persons he designated his successors (normally his descendants in the direct male line, or in the female line if there were no males) the perpetual right to select an incurable patient who would occupy the bed until his death. This new form of charity guaranteed the donor and his family direct and perpetual control over the use of the endowment, and this probably explains the very substantial growth in bequests and donations which the hospital received after the foundation of the new ward. It was, above all, this form of endowment which allowed the hospital to increase its capacity to around 220 curables and incurables in 1730, reaching 450 in 1792. Over 177 beds for incurables were set up by private benefactors between 1668, when the new ward was established, and 1754, when the board of governors started to restrict such endowments to encourage benefactors to found beds for curables instead. Despite these restrictions, another twenty-nine beds for incurables were endowed between 1754 and 1780.[14]

The number of beds for curables grew much more slowly. There were only fifty-eight beds for curables and twenty for convalescents given by private donors by 1754 (see Table 4.1). Furthermore, it should be noted that these seventy-eight beds were set up thanks to the generous donations from just two benefactors – the Marquis Villa (twenty beds for convalescents given in 1752) and Costeis, the banker, (forty beds for curables given in 1752). In the space of some eighty years or so, a total of only seventeen donors chose this form of charity, as against 114 who set up one or more beds for incurables. The benefactors' preference aggravated the imbalance between beds available for the sick and the increasing number available for incurables. The latter were soon as numerous as the former, and sometimes more so.

There were times in the eighteenth century when the board of governors was itself able to set up some beds for the curably sick, since the hospital's finances were in a healthy state; in 1713, six were set up, in 1723, another six, and then fifty in 1724.[15] Meanwhile, during the drawn-out economic crisis of 1734-50, due to famine, war, and epidemics, the hospital had to weather serious financial difficulties, added to, as we shall see, by imprudent policies foisted on the governors by government officials. The biggest burden of all was the building of the grandiose cross-shaped edifice that was supposed to serve as a new site for the Hospital of San Giovanni. For nearly a hundred years, from 1680 onwards, this absorbed most of the hospital's income, for although the board of governors had received the land as a gift from the Regent, it had to pay for all the building by itself.

It is true that beds for incurables were eventually turned into beds for the curable sick. The formula used for the endowment prescribed that when the founder's line of descent died out, the bed reverted to the board of governors, who had the power to change it into a bed for curables. This did increase provision for the sick, but only very gradually. Set up as one of the hospital wards, the Opera Incurabili had grown in a quite unforeseen way. The hospital was filled with old people and invalids whom the staff could do little for. In theory, the endowment conditions specified that persons nominated for a place as an incurable had to be examined by the hospital physician or surgeon to see whether they were really afflicted by an incurable disease.[16] In practice, however, the physician's opinion more often than not obsequiously concurred with the choice made by the donors, who were the hospital's principal benefactors. The incurables were, in consequence, the elderly governess and the coachman of the donor families, or persons who formed part of the protection network of these families, and so were provided with some insurance against old age.

The defects of this system did not escape observers at the time. As early as 1734, in a discussion of the measures to take in order to reorganize the city's poor relief structure, which had been under pressure in the wake of economic depression and epidemics, a complaint was made about the ward for incurables; it was said not to lack bequests, but

> in the name of being incurable . . . persons are accepted
> who are invalids rather than sick ranging from old age,
> blindness, lameness and other reasons, and are rightfully
> the responsibility of the Ospedale di Carità . . . since
> they have no need of any treatment for their ills, but
> only of food to satisfy their hunger.

In order to get the hospital to 'carry out its purpose, that is, to provide for the sick', it was suggested – without saying how – that the rules concerning the private nomination of patients be changed.[17] It is worth noting that the observer in question, the Prince of Francavilla, was himself a distinguished benefactor of the hospital. In 1725, he endowed some seven beds for incurables left to the hospital in his mother's will in 1711, and in 1731 he added two more beds to those already controlled by the family. Despite the strictures he expressed in his role as a state official, as a member of one of the wealthiest families in Turin he did not shun the advantages and influence that control of beds for incurables brought – as a source of prestige and a resource used to reward the fidelity of those under his protection.

In effect, benefactors continued to prefer this form of charity to the free bequest. For much of the century, the board of governors was not able to stop or regulate a practice that had attracted most of the donations and bequests enjoyed by the hospital. In 1744, for example, it was calculated that four out of five bequests (coming to a total of 214,945 lire) left to the hospital from 1729 were earmarked for the foundation of beds for incurables, while only one in four were free bequests.[18] So, on the one hand, measures were taken in 1754 and 1773 to limit the period of control over the nomination of patients, and in 1762 they went as far as to prohibit the acceptance of further endowments. Yet, when money was needed, the governors resorted to this means which they knew would procure funds from the public.[19] Finally, in 1780, even given the decrease in the number of foundations of beds for incurables (these being unwillingly accepted by the board of governors), the number of beds for curables that were founded still did not increase, and the existing provision fell well short of demand. It was therefore decided to grant the right of nomination for beds for curables as well.[20] The benefactors thus gained control over ordinary patients' access to the hospital, just as in the English voluntary hospital, where patients were admitted with a letter of recommendation. But, strangely enough, the measure existed on paper without having practical effect. After 1780, the right of nomination was not conceded to any of the new founders, except for the stipulation that the initial occupant of the bed would be nominated by the benefactor, after which the bed would be free. In practice, the beds were used for some years for incurable patients (even if the term 'incurable' was no longer mentioned), and they were then made available to the curable patients. So, beds remained under the control of the health personnel, as had previously been the case.

We do not know whether the physicians had a direct part in preventing the 1780 ordinance from being carried out. The fact is that the change that this made was alien to the way in which access to the hospital had been administered for over 200 years. In addition, the key role physicians had traditionally played was reinforced during the eighteenth century. Although the hospital's financial dependence on private charity had permitted the benefactor effectively to privatize a ward, using it for exercising influence, the Hospital of San Giovanni became neither a shelter for all and sundry nor a hospital for the care of the chronically sick. The ward for curables continued to be run by the medical staff and supervised by the board of governors. As we shall see, it can be taken as an early example of 'medicalization'.

If I have spent some time discussing the situation of beds for incurables, it is in order to demonstrate the inadequacy of the stereotypical notions of irrationality or religious motivation usually employed to explain Catholic charity. This is further confirmed if we examine the history of the bequests for beds. In the seventeenth century, the number of bequests did not increase in the climate created by baroque *pietas* and the devotion engendered by the Counter Reformation, nor did they decline in the subsequent century of 'dechristianization'.[21] Bequests grew in the mid-eighteenth century – the 'secular' years in which the absolute state was consolidated (see Table 4.2). If anything, trends registered the most acute phases in the conflict between elites and in the

Table 4.2   Endowments of beds
                for incurables per
                decade

Year	No. of beds
1668–77	8
1678–87	23 + u
1688–97	13
1698–1707	10 + u
1708–17	38
1718–27	9
1728–37	33
1738–47	28 + u
1748–57	27
1758–67	9 + 23*
1768–77	8 + 1*
1778–87	3
1788–97	4

See Table 4.1 for explanatory notes.

reordering of the social hierarchy. In fact, philanthropy
boomed precisely in those decades which saw the climax in
the conflict between the court and feudal interests, the new
stratum of officials (who were then busy taking over control
of the various city institutions and spheres of influence), and
the merchant class which was especially determined to
establish areas of control free from bureaucratic interference.
This complex confrontation between the social groups was
symbolically embodied, as we have seen, in the conflict over
who was entitled to be called a member of the shamefaced
poor.

Between 1720 and 1760, sizeable bequests gave the city
new institutions: a ward for patients with contagious diseases
(previously untreated by hospitals) at the Ospedale di Carità
in 1733; an institution for fallen women, built in 1747. In
addition, funds earmarked for the 'relative' poor were
increased via dowries and alms, as well as other initiatives.
In this period an unprecedented sum was spent on charity. In
relation to the Hospital of San Giovanni, it was the appearance on the scene of merchants, bankers, and shopkeepers as
founder of beds for incurables (previously the reserve of those
with court connections) that explains the increase in bequests
that took place. The merchant classes were able to break the
court monopoly on beds for incurables by systematically
making bequests, so that over a few years the control of some

fifty-six beds (thirty-five of which were in the hands of six families) were held by seventeen families.

It seems that philanthropy was inspired by profoundly secular aspirations and marked by rational calculation, even when the aims did not overlap with the interests of the sick and poor. The factors of prestige, influence and competition between social groups provide the best explanation for the trends in charitable donations. However, we should also consider the specific economic interests at work. If we examine the forms taken by charitable donations and the tenor of the contracts defining the terms of the agreement between the hospital and the benefactor, we can see how the act of charity was not always a one-way process, but often involved a more complex exchange in which the benefactor obtained (in return for his benefactions) the privilege of taking advantage of the availability of loans and investment opportunities offered by the hospital.

The development of the hospital's financial activities appears to have been connected with the project for a new hospital and the exceptional need for money that thereby ensued. Indeed, by the 1670s, the minutes of the board of governors' meetings were taken up with reports about credit and lending operations carried out with private individuals. Charity played a key role in those operations. The most common went as follows. The benefactor, while still alive, donated capital that after his death (and sometimes of others named) was used for charitable purposes, usually the setting up of beds for incurables. Meanwhile, a return (generally of 3–5 per cent of the capital invested, that is, the legal rate of interest) was paid annually during the lifetime of the benefactor or other persons designated in the will. The age of the donors, which tended to be fairly advanced, and the speed with which the hospital's obligations would be expedited figured highly in the calculations of the board of governors. These factors probably also served to establish the rate of interest. From the donor's point of view, such forms of charity largely represented an investment underwritten by the worthiness of the institution with whom the agreement was reached.

In this period, it should be noted, the opportunities for investing liquid assets were limited and full of risk. There was no banking system in the Savoyard state open to private investors, and savers were reluctant to lend to private banks because of their high failure rate; in fact, these banks dealt almost entirely with commercial credit.[22] The most common forms of investment were, therefore, the acquisition of credits. The main forms were: *censi* (guaranteed by income from property, land, and taxes); *tassi* (taxes owed by the communities); and the *Luoghi dei Monti di San Giovanni Battista* (shares of the public debt). Clearly, the annual income that could be obtained from the hospital was much less risky than the *censi*, which were invariably paid late, or the taxes, which often went uncollected (especially in times of war or bad harvests), while the issue of the *Luoghi dei monti*, which were much sought after by private individuals, were limited and insufficient to cover the demands of those with liquid capital to spare.

The shortcomings of the credit system meant that the Hospital of San Giovanni (as well as other charitable institutions, such as the Compagnia di San Paolo and the Ospedale di Carità) assumed an important role in the city economy, becoming an integral part of the financial structure. The hospital then reinvested the capital brought in, partly in land purchases, partly in other fixed assets, but above all it loaned considerable sums of money, usually at the legal interest rate of 3–5 per cent. In fact, a great number of private individuals turned to the hospital in search of an alternative to the normal high-interest loans. These transactions accounted for the major part of the hospital budget. In fact, only some 30 per cent of income came from rents from the institutions' properties and farms. The rest, apart from the small contribution made by alms and the foundlings' manufactures, came from its activities as a creditor.

Charity had become part and parcel of these financial dealings. A kind of exchange was undertaken between people who were either looking for a way of investing their money or for a loan on good terms, and the governors of the hospital, who were looking for ways to finance the institution. From the hospital's point of view, the profit did not flow so much from the difference between the interest on payments and withdrawals, as from the charitable gifts that formed the precondition for gaining entry to the hospital's system of credit. In 1735, for example, the board of governors granted a loan at 4 per cent interest to the Prince of Francavilla with the following words:

Although given the money shortage and the circumstances of the present war, the hospital could derive 5 or
even 6 per cent interest from a sum of 24,500 *lire*, since
it concerns a family so beneficent towards the hospital [it
had already founded nine beds for incurables], and so
that the undertaking is completely secure, the Board has
agreed to the request.[23]

Part of the advantages secured from agreements with the
hospital was then paid back in bequests and donations.
However, unlike the case with the high interest paid to a
moneylender, it did not involve a payment with no returns,
but, as we have seen with the beds for incurables, an investment accruing prestige and powers of patronage.

4

The existence of a large ward for incurable patients seems
once again to conjure up an image of the hospital-as-shelter
projected by historians, who refer to the Italian case in terms
of retarded 'medicalization'. However, if we analyse the ways
in which the ward for curables was traditionally run, then the
Hospital of San Giovanni appears in a very different light as
a forerunner in providing treatment of the sick. As a document of 1541 tells us, the hospital physician or surgeon had,
from the sixteenth century, been doing visiting rounds of
patients twice a day on a regular basis.[24] From the second
half of the seventeenth century, if not earlier, the duties of
the dresser (according to the chief surgeon's instructions)
were carried out by the younger surgeons resident in the
hospital. Originally, there were three of them, but their
number increased steadily, reaching thirteen by the 1730s, to
keep pace with the increase in beds. These surgeons were
assisted with simple duties by a group of nurses, who were
drawn from the ranks of ex-foundlings taken back by the
hospital. Moreover, in the late seventeenth century, a private
benefactor donated funds to create the post of assistant
hospital physician, which was reserved for a young man, who
had worked full time in residence in the hospital, 'to observe
the progress of diseases and report on them to the chief
physician'. Both the positions of dresser and assistant hospital

physician were occupied by young surgeons who wanted to enter the profession, not by apprentices or students. They were initially directly employed by the board of governors for a year, with the chance of having their period of service extended if they proved suitable.[25]

The hospital, therefore, already had a teaching function well before the university reforms completed between 1720 and 1739 made it compulsory for students of medicine and surgery to spend time in hospital as a precondition for entry into the profession. Judging by the number of candidates applying for this kind of practical experience, the post must have been considered prestigious and a good addition to the *curriculum vitae*. As it happened, some young physicians, after a long stint in the hospital, obtained important appointments, like that of chief regimental surgeon or even chief surgeon in the Hospital of San Giovanni. Many acquired more modest positions in the army medical service, and a great number went out to practice in the provinces. The chief physician and surgeon of the hospital were, as a matter of course, very prominent figures in Piedmontese medical circles. For instance, they usually held the chair of Practical and Theoretical Medicine at the university, and, in the case of surgeons, they held the office of anatomist. Some were even court physicians, but these duties normally passed to the physicians of the Hospital of San Maurizio and Lazzaro. So, even before the reforms, informal but solid ties existed between the Hospital of San Giovanni and the university.

It is worth noting that it was the board of governors that controlled the hiring of dressers and physicians and made sure that they carried out their duties as stipulated. They also took disciplinary measures in cases of irregularity or remissness. Certainly the opinions of the chief physician and surgeon had a significant bearing on the choice of dressers and medical assistants, who were often the physicians' pupils and sometimes even their relatives. One Alberto Verna, for example, who held the post of chief physician at the Hospital of San Giovanni for over forty years (serving seven as a dresser), established a veritable dynasty inside the institution. Two nephews succeeded him in his post, in 1739 and then in 1752, after long periods as his assistants, while a third nephew became assistant physician earlier in 1712. However, on paper, every decision on the various aspects of the hospital's life remained firmly in the hands of the governors; that is until the 1730s, when the authority of the board of governors became the object of fierce attacks. The attacks do not seem to have come so much from physicians demanding greater autonomy as from centralizers.

The governors' authority was also strengthened by life appointment, cut short only in cases of sickness necessitating resignation. So, we have examples of governors who managed hospital affairs for twenty or thirty years. As a rule the governors were regular in their attendance of board meetings, and carried out their duties with diligence. There were few cases of absenteeism or figurehead governors.

This, then, was more or less how hospitals worked and were managed when the university reforms transformed the system and syllabus of teaching, affecting the activities of the Hospital of San Giovanni too. As far as the Faculty of Medicine was concerned, the period of study was lengthened to five years, in line with the more established Faculties of Law and Theology. Particular importance was attached to practical medicine, which took up three of the five years' study. In addition, the students were required to follow demonstrations on cadavers and to attend hospital in the last two years of study. During this period, students would have received lessons at the patients' bedside and would have discussed the illnesses under observation and the most interesting cases in weekly meetings. Only those who had then been awarded a degree could practise medicine, and then only on completing two additional years of training with a hospital or an accredited physician. However, the most innovative of the reforms concerned surgery, which, from 1721, became a university faculty. The length of time studying was originally set at three years, but was lengthened to five years in line with the courses of the other faculties in 1738. For the students of surgery, too, practical experience in the Hospital became a crucial element in the curriculum.[26]

Consequently, the reforms made it clear that the hospital was a privileged place with regard to the teaching and research in medicine by greatly increasing the number of medical and surgical students in the hospital and requiring and making it compulsory for the hospital physicians to be members of the university faculty. Yet these reforms did not completely change the identity of the hospital, since, as we

have seen, it was already carrying out the functions of training and maintaining the profession, even if in a minor
capacity.

It is interesting to note how the Savoyard reforms came
several decades before the better-known reforms in Tuscany
and Lombardy that are usually seen as exemplifying and
pioneering reform in Italy. Furthermore, it is worth pointing
out that these Savoyard reforms were carried out despite the
absence of Enlightenment influences, and, instead, constituted a step in the construction of the absolute state. The
Turinese case disproves the argument, according to which
hospitals with 'modern' features developed in Italy thanks
largely to the Enlightenment-inspired reforms of the late eighteenth century. Greater weight should, instead, be attached
to the hypothesis advanced by some scholars suggesting
continuity in the Italian tradition in which the hospital was
used as a place of research, teaching, and medical practice.
According to them, the Morgagni clinic had its roots in a
practice started in Italian hospitals in the early sixteenth
century.[27]

As for hospital life, the real effects of the reforms were
political. They served as a vehicle for launching a violent
assault on the historical independence of the Hospital. These
reforms allowed state officials to extend their spheres of
influence in the Hospital and progressively usurp the traditional powers of the governors. In the 1750s, after more than
twenty years of conflict between the board of governors and
the central authorities, state officials became members of the
board itself.

This conflict had already begun to raise its head before the
reforms shook the hospital. In fact, in 1728 a project
presented as the King's personal wish was proposed to the
board of governors. It concerned the establishment of a
maternity ward and a school of midwifery under the direction
of a French midwife, who had undertaken training in Paris
for the purpose. The project sounded to the governors like an
unprecedented and aggressive intrusion of royal power into
the administration of the hospital, and provoked a strong
reaction on the part of the governors. They tried several
times through representations to the King and his representative to have the project disowned. The clash took a violent
turn, with the governors appealing to the Hospital's tradition

of independence, and the central government representatives insisting that the wishes of the sovereign be respected. In the end, an investigation was set up on the Senate's orders to establish the origins of the charity and whether the Hospital should be considered a secular or an ecclesiastical body, or a combination of the two. It was summarily concluded that the Hospital of San Giovanni was secular, and therefore subject to the sovereign. It thereby followed that the claims advanced by the board of governors were invalid. After some delay, the Opera Partorienti with ten beds was finally set up, and the Hospital had to foot the bill.[28]

The decision on the legal status of the hospital cleared the way for more systematic interventions by the central authority. Soon afterwards, in 1730, a 'protector' was appointed to the Hospital of San Giovanni, as shortly occurred in all charitable institutions. The protector was a high official (in this instance, the first president *pro tempore* of the Senate) who was supposed to serve as the link between the everyday running of the hospital by the board of governors, the needs of the institution, and the policies of the central government.[29] The imposition of an external authority was obviously greeted with hostility by the governors. Yet again, in 1740, an important *rappresentanza* was presented to the King in which the governors described the course conflicts had taken over several years. It included proposals for the restoration of the board's prerogatives, headed by the call for the reconsideration of the post of protector. It requested 'the First President of the Senate continue as Protector of the Hospital, providing counsel, favour and help, when the Governors and administrators so request and without interfering in the affairs and management of the Hospital'.[30] The most serious causes of the conflict date back to 1734. When faced with a grave crisis resulting in a large increase in patient admissions to the Hospital, the protector, Caissotti, imposed solutions that were at odds with the normal financial prudence of the board, leaving the Hospital deep in debt until the 1750s.[31]

Therefore, the reforms were carried out in an already highly-charged atmosphere, and represented an opportunity for further reducing the governors' authority. With the pretext of wanting to avoid straining the Hospital's finances, it was established that only a fraction of the salaries of the four physicians (whose numbers had been increased to meet the growth in teaching duties) would be paid by the Hospital itself, and the rest by the university. This seems to have had the effect of cutting down the governors' authority over the physicians and emphasising their role as teachers, as against their obligations towards the sick. Then, in 1739, the board was suddenly deprived of its traditional prerogative of selecting physicians. The central authority claimed that the physicians recently selected by the board were not up to the standards required of the post.[32] The same year it was established that the dressers would no longer be provided by the board but by the *magistrati della riforma* (the officers who governed the university),[33] and they would be chosen instead from among the surgical students at the Collegio delle Province (an institution created to promote university education via the provision of scholarships to over 200 students). The governors, in the 1740 *rappresentanza* cited above, give the impression that they were less and less in control of the management of the hospital, which was said to be slipping into chaos:

> Physicians of the hospital occasionally delegate their rounds to one another, sometimes to no one, and then send the assistant physician out on the rounds, and the chief physician comes in the evening when he can. The surgeon is deemed to have great theoretical ability but insufficient practical experience, and although it is his duty to carry out the difficult operations of removing gall stones, cleansing cataracts, suturing arteries or performing surgery on what is called the 'king's evil' [scrofula] and similar things, these duties are actually performed by former surgeons of the hospital – the Vernas, uncle and nephew. . . . The hospital is full of praise for royal provision that physicians and surgeons also be professors at the University. However, conscience requires it be reported that it is not advantageous to the Hospital because neither the physician nor the surgeon has a real dependence on it, and is harmful to the sick because they are no longer served with the punctuality and charitable feeling of before.

The very midwife of the maternity ward and school for

midwifery mentioned earlier is referred to as someone who:

> does not think of herself as depending on the Governors
> of the Hospital but on the Reform officers. She has not
> rendered service in keeping either with the rules or with
> her duty. Considerable disorder has taken place, and she
> has been absent for over three months from her post,
> having returned to her country with the intention of
> coming back the following spring. She has delegated her
> duties to another Frenchwoman, and left asking permis-
> sion only of those under whose authority she believes to
> be.

Although authority remained in the governors' hands on
paper, in practice the influence of the state officials was
greatly extended, so that the two confronted one another
inside the Hospital. Confrontations also took place at a
symbolic level, as can be seen in the episode recounted (with
a touch of irony) in the *rappresentanza*. A visitation occurs in
response to the governors' complaints that the sick were not
properly cared for by the young medical students of the
Collegio delle Province:

> Leaving aside the various acts of insolence committed,
> the First President, Protector and Head of the Reform
> came with all the Reform officials to see about the above
> mentioned inefficiencies, but did not manage to, and so
> returned a second time, with full pomp and ceremony,
> once more accompanied by all the Reform officers and,
> in addition, the Secretary of the Reform, in the light of
> which the governors argued that from then on the run-
> ning of the Hospital should fall to him, or at least the
> presiding over the governors.

We know now that what was proposed in this instance as a
possibility not without paradoxes shortly became a reality.
From the 1750s, a *magistrato della riforma* sat regularly on the
board of governors, which, by this time, no longer represented an expression of municipal power.

The reforms, it can therefore be said, did not lead to a
rationalization of the hospital's operation, but did lead to a
fairly prolonged period of confusion and poor organization

following the collapse of the traditional supervision of the medical staff's activities. The reforms were not an aspect of a conflict between 'progress' and 'backwardness', nor did they add up to a 'modernization' of the Hospital. Rather, they allowed a change of power that also occurred in other charitable institutions, not to mention the various centres of government in the city (the council, the different courts of law, and so on). The state was increasingly involved in the management of the Hospital of San Giovanni, but this did not entail any major changes in the methods of management. Inadequate provision lasted until the end of the century; 'The professors of the University do only one round a day, some go months, others years without setting foot in the Hospital. . . . The result is that the sick get inexpert and improper treatment from the two young physicians'.[34] Moreover, the innovations introduced in the financial running of the Hospital, as we have seen, turned out to be a failure. Nor was an effort made to resolve the problem of the disproportionate number of beds for incurables; on the eve of the French takeover, there were still some 218 for incurables and 232 beds for curable patients.

The shifts in the administration of charity into the hands of the state is usually in itself considered a sign of progress and rationalization. When the outcome does not meet expectations, the explanation is sought in the persistence of old forms of management, such as the continued presence of religious staff in the hospitals. My reconstruction, however, demonstrates how this shift should, in actuality, be seen as the substitution of an old elite by a new one, and as the affirmation of a new social group. In this instance, we have the state officials who concentrate power in their hands that had previously been divided up in a more complex way between different *milieux*.

It is undeniable that the appearance of a new group whose identity was now completely defined in relation to state service led a professionalization to the forms of public administration. However, it is important also to turn this perspective on its head, and observe how the rhetoric of reform and public welfare itself largely constituted a 'language' or 'discourse' that permitted or legitimized the creation of new functions and duties enlarging the scope for intervention by public administrators and the bureaucratic class itself. We have seen this in the innovations introduced in the Hospital of San Giovanni, such as the Opera Partorienti, the school of midwifery, the introduction of university education to the whole hospital. These innovations can be seen as important moments in the evolution of the hospital, but they were also prongs in the attack which allowed state officials to substitute themselves for a multiplicity of different centres of power. Necessary importance should therefore be accorded to conflict as a motor of change. The clash between different groups of elites has reappeared throughout the course of this reconstruction as a crucial element in explaining developments in philanthropic practices, changes in institutional structures, and in the social composition of recipients of relief. The transformation undergone by the governing bodies of the institutions led, among other things, to a redefinition of the categories and contents of privilege. In the second half of the eighteenth century, state officials and the military progressively gained preferential access to charitable resources. In short, the establishment of state control did not entail the suppression of particularist interests in public administration, but a shift in the traditional system of protection and patronage in favour of different social groups.

Notes

1. The tendency to consider the problem of relief as the product of religious and state policies and ideologies is, above all, a feature of historiography of the 1970s, which saw a renewal of interest in the subject after a period of neglect. The findings of this research are analysed by M. Rosa in 'Chiesa, idee sui poveri e assistenza in Italia dal Cinque al Settecento', *Società e Storia*, 10 (1980). Some general syntheses on systems of poor relief in Italy come under the same heading: B. Geremek, 'Il pauperismo nell'Italia pre-industriale (sec. XIV–XVIII)', *Storia d'Italia*, vol. 5:1, *I Documenti* (Turin, 1973); B.S. Pullan, 'Poveri, mendicanti, e vagabondi (secoli XIV-XVII)', *Storia d'Italia, Annali I, Dal feudalesimo al capitalismo* (Turin, 1978); S.J. Woolf, 'La formazione del proletariato (secoli XVIII–XIX), op. cit. See also the collection of essays *Ricerche per la storia religiosa di Roma*, 3 (1979). More recently an approach that is more attentive to social dynamics is E. Grendi, 'Ideologia della carità e società indisciplinata. La costruzione del sistema assistenziale genovese', in G. Politi, M. Rosa, and F. della Peruta (eds),

Timore e carità. I poveri nell'Italia moderna (Cremona, 1982), and the number of *Quaderni Storici* edited by the same author 'Sistemi di carità. Esposti e internati nella società di Antico Regime', *Quaderni Storici*, 53 (1983). See, furthermore, the studies indicated in note 8, and the remarks by S.J. Woolf in the Introduction to his *The Poor in Western Europe in the Eighteenth and Nineteenth Centuries* (London and New York, 1986).

2. A. Scotti, 'Malati e strutture ospedaliere dall' età dei Lumi all' Unita', in F. della Peruta (ed.), *Storia d'Italia. Annali 7. Malattia e medicina* (Turin, 1984); E. Brambilla, 'La medicina nel settecento: dal monopolio dogmatico alla professione scientifica', op. cit.; P. Frascani, *Ospedale e società in età liberale* (Bologna, 1986); G. Cosmacini, *Storia della medicina e della sanità in Italia* (Bari, 1987). A different approach is developed by F. Giusberti, in the article 'La povertà e malattia. Il Sant' Orsola a Bologna dal XVII al XVIII secolo', *Annali della Fondazione Luigi Einaudi*, 13 (1979).

3. The Savoy Kingdom included after the treaty of Utrecht (1713) the territories of Piedmont, Savoy, Nice, Oneglia, Aosta, and, after 1720, Sardinia. For a classic interpretation of its political system see G. Quazza, *Le riforme in Piemonte nella prima metà del Settecento* (Modena, 1957), and more recently G. Symcox, *Victor Amadeus II. Absolutism in the Savoyard State 1675–1730* (London, 1983).

4. For histories of the two hospitals, see S. Solero, *Storia dell' Ospedale Maggiore di San Giovanni Battista e della Città di Torino* (Turin, 1959); T.M. Caffaratto, *L'Ospedale Maggiore di San Giovanni Battista e della Città di Torino. Sette secoli di assistenza secoli-sanitaria* (Turin, 1984); also 'Storia dell' Ospedale Maggiore di Torino della religione e ordine dei SS. Maurizio e Lazzaro', *Annali Ospedale M. Vittoria di Torino*, XXII (1979), 7–12. During the eighteenth century the number of beds in the Hospital of S. Giovanni rose to 450 (for both curables and incurables), while the number at SS. Maurizio e Lazzaro remained at fifty to sixty.

5. These measures are mostly concentrated in the second half of the sixteenth century; T.M Caffaratto, *L'Ospedale Maggiore*, 15–16. But already, by the beginning of the seventeenth century, the city council's request that the hospital concern itself with the poor provoked the governors' protests; Archivio Comunale di Torino (henceforth ACT), *Ordinati*, 13.12.1601, 26.12.1601, 11.1.1602. The hospital, in as much as it was dependent on the municipality, carried out its duty of taking in foundlings abandoned in the city. They were then sent to the villages of the Canavese area for wet-nursing at city expense. When 10 years old, they returned to the hospital which tried to place them in apprenticeships or in service, or put up for adoption. However, with the increase in abandoned children, it became more and more difficult to find an occupation for all of them. Thus, small manufactories were organized, initially in the hospital itself, then, in the second half of the eighteenth century, on a larger scale outside the hospital.

6. As far as the Ospedale di Carità is concerned, see my article 'Conceptions of poverty and poor relief in Turin in the second half of the eighteenth century', European Institute, Florence (forthcoming). The research is based in particular on analyses of the wealth of information found in the registers of inmates kept from 1742 onwards.

7. C. Bloch, *L'assistance e L'État en France à la vieille de la Révolution, 1764–1790* (Paris, 1908); C. Jones, *Charity and Bienfaisance. The Treatment of the Poor in the Montpellier Region, 1740–1815* (Cambridge, 1982); M. Jimenez Salas, *Historia de la asistencia social en Espana en la edad moderna* (Madrid, 1958); A. Highmore, *Pietas Londiniensis* (London, 1814).

8. An important exception is the work of R. Trexler, 'Charity and defence of the urban elites in the Italian communes', in S.C. Jaher (ed.), *The Rich and the Well-born and the Powerful* (Urbana, 1973), and of G. Ricci, 'Povertà vergogna e povertà vergognosa', *Società e Storia*, 5 (1979). Worth noting is also the article by G. Muto, 'Forme e contenuti economici dell' assistenza nel Mezzogiorno moderno: il caso di Napoli', in G. Politi, M. Rosa, and F. Della Peruta (eds), *Timore e carità*. Great interest has been shown in the last few years in the study of women's institutions: L. Ciammitti, 'Fanciulle, monache, madri. Povertà femminile e previdenza a Bologne nei secoli XVI–XVIII', in *Arte e pietà. I patrimoni culturali delle opere pie* (Bologna, 1980), and 'Quanto costa essere normali. La dote nel conservatorio femminile di Santa Maria del Barracano (1630–80)', *Quaderni Storici*, 53 (1983); S. Cavallo, 'Assistenza femminile e tutela dell'onore nella Torino del XVIII secolo', *Annali della Fondazione Luigi Einaudi*, XIV (1980); L. Ferrante, 'L'onore ritrovato. Donne nella Casa del Soccorso di San Paolo a Bologna (sec. XVI–XVII)', *Quaderni Storici*, 53 (1983), D. Lombardi, 'L'ospedale dei mendicanti nella Firenze del Seicento. "Da inutile serraglio dei mendici a conservatorio e casa di forza per le donne"', *Società e Storia*, 24 (1984).

9. R. De Maio, *Società e Vita religiosa a Napoli* (Naples, 1971), 368; L. Guidi, 'Onore e status femminile negli istituti di reclusione napoletani dell' Ottocento', in *Quaderni del Dipartimento di Scienze Sociali dell' Istituto Universitario Orientale di Napoli*, 2 (1988); S. Cavallo, 'Assistenza femminile'.

10. For an interpretation of women's institutions as a product of the cultural climate of the Counter Reformation see B. Pullan, *Rich and Poor in Renaissance Venice: The Social Institutions of a Catholic State to 1620* (Oxford, 1971), 385–94, and 'The old Catholicism, the new Catholicism and the poor', in G. Politi, M. Rosa, and F. della Peruta (eds), *Timore e carità*, 16–17. For explanations of the widespread relief to the shamefaced poor see G. Ricci, 'Povertà, vergogna', 328–9.

11. Archivio Storico San Paolo, *Ordinati*, vol. III, n. 57, 21.2.1734.

12. Archivio Storico San Paolo, *Repertorio dei lasciti*, vol. 160–163.
13. Archivio Ospedale San Giovanni (henceforth AOSG), *Ordinati*, 26.6.1667, 9.3.1668.
14. The endowments of beds for incurables have been reconstructed using various sources: the fund *Letti Incurabili* (AOSG, Categoria 10, Classe 3, vols 1–7) has in fact turned out to be incomplete. Further documentation was obtained therefore from the fund *Eredità Legati* (AOSG, Categoria 4, Classe 1, vols 1–69), and from the *Ordinati* of the hospital from 1668 onwards. The beds were put up either by donations of living donors, or left in wills; in this second case a rather long time possibly passed from the disposition to the actual foundation. Note that the dates given here (including those that appear in Table 4.1) refer to the disposition; that is the official act which the benefactor provided for the immediate or future foundation.
15. AOSG, *Ordinati*, 10.4.1713, 10.12.1716, 6.12.1723, 30.12.1724.
16. The formula for the endowment of beds stipulated that incurables be expelled if they failed to show respect for hospital officials or caused disorder. There are actually some cases of expulsion documented.
17. Archivio di Stato di Torino, *Luoghi Pii di qua dai Monti*, m.19, fasc.7, 'Sentimenti sugeriti dal principe di Francavilla e dal Padre Perardo. . . circa il modo di promuovere il sovenimento dei poveri', 1734.
18. AOSG, *Ordinati*, 21.5.1744.
19. AOSG, *Ordinati*, 21.1.1754, 27.5.1775. In January 1760, for example, since money was needed for the completion of the hospital buildings, the governors put twenty-three entitlements for the nomination of beds for incurables up for sale at 3,000 lire each following their reversion to the hospital on the death of the testators' descendents. Some twenty-one were sold within a year. AOSG, *Ordinati*, 16.1.1760.
20. AOSG, *Ordinati*, 20.4.1780.
21. See M. Vovelle, *Piété baroque et déchristianisation en Provence au XVIIIe siècle* (Paris, 1978).
22. G. Prato, *Problemi monetari e bancari nei secoli XVII e XVIII* (Torino, 1916).
23. OSG, Cat. 10, Cl. 3, vol. 2.
24. 'Il modo et governo de la Congregatione de poveri in l'hospitale di San Giovanni', 1.5.1541, published in T.M. Caffaratto, *L'Ospedale Maggiore*, 195, *passim*.
25. All information about the extent and increase of the medical staff, the careers of physicians and surgeons, was obtained through examination of the hospital *Ordinati*. Some biographical information relative to physicians and surgeons can be found in G.G. Bonino, *Biografia medica piemontese*, 2 vols (Turin, 1925).
26. F.A. Duboin, *Raccolta per ordine di materie delle leggi . . . emanate*

negli stati di terraferma fino all'8 dicembre 1798 dai sovrani della real casa di Savoia (Turin, 1818–68), T. XIV, Capo IV, 'Dell'insegnamento della medicina', 643–49; Cap V, 'Dell' insegnamento della Chirurgia', 655–66; Articolo IV, 723; Articolo V, 733. T. Vallauri, *Storia delle Università degli Studi del Piemonte*, 3 vols (Turin, 1816). D. Balani, D. Carpanetto, and F. Turletti, 'La popolazione studentesca dell' Università di Torino nel Settecento', *Bollettino Storico Bibliografico Subalpino*, LXXVI (1978).

27. J.J. Bylebyl, 'Commentary', in J.H. Stevenson, *A Celebration of Medical History* (Baltimore and London, 1982). For a re-evaluation of the hospital's role as a place for medical practice, research, and training in other areas of Europe besides Paris in the eighteenth century, see O. Keel, 'The politics of health and the institutionalisation of clinical practices in Europe in the second half of the eighteenth century', in W.F. Bynum and R. Porter (eds), *William Hunter and the Eighteenth-Century Medical World* (Cambridge, 1985). For reforms in Tuscany and Lombardy during 1770s and 1780s see A. Scotti, 'Malati e strutture ospedaliere', 250 *passim*; G. Cosmacini, *Storia della medicina*, 234 *passim*.

28. The conflict over the foundation of the Opera Partorienti can be followed in the minute books (*Ordinati*) from the board of governors meetings.

29. F.A. Duboin, *Raccolta*, T. XII, 647, 'Regie Patenti di nomina del Primo Presidente del Senato di Piemonte, con autorità di vegliare al buon governo dell'ospedale di San Giovanni in Torino', 10.8.1730.

30. ACT, *Ospedale di San Giovanni*, N.666, 'Rappresentanza del venerando spedale maggiore di San Giovanni Battista e della città di Torino', 1740.

31. Caissotti ordered that the hospital, already overflowing with patients, should try to accept all the sick who asked to be admitted, by creating new beds, transforming areas used for other purposes into patient-care areas, and increasing the number of physicians and nurses. To this purpose all of the hospital income had to be used (including the reserve that the board of governors usually kept intact) and the hospital had to resort to loans for further financing (AOSG, *Ordinati*, 29.6.1734).

32. AOSG, *Ordinati*, 9.8.1739.

33. AOSG, *Ordinati*, 2.8.1739.

34. T.M. Caffaratto, *L'Ospedale Maggiore*, 143, 'Relazione anonima', toward the end of the century.

5

Politics and the London Royal Hospitals, 1683 – 92[1]

Craig Rose

Between 1546 and 1552 Henry VIII and Edward VI established, on the site of dissolved monastic foundations, the five London royal hospitals: St Bartholomew's, St Thomas's, Christ's, Bridewell, and Bethlem. Although they were the largest and wealthiest charitable institutions in early modern London, their early history has been virtually ignored by professional historians. Those interested in the hospitals are thus still largely dependent on the staid and reverential institutional histories written in the first decades of this century.[2] The lack of interest of social and medical historians in the royal hospitals is understandable; prior to the late eighteenth century the hospital records contain only minimal information on medical practices and the conditions of patients and inmates. The neglect of political historians is less excusable. The royal hospitals were important civic institutions, and were bound to be affected by major crises in civic politics. One such crisis in London politics broke out in the last years of the reign of Charles II.

The early 1680s witnessed a vicious struggle for power in London between the emergent Whig and Tory parties. When victory in that battle had gone to the Tory supporters of Charles II, the King and his government launched a systematic effort to drive the Whigs from public life. With their extensive property-holdings and substantial revenues, the royal hospitals, especially Whig-dominated St Thomas's, soon drew the attention of the authorities. In 1683 the Crown intervened in the administration of the hospitals, and purged those governors and staff members who supported the Whigs. After 1683 the Stuart monarchy and the political parties experienced many vicissitudes, which were also reflected in the affairs of the hospitals. In this essay, I shall explain how and why these philanthropic institutions were drawn into the bitter conflict between Whigs and Tories.

The administration of the Royal Hospitals

The royal hospitals established in the mid-Tudor period were apparently London's response to the municipal relief institutions which had recently been opened at Lyon and Geneva.[3] The hospitals were each allocated specific tasks: St Bartholomew's, West Smithfield, and St Thomas's, Southwark, the two greatest of the medieval hospitals, were to provide relief for the sick poor; Christ's Hospital was to cater for the orphaned children of poor City freemen; Bridewell, a former royal palace, was converted into a correction centre for vagrants; and Bethlem retained its pre-Reformation role as a lunatic asylum.

Although the hospitals were royal foundations, their administration was placed in the hands of the Corporation of London. At first the hospitals were closely supervised by the City authorities. An Act of Common Council of 1557 required yearly joint elections of governors, under aldermanic supervision, at Christ's Hospital on St Matthew's Day (21 September); in the same year a joint rule book was issued.[4] In practice, apart from Bridewell and Bethlem which shared a single administration, the hospitals soon went their separate ways. Aldermanic supervision of the governors had lapsed by 1615, and though the St Matthew's Day Court continued, its function had become purely ceremonial.[5] By the early years of the seventeenth century, though they continued to receive certain customary revenues from the City, the hospitals had become virtually independent corporations.

Each hospital was ruled by a court of governors, which elected its own members, appointed hospital staff, and chose a new president from the ranks of the City aldermen upon the death or retirement of the incumbent. The president himself had sole power to convene meetings of the General Court of Governors, and a dominant president could have a decisive influence on its proceedings. The General Court met relatively infrequently, and day-to-day administration was in the hands of a committee of governors centred on the treasurer. Its decisions were provisional, and required the approval of the General Court for ratification.

Most of the governors' time was taken up with mundane administrative matters: renewing leases on hospital property; entering into contracts with tradesmen; and ensuring the maintenance of the hospital buildings. They do not appear to have supervised the welfare of patients and inmates closely. The relief activities of the hospitals, however, were considerable. In 1677–8 St Bartholomew's Hospital provided treatment for 1,967 patients, and its sister hospital of St Thomas's for 2,080. Both hospitals also gave 'money and other necessaries' to patients on their discharge. Christ's Hospital was providing for the education and upkeep of 663 poor children in 1684.[6] To finance these activities, the hospitals relied upon their own large, independent revenues, derived primarily from endowed property. Thus by the 1680s the annual revenues of St Bartholomew's and Christ's Hospitals both exceeded £7,000, while those of St Thomas's totalled more than £4,000.[7]

The independence of the hospitals, though, was largely illusory. Aldermanic control of the hospitals, embodied in the original royal grant of the institutions to the City, had lapsed but had never been legally revoked. Even more importantly, as royal foundations the hospitals were ultimately subject to the authority of the Crown. Indeed, in the letters patent of 1552, by which he granted Christ's, Bridewell, and Bethlem to the City, Edward VI specifically reserved the right for his 'Heirs and Successors' to appoint commissioners, if they saw fit, 'to visit the Hospitalls . . . and to doe and execute' all matters relating to their management.[8] The hospitals' double vulnerability to outside intervention was to be graphically exposed during the political crisis that racked the nation after the Popish Plot revelations of 1678.

Sir John Lawrence and St Thomas's Hospital

From 1679 to 1681 the Earl of Shaftesbury's exploitation of the mass hysteria generated by the Plot seemed to have the throne of the Stuarts once again teetering on the edge of collapse. In three successive general elections Shaftesbury's

Whigs had gained victory, but they had not achieved power; by skilful use of his prerogative rights of proroguing and dissolving Parliament, Charles II had thwarted the Whigs' efforts to exclude his Catholic brother and heir, James, Duke of York, from the succession to the throne.[9] By 1681 the Crown's steadily improving financial position enabled Charles to rule without Parliament, and he launched a counter-attack against his enemies. In the last four years of his reign, the so-called Tory reaction, the King co-operated with his Tory supporters in systematically driving the Whigs from public life. The Whig leaders were struck down one by one. Protestant dissenters, the strongest supporters of the Whigs, were persecuted with relentless zeal by Tory justices.[10] The most ambitious aspect of the royal offensive was a wholesale attack on parliamentary corporations. Through the issue of writs of *quo warranto*, corporation charters were forfeited and remodelled by the Crown to bring them under its control.

The dominance of London in the nation's affairs naturally made it a focal point in the Crown-Tory campaign. In the capital the battle between Whigs and Tories was particularly fierce, and from 1682 began to run decisively in favour of the Tories.[11] Victory in a bitterly contested shrieval election brought the Tories control of the City's law courts. The charters of several City livery companies were forfeited, and hundreds of Whig liverymen were purged, thus disqualifying them from voting in mayoral, shrieval, and parliamentary elections. Most dramatically of all, a *quo warranto* was issued against the Corporation of London itself. As a result, in October 1683 the City's charter was forfeited, the Corporation of London dissolved, and the City was placed directly under the control of royal commissioners.[12] As we shall soon see, one of the tasks entrusted to the commissioners was to purge the royal hospitals of all parties disaffected to the government.

The first sign that the Tory reaction in London would extend as far as the hospitals had come in 1682. On 9 February the Tory-controlled Court of Aldermen issued an order that the hospitals should appoint no further governors without the Court's approval, thus reasserting a power that had lapsed for over sixty years. Two weeks later an aldermanic committee was established to investigate the hospitals' administration.[13]

Within a few days these sudden efforts of the aldermen to reassert their ancient authority over the hospitals were overtaken by a more serious development. On 27 February the General Court of Governors of St. Thomas's Hospital received the stunning news that a Royal Commission of Visitation had been established to examine the affairs of that hospital.[14] This initial royal intervention does not appear to have progressed very far, and no action was taken against St Thomas's. Nevertheless the events of spring 1682 had shown that both the Court of Aldermen and the Crown were concerned about the hospitals, and that St Thomas's was the primary object of their concern.

Why had St Thomas's attracted such undesired attention? The answer lies primarily in government suspicion of Alderman Sir John Lawrence, president of St Thomas's since 1668. A wealthy City merchant, Lawrence was a man of strength and courage; Lord Mayor during the Great Plague of 1665, he had been one of the few to stay at his post throughout that terrible episode.[15] He was also an inveterate and tactless opponent of Charles II's regime; as early as 1672 a government informant was warning of the 'imperious and insolent behaviour' of the 'ill minded' Lawrence, and of his attempts to fan hostility to the government in the City.[16] During the exclusion crisis Lawrence was a senior figure among the City Whigs, and in 1681 he had been foreman of Shaftesbury's *ignoramus* jury.[17]

According to complaints made to the King by some disgruntled Southwark Tories, Lawrence's Whiggery was having a major impact on the administration of St Thomas's. The Tories claimed that Sir John and the hospital's Nonconformist treasurer, James Hayes, had appropriated to themselves the power to appoint governors. Consequently 'a very great Majority [of the Court]' were said to be 'persons avowedly disaffected to the Government established'.[18] This appears to be something of an exaggeration. I have identified 102 of the governors of St Thomas's in 1683, although the total number was probably closer to 130.[19] Of these 102 I have labelled forty as Tories and forty-two as Whigs, with at least ten of the latter being dissenters.[20] However, holding the key positions of president and treasurer, the Whigs certainly exercised a dominant influence on the hospital's affairs. Their power was clearly reflected in the composition of the hospital's staff and appointees. Although the rector of the parish of St Thomas was 'a person of inflexible loyalty' to the government, the remaining hospital appointees, from the chaplain, William Hughes, and the physician, Richard Torlesse, 'down to the porters', were all said to be persons of 'factious principles'.[21]

This was most obviously so in the case of the chaplain, or hospitaller, William Hughes. During the Civil War Hughes had been a chaplain in the parliamentary army, and as a reward had gained the rich living of Hinton in Berkshire.[22] In 1651 he had delivered a sermon in which he argued that the age of the fifth monarchy was dawning, and that the regicide was 'not so uncouth as some do render it', having 'cured the wound' of monarchy, that persecutor of the saints.[23] When that 'wound' was reopened in 1660 Hughes was ejected from Hinton, and for some time thereafter was patronized by Lord Wharton, the leading Presbyterian peer.[24] By 1680, the year in which he was appointed chaplain of St Thomas's, Hughes was edging towards conformity.[25] But it was not until three years after his appointment to St Thomas's that he conformed to the Church of England and was ordained.[26] It is clear, though, that Hughes was an unenthusiastic Anglican, for in July 1683 the King ordered the Bishop of Winchester to investigate complaints 'of the great disorderliness in the Church service as now performed in St Thomas' Hospital, Southwark, to the great discouragement of loyal and conformable subjects'.[27] A later report gave a colourful if somewhat jaundiced account of Hughes's unease with the Church of England: 'the Form of Prayer made him puke, he sweat at the Litany . . . and he still hates every thing in the Church but its Preferments'.[28]

The maintenance of a Nonconformist chaplain is the most blatant sign of the political and religious sympathies of the dominant group of governors led by Sir John Lawrence. More important was the Whigs' exploitation of the hospital's extensive properties and revenues as a means of political influence and patronage in Southwark. St Thomas's owned 170 rents in the borough, 110 of these in the parish of St Thomas itself, where virtually all property was in the hospital's hands.[29] The parliamentary franchise in Southwark was vested in all householders not in receipt of alms,[30] so the hospital's property gave it a major influence over a considerable number of votes. According to the Tories the governors had fully exploited this influence on behalf of the Whig candidates in the hard-fought Southwark election of 1681, 'showing favour or using Rigor in renewing leases' to tenants, 'accordingly as they act agreeably or contrary to their dictates'.[31]

Another major source of local patronage for the governors was the disbursement of the hospital's revenues. In 1681–2 St Thomas's income amounted to £4,147, derived primarily from its rentals. Disbursements in that year totalled almost £4,000, of which £2,130 were expended on tradesmen's contracts, mainly for food and other supplies for the patients.[32] With such spending power, the governors could exercise a major influence over local traders. Indeed in October 1683 a government informant had warned secretary of state Jenkins that the disposal of hospital revenues was of great importance to London tradesmen, and that where a hospital's 'officers are factious, the revenues are disposed of to their own party to the discouragement of loyal citizens'. He concluded, 'I need not mention St Thomas, where the whole revenue is and has been distributed amongst the enemies of the government.'[33]

By 1683 Tory fears about St Thomas's role in fomenting and sustaining Whiggery in Southwark had reached fever-pitch. In January the Southwark grand jury urged local justices 'to increase the number and strengthen the interest' of the loyal party in the borough, who were 'labouring more particularly under the grievance, that persons notoriously disaffected are become the majority of governors of an hospital of royal foundation among them and so the disposers of all offices relating thereto and the managers of a large revenue belonging thereto'.[34] That summer it was reported that the loyalty of Southwark was 'preserved only by the care of a few honest and active men'; among the measures recommended to curb opposition was the visitation of St Thomas's.[35]

The Commission for Hospitals 1683–8

The opportunity to take action against St Thomas's and disaffected elements in the other hospitals came in October

1683, when the dissolution of the Corporation of London and the purge of the Whig minority on the aldermanic bench marked the complete defeat of the City Whigs. On 15 October it was urged upon secretary Jenkins that 'In the regulation his Majesty is now about concerning the City, great care should be taken in the government of the hospitals.'[36] On 20 October, Lord Mayor Sir William Pritchard instructed the Common Sergeant of London to search the poll books, in order to discover how the hospital staff had voted in elections; the previous day the Common Sergeant and the Recorder had 'settled a commission for the government of the hospitals'.[37] A royal warrant was issued on 23 October, appointing the Commission, whose membership was identical with that of the Commission to rule the City – the Crown and the City law officers, the Lord Mayor, and the purged Court of Aldermen.[38] It appears that no independent action was thought necessary against the hospital charters, since their fate was deemed to be bound up with that of the demised Corporation of London.

The first meeting of the Commission for Hospitals took place on 10 November, when the royal hospitals were purged of the Whigs among their governors and staffs, and their replacements appointed.[39] Heeding the informant's recommendations on the revenues, the Commissioners ordered that the hospitals should only employ such tradesmen 'as are truely Loyall and well affected to the government'. They also required the clerks of the hospitals to furnish lists of their tenants. This indicates that the commissioners were fully aware of the political significance of the hospitals' property, and that they perhaps intended to cow disaffected tenants by threat of eviction. Since 1682 the Tory justices in the London area had been fighting an economic war against the dissenters, linking the licensing of innholders and the payment of poor relief to church attendance; the commissioners' orders on tradesmen and tenants should be seen in this context.[40]

The impact of the Commission varied greatly from hospital to hospital. Not surprisingly St Thomas's, which had prompted the intervention in the first place, was the worst hit. The president, Sir John Lawrence, was replaced by Sir William Hooker, a Tory alderman, while the treasurer was also displaced. The total number of governors ejected is unknown, but was probably well over forty.[41] To replace them the commissioners appointed a large number of new governors.[42] Virtually the entire staff was ejected. Out went William Hughes, the chaplain; Dr. Richard Torlesse, the physician; Thomas Hollyer, one of the surgeons; the steward; the clerk and his rent-gatherer, the porters, and the beadle.[43] In August 1684 the hospital's remodelled Court of Governors was also to dismiss six of the nursing staff, including three sisters, for 'incorrigible ill behaviour' and 'non complyance with the rules and orders of this House'.[44]

For Whigs and Nonconformists in Southwark, the loss of hospital contracts and the threat of eviction must have been a severe blow. As early as 27 October the Surrey justices, three of whom were Tory governors of St Thomas's, reported that vigorous prosecution of the penal laws had forced many Southwark dissenters to 'leave their trades and habitations'. 'This prosecution being continued', they wrote, 'and our Hospital Regulated (a matter of so great Consequence in the whole affair, that we cannot omit to mention it whenever we speak of Southwark), we shall shortly be able to give you as good an account of this borough as you can wish'.[45]

Were there also attempts to bar dissenters from entering the hospital as patients? From 1689 to 1690 John Turner, the chaplain appointed by the commissioners in 1683, fought a desperate battle to prevent his dismissal by the resurgent Whigs.[46] During this struggle he twice expressed his hostility to discrimination against patients on the grounds of religion, which at least suggests that such an accusation had been made.[47] However, in the absence of any firmer evidence it seems best to deliver a 'not proven' verdict on this issue.

Of the other hospitals, Christ's was the next worst affected by the rule of the commissioners. The president, Sir John Frederick, was a Whig alderman, while the treasurer and several of the governors were described as 'old Cromwellists'.[48] All were dismissed. Three new governors were appointed by the commissioners, and on 11 December the remodelled Christ's General Court appointed nineteen more. Only two of the hospital's employees were dismissed – the girls' school mistress, and the master of a school administered by the hospital at Ware in Hertfordshire.[49] At Bridewell, where Sir William Turner, a devout churchman, was president, the only major casualty was the hospital's treasurer.[50]

The hospital least touched by these events was St Bartholomew's. During the Civil War St Bartholomew's apparently acquired a reputation as a stronghold of Anglican royalism, and in the early 1680s its Court of Governors was composed almost entirely of Tories.[51] In November 1682 the governors anticipated a later measure by the commissioners, when they ordered 'That noe person or persons whatsoever that shall dissent from the Church of England or are disaffected with the Government as is now established by law shall serve this Hospitall with any Comoditties'.[52] With such fervent loyalty among the governors there was little for the commissioners to do, and hospital affairs after November 1683 were conducted much as before.

In February 1685 the Catholic James II succeeded to the throne. For the first year of his reign the Anglican *status quo* was maintained, but by early 1686 the King had made it clear that he wished to introduce toleration and civil equality for his co-religionists. When his Tory allies refused to accept such a policy, James began to co-operate with his erstwhile enemies, the Whigs and Nonconformists. Thus from late 1686 it was the Tories who were to find themselves under attack from royal power.

The first hospital to feel the effects of King James's policies was staunchly Tory St Bartholomew's, whose governors now faced a far greater degree of intervention in their affairs. Although power to appoint governors and staff lay with the commissioners, it is clear that prior to 1687 they only confirmed selections presented to them by the Court of Governors. However, in March 1687 the commissioners appointed an officer without reference to the governors.[53] Three months later the governors were informed that it was 'his Majesties pleasure' that his personal druggist, a certain Staines, be appointed the hospital druggist. The governors were disgruntled; though they 'frankly complied' with the King's command, they warned Staines to 'serve the house with as good drugs and att as reasonable price as any other person, hath, or will do'.[54] In November, when the King appointed Timothy Sutton assistant surgeon, the governors' unhappiness was even more evident. Most unusually, they pointedly warned Sutton 'to be carefull in the Busienesse that shalbe assigned him'.[55]

The governors could do little to oppose the King's orders, but they responded to his religious policies by reasserting St Bartholomew's traditional Anglicanism. In April 1686, when the vicar of the hospital parish of St Bartholomew the Less asked the governors to provide a new surplice, he was told to go to the churchwardens; a year later a surplice was 'appointed to be provided at the charge of this house'.[56] In October 1685 the parishioners of Christ Church, Newgate Street, the presentation to which lay with the hospital, asked the governors to contribute to the pewing of the church, only to receive the brusque reply that 'it did not concerne this Hospitall neither was the house in a condition to answer this request'.[57] In June 1687, shortly after James had officially granted toleration to Catholics and dissenters, the governors ordered the construction of a new altar for Christ Church at the cost of £100 to the hospital.[58] This reassertion of Anglican values was also reflected in the governors' decision in January 1688 to introduce compulsory daily prayers for the patients.[59]

By that time the King had further intervened in the affairs of the royal hospitals. In October 1687 James removed the recalcitrant Tories from the Court of Alderman.[60] Among these were the presidents of Bridewell, Christ's, and St Bartholomew's. They were now dismissed from their presidencies by the hospital commissioners, and replaced by supporters of the King.[61] The presidents were the sole victims of the purge, for there were no mass removals of governors and staff as in 1683. However, at Christ's Hospital some of the Whig governors ejected in 1683 had been restored in March 1687, and several more were reappointed a year later.[62] At St Thomas's some of the governors removed in 1683 also appear to have been restored early in 1688.[63]

The struggle for St Thomas's 1689–92

If the King had plans for a more ambitious remodelling of the hospitals' administration, then these, like his far grander designs, were swept away by the Glorious Revolution of November 1688. A month earlier, in a forlorn effort to conciliate his opponents, James had already restored the City of London's charter, thus re-establishing the Corporation and, *inter alia*, dissolving the Commission for Hospitals.[64] On 6 November the Court of Aldermen, now restored of its members purged by King Charles in 1683 and King James in 1687, set up a committee to investigate the appointment of the hospital presidents. The governors of Christ's, Bridewell, and St Bartholomew's did not await the outcome of the committee's deliberations, and swiftly restored the Tory presidents deposed in 1687.[65]

Events at St Thomas's Hospital were far more complicated. The president, Sir William Hooker, had been the only hospital president to escape the anti-Tory purge of 1687. But he now faced the challenge of Sir John Lawrence, the Whig president deposed in 1683. The Court of Governors was still composed mostly of those appointed by the commissioners in 1683. They were likely to resist fiercely the restoration of Lawrence, for if Hooker were not the rightful president then they could hardly be the rightful governors. For his part, Lawrence could rely on the support of the surviving Whig governors ejected with him in 1683 in any attempt to overthrow the work of the commissioners. A clash was inevitable.

Lawrence forced the issue by summoning a General Court, which he hoped would recognize him as president. The Court met on 10 January 1689, and was attended both by those governors ejected by the commissioners in 1683 and those that had been appointed to replace them. Immediately 'reflections and hott debate did arise', the rival groups presumably questioning each other's legality.[66] A later report alleged that the Commission governors made 'a very great disturbance', and 'would not suffer any settlement to be made'.[67] As well as refusing to accept Sir John Lawrence as president, it would appear that the Commission governors were determined to prevent the restoration of the hospital staff deposed in 1683.

On 14 January Sir William Hooker, who had avoided the meeting thanks to a strategically timed cold, wrote a letter to the aldermanic bench outlining his position on these events.[68] He regretted the altercations between the rival groups of governors, 'it being not the way to heale a Nation'. However, Hooker insisted that Sir John Lawrence could only be restored by a direct order from the aldermen. His only personal desire was that the Court of Aldermen 'take such a measure and way of settling this businesse, as that it may take away all animosities'. To this end Hooker was willing to give up the presidency. But this was only on the proviso that Lawrence 'will not insist upon any matter whereby others may suffer'; by this he meant any attempt to eject the staff appointed by the commissioners in 1683.

There was never any direct order restoring Lawrence as president, but the Court of Aldermen seem to have accepted him as such. Sir John's initial aim was to restore the hospital staff dismissed in 1683. Unable to call a General Court of Governors because of the presence of the Commission governors, Lawrence decided to work through the aldermanic bench where the Whigs were gaining the ascendancy. On 24 January the aldermen ordered the reinstatement of all ejected officers, probably on the grounds that they were legally restored by virtue of the restitution of the City charter.[69] Some of the existing hospital staff who were to be displaced by the order resisted the restoration of the former officers. This resistance was led by John Turner, who had been appointed hospital chaplain by the commissioners in 1683. In the course of 1689 he launched into a series of unavailing appeals to the aldermen to revoke their January order.[70] Finally, in the early summer of 1690 he joined forces with Dr William Briggs, the recently deposed hospital physician, in a petition to King William and Queen Mary. Their petition was referred to Lord Chief Justice Holt who settled matters by judging against Turner and Briggs in December 1690.[71]

By 1690, thanks to the Court of Aldermen, St Thomas's had been cleared of the officers appointed by the commissioners in November 1683, and those purged at that time had been restored. However, Sir John Lawrence and his supporters among the governors had not fully regained control of the hospital and its patronage. The governors appointed by the commissioners were still in the majority, and it was effectively impossible for the president to call a General Court. During this period the hospital was administered by the Grand Committee, the body of governors which normally ran affairs between Courts. Composed of governors from the rival groups, the Committee had kept St Thomas's functioning, but no binding decisions could be made without the approval of a General Court.[72] It was thus imperative for Lawrence to remove the Commission governors if he were to regain control of the hospital and its patronage.

The first moves were made in the summer of 1690. On 1 July Lawrence gained the approval of the aldermen for the appointment of fifty-nine new governors.[73] I have identified the probable political affiliation of thirty of these men: one was a Tory; two were Tories by 1700, but were political waverers in 1690; twenty-seven were Whigs.[74] Among these twenty-seven were many of the leading names of London Whiggery. Eleven of them were aldermen, virtually the entire Whig component of the aldermanic bench. Ten of the twenty-seven had had action taken against them during Monmouth's rebellion.[75] No fewer than fourteen of the twenty-five men identified by G.S. De Krey as the leaders of the London Whigs in 1690 can be found among these twenty-seven governors.[76] On the basis of such evidence there can be little doubt that most of the twenty-nine new governors whose political allegiance has proved unidentifiable were Whig in their sympathies.

His support among the governors powerfully reinforced, Lawrence was ready to take direct action against the Commission governors. The obvious method was to work through the Court of Aldermen, controlled by the Whigs since 1689.[77] Sir John had already exploited the ancient aldermanic power over the hospitals in gaining the removal of the Commission-appointed staff and the appointment of the new Whig governors; now he brought the issue of the Commission governors before the aldermen.[78] It was claimed that since January 1689 the business of the hospital had been obstructed by the Commission governors, and that the president would be unable to hold court 'until those Commission Governors were many of them laid aside'. Their original appointment had been illegal, for many were said to be 'not free of the City'. Moreover they were politically obnoxious, 'severall of them being actors in Cheife for the turning out of the ancient worthy Citizens that were Governors before the avoydance of the Charter'. In fact they had been 'the only forward men to have the Charter delivered up to the then King', and others were 'knowne to be profest Papists'. In addition the Commission governors were alleged to be indisposed to charity, being men of 'very mean estates and of a covetous mind'. It was therefore requested that the aldermen depose the Commission governors, and that in future only 'those that were Governors before the Judgement in the Quo warranto And those approved by the Court of Aldermen in July last 1690' be summoned to attend hospital courts.

On 23 October a committee of nine aldermen was established to investigate not only the St Thomas's controversy, but also the method of appointing the governors of the 'severall hospitals'. Seven of its members were governors of St Thomas's Hospital; two were Tories who had been governors since the 1670s, while five were Whigs appointed in July 1690. This left two outsiders, a Whig and a Tory, who were immediately made governors by Lawrence in an obvious bid for their support.[79]

The extension of the committee's terms of reference to the other hospitals raised the suspicions of the governors of Tory St Bartholomew's. They seem to have feared, with some justification, that it was a Whig attempt to purge all the hospitals of large numbers of Tory governors. Throughout 1691 Alderman Sir William Pritchard, president of St Bartholomew's, procrastinated in the face of repeated aldermanic commands that the hospital deliver to the committee its charter and a list of its governors. In September a compromise was at last reached; the names of the governors would be presented to the Lord Mayor, but only within the framework of the traditional and purely ceremonial St Matthew's Day Joint-Court at Christ's Hospital. Little wonder that Pritchard was thanked by the governors of St Bartholomew's for successfully 'asserting the Rights of this Hospitall'.[80]

The aldermanic committee itself was divided over the issue of the St Thomas's Commission governors. On 8 January 1691 Sir John Lawrence was informed 'that the Committee of Aldermen had a meeting last night wherein they much debated the business of our Governors but could com to no issue'. Lawrence was urged to attend the committee, for 'with your Assistance it would be carried to lay asid the Commission Governors'.[81] It appears likely that the Tory minority on the Committee was putting up a stiff defence of the Commission governors, or that some of the more moderate Whigs were wavering. It was not until 10 March that the committee reached its verdict, declaring the appointment of the Commission governors to be illegal. But the report was signed by only five of the committee's nine members, all of them Whigs.[82]

Armed with the aldermanic decision against the Commission governors, Sir John Lawrence called a General Court of St Thomas's Hospital, summoning only those governors appointed prior to the *quo warranto* or since July 1690. The Court met on 27 March 1691, the first since September 1687, and, in the opinion of Sir John and his supporters, the first legal Court since June 1683. A committee was immediately established to investigate fully the hospital's administration in the intervening eight years, but its primary purpose was to consider how many of the Commission governors 'are fitt, and propper, to be continued governors'.[83] At the next General Court on 26 May the committee presented its report, 'which being read and debated upon after some amendments was approved'. Only forty-three of the 137 Commission governors were to be retained, and few of these were to play an active part in hospital administration.[84] Lawrence and the Whigs had regained control of St Thomas's.

In only one area at St Thomas's had the events of 1683 to 1688 not yet been overturned. Three of the hospital's four surgeons had been appointed during the rule of the commissioners, although not in the original intervention of October/November 1683.[85] It seems that as they had not been appointed directly upon the forfeiture of the City's charter, it had not been possible to remove them in 1689 upon the charter's restitution. The fourth surgeon, John Browne, had in fact been appointed by the governors in June 1683, prior to the *quo warranto*. But his appointment had been due to strong royal pressure at a time when the governors were hardly in a position to resist.[86]

In May 1691 a committee of governors reported that there were 'great animosities between the Chirugeons', and that all four were guilty of a 'breach of orders and neglect of their duty to the great prejudice of the patients'.[87] There may well have been some validity in these charges; in October 1689 the Grand Committee had suspended Browne for performing 'considerable operacons' without the approval of the physician and the other surgeons,[88] while it is possible that the surgeons were quarrelling over seniority.[89] However, the issue was complicated by the political considerations. The governors alleged that the 'cheife cause' of the surgeons' misconduct was

> the methods by which they came into their places, every one of them haveing been chosen or placed either with regard to Recomendatory Letters [as in Browne's case] or by Mandamus as in the time when Governed by Commissioners, which has made some of them say often That they were not chose by the Governors and therefore were not to obey them.[90]

On 7 July the General Court decided that the surgeons' reported misbehaviour was 'a sufficient ground for the Court to proceed to a new Election of surgeons'. Fearing the worst, John Browne then appeared, and pleaded the court's favour as 'hee was chose at a General Court'. The governors, though, were set on their course; Browne and his three colleagues were summarily dismissed.[91] Sir John Lawrence and his governors must now have fondly believed that they had finally cleansed the hospital's Augean Stables: they were soon to be proved sadly mistaken.

John Browne had been Charles II's surgeon-in-ordinary, and was a passionate high Anglican.[92] In 1684 he had written *Charisma Basilicon*, a major book on touching for the king's evil, in which ceremony he played a leading part. After the Revolution he had managed to retain royal favour, and had been appointed William III's surgeon. He was not the sort of man to take dismissal lightly. Thus, within days of their dismissal, Browne and his three colleagues had petitioned the Privy Council to overturn the governors' actions.[93] The surgeons claimed that they had been ejected 'for no other reason than that they came in by Mandates'. Some of the governors, they alleged, had 'been willing to introduce their own friends', and 'formed parties', an allusion to the appointments of July 1690. Nearly 100 rightful governors had not been summoned to the court at which the surgeons had been dismissed, a reference to the deposition of the Commission governors. Even so, they claimed, some of the governors had protested against the court's proceedings, a fascinating glimpse of possible conflict between the Whig and the few remaining Tory governors. Finally the surgeons alleged that their replacements were inexperienced, and totally unqualified for their places.

The surgeons' petition was considered by the Privy Council on 17 July. At a meeting attended by only Queen Mary and Lord President Carmarthen, it was decided to summon the governors to explain their actions at the next meeting of the Council.[94] A week later, at a much fuller meeting attended by the King, the governors presented their defence. It failed to impress the Privy Council, which decided to establish a Commission of Visitation to investigate the affair.[95] Two factors probably account for the Council's decision. In the first place St Thomas's was packed with soldiers and seamen wounded during the war with France[96]; the surgeons made great play of their services to these men, and such a dramatic turnover in the surgical staff was bound to alarm the King and the Council. This was especially so if the surgeons had been dismissed on political rather than medical grounds, and this leads naturally to the second aspect of the Council's reasoning. Since 1689 King William had become increasingly suspicious of the partisanship and radicalism of his London Whig allies, viewing their vengeful attacks on the Tories as an obstruction to the efficient prosecution of the French war. In consequence the King had turned to the Tories, still further alienating the Whigs, who now had a sense of betrayal added to their other grievances.[97] As we have seen, many of London's leading Whigs were governors of St Thomas's Hospital; the Privy Council may have interpreted the dismissal of the surgeons as a further illustration of the irresponsible partisanship of the City Whigs, not to mention a breach of the spirit of the May 1690 Act for reversing the *quo warranto*.[98]

On 18 August a warrant was issued, establishing a Royal Commission to investigate all hospitals of royal foundation in the kingdom. The commissioners were to investigate 'all Crimes, Defects, Abuses, Corruptions, Irregularitys and Enormitys' in the hospitals, and given full powers to deal with them, including if necessary the removal of 'any Master, Head, Governor, Officer or Officers'.[99] Although the Commission covered all royal hospitals, its only visible target was St Thomas's.

Thus by a strange irony, having struggled so hard to regain control of the hospital, Sir John Lawrence was now faced with an almost exact repetition of the events of

October/November 1683. In September the aldermen appointed a committee composed solely of St Thomas's governors 'to consider how farre the said Commission may affect the Rights and Interests of this City'.[100] The governors of St Thomas's prepared to defend their position, arguing that the Commission was invalid, because Edward VI's letters patent had left ultimate power over hospital affairs with the Court of Governors.[101] Yet there was an undeniable air of panic at St Thomas's. Samuel Smith, one of the hospital's new surgeons, beseeched Alderman John Wildman, a leading City Whig and a St Thomas's governor, to come to the assistance of 'a usefull and Antient Body of men almost ruind by some pretended Friends, and undermining enemyes', and so 'bridle the like arbitrary and despoticke practice Creept into the hospitall'.[102] Events were soon to render Smith's hysteria needless.

The Lords Commissioners of the Great Seal at first delayed and finally refused to pass the Commission of Visitation under the Seal. In a report delivered to King William on 31 December 1691, they argued against the Commission on a variety of technical and legal grounds.[103] But their diffidence was based above all on considerations of political prudence; such a Commission they argued, was 'Unpresidented, Arbitrary, of Dangerous consequence', and indeed

> may be of as evill consequence, as the late Commission in the late Reign [of James II] for the Visitation of Magdalen Coledg in Oxford, and in all probability would bee used by ill men to rayse Feares, Jealousyes, and discontents and cause a greater Fermentation amongst the Citizens of London and parts adjacent, than that did in the universityes.[104]

This was an amazing statement. It tells us much both of the government's fears of the City Whigs in the early 1690s, and the extent to which St Thomas's was seen as one of the focal points of London Whiggery.

The warnings of the Lords Commissioners were heeded. The King referred the 'legall part' of the report to the consideration of the Crown's law officers, but no further action was taken.[105] Early in the new year John Browne appealed directly to the Marquess of Carmarthen, the Tory

Lord President of the Council, to intervene on behalf of the surgeons. In a vituperative letter, he viciously denounced the governors and staff of St Thomas's as dissenters and republicans, that same breed of men who had 'made the best of Princes [Charles I], the celebrated Martyre of their inextricable malice'.[106] Browne's most splenetic outburst was reserved for the Lords Commissioners of the Great Seal, for they had advised the King 'to stand still with his arms claspt about him, whilst his enemyes are buffetting him'.[107]

But Browne was fighting a lost cause. Although there appears to have been a minor flurry of activity in August 1692, no action on his behalf was forthcoming from the King and his ministers.[108] In that same month, upon the death of Samuel Smith, Browne applied unsuccessfully to the St Thomas's governors for the vacancy; in 1699 he was still engaged in a solitary and forlorn battle for restoration.[109]

Sir John Lawrence survived just long enough to see off the renewed threat of royal intervention in St Thomas's affairs, for he died on 26 January 1692. It is in the figure of Sir John that the vicissitudes of St Thomas's hospital between 1683 and 1692 are best encapsulated. In the early 1680s he had used the hospital's patronage to foster dissent and Whiggery in Southwark. As a result he had been ejected in 1683, together with the many of the governors and staff. From 1689 to 1691 he led the struggle to reverse the actions of Charles II's commissioners, but by his zealous and pigheaded partisanship had helped to provoke the prospect of further Crown intervention. Above all he was responsible, more than any other, for ensuring that St Thomas's Hospital remained a Whig stronghold. When the governors met to elect Lawrence's successor in February 1692, it was fitting that they should choose Sir Robert Clayton, the most magnificent figure in London Whiggery.[110]

Conclusion

The events of 1683 to 1692 had shown that the London royal hospitals could not stand aloof from wider political developments. In October 1683, when the Corporation of London was dissolved, Charles II had also felt it necessary to intervene in the administration of the hospitals. The property they owned and the revenues they controlled gave the hospitals important local influence, an influence that the King would not allow to be exploited by his enemies. A Royal Commission was established to supervise the administration of the hospitals, ensure the loyalty of their governors and further the economic war against the dissenters. At St Thomas's Hospital, where the dominant group of Whig and Nonconformist governors had long worried the government, a severe purge of governors and staff ensued. Christ's Hospital was also badly hit by the Commissioners, but Bridewell was relatively unscathed. At St Bartholomew's Hospital, whose governors were fervently loyal to the Crown, there was no need for any action. However, it was Tory St Bartholomew's which was worst affected by royal intervention in the reign of James II, although that King's purge of Tory hospital presidents in 1687 was of less consequence than the purge of 1683. The Glorious Revolution led to a reversal of King James's intervention of 1687, and at St Thomas's it also eventually resulted in the overturning of all the Commission's actions since 1683. After a hard struggle St Thomas's and its patronage were regained by the Whigs in 1691, only for William III's government, fearful of Whig radicalism, to threaten further intervention in the hospital's affairs. That threat was seen off, and St Thomas's was to remain a bastion of London Whiggery. In contrast London's other great medical hospital, St Bartholomew's, was committed even more firmly to the Tories. In 1692 the contrast between the two hospitals was no better symbolized than in the figures of their respective presidents: at St Thomas's, Sir Robert Clayton, the Whig who had led the defence of the City's charter in 1683; at St Bartholomew's, Sir William Pritchard, who as Lord Mayor in 1682-3 had been Charles II's principal ally in gaining its surrender.

Notes

1. I would like to thank Mark Goldie, John Morrill, and Roy Porter for criticizing earlier drafts of this essay. I am also grateful to those who commented upon versions of this essay, which were read to seminars in Cambridge, Exeter, and London in 1986 and 1987.

2. For example, see Sir Norman Moore, *History of St Bartholomew's Hospital*, 2 vols (C. Arthur Pearson, London, 1918); F.G. Parsons, *History of St Thomas's Hospital*, 3 vols (Methuen, London, 1933–6); E.H. Pearce, *Annals of Christ's Hospital* (Hugh Rees, London 1901); E.G. O'Donoghue, *Bridewell Hospital*, 2 vols (Bodley Head, London, 1923–9), and *The Story of Bethlem Hospital* (T. Fisher, Unwin, London, 1914).

3. Paul Slack, 'Social policy and constraints of government, 1547–58', in Jennifer Loach and Robert Titler (eds), *The Mid-Tudor Polity c. 1540–1560* (Macmillan, London, 1980), 108–13.

4. Moore, *St Bartholomew's Hospital*, vol. 2, 182–7.

5. British Library Sloane MS 2728A, fos 2–3.

6. *Calendar of State Papers Domestic*, March-December 1678, 87–8; Pepys Library MS 2,612, fo. 721. The two medical hospitals had about 250 patients each at any one time.

7. St. Bartholomew's Hospital HB 1/9, fo. 141, Pepys Library MS 2,612, fo. 723. For St Thomas's, see p. 129.

8. Greater London Records Office H1/ST/A 91/5.

9. For the general political background, see J.R. Jones, *The First Whigs* (Oxford University Press, 1961).

10. G.R. Cragg, *Puritanism in the Period of the Great Persecution 1660–88* (Cambridge University Press, 1957), 24–6; John Miller, *Popery and Politics in England 1660–88* (Cambridge University Press, 1973), 189–95.

11. D.F. Allen, 'The Crown and the Corporation of London in the exclusion crisis', unpublished PhD thesis, University of Cambridge, 1978; A.G. Smith, 'London and the Crown, 1681–5', unpublished PhD thesis, University of Wisconsin, 1967.

12. Smith, 'London and the Crown', 285–309, 336–9.

13. Corporation of London Records Office Repertory 87, fos 86, 93.

14. Greater London Records Office H1/ST/A1/6, fo. 23.

15. Parsons, *St Thomas's Hospital*, vol. 2, 102; W.G. Bell, *The Great Plague of London in 1665* (Bodley Head, London, 1924), 70, 227–8. For general biographical details, see J.R. Woodhead, *The Rulers of London 1660–89* (London and Middlesex Archaeological Society, London, 1967), 106.

16. British Library Stowe MS 186, fos 5–9.

17. Tim Harris, *London Crowds in the Reign of Charles II* (Cambridge University Press, 1987), 178.

18. Bodleian MS Tanner 140, fo. 111.

19. British Library Sloane MS 2,728A, fo. 64, is a list of the hospital governors prior to the purge of 1683. Like most of the governors' lists, it was probably drawn up during the struggle for control of the hospital after 1689. Because of this, it only listed those governors still alive in 1689–90, and contains seventy-four names. However, the names of a further twenty-eight governors of 1683, who had died by 1690, have been discovered thanks to another list

in fos 55–6 of the same MS. This list dates from 1679, with additions for 1680 and 1681. From this second list, it has been deduced that the hospital had 130 governors in 1681.

20. The principal source for identifying political allegiance is the biographical data contained in Woodhead, *Rulers of London*. The *Dictionary of National Biography* and B.D. Henning (ed.), *The House of Commons 1660–90*, 3 vols (Secker & Warburg, London, 1983) were also consulted. Where these sources failed to identify the political allegiance of a governor, I have assumed that if he attended any hospital business after the purge of October 1683, then he was probably a Tory. Conversely, if a governor attended no hospital business during the rule of the commissioners but did so after 1688, I have assumed that he was a Whig ejected in 1683. This method is certainly not foolproof, and so the total figures should be treated with some caution. It should also be noted that the nature of the sources makes it easier to identify Tories than Whigs. There will be a full discussion of biographical methods and pitfalls in the relevant chapter of my PhD thesis.

21. Bodleian MS Tanner 140, fo. 111.

22. Anthony Wood, *Athenae Oxonienses*, ed. Philip Bliss, 4 vols (London, 1813–20), vol. 4, cols 541–4.

23. William Hughes, *Magistracy and Ministry, or a Rule for the Rulers and People's due Correspondence* (1652), 13, 20.

24. Wood, *Athenae*, vol. 4, col. 542.

25. See Hughes' pamphlet, *An Endeavour for Peace Among Protestants* (1680), which urged the comprehension of dissenters within the Church of England.

26. John Turner, *A Second Representation of the Hospitaller of St Thomas Southwark's Case* (1689), 5.

27. *Calendar of State Papers Domestic* July–September 1683, 235.

28. John Turner, *An Argument in Defence of the Hospitaller of St Thomas Southwark* (1689), 19.

29. Greater London Records Office H1/ST/E29/5, fos 228–30.

30. Henning, *The House of Commons*, vol. 1, 414.

31. Bodleian MS Tanner 140, fo. 111.

32. Greater London Records Office H1/ST/E29/5 fos 231–4.

33. *Calendar of State Papers Domestic*, October 1683–April 1684, 36.

34. Op. cit. January–June 1683, 10–11.

35. Op. cit. July–September 1683, 235.

36. Op. cit. October 1683–April 1684, 36.

37. Op. cit. 44–5.

38. Op. cit. 56. The commissioners are listed in St Bartholomew's Hospital Ha 1/7, fo. 137.

39. St. Bartholomew's Hospital Ha 1/7, fos 135–7 records the proceedings of the commissioners.

40. Smith, 'London and the Crown', 266; Harris, *London Crowds*, 210.

41. Other than Lawrence and the treasurer, we only know the

identity of eight of the ejected governors, who in 1688 wrote a memorial on behalf of the displaced officers. See British Library Sloane MS 2,728A, fo. 15.

42. Lists of the Commission governors can be found in British Library Sloane MSS 2,728A, fos 74–5, and 2,728B, fo. 214. The lists each contain approximately 140 names, with all but ten or so appearing in both lists. It is unlikely that so many governors were appointed at one time, so it probably includes all the governors appointed during the rule of the commissioners.

43. British Library Sloane MS 2,728A, fo.15.

44. Greater London Records Office H1/ST/A1/6, fos 27–9.

45. Bodleian MS Tanner 140, fos 112–13. The dismissal of the 'Brewers, Bakers, Artificers and others that sold provisions to the house for the use of the poore' is mentioned in British Library Sloane MS 2,728A, fo. 15.

46. See p. 135.

47. Turner, *Second Representation*, p. 7; Turner, *A Memorial Humbly Presented to the Right Honourable The Lord Chief Justice Of the King's-Bench In Behalf of the Hospitaller and His Friends* (1690), epistle dedicatory.

48. Woodhead, *Rulers of London*, 73; *Calendar of State Papers Domestic*, October 1683–April 1684, 36.

49. Guildhall Library MS 12,806/7, fos 495–9.

50. O'Donoghue, *Bridewell*, vol. 2, 159.

51. Nellie J.M. Kerling, 'The parish of St Bartholomew the Less', in Victor Cornelius Medvei and John L. Thornton (eds), *The Royal Hospital of St Bartholomew 1123–1973* (St Bartholomew's Hospital, London, 1974), 40–1. British Library Sloane MS 203, fo. 130, is a list of hospital governors in about 1682. It contains the names of 221 governors, of whom seventy-eight can be identified as Tories from the biographical sources cited in note 20. A further sixty-six governors can be labelled probable Tories on the basis of continued involvement in hospital business after 1683. Only ten of the governors can be identified as Whigs.

52. St Bartholomew's Hospital Ha 1/7, fo. 126.

53. Op. cit., fo. 169.

54. Op. cit., fo. 198.

55. Op. cit., fo. 302.

56. Op. cit., fos 172, 192.

57. Op. cit., fo. 162.

58. Op. cit., fos 195–9.

59. Op. cit., fo. 307.

60. J.R. Jones, *The Revolution of 1688 in England* (Weidenfeld & Nicolson, London 1972), 164.

61. St Bartholomew's Hospital Ha 1/7, fo. 208.

62. Guildhall Library MS 12,806/7, fos 780, 837.

63. Two of the governors definitely ejected in 1683 appear after March 1688 on the register of hospital takers-in, those governors

who supervised the admission of patients. Three other governors appear on this register after March 1688, having had nothing to do with the hospital since 1683. One of these was a Presbyterian. Greater London Records Office H1/ST/A62, fo. 46.

64. Jones, *Revolution of 1688*, 263.

65. Corporation of London Records Office Repertory 94, fos 38–9; St Bartholomew's Hospital MS Ha 1/7, fo. 320; Guildhall Library MS 12,806/7, fo. 879; O'Donoghue, *Bridewell*, vol. 2, 161.

66. Corporation of London Records Office MS 58.4.

67. British Library Sloane MS 2,728A, fo. 59.

68. Corporation of London Records Office MS 58.4.

69. Corporation of London Records Office Repertory 94, fo. 91.

70. For Turner's case, see the pamphlets cited in notes 26, 28, and 47.

71. Greater London Records Office H1/ST/A1/6, fo. 36; Public Records Office PC2/74, fos 82-3.

72. Greater London Records Office H1/ST/A1/6/2, fos 76 *passim*, for the committee's proceedings in 1689–90; British Library Sloane MS 2,728A, fo. 66, for its composition.

73. Greater London Records Office H1/ST/A1/6, fo. 33; Corporation of London Records Office Repertory 95, fo. 159.

74. For the main biographical sources, see note 20.

75. See Smith 'London and the Crown', Appendix, table 7, for a list of London Whigs against whom action was taken during Monmouth's rising.

76. G.S. De Krey, 'Political radicalism in London after the Glorious Revolution', *Journal of Modern History*, 55 (1983), 585–617, at p. 594. Another two of the Whig leaders were already governors of St Thomas's.

77. G.S. De Krey, *A Fractured Society* (Oxford University Press, 1985), 16.

78. British Library Sloane MS 2,728A, fo. 59.

79. Corporation of London Records Office Repertory 95, fo. 181; British Library Sloane MS 2,728B, fo. 178.

80. Corporation of London Records Office Repertory 95, fos 208, 305, 318, 324; St Bartholomew's Hospital Ha 1/8, fos 47, 58, 60.

81. British Library Sloane MS 2,728A, fo. 61. For Lawrence's reply, see British Library Sloane MS 2,728B, fo. 120.

82. Corporation of London Records Office Repertory 95, fos 233–5; British Library Sloane MS 2,728A, fos 2–3.

83. Greater London Records Office H1/ST/A1/6, fos 33-4.

84. Op. cit. fo. 36; British Library Sloane MS 2,728A, fo. 63.

85. These three were Michael Court and Thomas Elton, senior surgeons, and William Pepper, junior surgeon.

86. Greater London Records Office H1/ST/A1/6, fo. 25.

87. Op. cit., fo. 34.

88. Greater London Records Office H1/ST/A6/2, fo. 87.

89. In 1699 two of the surgeons resorted to fisticuffs while

attending patients, because of a dispute over seniority. The senior surgeon marched in front of the others at the Easter Spittle Sermon, given for the aldermen and the hospital governors. See E.M. McInnes, *St Thomas' Hospital* (George Allen & Unwin, London, 1963), 65.

90. Greater London Records Office H1/ST/A1/6, fo. 35.

91. Op. cit., fo. 37.

92. *Dictionary of National Biography*.

93. Greater London Records Office H1/ST/A91/9.

94. Public Records Office PC2/74, fos 210–11.

95. Op. cit., fo. 213.

96. British Library Harleian MS 6,190 is a register of the seamen treated in the hospital between 1689 and 1693. These numbered 1,943.

97. For William III and the City Whigs, see De Krey, *Fractured Society*, 61–3, and 'Political radicalism', 599–600. E.L. Ellis, 'William III and the politicians', in Geoffrey Holmes (ed.), *Britain after the Glorious Revolution* (Macmillan, London, 1969), 115–34, gives a succinct account of the King's relationship with the parties.

98. For the Act for reversing the *quo warranto*, see De Krey, *Fractured Society*, 64. The Act restored all charter officers deposed at the time of the *quo warranto*, but confirmed in their places those appointed thereafter.

99. Corporation of London Records Office Misc. MS 27.14.

100. Corporation of London Records Office Repertory 95, fo. 341.

101. Greater London Records Office H1/ST/A91/7; Pepys Library MS 2612, fos 730c–e.

102. British Library Sloane MS 1,731A, fo. 56.

103. Pepys Library MS 2,612, fos 730e–i. The report also appears, together with John Browne's comments, in British Library Egerton MS 3383, fos 108–15.

104. Op. cit., fos 111-12. For the Magdalen College affair of 1687, see Jones, *Revolution of 1688*, 119–21.

105. British Library Sloane MS 2,728A, fo. 8.

106. British Library Egerton MS 3,383, fo. 108.

107. Op. cit., fo. 112.

108. Greater London Records Office H1/ST/A1/6, fo. 42.

109. Op. cit., fo. 68.

110. Op. cit., fo. 40.

6

The gift relation: philanthropy and provincial hospitals in eighteenth-century England

Roy Porter

Laurence Sterne's *A Sentimental Journey* (1760) opens with a sentimental yet disturbing vignette about giving. Solicited in Calais for alms by a mendicant monk, the hero resolves in his head not to give, on the grounds that stout Protestant Englishmen properly offer charity only to those who 'eat the bread of their own labour' not those who 'eat the bread of other people's'. Yet he longs to give – 'my heart smote me'.[1] His emotions gain the day, but with a whimsically arbitrary outcome; the hero gives the monk his snuff-box, and they part soul mates in sentimental floods of tears.

The cameo captures the equivocations of charity in Georgian England. Philanthropy was assuredly in fashion. As Henry Fielding put it in 1749, 'Charity is the very characteristic virtue at this time' – adding rather uncharitably, 'I believe we may challenge the whole world to parallel the examples we have of late given of this noble, this Christian virtue'.[2] Yet the age was also perturbed by its enigmas. If charity sprang from spontaneous feeling, what if the heart – as with the heart of Sterne's hero – was wayward in its objects? If the heart seemed to have reasons of which the reason knew nothing? Both sentimentalists and dismal economists could foresee the generous impulse opening a Pandora's box of evils. And so the Georgians preoccupied themselves with plotting the proper pathways from impulse to action, from causes to consequences, weighing good intentions alongside value for money. Springing from the heart, benevolence could all too easily be wasteful or even counterproductive, demoralizing to the recipients, and the dupe of fraud. Yet however precarious and liable to abuse, charity

149

was something that had to be dispensed, rather than dispensed with. It was after all the cardinal Christian virtue, the hallmark of humanity and, not least, of the gentleman, a generosity soaring above the sordid miserliness of the vulgar, above the institutionalized, anonymous, halfpenny dribblings of the parish poor law.[3]

Thus aware of Sterne's dilemma, the Georgians hoped to sail the course between the Scylla of sentiment and the Charybdis of calculation, fusing the heart of generosity with the brain of utility into practical outlets. One of the most popular instruments devised for this purpose – pretty much a Georgian invention – was the voluntary hospital; or, as John Aikin rather insistently called it in his *Thoughts on hospitals* (1771), the 'infirmary', thus underlining its specifically medical nature and clearly distancing it from the traditional association of 'hospital' with 'almshouse', with its connotations of poor law provision for indigent paupers.[4] In this paper I shall explore the resonances of giving, and of receiving, as they formed the order of the Georgian provincial infirmary, viewed both ethnographically, as a symbolic meaning system, and practically, as a microeconomy of exchange; and I shall do so in the light of Ferdnand Braudel's dictum 'he who gives, dominates'. This is not a study of the workings of the eighteenth-century hospital; rather an analysis of its underlying ideology.

If my rehearsal of contemporary rhetoric and rationalizations for charity to the sick sound hackneyed, echoing soporific platitudes, this is (I fear) as it ought to be, and forms an integral part of the story. For there was indeed a striking uniformity to the provincial infirmary. The early foundations in the 1730s – Winchester, Bristol, Exeter, York, etc. – were cloned again and again throughout the nation; Bath, Northampton, Worcester, Shrewsbury, and Liverpool had followed before 1750, and then in the second half of the century, Newcastle, Manchester, Gloucester, Cambridge, Salisbury, Leeds, and many others followed suit.[5] Whereas there were none in 1735, sixteen provincial voluntary hospitals existed by 1760 and thirty-eight by 1800, and all followed the same model, framed similar rules, and made identical appeals to the passions, piety, prudence, and pockets of the locals. Indeed, the first founder, the Reverend Alured Clarke, was to repeat himself when he was ecclesiastically translated from

Winchester to Exeter; and partly because his benevolent schemes were fanfared throughout the pages of the *Gentleman's Magazine,* Clarke's own rules and persuasives were taken up verbatim as blueprints across the nation.[6] For example, when the Salop Infirmary was established in 1747, the governors recommended[7]:

> For the better conducting it, the Rules and Orders drawn up for the government of *Winchester Hospital,* which are published by Dr. Alured Clarke, may be consulted; and what further information can be had from the Hospitals and Infirmaries in London, will be ready to be laid before the Subscribers for their consideration; from which helps it will be easy to draw out such a plan, as (with the blessing of God) will not fail to answer the charitable ends intended.

In points of detail the provincial infirmaries evolved differentially during the century, some sprouting fever wings, some lunatic asylums, bath-houses, electric machines, and others chapels, but the vital force remained the reciprocity of giving and receiving. For the annual infirmary sermons (perhaps delivered to Hogarthian sleeping congregations), dinners, and public collections at the assizes and the races, all helped keep the guineas jingling in. Only exceptionally did the Georgian infirmary suffer financial collapse or a major crisis of public confidence.

If infirmary publicity promoted in sermons, annual reports, and the newspapers, wears a familiar and bland face, that is precisely because it was meant to be uplifting, uncontroversial, and soothing. The hospital was there to heal the sick; but it was intended to function as a social balm as well. Throughout the Tudor and Stuart age, the springs of doing good had become polluted through sectarian theological warfare (after all, the Reformation had put the very doctrine of good works under a cloud, as a Popish deviation, and had asset-stripped much of the medieval machinery of organized charity).[8] Hence charitable action in the seventeenth century frequently had a sectarian sting in the tail. When early Stuart corporations funded town preachers, it would be seen by Laudians as a Puritan gesture against the hierarchy. The Georgians by contrast breathed a sigh of relief to discover in the infirmary a vehicle for practical benevolence which seemed proof against theological sniping (more so, for example, than smallpox inoculation), and which did not arouse the same sociopolitical anxieties as schemes to teach the poor to write, or workhouses, or model colonies abroad. It seemed Alexander Pope's pieties came true[9]:

In Faith and Hope the world will disagree,
But all mankind's concern is Charity.

Georgian opinion vested great faith in the hospital as a symbolic clasping of hands between the social ranks. Capitalism was arguably constantly widening the gulf between masters and men, and all the more so as the science of political economy replaced the ethics of the 'moral economy'. Recognizing the perils of naked class antagonisms, the propertied, as E.P. Thompson has argued, fabricated elaborate and spectacular rituals of paternalistic care – specious, but theatrically effective.[10] Thus the severe – indeed increasingly severe – justice and majesty of the law were tempered by displays of the quality of mercy; wage labour was to be softened once in a while by the harvest supper and yuletide largesse. An act of conspicuous, self-congratulatory, stage-managed *noblesse oblige* similarly underlay the infirmary. Poverty, malnutrition, premature ageing, occupational accidents, and diseases would remain the abiding realities of life for the labouring classes, as would the coercive, police functions of the poor law for ensuring a tractable labour force. But the infirmary threw a cloak of charity over the bones of poverty and naked repression.[11] It enabled the polite and propertied to pose as tender souls, as those, indeed, who were fired by a generous disdain for the flinty provisions of the poor law, the workhouse, and the bridewell. Alured Clarke at Winchester, and all those who subsequently parrotted and paraphrased him, dismissed care for the sick in the workhouse as inadequate to meet the need. Subscribers clearly sought a conspicuous monument of prestigious charity, distinct from the tainting and compulsory housekeeping of the poor law system. By patronizing voluntary hospitals as a separate additional stratum on top of the parish system, donors got the best of both worlds. In the poor law workhouse they showed the hand that disciplined; in the infirmary, the hand that gave, for in the infirmary, as Bishop Isaac Maddox, founder of the Worcester Infirmary, put it in 1743, 'the poor and the rich meet together'.[12]

The infirmary was thus in some measure to close the rift, or at least to paper over the cracks, between patricians and plebeians. But no less important a function was that of healing the wounds within the propertied classes themselves, as Maddox acknowledged in the same sermon when he referred to the 'asperities' so dangerous in civil society which would be smoothed down by 'mutual intercourse in works of charity', providing a 'friendly cement'.[13] Contemporaries were perturbed by the tensions in what Holmes and Speck have dubbed 'the divided society'.[14] In the Stuart century the governing classes had been split by struggles between Anglican, Papist, and Puritan, between Royalist and Roundhead; by the early eighteenth century these had become the dogfights of Hanoverian *versus* Jacobite, Whig *versus* Tory, established church *versus* dissenter, ministerialist *versus* the backwoods squirearchy, town *versus* country, landed *versus* moneyed wealth and trade. Opinion leaders – pre-eminently Addison and Steele in the *Spectator* – were making a concerted appeal for the ruling orders to close ranks and pull together (Mr Spectator's own club being the epitome of this, where all gentlemen of good will – Tory and Whig, ancients and moderns, landed and trading – could smoke a pipe of peace together). The hospital was promoted as precisely the engine to unify and integrate the propertied of every hue and all the gradations of rank. Thus in 1766, making an appeal for an infirmary in Leicester, William Watts claimed it would help quieten 'the vile, and most Unchristian Spirit of Party itself'.[15] But the religious hatchet also should be buried. The governors' publicity for the Devon and Exeter Infirmary thus argued that it would 'unite Good Men of all Denominations more firmly with us in a common cause',[16] and Joseph Priestley made the same point quite explicitly in his 1768 sermon on behalf of the Leeds Infirmary[17]:

> It is a recommendation of this scheme, that the benefits of it are not confined to any particular sect or party in religion; but that it is equally open to all who may stand in need of it. It has therefore a natural claim to the patronage and support of all those who make pretensions

to catholicism; and who while they profess to be *Christians* forget not that they are *men*, but bear an affectionate regard to all their brethren of mankind, however distinguished by religious epithets and denominations.

The hope that men of good will would bury their differences and remember the good Samaritan was in fact often realized. Thus at Northampton the two leading promoters of the hospital, working cheek by jowl, were the Anglican, Dr James Stonhouse, and the eminent dissenter, Philip Doddridge[18]; while at Exeter and elsewhere, both the Anglican and the dissenting clergy agreed to hold collections at their services (infirmary doors were of course to be open to all denominations).[19] And in Bristol, newspapers were pleased to report that subscribers to the infirmary included 'Persons of all Persuasions'.[20]

Of course, so entrenched and spiteful were local factions that such reconciliations through giving were not achieved everywhere. In Leicester, for example, the hospital pressure group came to be identified with Whiggish country gentlemen, who used it as a vehicle for their opposition to the oligarchic Tory corporation.[21] In fact, the Leicester corporation gave not a penny towards the founding of the infirmary, which was managed by a cabal of prominent Whigs – the Duke of Montagu, the Earl of Stamford, and Lord Wentworth. Something rather similar transpired at Exeter. There the City Hospital had been founded in 1701, as a poor law almshouse under the auspices of the corporation. A rival infirmary (i.e. medical hospital), the Devon and Exeter, was then launched in 1741, following the promptings of country gentlemen and leading clergy, especially Alured Clarke. Fierce contention flared for a few years, as is described by a contemporary surgeon, Bartholomew Parr[22]:

> The contest between the two institutions was carried on for some time with unabating rancour. The Chamber [i.e. the City Council] subscribing £100 to one annually. The country gentlemen and the Church as liberally supported the other. The surgeons supplied in the County Hospital their own dressings and the apothecaries of the town their own medicines. The Chamber published a plan of Exeter which showed their

favourite institution with a prospect of fields and a dairy maid milking a cow, while that of the County Hospital displayed the graveyard and a funeral procession.

The City Hospital eventually collapsed, and the Devon and Exeter went on to thrive.

Factions also occasionally arose within the infirmaries. Thus a movement gained ground in the 1760s at the Bristol Infirmary for remunerating a clergyman for his services.[23] In 1773 a decision was taken to salary an Anglican chaplain out of general infirmary funds, which provoked a threatened walkout by Quaker and dissenter subscribers before a compromise was reached. And at the Manchester Infirmary a secession actually occurred. As Pickstone and Butler have shown, by the late 1780s a radical and Whiggish ginger group amongst the subscribers was trying to make its presence felt, by moving that the infirmary should reach out more into the community, in particular by establishing a lying-in service. In retaliation, the leading lights of the honorary medical staff, all Tories – Charles White and his son, and Edward Hall and his son – quit the institution and set up their own rival, the St Mary's Lying-in Hospital.[24]

These instances are however exceptional. But they attest to the corrosiveness of local passions, and, in doing so, indicate the wisdom of infirmary promoters in making their institutions as accommodating and ecumenical as possible, and point to the broad success of the infirmary movement in reconciling the divided society by gift-relations.[25] For infirmaries actually became foci of civic loyalties, escaping the opprobrium of cabal warfare and the worst accusations of jobbery and nepotism which dogged the Georgian corporation and many long-standing charitable trusts.[26] Whereas in London the multiplicity of hospitals led each to acquire some colour of party loyalty – thus St Thomas's was visibly pro-Whig and dissenter, whereas Bart's was high church and Tory, as Craig Rose's preceding chapter shows – the fact that provincial towns housed only a single infirmary encouraged locals to sink their differences. Thereby the infirmary became a proud manifestation of civic spirit and achievement in an age when, with the urban economy booming, citizens could afford to give more to charity, while signalling that they were not boorishly money-mad but participants in a cosmopolitan emulative and fashionable culture of science, benevolence, and humanity, of which the infirmary was a prize bloom.[27]

The infirmary was also an expression of a wider movement for institutional renewal. Traditional institutions – Parliament, the established church, the corporations, urban, and medical – had grown hidebound, torpid, oligarchic, unable to meet the challenges of the emerging new society (for example, in expanding towns the demand for better paving, lighting, and drainage). Free associations of influential public-spirited gentlemen and citizens were coalescing to meet these needs. The voluntary hospital was just such a creation, owing little to official initiatives, local or central. Thus, for example, of the £4,000 or so subscribed to the Newcastle Infirmary, just £100 came from the corporation.[28] The infirmary thereby marks pregnant new allegiances of the polite and moneyed, brought together in the name of giving.

What form, then, did the infirmary actually take? Its key features were that it mobilized collective, not individual, charity, and giving by the living rather than through bequest. The main pattern of charity established in the middle ages, and continued thereafter, was the endowment set up by individual munificence, often perpetuating the family name, usually not taking effect till after the donor's death, and frequently with a view to settling accounts with God.[29] Most Tudor and Stuart schools and almshouses were of that kind. But hardly any Georgian infirmaries were. Guy's is the outstanding exception. But the only provincial hospital following that pattern is Addenbrooke's in Cambridge, and the fact that it was set up by private bequest surely explains its uniquely sickly early career – established in 1719, it did not open its doors till 1766.[30]

Rather, the Georgian infirmary, like most other Georgian charities, operated on a kind of joint stock principle. The donors were numerous; they were typically the living (though of course bequests were gratefully accepted as well); and they were encouraged to be long-term subscribers, giving, say, two guineas a year for life. This arrangement amounted to a clever and extremely successful instrument of charity. Ever suspicious of human nature, the Georgians recognized that the lump-sum bequest from an individual almost inevitably fell prey, after his death, to misappropriation, malversation, or embezzlement – in short, as Joseph Priestley put it,[31] 'to those abuses which we see, by lamentable experience, never fail to creep into the disposal of fixed revenues'. But the infirmary's magic formula was proof against that. Because it was by the living, giving purchased a stake in the infirmary's management and resources. A substantial donation (at the Salop Infirmary the minimum was 20 guineas) made one a manager or trustee, with a right to sit on the board of governors; a smaller offering – a couple of guineas a year was typical – bought lesser rights to nominate in- or outpatients. Thus the simple device of attaching rights, privileges, and duties to philanthropy ensured that the donor's interest lay in avoiding mismanagement of his own moneys. That this was intended as a prophylactic against corruption was clearly spelt out at the time, as by the managers at the Salop Infirmary[32]:

> To prevent any misapplication of the Charity, the government of it must be placed in the hands of the *Principal Benefactors* to it, who will of consequence be most interested in its success; and a state of the accounts must be published from time to time, for the satisfaction of all the *Contributors*.

And because the institution depended on repeated annual gifts, regular and careful housekeeping was essential. Thus the cunning of the infirmary gift-relation lay in the fact that charitable giving was not the discharging of a responsibility once and for all, but the acquisition of one. The donation of money merely opened the doors to the donation of time, expertise, and involvement.

Who then was it who gave? It was essential to the wider social purposes of the infirmary that a broad social spectrum should be encouraged to give; the more donors, the more the community consensus, and the healthier the revenues. Community pockets were tapped in an inventive variety of ways, anticipating later 'flag days'. Annual charity sermons were preached, followed by silver collections, which often raised up to £100; routine Sunday church collections were sometimes earmarked for the infirmary. Collections were held at the assizes, assemblies, and the races. Special gala concerts and charitable theatre performances were mounted – thus from the beginning the Birmingham Music Festival was a fundraiser for the General Hospital.[33] The secretary of the Worcester Infirmary personally rode round the county on special fund-raising tours. And, to reach the lower ranks, collecting boxes were padlocked to the walls of inns, and house-to-house collections were even staged.[34] Apparently gifts did indeed flow in from people not specially affluent, and hospitals commonly welcomed benefactions in kind rather than in cash. The benefaction book at Northampton includes, for example, the gift of a large knife and fork from a Mr Bignall, and a candle box and a dripping pan from another donor, both quite possibly small tradesmen or shopkeepers.[35]

But who gave the princely sums? A well-established view amongst historians of hospitals attributes the greatest generosity to the middle classes, proverbially rising. As Leader and Snell put it in their account of the Sheffield Infirmary,[36]

> The Hospitals and Infirmaries founded during the 18th century owed their birth, not so much to the great land-owners as to the prosperous manufacturers and merchants. It was a popular movement not an aristocratic one.

In a more general context this view has been supported by David Owen[37]:

> Associated philanthropy was, in a large measure, middle class in its support and Puritan in its temper . . . donors came overwhelmingly from trade and commerce rather than from the great families.

But these conclusions seem dubious for the infirmaries, particularly at the time of the great fund-raising drives needed to get them off the ground. Certainly their publicity targeted overwhelmingly on the landed orders and the upper clergy, as witness this appeal for the Norfolk and Norwich in 1744[38]:

> Let me therefore propose to your consideration, amongst other Motives to this Charitable Undertaking, the follow-ing: – THAT Norfolk is abundantly able to provide for

the Support of this Charity by Voluntary Contributions, and which therefore would be burdensome to NONE, but highly beneficial to MANY: – THAT we have several Noble Families and Gentlemen of large Estates and Influence, who would, as we may justly hope, be filled with a charming Emulation to deserve the Regards of their County by a distinguishing Benevolence on this occasion; whose skill is to direct, – whose Bounty to feed, – whose Example to dignifie and recommend this much-wanted Charity, all incourage us to hope for the happiest success.

The landed classes were indeed prominent in all the stages of seeding the infirmaries. Thus the foundation meeting of the Gloucester General Infirmary in 1754 was attended, so the newspapers reported, by 'the nobility, gentry and clergy of the county'.[39] The composition of the steering committee for the Norfolk and Norwich Hospital in 1770 consisted entirely of the landed and the higher clergy, i.e.

the Earl of Rosebery, the Earl of Albemarle, the Earl of Oxford, the Earl of Buckingham, Viscount Townshend, Lord Walpole, the Bishop of Norwich, Sir Edward Astley, Bart., Thomas de Grey, Esqre., Edward Bacon, Esqre., and William Fellowes, Esqre.[40]

Similarly, the list of governors of the Nottingham General Hospital for 1782 was headed by[41]:

The Most Noble Henry Fines Pelham Clinton, Duke of Newcastle, Lord Lieutenant of the County.
The Most Noble William Henry Cavendish Bentinck, Duke of Portland.
His Grace the Lord Archbishop of York.
The Right Honourable Henry, Lord Middleton.
Sir George Saville, Bart.,

and so forth. And Sir Francis Hill's verdict on the Lincoln County Hospital is that[42]

apart from the mayor and aldermen, who were governors *ex officio*, the hospital was wholly in the hands of the gentry and clergy. An annual sermon was preached in aid of it at the cathedral, at which ladies or gentlemen solicited contributions, and an annual charitable assembly was held for it in race week.

Not surprisingly, then, the big money came from the grandees. Take the Salisbury Infirmary, an institution which probably would not have been founded at all without a handsome aristocratic donation. When Lord Feaversham died in 1763, he bequeathed £500 'to the first infirmary that should be established in the County of Wilts, within five years of his decease'.[43] Acting on this spur, the city corporation immediately wrote to Lord Pembroke, Lord Radnor, and the Bishop of Salisbury, to get plans moving. Similarly, at the founding of the Nottingham General Hospital, the Hon. Henry Cavendish gave, anonymously, a staggering £6,337; the Duke of Newcastle gave £300, as did the Duke of Portland; whereas the largest local employer, the opulent mill-owner Richard Arkwright, gave £200.[44] Likewise when the Cornwall Infirmary was floated in 1799, the Prince of Wales gave £500, the Duke of Leeds and the Earl of Mount Edgecombe both £200, but none of the local tin and copper mining companies – surely the largest beneficiaries of the institution – gave more than 50 guineas.[45]

Why was this? It is partly because the grandees in general had more to give. It is importantly also because the infirmary movement, though building in town centres, was, both in inspiration and in actuality, very much a 'county' movement, galvanizing the local community at large and commonly involving the quite specific provision that the infirmary was not to be restricted to the sick poor resident in the home parish or town, but was to fling its doors wide open to the sick from everywhere – a 'generous' gesture of great benefit to the county. Thus the very masthead of the Sheffield General Infirmary stated that it was 'For the Reception of Sick and Lame Poor of any County'.[46] Indeed, a large proportion of the infirmaries either included the name of their county in their title – the Devon and Exeter Infirmary, the Norfolk and Norwich Hospital, the Salop Infirmary, the Durham County, the Lincoln County – or were known as 'general' hospitals (e.g. the Leeds General, the Sheffield General), the word 'general' signalling that the institution was not restricted, as were the poor law medical services, to labourers with a settlement in the home parish. In the voluntary infirmary the passport securing entry was not the parish settlement but the admission letter of the subscriber.

Moreover, the conspicuous show of *noblesse oblige* stemming from giving and serving was a highly effective means of asserting grandee cultural hegemony. David Cannadine has rightly stressed the eagerness of the Victorian aristocracy to serve as patrons of multitudes of good causes and local voluntary associations; as their economic and political grip on the nation slowly relaxed, cultural dominion came to count for more.[47] But in doing so, they were only sitting in seats already warmed by their grandfathers. The Duke of Portland was one of the founding fathers of the Nottingham General Hospital. In 1944 the Duke of Portland was still the president of what was still the voluntary hospital.

The landed classes were thus prominent patrons of the infirmaries. The Anglican clergy likewise sought to seal the bond between healing and holiness, by playing an active role. Several infirmaries owed their existence to clerical enthusiasm; both the Winchester and the Devon and Exeter arose largely through the energies of Alured Clarke, while Bishop Maddox founded the Worcester; and it is noteworthy how many cathedral cities got their infirmary in the first wave of foundations. Worcester, Hereford, Exeter, Salisbury, Winchester, all built their hospitals long before big, prosperous mercantile Hull, which had to wait until 1782, or Sheffield, which had no hospital till 1797. By contrast, the medical professions were perhaps less conspicuous in the launching of infirmaries than one might have supposed, confirming the impression that hospitals sprang more from a lay desire rooted in the community to generate appropriate charity than from strict evaluations of overwhelming medical need or even from the professional ambitions of the practitioners. Rather few infirmaries owed their origin to the campaigning zeal of practitioners (the Birmingham General, promoted by Dr Ash, is one exception).[48] But once an infirmary was launched, the medical staff took their place alongside the donors, wedded to charity not profit. It was the universal practice that the physicians and surgeons should be honorary, giving their services freely (though commonly they received a token honorarium). Infirmary rules often spelt this out: 'No fee or reward of the least kind shall be given to any person belonging to the hospital on any occasion' commanded one of the by-laws of the Devon and Exeter.[49] That the upper echelons of the medical staff should have been eager to serve *gratis* is no surprise. For, on the one hand, as Holmes and Loudon have argued, by the mid-eighteenth century, provincial practitioners were far more prosperous than ever; they could afford a generous philanthropic gesture.[50] While on the other, their 'gentlemanly' status in the community was still, however, somewhat less than assured, and they were in danger of being looked upon as a class of superior tradesmen; in such circumstances, an honorary appointment to a hospital would help elevate a practitioner into the genteel bracket as well as affording him close contact with his betters and the prospect of new lucrative high-class custom from the subscribers.

Having discussed who gave, I turn to the question of why they gave. The professed motives were many, varied, and overlapping. Everyone who argued the cause of charity stressed the pole star of duty – duty to God, duty to humanity. As the Revd Isaac Maddox put it in 1743, neatly dovetailing both: 'It is a *Christian* duty no less than a *social obligation of citizenship* to relieve the distress wrought by sickness and poverty.'[51] In the classical mode of Enlightenment utilitarian piety, it was also suggested that giving today was in fact a form of investment for the hereafter. Confirming this, one of the favourite texts used for hospital sermons was Psalm xli, 1, 'Blessed is the man that provideth for the sick and needy, the Lord shall deliver him in the time of trouble', a sentiment endorsed by Bishop Edmund Gibson, who preached in 1716 that 'whatever is laid out in Charity, God accounts an Offering and a Loan to himself: and accordingly he engaged to repay it'.[52] 'These poor people', Bishop Maddox assured his congregation, 'cannot recompense you; but you *will be recompensed at the resurrection of the just*'.[53]

But if charity was a duty, it was also a pleasure. The egotistical joys of giving were not denied or found embarrassing by the Georgians. Individually they liked to savour what the *Gentleman's Magazine* in 1732 called 'the most lasting, valuable and exquisite pleasure' of charity.[54] And collectively they plumed themselves that in giving so unstintingly they thereby proved themselves more civilized, sensitive, and tender, than their forebears or, doubtless, their inferiors. As the Annual Report of the Leeds Infirmary expressed it in 1784, the generosity of donors proved that 'the charity of Mankind . . . has been progressive, and reflects peculiar Lustre on the present Period'.[55] Joseph Priestley argued that in giving freely we 'reap all the advantages of the real refinements and true polish of the present age',[56] and, in a similar vein, William Watts urged his Leicester citizens, 'we are called to be charitable in an age, and nation, and instance, in which Charity abounds', in acts of benevolence in which 'public and private good are most intimately mixed'.[57]

Duty and pleasure, but also prudence. As the future Archbishop Secker – himself trained as a doctor – put that trinity: 'Religion, humanity, common Prudence, loudly require us to rescue' the sick poor.[58] The appeal to give from reasons of mercantilist self-interest was compelling. The sick poor could not afford medical treatment, or, as Bishop Maddox stressed, at best they went to quacks who were likely to disable them permanently. But they were the nation's workforce. If kept from work through disease or injury, the loss of their labour represented a direct debit to the community, with the risk of further charges if they and their families fell on to the parish. It was false economy not to help restore them to labour as speedily as possible. Thus, as Priestley phrased it, in the light of these arguments, the infirmary was 'the cheapest of all charities, the most great good being done with the least expense'.[59] The economics of the matter seemed decisive; infirmary treasurers calculated that the average cost of an inpatient amounted to about £3 12s. (these figures are from the Northampton Infirmary),[60] whereas at the beginning of the century the Quaker philanthropist John Bellers had calculated that the death of a labouring man, capable of bearing children, represented a capital loss to the community of some £200.[61]

Moreover, giving to the hospital meant saving in an additional way, for the hospital was represented as highly efficient on account of economies of scale. More of the sick poor could receive treatment there for less outlay, as compared with outdoor relief or one-off parish action. This persuasive argument runs like a watermark through the propaganda of the voluntary hospitals. Thus, noting that the poor, as much as we are apt to overlook them, are a very necessary and useful Part of the Community, nor ought it to be forgotten that to the Sweat of their Brows, and to the labour of their Hands, it is owing, that the Rich enjoy the Accommodation of Ease and Pleasure

the managers of the Nottingham General Hospital went on to argue how economically they could be relieved in hospitals[62]:

It has been laid down as Matter of Fact, confirmed by Experience, that distressed Objects are taken care of in Infirmaries, for a tenth Part of what must necessarily be spent for them at their own Habitations: so that the same Contributions which if disposed of separately, and in a private Manner would barely be sufficient for the Relief of Forty or Fifty Persons, when collected together and providently Managed, will answer the Distress of three or four hundred. And what is still more, supposing this Collection to be doubled, it will then extend to the Relief not of twice only, but of three Times the Number. For the larger the Contribution is upon the whole, the more is the Expense of each Patient abated.

Though all this had been said long before and more briefly by the patriarch of the movement, Alured Clarke: 'For a thousand persons will be relieved here at a less expense, than would be required for an hundred in the ordinary way of giving Alms.'[63]

Charity must come from the heart. But, the Georgian *Homo economicus* never tired of reminding himself, erratic, impulsive, blind benevolence would do more harm than good. Give thoughtlessly, warned Joseph Priestley, and[64]

with the best intention in the world, you may be doing nothing better than encouraging idleness, profligacy and imposture: but in the cases for which this infirmary is provided, there can be no imposition, and avarice has none of its usual paltry excuses to avail itself of.

There is no denying, as Lewis and Williams stressed,[65] that personal, *ad hominem* charity flourished in Hanoverian times. Yet as Sterne's *Sentimental Journey* suggests, there was also a rising horror against personal mendicancy, no sympathy for the old Popish image of the holy beggar, and a great terror of being duped by imposters (newspapers often carried warning stories of fraudulent beggars at large). These fears were crystallized by Bishop Maddox[66]:

> The more difficult it is to distinguish real from pretended objects of charity; and the greater inconveniencies arise from encouraging laziness and debauchery, under the appearance of distress, the more requisite it is to employ the strictest caution, that the clamorous and unworthy may not eat the bread of the poor; no idleness and imposture riot in that relief, which is justly due to actual want and sickness.

The great virtue of the hospital, by contrast, was that it institutionalized an effective, double-sifting procedure, to ensure that charity was properly dispensed, and thus was neither demoralizing nor wasteful, but rather expended on worthy objects for tangible benefits. For on the one hand there was a medical screening process, which barred patients suffering from chronic, terminal, or infectious conditions, for which the hospital could do nothing. As the Salop Infirmary rules put it[67]:

> that no woman big with child, no child under seven years of age (except in extraordinary cases such as Fractures, Stone or where Couching, Trepanning or Amputation are necessary), no persons disordered in their senses, suspected to have the small-pox or other infectious distempers, having habitual Ulcers, Cancers not admitting of Operation, epileptic and convulsive Fits, consumptive Coughs and Consumptions, or Dropsies in their last stages, in a dying condition, or judged incurable, be admitted as In-patients.

An embargo which sometimes had seemingly heartless consequences – 'Margaret Barnfield rejected as a patient being in a dying condition with dropsy and Gutta Serena'[68] – but which was designed to maximize bed-room for conditions which could profitably be treated – scurvy, abscesses, burns, skin complaints, leg ulcers, rheumatism, broken limbs, and the like.

And, on the other hand, there was the personal test. Patients were expected to be known to, and scrutinized by, the subscriber nominating them, to ensure that they indeed fell within the intended clientele, i.e. the labouring poor, being neither frauds, nor those who could afford to pay for their own treatment (for that would be taking bread out of the mouths of the physicians), nor the domestic servants of gentlemen who ought to foot the bill themselves (though rules against admitting the personal servants of subscribers tended to become relaxed in the course of time).

Ensuring strict propriety of admission was a constant headache. As the governors of the Norfolk and Norwich Hospital complained in 1788[69]:

> It is earnestly requested that every gentleman would inform himself of the circumstances of the person he recommends, as several have been admitted into the Hospital, of ability, it is believed, to have paid for their cure; whilst others have endeavoured to get admission whose circumstances have been known to be good; and some have made pecuniary offers to the Faculty for their attendance and skill, provided they would not oppose their admission in the Hospital. The injury the Charity must sustain if attempts of this sort are not speedily crushed, is too obvious to be insisted on, not to mention the injustice of breaking in upon the private practice and emoluments of many gentlemen in the profession of Physic and Surgery in the country.

Nevertheless the principle of individual charity, filtered through appropriate tests, absolutely matched the mood of the times. For the personal touch was vital, since, as Priestley told potential subscribers, the nominated patients 'will be your neighbours and acquaintances, in whose afflictions you will have previously sympathized and in whose relief you can heartily rejoice . . . you soon see the effect of your benevolence'.[70]

What, then, were the sick to do in return for being on the receiving end of the gift relation? How were they to perform 'gratitude'? First, patients were to be obedient and docile. Every hospital had its elaborate decalogue of house rules. At the Salop Infirmary two lists were posted on the walls, '*What*

The Patient May Expect' and '*What The Charity Requires*', the latter far longer and including bans on cursing, gambling, smoking, going out without leave, or smuggling in hard liquor, and an absolute prohibition upon the mingling of male and female patients.[71] Patients could expect little say in their treatment. In his pioneering *Medical Ethics*, Thomas Percival explained that the sick poor in hospitals were not entitled to the same privileges as paying patients in the outside world, such as the right to choose their own physician.[72] And obstreperous patients clearly got short shrift, as this example from the Newcastle Infirmary suggests[73]:

> In May, 1754, a complaint as to the meat and beer was judged to be unfounded. The complaining patients were severely reprimanded, and ordered to have toast and water for a week.

Second, patients were expected to do their share in the domestic running of the hospital, so far as was compatible with their condition. For example, a resolution at the Leicester Infirmary in 1800 stated that 'such patients as are able, shall be employed in nursing the other patients, washing and ironing the linen', etc.[74]

Third, patients were to submit to moral and religious improvement. As a 1747 report of the Northampton Infirmary boldly states[75]:

> That the benefit of a Reformatory may as far as possible be added to those of an infirmary. The clergy of Northampton attended in their turn to visit the sick, to read prayers in the wards and to give communion at the proper times, for which purpose a Chalice and paten have been presented to the Society by an unknown benefactor and care is taken that the patients of all persuasions may be attended in the manner they desire.

To this end, another valued form of donation to the hospital were Bibles and other improving literature. The new wards at the Devon and Exeter, for example, were provided with 'three Bibles, three Common Prayer Books and three Books of the Whole Duty of Man',[76] while the Leicester Royal Infirmary took no fewer than 200 copies of Dr James

Stonhouse's *Friendly Advice to a Patient* and his *Spiritual Directions to the Uninstructed.*[77]

Lastly, patients who were relieved or who recovered were expected to make a public show of gratitude. Often the mode of this display was specified. At the Norfolk and Norwich for example the rule was[78]:

> that those patients discharged who have received important cures, be directed by the Chairman of the weekly Board to return public thanks at their respective places of worship, and that in any extraordinary cure the nature of the case, when proper, may be specified

and in a similar vein in Newcastle[79]:

> That when patients are discharged cured, they shall be strictly enjoined by the Chairman of the Committee, to return thanks to Almighty God in their respective places of worship and to the subscribers who recommended them.

As suggested already, the one thing the patient was not to do was to pay for his treatment. The Northampton Infirmary specified in bold type[80]:

> **HERE ARE NOW ADMITTED THE POOR, SICK LAME** (being recommended according to the rules following) and supplied with advice, medicine, diet, washing and lodging, **AND NO MONEY GIFT OR REWARD** is taken of them or their friends on any account whatever.

For monetary payment would instantly have thrown the delicate boundaries between donor and donee into utter confusion, sullied grace with commerce, and destroyed the ritual of the gift relation upon which the whole superstructure depended.

But what did all this mean in the concrete case? Did the hospitalized sick enact their prescribed roles? What was the patient's point of view? Alas, I know of no account, in any Georgian diary, autobiography, or series of letters, recording in the first person what patients actually made of their experiences of the hospital and its philanthropic scenarios. We do, however, have the next best thing, a sixty-page poem in blank verse dramatizing such experiences, written and published, by a travelling comic actor, Joseph Wilde, who spent nine weeks in the Devon and Exeter Hospital at the beginning of the nineteenth century with some kind of unspecified leg complaint.[81] Wilde's account reads as panegyric, and it presents severe interpretative problems if we try to sift fact from stereotypes served up for public consumption. Arguably, however, Wilde's text is peculiarly revealing precisely because, as an actor, he knew just how to act out the part of the grateful recipient of philanthropy within that ritual institution.

Wilde's poem reveals many details of incidental interest which illuminate the order of the Georgian infirmary. We see him, first of all, failing to gain admission at all because of the lack of a letter of recommendation (a friendly parish clerk overcomes that problem).[82] We see the medical staff visiting the wards at fixed hours each day, attended, be it noted, by a train of medical students who are their pupils.[83] We see regular visiting hours for the sufferers' friends,[84] and we see the convalescent patients expected to clean the wards, serve food, mix medicines, and generally to minister to the needs of the bedridden and the seriously sick[85]:

Now all arise, whose ills will let them rise;
And now, the sound of crutches and of staves
Is heard through all the ward; but not to sloth,
Or listless sauntering as they uprose;
All who can wield an instrument of labour
Are busily employ'd in cleanliness;
Till the whole ward, for neatness, might compare,
And wholesome sweetness, with a monarch's palace.

But, above all, perhaps, we see – because this is what Wilde dwells upon – the emotional economy of the infirmary. This has four elements. First there is Wilde's virulent antipathy to the nursing staff, scourges and scolds, unfeeling and ungracious women who for him are the veritable embodiment of uncharitable behaviour.[86] The Devon and Exeter has a complaints procedure, and Wilde records that he registered his protests against the unfeeling, uncaring nurses before that panel[87]:

'See yon poor wretch, o'erwhelm'd by dire disease,
'And long experience of the world's indifference,
'Or worse, its cruelty – his last resource
'Is in this mansion – here he hopes to find,
'At least, alleviation of his woes:
'He knows his gen'rous patrons have provided
'One of the gentler sex, in ev'ry ward,
'To be his more immediate consolation:
'How great his disappointment and dismay,
'When, for the comfort which he hop'd to meet,
'He finds, or thinks he finds, the world all bad!
'Alike inimical to poverty!
'Then sinks life's wav'ring balance, hope expires –
'Struck to the heart – he dies in deep despair.'

He doesn't report on the outcome.

Second, Wilde praises the patient community itself for its generous fund of warmth, sympathy, and kindness ('Delightful picture of humanity').[88] He presents a glowing portrait of patient mutual support, both tangible and moral, and clearly believed the psychological boost given by shared humour and cheerfulness amongst the community had great therapeutic importance[89]:

Design'd by Providence for social bliss,
The mind of man, how wonderfully fram'd,
And fitted to enjoy this feast of nature!
If for a few short days, together pent
In the same vehicle, souls sometimes mix
With souls, till both are quite averse to part;
How much more closely drawn did Thespis feel
This mortal tie, for nine long weeks immur'd
In one apartment, not a moment absent
From these his dear companions in affliction.

Join'd in one common mis'ry, grief attracts
By stronger bonds than pleasure ever knew;
The bonds of pity! What though diff'rent far
The scenes each diff'rent man is doom'd to act;
The play of life is still the same to all,
And still the same its most essential duties;
The same its natural wants, the same its end.

Fill'd with these genuine, best of human feelings,
This wide philanthropy, embracing all,
His heart expanding rises to his lips,
And thus, in tender accents, he bespeaks them:

'My dear companions, partners in mischance,
'Brothers by nature, by afflictions friends,
'And dearer grown by mutual acts of kindness,
'Full many a day, together we have past
'In friendly intercourse, not uninstructive;
'Where I've endeavour'd, and I hope not vainly,
'To merit and to gain your approbation.
'Your kind assistance in my weak condition,
'Has often fill'd my heart with gratitude;
'And such return as I had pow'r to make
'I still have made, and made it cheerfully.
'My hands, my eyes, my thoughts have been employ'd
'To aid your correspondence with your friends,
'T' explain to them your wants and speak your love:
'I know your kind concern will follow me,
'And earnest prayers for my restoration.'

Third, Wilde was positively glowing about the physicians.
His poem presents them as punctual, tactful, attentive,
finding time for cheery words to all their sufferers, and
respectful towards the battered feelings of the sick. Dr Patch
was, he says, a 'sage', but still more, he was a man. Wilde
recalls Patch's verdict on him[90]:

'Beyond all surgery' – for pity then,
The skilful doctor for awhile was lost
In the more noble character – the man:
And though inur'd to sights of deepest woe,
The starting tear proclaim'd the feeling heart:
This tribute paid to sweet Humanity.

Clearly, to judge from Wilde's account, the medical staff
perfectly acted out their role as benevolent dispensers of
science and sympathy.

And, last, Wilde had nothing but praise for the hospital
itself ('blest institution'),[91] both in its objects and their
execution. Indeed he dedicated his work to its supporters.

There is not a hint in his lines of the reservations and second thoughts about the efficacy of infirmaries one finds expressed by John Aikin, or, somewhat later, by Thomas Beddoes.[92] For Wilde, no praise was too high for the humanity of the subscribers; and gratitude duly poured from his lips.[93]

'When I reflect on all I have beheld,
'On all I have experienc'd in this mansion,
'When I survey the heart-affecting sight,
'Which now presents itself before mine eyes,
'These, the restor'd, and you their blest restorers,
'My heart, o'erwhelm'd, becomes too full for praise;
'And praise, if I could utter, were presumptuous,
'Where thanks and blessings only should be pour'd.
'That I am thankful for the kindness shewn me,
'Witness these tears which flow not now for grief,
'Or disappointment at my loss of hope:
'My heart has long been satisfy'd in this,
''Tis not in Science to avert my fate,
'Else had I found my restoration here.'

At one level, of course, the hospital gift relation was nothing other than traditional paternalism institutionalized, the stewardship of the rich towards the poor, humanitarian but ultimately conservative. But also, in a slightly more refined sense, the voluntary hospital represented a subtle device whereby the governing classes could enjoy the advantages of treating most of the poor most of the time through the repressive policing mechanisms of the poor law, while also being able personally to lend their names to more prestigious institutions for handpicked members of the labouring classes, institutions of which they could be visibly proud, and which put an idealized gloss upon their relations with the poor. And at the same time the voluntary hospital represents the classic medium through which, by joint subscription action, the polite and propertied initiated their own act of national renewal, meeting through association, philanthropy, and culture new social challenges, which could no longer be met by the established institutions of old corruption. It is a measure of the satisfactoriness – to the donors – of all those moves that the voluntary hospital system lasted with minimal alterations for no less than two centuries.

Notes

1. Laurence Sterne, *A Sentimental Journey*, ed. by G. Petrie (Penguin Books, Harmondsworth, 1982), 31.
2. Quoted in David Owen, *English Philanthropy 1660–1960* (Cambridge, Mass., Belknap Press, 1965), 11; see also Donna Andrew, 'London charity in the eighteenth century' (PhD thesis, University of Toronto, 1977).
3. See Owen, *English Philanthropy*, note 2.
4. J. Aikin, *Thoughts on Hospitals* (London, Johnson, 1771).
5. See J. Woodward, *To Do the Sick No Harm: A Study of the British Voluntary Hospital System to 1875* (London, Routledge & Kegan Paul, 1974); F.N.L. Poynter (ed.), *The Evolution of Hospitals in Britain* (London, Pitman, 1968); S.G. Cherry, 'The role of the English provincial hospitals in the 18th and 19th centuries' (PhD thesis, University of East Anglia, 1977); W.H. McMenemey, 'The hospital movement of the eighteenth century and its development', in Poynter, *The Evolution of Hospitals in Britain*, 43–72. Note that the present essay confines itself to English provincial hospitals. Nothing is said about either London or Scotland. Nor is it intended to be a general survey of the functions fulfilled by the voluntary hospital.
6. Quoted in Owen, *English Philanthropy*, 14. See also Alured Clarke, *A Sermon preached in the Cathedral Church of Winchester before the Governors of the County Hospital at the opening on October 18th 1736*, Winchester, and *A Sermon preached before the Trustees of the Charity Schools at the Cathedral Church of Exeter on 13th October 1741*, Exeter.
7. H. Bevan, *Records of the Salop Infirmary* (Shrewsbury, by order of the Board of Directors, 1847), 6.
8. R.M. Clay, *The Medieval Hospitals of England* (London, Methuen, 1909).
9. Alexander Pope, *Essay on Man*, epistle III.
10. E.P. Thompson, *Whigs and Hunters* (London, Allen Lane, 1957); D. Hay, P. Linebaugh and E.P. Thompson (eds) *Albion's Fatal Tree* (London, Allen Lane, 1975).
11. Betsy Rodgers, *Cloak of Charity. Studies in Eighteenth Century Philanthropy* (London, Methuen, 1949).
12. I. Maddox, *The Duty and Advantages of Encouraging Public Infirmaries*, 3rd edn (London, J. Brotherton, 1743), 6.
13. Maddox, *Duty and Advantages*, 17. Maddox writes:

The various apprehensions of mankind, the different opinions entertained upon points of government and policy, as well as upon subjects of a higher nature, are too often apt to inflame the passions, create animosities, and produce, at best, a cold disregard; sometimes, it is to be feared, much rage and fierceness: but this mutual intercourse in works of charity, smooths and rubs off these asperities. A joint labour of love, by uniting in some measure the views of different persons, forms a kind of friendly cement; softens the angry passions, and abates that severe and harsh opinion, which men of disagreeing sentiments and views are too ready to entertain and propagate upon the whole character of one another.

14. Geoffrey Holmes and W.A. Speck, *The Divided Society. Party Conflict in England 1694–1716* (London, Edward Arnold, 1967).

15. E.R. Frizelle and J.D. Martin, *The Leicester Royal Infirmary 1771–1971* (Leicester, Leicester No. 1 Hospital Management Committee, 1971), 26.

16. J.D. Harris, *The Royal Devon and Exeter Hospital* (Exeter, Eland, 1922),16.

17. J. Priestley, *A Sermon On Behalf of the Leeds Infirmary preached at Mill Hill Chapel* . . . (Leek, 1768), 19.

18. F.F. Waddy, *A History of Northampton General Hospital 1743 to 1948* (Northampton, Guildhall Press, 1974). See also Philip Doddridge, 'Compassion to the sick recommended and urged', in Job Orton (ed.), *The Works of Philip Doddridge, D.D.*, vol. iv (London, 1804).

19. J.D. Harris, *The Royal Devon and Exeter Hospital*, 13.

20. G. Munro-Smith, *A History of the Bristol Royal Infirmary* (Bristol and London, Arrowsmith, 1917). See also Jonathan Barry, 'The cultural life of Bristol, 1640–1775' (DPhil thesis, University of Oxford, 1985).

21. Frizelle and Martin, *The Leicester Royal Infirmary*, 27.

22. P.M.G. Russell, *A History of the Exeter Hospitals, 1170–1948* (Exeter, Exeter Medical Post-Graduate Institute, 1976).

23. Munro-Smith, *Bristol Royal Infirmary*, 37.

24. J.V. Pickstone and S.V.F. Butler, 'The politics of medicine in Manchester, 1788–1792: hospital reform and public health services in the early industrial city', *Medical History*, 28 (1984), 227–49; W. Brockbank, *Portrait of a Hospital 1752–1948* (London, Heinemann, 1952); John V. Pickstone, *Medicine and Industrial Society. A History of Hospital Development in Manchester and its Region, 1752–1946* (Manchester, Manchester University Press, 1985), 10ff., and, for nineteenth-century charities, 42–62.

25. For conceptual background see R.H. Titmuss, *The Gift Relationship* (London, George Allen & Unwin, 1970).

26. See W.F. Bynum, 'Health, disease and medical care', in G.S. Rousseau and Roy Porter (eds), *The Ferment of Knowledge* (Cambridge, Cambridge University Press, 1980), 211–54.

27. For discussion of that culture see P.J. Corfield, *The Impact of English Towns, 1700–1800* (Oxford, Oxford University Press, 1982).

28. See G.H. Hume, *The History of the Newcastle Infirmary* (Newcastle-upon-Tyne, Andrew Reid & Co., 1906).

29. Carole Rawcliffe, 'The hospitals of later medieval London', *Medical History*, 28 (1984), 1–21.

30. Sir Humphry Rolleston, *The Cambridge Medical School* (Cambridge, Cambridge University Press, 1932).

31. Priestley, *A Sermon*, 11.

32. Bevan, *Salop Infirmary*, 6.

33. J. Money, *Experience and Identity. Birmingham and the West Midlands 1760–1800* (Manchester, Manchester University Press, 1977), 84; see also Frizelle and Martin, *Leicester Royal Infirmary*, 74–5.

34. J. Latimer, *The Annals of Bristol in the Eighteenth Century* (reprinted, Bath, Kingsmead Reprints, 1970), ii, 318.

35. Waddy, *Northampton General Hospital*, 6.

36. J.D. Leader and S. Snell, *Sheffield Royal Infirmary, 1797–1897* (Sheffield, Sheffield Infirmary, 1897), 6.

37. Owen, *English Philanthropy*, 12–13.

38. Sir P. Eade, *The Norfolk and Norwich Hospital 1779–1900* (London, Jarrold, 1900), 17. See also E. Copeman, *Brief History of the Norfolk and Norwich Hospital* (Norwich, 1856).

39. G. Whitcombe, *The General Infirmary at Gloucester* (Gloucester, John Bellows, 1903), 9.

40. Eade, *Norfolk and Norwich Hospital*, 36.

41. F.H. Jacob, *A History of the General Hospital near Nottingham* (Bristol and London, Wright, 1951), 16. For the same at Northampton, see Waddy, *Northampton General Hospital*, 5.

42. Sir F. Hill, *Georgian Lincoln* (Cambridge, Cambridge University Press, 1966), 71. See also T. Sympson, *A Short Account of the Old and of the New Lincoln County Hospitals* (London, J. Williamson, 1878). The genteel nature of such hospitals is emphasized in Charles Webster, 'The crisis of the hospitals during the industrial revolution', in E. Forbes (ed.), *Human Implications of Scientific Advance* (Edinburgh, Edinburgh University Press, 1978), 214–23.

43. Salisbury General Hospital, *Salisbury 200 – The Bicentenary of Salisbury Infirmary, 1766-1966* (Salisbury, Salisbury General Hospital, 1967), 15.

44. Jacob, *Nottingham General Hospital*, 25.

45. C.T. Andrews, *The First Cornish Hospital* (Truro, the author, 1975).

46. Leader and Snell, *Sheffield Royal Infirmary*, 12; for the parallel at Nottingham, see Jacob, *Nottingham General Hospital*, title page.

47. David Cannadine, *Lords and Landlords. The Aristocracy and the Towns, 1774–1967* (Leicester, Leicester University Press, 1980).

48. See Money, *Experience and Identity*; see also C. Pye, *A Brief Account of the General Hospital near Birmingham* (Birmingham, 1820); J.M. Hall and V.C. Harral, *The General Hospital, Birmingham* (Birmingham, University of Birmingham Hospital, 1967). For Yorkshire see H.H. Marland, *Medicine and Society in Wakefield and Huddersfield 1780–1870* (Cambridge, Cambridge University Press, 1987).

49. Russell, *Exeter Hospitals*, 26.

50. Geoffrey Holmes, *Augustan England, Professions, State and Society*

1680–1730 (London, George Allen & Unwin, 1982); I. Loudon, 'The nature of provincial medical practice in eighteenth century England', *Medical History*, 29 (1985), 1–32.

51. W.H. McMenemey, *A History of the Worcester Royal Infirmary* (Worcester and London, Press Alliances, 1947), 20.

52. Rodgers, *Cloak of Charity*, 7.

53. Maddox, *Duty and Advantages*, 24.

54. Rodgers, *Cloak of Charity*, 8; Owen, *English Philanthropy*, 14.

55. J.T. Anning, *The General Infirmary at Leeds*, vol. 1, *The First Hundred Years* (Edinburgh, E. & S. Livingstone, 1963), 1.

56. Priestley, *A Sermon*, 10.

57. Frizelle and Martin, *Leicester Royal Infirmary*, 24. Watts continued:

> Herein public and private good are most intimately combined. Herein we are called to be charitable in an age, and nation, and instance, in which Charity superabounds. These inducements therefore it is to be hoped accompanied with that inward Testimony which cannot but arise in every compassionate breast, will effectually actuate all, each according to their circumstances and degree, to prove themselves truly friends to the poor, to the county, to the kingdom, to mankind. In *this*, and every other humane, polite, charitable, and christian, regard, may the very respectable county of Leicester ever, under the divine influence, be an example and praise to this land of Liberty and social Virtue: This land of Liberty and social Virtue ever, under the divine Influence, be an example, and praise, to the whole Earth!

58. Owen, *English Philanthropy*, 38.

59. Priestley, *A Sermon*, 10.

60. Waddy, *Northampton General Hospital*, 6.

61. Owen, *English Philanthropy*, 38.

62. Jacob, *Nottingham General Hospital*, 18. Compare the same argument used by the advocates of the Leicester Infirmary:

> Whereas many sick and lame persons languish (deprived even of the due Necessaries of Life at a time when more particularly required) and too often die miserably partly for want of Accommodations and proper Medicines in their own Houses or Lodgings, and partly by the inprudent laying out of the small Pittance allowed by their Parishes and by the Ignorance or ill Management of those about them, thro' which they suffer extreamly, nay are sometimes lost. (Frizelle and Martin, *Leicester Royal Infirmary*, 33.

63. See Woodward, *To Do the Sick No Harm*, 14.

64. Priestley, *A Sermon*, 18.

65. W.S. Lewis and R.M. Williams, *Private Charity in England 1747–1757* (New Haven, Yale University Press, 1938).

66. Maddox, *Duty and Advantages*, 3.

67. W.B. Howie, 'The administration of an eighteenth century provincial hospital', *Medical History*, 5 (1961), 34–55, 50. For a European perspective on the population of eighteenth-century hospitals, see A. Imhof, 'The hospital in the eighteenth century: for whom?', *Journal of Social History*, 10 (1970), 448–70. For Scotland see Guenter Risse, *Hospital Life in Enlightenment Scotland* (Cambridge, Cambridge University Press, 1986), especially Chs 1 and 2.

68. Howie, 'Administration', 37.

69. Eade, *Norfolk and Norwich Hospital*, 56.

70. Priestley, *A Sermon*, 18.

71. Howie, 'Administration', 52.

72. T. Percival, *Medical Ethics* (Manchester, J. Jackson, 1803).

73. Hume, *Newcastle Infirmary*, 25.

74. Frizelle and Martin, *Leicester Royal Infirmary*, 58. Howie, 'Administration', records the following (53):

> In 1786 the Nurse in the Male Ward complained to the Weekly Board of Thomas Virnall, a patient in the Ward 'for refusing to give her the customary assistance in fomenting such Patients as are not able to do it for themselves.' He pled in his defence 'that his hands were so very tender that he could not bear the operation'. He was reprimanded. (*Minutes*, 17 July 1786)

75. Waddy, *Northampton General Hospital*, 9.

76. Harris, *Devon and Exeter Hospital*, 29.

77. Frizelle and Martin, *Leicester Royal Infirmary*, 60. See also J. Stonhouse, *Friendly Advice to a Patient*, 9th ed. (London, J. Rivington, 1750).

78. Eade, *Norfolk and Norwich Hospital*, 61.

79. Hume, *Newcastle Infirmary*, 11.

80. Waddy, *Northampton General Hospital*, 6.

81. Joseph Wilde, *The Hospital, a Poem in Three Books, Written in the Devon and Exeter Hospital, 1809* (Norwich, Stevenson, Matchett, and Stevenson, 1809). See W.B. Howie, 'Consumer reaction: a patient's view of hospital life in 1809', *British Medical Journal*, 3 (1973), 534–6.

82. Wilde, *The Hospital*, 6–7.

83. Op. cit., 17.

84. Op. cit., 42.

85. Op. cit., 27, 31.

86. Op. cit., 56.

87. Op. cit., 58.

88. Op. cit., 29.

89. Op. cit., 61–3.

90. Op. cit., 18.

91. Op. cit., 55.

92. John Aikin, *Thoughts on Hospitals* (London, Johnson, 1771); J.E. Stock, *Memoir of the Life of Thomas Beddoes, M.D.* (London, J. Murray, 1811), appendix 3, 'Considerations on infirmaries'.

93. Wilde, *Hospital*, 67.

III

Modern

7

An historical survey of children's hospitals[1]

Eduard Seidler

The development of the children's hospital has received systematic appraisal from neither historians of pediatrics nor historians of medicine and medical institutions. In particular, we lack any in-depth studies on the motives which have spurred both medicine and wider society to establish this distinctive institution.

This paper does not pretend to compensate in any comprehensive manner for this gap in the literature, but it does hope at least to draw attention to a number of elements peculiar to the history of the children's hospital and worthy of more detailed study. Speaking from the standpoint of a pediatrician, all too conscious of the problems plaguing the concept of the children's hospital today, my strategy here is not to construct some abstract chronology, but to attempt a critical overview of the various approaches people under different historical circumstances have adopted to the problem of the children's hospital. The question at hand cannot be formulated simply enough: What leads people to establish institutions for sick children, what form do these institutions take, and what is their function understood to be?

The child in hospital

The children's hospital has its roots in the eighteenth century's radical transformation of the old 'hospital' – home of refuge, into the '*Krankenhaus*' – institution for the care of the sick. Before the eighteenth century, it would not be correct to call any institution of the Christian social service system a

181

'hospital' as we understand the term today. It cannot be stressed enough that the setting up of homes of refuge for pilgrims, misfits, the poor, the lame – and also certain groups of children – must be understood in the context of a Christian culture dedicated to the protection of the helpless. As such, the old hospital was not, or only incidentally, concerned with special care for the ill. In principle, it was still the same institution for the poor and needy which the council fathers in Nicaea had established when, in the year 375 AD, they made it the duty of every diocese to address itself to the physical, mental, and social sufferings of its flock. This old concept of the hospital, while manifesting itself institutionally in a variety of forms over the succeeding centuries, never ceased to be strictly an organization for the care and refuge of the poor and sick; it was never conceived as an institution of medicine. It belonged, rather, to the Church, the lay sisters, and later the towns, the princes, or the state.

If we look for children in this hospital system, we find the unwanted, the abandoned, the orphaned, but hardly any truly sick children. This is not the place to involve ourselves in the complex history of foundling hospitals and orphanages, in which this hospital system certainly played a role. It will suffice at this juncture simply to note that, as long as an extremely high rate of child mortality was tolerated by society, so long as the long-term survival of every newborn child was not perceived as part of the medical profession's responsibilities, as long as the state also saw no reason to look upon child mortality as a problem with which it should concern itself, then it was left to humanitarian and charity groups to take on a child if its parents – for whatever reason – were no longer able or willing to care for it. To just what extent, then, the history of the children's hospital can be simply understood in the broad context of social history, and how far it touches on the deeper biosocial problem of human ambivalence towards the weakness and absolute dependence of the child, can here only be posed as a question.[2]

Before the eighteenth century, our knowledge of everyday life, including the everyday life of the sick or helpless child, whether at home or in a hospital, is so meagre that it is impossible to make any sort of authoritative statement. We know though, if only sketchily, that coexisting with the special foundling hospitals and orphanages, there were apparently nurseries in many general hospitals. This was especially true of the larger hospitals, such as the Hôtel-Dieu in Paris, St Bartholomew's in London, Heilig-Geist in Nürnberg, Juliusspital in Würzburg, just to mention a few. These nurseries, however, simply acted as an additional component of a complex network of social services for the poor and needy; they were not specially conceived as medical units, i.e. as special institutions for the care of sick children.

All this began to change only in the time of the European Enlightenment, when the child as a concept, as a social entity, began to take on a new significance. Briefly put, we are concerned in this period with a society which, caught in the throes of a growing sense of nationalistic sentiment, no longer looked upon the child as a poor weak wretch who might as well die as live, but which increasingly celebrated its children as the bearers of its hopes for the future; and which consequently came to see the survival and healthy development of its children as the only guarantee of its own continuing existence. The imperative of national survival, then, implied that the medical profession (working with the schoolteachers) was duty bound to help the vulnerable child raise itself to a level of physical integrity and intellectual independence sufficient to allow it ultimately to take its place in society as a responsible adult.

The change from hospital to *Krankenhaus*

In the eighteenth and early nineteenth centuries, the medical profession took it upon itself to reorganize the old hospitals in three ways. Where previously doctors had visited these institutions only occasionally as consultants, now these hospitals were increasingly used:

1 as centres for medical training;
2 as clinical laboratories for medical research – a development with especially wide-reaching consequences; and
3 finally, though rather later, as an organization of healing concerned with the welfare of the population.

All these developments were part and parcel of a more general splintering and reorganization of the old hospital of refuge and care into a conglomerate of new specialized institutions of social welfare, one of these being medical. The *Krankenhaus*, with its broad aim of admitting and healing sick persons, thus came into being, along with a wide range of other new social institutions, asylums, and homes. Under the influence of the *égalité* of the French Revolution, moreover, these new institutions aimed, at least in principle, to extend their services to every citizen.[3]

For sick children, two competing systems of care and treatment were offered, the modern-day descendants of which have remained in conflict to the present day.

1 Outpatient care, or care for the child by the medical profession which allows it to remain in its own familiar surroundings at home.
2 Inpatient care, which takes the sick child into a special institution with the aim of re-establishing its health before returning it to its family.

Three well-known historical examples will allow us to see the concrete working-out of this two-pronged system. The first *ambulatorium*, or outpatient dispensary for sick children, established in 1769 by George Armstrong in London (7 Red Lion Square), normally receives merely glancing attention from historians of pediatrics, especially since it was forced to close in 1782 for 'lack of public interest and support'.[4] Yet this institution's conceptual importance earns it a key place in the history of the children's hospital, since it established the basic idea that sick children require a type of institutionalized care distinct from that called for in the case of adults.

'To administer advice and medicines gratis to the children of the Industrious Poor, from the birth to the age of 10 or 12 years' – this was the high ideal of this new dispensary, which Armstrong saw as 'charity of the greatest consequence to the Public'.[5] Not the increase of medical knowledge, but the saving of 'a great many lives very useful to the Public' was the aim. Among an intellectual elite, keen to maintain the more mundane cogs of their comfortable society in good working order, the Armstrong dispensary was conceived as a 'nursery for labourers, tradesmen, soldiers, and sailors'. A proud figure of nearly 35,000 children – or about eight children per day – treated by Armstrong's unit between 1769 and 1781, speaks volumes for the success of the experiment:

> As persons in the lower stations of life have a more free intercourse and communication with one another, than those of a higher rank, and make their children a more frequent topic of conversation, for want of other subjects, and being also less liable to dissipation, it is natural to imagine, that by means of this charity the above mentioned instructions are now become generally known and observed by the Industrious Poor in and about London.[6]

After Armstrong's institution was forced to close its doors, one sees, both in England and on the continent, a number of further attempts – today mostly forgotten – to develop the idea of the dispensary as an ideal institutional model for the medical treatment of sick children. The Royal Infirmary for Children, founded in London in 1816 by Davis, had three departments in the city and was almost entirely devoted to the treatment of outpatients. On the other hand, in 1852 when Charles West in Great Ormond Street in London, began to realize his long-cherished wish for a real children's hospital, this was no further development of the Armstrong 'social-pediatric' dispensary, but was an expression of the larger attempt of the time to raise English institutions to the standard of scientific excellence represented by the Paris and Vienna schools of clinical pathology.[7]

Meanwhile, on the continent, Joseph Johann Mastalier's *Kinderkrankeninstitut* had emerged in 1788 as an expression of the philanthropic impulses of an enlightened Viennese absolutism, with much family resemblance to the (now-defunct) British dispensary of Armstrong.[8] In a petition to the Emperor dated 1792, the order of priority of Mastalier's concerns was clearly delineated. At the top of the list was the 'charitable act' of providing children 'with necessary aid in the simplest, swiftest manner, and involving the minimum of costs'. Ranking second was the issue of wider social benefit; it was clear that the nation as a whole would 'profit greatly' if its mothers were better informed on the rules for healthy living. Finally – and clearly of lesser significance – it was noted that the new institute would offer 'an important advantage for the medical sciences', allowing them the opportunity to make 'some useful discoveries' through 'closer observation of children's illnesses'. In ·contrast to the London experiment, Mastalier's small institution proved itself robust; out of its humble beginnings emerged, under Leopold Anton Gölis, the 'first public children's hospital' in Vienna. This institution, however, was finally completed only in 1837 by Ludwig Wilhhelm Mauthner, who had been prodded into action by the founding of the first children's hospitals in Germany and Austria.

I have chosen to focus on these two small institutions because they are illustrative of one type of child medical care which would continue to find form throughout the later history of the children's hospital. The underprivileged ('deserving poor') child represented the first object of structured pediatrics. Only much later, as we well know, would the general outpatient clinics, concerned all along with children and the poor, spawn their specialized pediatric facilities and children's clinics. Indeed, much of what is said today about 'social pediatrics' as a supposedly new dimension of child medical care, was – from prevention to after-care – clearly anticipated in these early pediatric institutions.

At this point, it is necessary to take a closer look at those two institutional 'types' with which the true children's hospital would most intimately come to identify, and whose beginnings are to be found at the Hôpital des Enfants Malades at the Rue de Sèvres in Paris.

The history of this institution, so pertinent to our problem, has unfortunately hardly been investigated. The brief official canons tell the proud story of how the decree of the 9th Floréal of the tenth year of the Revolution (29 April 1802) effected the transformation of the orphanage Maison de l'Enfant Jésus into the first children's hospital in the world.

As might be expected, the real situation was much more complex, emerging in the first instance more as an administrative and social drama than a medical one.[9] In France, since the Renaissance, since the days of François I and Vincent de Paul, it had been widely agreed that children had no business in hospitals and other institutions designed for adults. The fact that they were in fact sent to such places was repeatedly denounced as a scandal and a disgrace. Among the widely discussed reports was one from the Hôtel-Dieu, where not only in the nursery, but also in the adult wards, up to eight children were forced to share one bed – with over 90 per cent becoming prey to certain death as a result of infection. The famous, and for hospital history so important, memorial written by Jacques René Tenon in 1788 strongly argued for at least equipping the new hospitals with special wards for children under 12 years old.[10]

By setting aside 250 beds for children under 15 in a large building 'vaste, aéré et propre', the new hospital hoped to achieve three things: first, to set up a precise line of demarcation between the adults and children; second, to put itself in a position to achieve a more precise classification of the children according to illness; and third, to encourage the ethically-desirable possibility of discharging the children less 'corrumpus' than had been the case when they were mixed indiscriminately in with the adults in general hospitals.

For some time, then, we hear nothing about a children's hospital based on a medical conception, if we disregard the fact that only acutely ill children were to be admitted to the new hospital, while those with infectious diseases and the chronically ill were to be taken to the Hôpital des Vénériens or the Hôpital Saint-Louis.

The large Parisian clinics, which arose during the post-Revolutionary years, e.g. by converting large monastery buildings, aimed to provide the increasingly prestigious clinical/pathological Paris School with new scientific knowledge and facts.[11] The large number of patients and conveniently high mortality rate offered French doctors the opportunity of perfecting their clinical-anatomical localizationist approach to illness and its treatment, which had been steadily gaining adherents since the days of Morgagni. Paris became the centre of this revolution in medical methodology, with men such as Corvisart, Laënnec, Bichat, and Broussais paving the way for later workers.

The pediatric institution at Rue de Sèvres established itself in this school soon after its foundation. In fact, fundamental scientific research into children's diseases based on the new methods began here. Soon it was almost exclusively oriented towards the gaining of knowledge for medical science, with comparatively little concern for the care of the afflicted.

Pediatrics is indebted to these efforts to correlate the first complete descriptions of children's illnesses with pathological/anatomical findings. The impact of this pioneering work continues to make itself felt in nosology up to the present day. It should be said, however, that even while doctors of the time prided themselves on their advanced research methods, a basic rationale for the founding of the Hôpital des Enfants Malades, i.e. systematic separation of the children from one another according to illness, was completely forgotten. Up to the end of the century people complained of hospital epidemics; however, for the enterprising physicians these were an object of scientific interest no less than the range of primary diseases. 'One has,' the famous Tübingen clinician Carl August Wunderlich wrote home in 1841, 'ample opportunity to study especially infectious diseases, which do not die out even after all possible measures of containment are applied'.[12] Even today we have very little information about this hospital, described later by Rauchfuss as an 'excellent organisation of *traitement externe*'.[13] These words of praise can be put into perspective by noting that this outpatient treatment mentioned by Rauchfuss apparently played only a minor role in the functioning of the institution as a whole.

I have deliberately discussed the background of the founding of these institutions of child medical care in considerable detail because I believe we cannot discuss such institutions as abstract isolated historical curiosities, but must attempt to integrate them into the constitutional structure of the children's hospital as a concept. Back in the nineteenth century, Franz Seraphim Hügel had already identified the three types: the *Kinderkrankeninstitute*, the *Kinderkrankenhäuser*, and the *Kinderbewahrungsinstitute*, thereby specifying that children might either be visited at home, admitted to an institution as outpatients and given specific treatment, or taken out of their family environment into care.[14]

Up to this point, we have seen that different institutions were established to deal with all these tasks. Whereas all forms of day nurseries were seen as 'sickness/palliative institutions', the institutes for children's diseases were concerned with outpatient consultation and home visits. Over time, the children's hospital, conceived for the purpose of diagnosing and treating sick children, came to dominate these other institutions, largely as a result of its association with pediatric research. Unfortunately, it did not take long before the dangers as well as the opportunities afforded by this development made themselves felt, notably in the pernicious phenomenon which would come to be known worldwide as 'hospitalism'.

Structural elements of the children's hospital

In 1877, the German-Russian pediatrician Carl Rauchfuss presented his detailed analysis of the children's hospital in the first international *Handbuch der Kinderkrankheiten*.[15] By this time, so many individual examples of the institution had arisen internationally that he could venture to construct what, to his mind, would represent the optimal model.

> If one were simply to build children's hospitals along exactly the same construction and with the same furnishing, equipment and organization as the general hospitals, then it would not be worthwhile building them at all; it would then be advisable to recognise the appropriateness of expanding on the practice of many already established general hospitals of treating sick children in a children's ward. The requirements of a children's hospital are, however, more complicated than those of a general hospital, and these incorporated children's wards are compelled under the circumstances to do without.[16]

Rauchfuss, who here unremittingly propagated the model for an independent children's hospital, wanted to unite all elements of child care under one roof. With a capacity of ten beds and 500 outpatients per 10,000 inhabitants, he believed it would be possible to cope, providing the following structural elements were established:

1 An outpatients' department, separate from that of the inpatients. The main advantage of such a department 'is self-evident', meriting the greatest attention and interest from all involved. Rauchfuss stressed, however, that it should not be serviced by already exhausted physicians

from the inpatient department.

2 An observation or quarantine ward, connected to each of the different main wards.

3 Isolation houses serving, if possible, every conceivable form of illness, including mixed cases.

4 Play and gymnastic halls, rooms for physiotherapy, and garden areas.

Reactions to Rauchfuss's proposals instructively highlight the massive objections to which the concept of the children's hospital at this time was susceptible. The high rates of infection and mortality within these institutions had raised the question, not only among the general population but in the medical world as well, as to whether children's hospitals deserved to exist at all. A more subtle objection had been raised by Florence Nightingale, who – exploiting the full weight of her authority – had made the case that children collectively were incapable of mature analysis and assessment, and so their complaints could not be taken into consideration as a guideline for assessing the care they required. Without such a feedback from the charges, however, it would be difficult to run a hospital efficiently. These considerations led Nightingale to recommend that sick children be put alongside the adults once more, preferably in the women's wards.[17]

The main problem, though, was and remained that of infection, a fact which led Rauchfuss and his generation to envisage the future of the children's hospital exclusively as a decentralized institution dedicated to 'the perfecting of the construction, furnishing, equipment and staffing' of the isolation houses.

The isolationist trend dreamt of by Rauchfuss would in fact become the favoured trend among builders of children's hospitals, as knowledge from bacteriology helped pediatric research achieve its first publicly recognized breakthrough – the decline of child mortality. The questions raised as to the value of the children's hospital increasingly had to be weighed against the plainly growing improvements in the institution's infrastructure: the introduction of cubicles, increased decentralization, measures for antisepsis and asepsis. The growing number of scientific arguments supporting all these measures not only helped relieve the hospitals of the accusation that they were little better than houses of death, but also permitted them to admit certain classes of children which had previously been treated only as outpatients or not at all, especially infants.

When Arthur Schlossmann, one of the most famous German pediatricians of his time, opened his 'Säuglingsheim' in Dresden in 1904, he had to give it this name instead of the originally intended 'Säuglings-Heilanstalt', in order to avoid the intrigue aimed against him on the grounds of unfair competition.[18] It was his belief that an

> institute run by specialists for sick infants [should] be established, which – in a fully self-contained fashion – should fulfil the special demands of infant hygiene, have its own trained nursing staff and specially trained doctors and management and, if at all possible, not be affiliated with a large hospital, but rather with an obstetric institution in order to have access to wet nurses or breast-feeding by the mother.

Not to be withheld in this connection is the fact that other pediatricians at this time were making the case for the infant hospital in candid social Darwinistic tones. The fact that more interest had been devoted to 'worthless' idiots, deaf-mutes, and cripples than to 'preventing the demise of normal human beings' was denounced as a pernicious consequence of the 'singular confusion [produced by] the emotion of humanitarianism'. Far better if society directed its philanthropic instinct to improving its system of infant care. 'If the century just begun is to become a century for the child', wrote the Aachen paediatrician J.J.G. Rey in 1906, then the first task of pediatrics lay in infant care.[19]

Yet the idea of separate infant-care institutions was not to be realized. On the contrary, the children's hospitals strived increasingly to take advantage of this new opportunity to put their capabilities to the test, either by establishing their own infant departments or by setting up day nurseries. Having taken over responsibility for infants, the children's hospital gained a new reputation for self-centredness and aloofness, and it cannot be denied that its further development was in fact increasingly inward-looking and oriented towards its own needs. The old interest in outpatient treatment declined markedly; the outpatient stations gradually turning into selective admission departments. Special departments for convalescence, for chronically sick children, and for the incurable were established. There was hardly any children's hospital which did not work in close co-operation with one or another children's sanatorium for tuberculosis, scrofula, anaemia, or rickets; or did not have its own salt-water spa, seaside hospital, or high altitude health resort. This specialization, with its useful and its problematic consequences, led in turn to something else: the operating theatres (along with their special patients) migrated from the children's clinics to newly-established special children's departments in surgical hospitals.

When the Deutsche Gesellschaft für Kinderheilkunde offered the opportunity in Hamburg in 1928 to discuss, on an international level, the problem of the children's hospital, hardly any aspect of the new infrastructure of this institution received a mention.[20] Emil Feer emphasised merely two features as relevant compared to the general hospital: first, the establishment of specially strict measures to be taken when admitting child patients with an infectious disease, in order to prevent the infection of the other patients; and, second, the establishment of special infant-care stations, milk kitchens, and a system facilitating access to wet nurses. Otherwise, the demands raised in 1928 for separate isolation departments or department houses and for the setting up of isolation wards were the same as those of fifty years previously. The only thing that strikes one's attention in this new report is that outpatient treatment is no longer specifically mentioned as a goal of the children's hospital. A planner has to decide, said Feer, whether he prefers centralization or decentralization; he himself was in favour of a series of self-contained units operating within a system of linking corridors. Finally, Feer appealed to the likely financial backers of such an institution, declaring that, after all, a good children's hospital must be able to meet the most exacting of standards, for 'the responsibility is too great for us to undertake to run a children's hospital with inadequate means and facilities'.[21]

The home for sick children

Arthur Schlossmann, whose official task it was to report on the care of children suffering from infectious diseases, chose in the 1928 meeting to swing back and strike a surprise blow by reproving the isolated hospital and its sterile historical developments – with emphasis on both senses of the word. 'The children's hospital is dead!' he cried out. 'Long live the home for sick children!'[22] To the horror of many colleagues, he demanded, in place of independent children's hospitals, large pediatric departments in general central hospitals, which he held to represent the ideal and most economic institution for public health care. The long-bemoaned problem of infection he noted, was in the present age principally under control, and matters could only improve. Thus, all individuals under the age of 14 should, with respect to 'hygiene, finance and general medical management . . . come under the supervision of the pediatrician'. Moreover – and here Schlossmann touched on a problem he considered particularly important – 'children have no business in eye clinics, ear clinics, so-called surgical tuberculosis wards, or even skin clinics; [all such child patients] belong together in children's departments'. Schlossmann was convinced 'The best care for our patients stems from cooperation with other specialists. With the integration of the children's departments into the large general hospitals, we have the possibility of ensuring the best specialist treatment and assistance at any hour.' In those cases where the internist or surgeon on his own attempts treatment, it becomes all too easy to lose sight of the fact that the individual, not the illness, is the ultimate object of medical care.

It would take us too far afield to give a report on the extremely interesting international discussion which ensued as a result of both the above-mentioned contributions and the other lectures; one can read them in the 1928 issue of the *Monatsschrift für Kinderheilkunde*. It remains only to mention the comment made during the discussion by the famous Munich pediatrician Meinhard von Pfaundler who, with his demand for a special pediatric surgeon under one's own roof, anticipated the new trend towards super-specialization familiar to us today.

Before we finally ask whether this historical overview of the development of the children's hospital has provided any useful data for helping us cope with the problems of today and tomorrow, let us briefly cast a glance at the closing main points of discussion which were given consideration at a 1957 meeting of the Deutsche Krankenhausinstitut and the pediatricians.[23] This is quickly accomplished, as we can readily ascertain that hardly any significant new issues were raised, though a great many unimportant ones insisted on making themselves heard. The problem of infection – here Schlossmann had been proved right – was no longer associated with the classical 'children's diseases', but had instead become the stigma of care for premature infants. Fanconi saw the age of single cubicles and lobbies as at an end, and argued for the establishment of four- and six-bed rooms or even wards, where the children might feel 'very happy'.[24] He went on to say that a distinction should be made between hospitals for the chronically sick, in which 'family life should be reproduced as far as possible', and hospitals for patients with acute conditions, for whom the optimal solution was a 'self-contained high-rise building', allowing the shortest possible travelling-distance from one department to another. In addition, larger children's hospitals should be built, he thought, as it was only there that recently-developed expensive specialized equipment could properly be put to use. For the same reason, a small children's hospital could only really function efficiently in liaison with a larger general hospital. As things turned out, psychological and administrative pressures on the children's hospital have led to a situation in which social customs and living standards define the parameters within which decisions and plans are made, far more than advances in medicine.

In the same discussion of 1957, in the course of an extensive survey outlining once again general operational principles for the running of a children's hospital, Joachim Wolff and Horst Sahl expressed their desire to create a 'Lebensraum' for each patient in accordance with his or her condition, age, and illness.[25] They reasoned that the children's hospital had basically to cater to the needs of four classes of patients: 'the premature infant, the baby, the toddler, and the school-age child with internal complaints and infectious diseases'. From their analysis, they attempted to design an ideal multi-faceted sickroom which would meet the needs of the children of the different age groups, and, out of this, to organize care-groups, and finally wards. They remained convinced, however, that 'concerning the question of children's hospitals,' there 'will continue to be differing opinions'.

By this time, the old idea of the outpatient unit had been practically abandoned, even though Bessau had stressed as late as 1928 that 'outpatient clinics acting as university teaching hospitals' are 'an absolute must'. In institutions not affiliated with a university, the issue had become a problem of professional politics. Bessau was nevertheless of the opinion that one should continue to support the concept of an outpatient department, and to be able to say of the medical directors: 'Ye shall know them by their out-patient departments'.[26]

The opening of this paper posed the deceptively simple question: Why, to what end, and in what form were institutions for sick children established? Based on our historical analysis, we are now in a position to propose the following reply.

The reason for children's hospitals coming into being must be linked to the coincidence of the rise of Enlightenment values, leading to public protection of children on the one hand, and the interest of the medical profession in exploiting the children in the service of its new scientific orientation on the other.

Consequently, the end or purpose of the children's hospital was never strictly bound up only with the effort to advance clinical knowledge, to teach students, and to cure diseases, but had as much to do with society's growing interest in its children as social resources, to be entrusted to medical care for individual and social survival.

The development of the structure and the functioning of the children's hospital vacillated between the self-interest of the medical profession and the proper needs of the sick children. The history of this institution thus reflects both these competing factors at every time, if in very different forms.

Given all these competing forces shaping the history of the children's hospital, we are left with no 'ideal model' of the institution, neither in its outward appearance nor in its inner organization. Indeed, I am personally convinced that the search after such an 'ideal type' must be ultimately fruitless, because in the end the needs of a sick child are not met simply through institutionalized cure and care.

Notes

1. I am grateful to Dr Anne Harrington for her assistance in the English translation and revision of this paper.
2. E. Seidler, 'Das kranke Kind. Historische Modelle einer Medizinischen Anthropologie des Kindesalters', in J. Martin and A. Nitschke (eds), *Zur Sozialgeschichte der Kindheit. Historische Anthropologie*, vol. 4 (Freiburg/München, 1986), 685–709.
3. D. Jetter, *Grundzüge der Krankenhausgeschichte (1800–1900)* (Darmstadt, 1977).
4. G. Fr. Still, *The History of Pediatrics* (London, 1965), 422. See also W.J. Maloney, *George and John Armstrong of Castleton: Two Eighteenth-Century Medical Pioneers* (Edinburgh, 1954); F.N.L. Poynter, 'A unique copy of George Armstrong's printed proposals for establishing the dispensary for sick children, London 1769', *Medical History*, 1 (1957), 65–6.
5. G. Armstrong, 'A general account of the dispensary for the relief of the infant poor', in *An Account of the Diseases Most Incident to Children, from the Birth till the Age of Puberty, with a Successful Method of Treating Them*, new edn (London, 1783), 179–200.
6. Op. cit., p. 197.
7. Ch. West, *On Hospital Organisation, with Special Reference to the Organisation of Hospitals for Children* (London, 1877).
8. H. Dorschel, *Die frühe Wiener Pädiatrie* (Med. thesis, Heidelberg, 1957).
9. P. Vallery-Radot, *Deux siècles d'histoire hospitalière de Henri IV à Louis-Philippe (1802–1836)* (Paris, 1947).
10. J.R. Tenon, *Mémoires sur les hôpitaux de Paris* (Paris, 1788).
11. E.H. Ackerknecht, *Medicine in the Paris Hospital, 1794–1848* (Baltimore, 1966).
12. C.A. Wunderlich, *Wien und Paris. Ein Beitrag zur Geschichte und Beurtheilung der gegenwärtigen Heilkunde* (Stuttgart, 1841).
13. K. Rauchfuss, 'Die Kinderheilanstalten', in Carl Gerhardt (ed.), *Handbuch der Kinderkrankheiten*, vol. 1 (Tübingen, 1877), 463–528.
14. F.S. Hügel, *Beschreibung sämmtlicher Kinderheilanstalten in Europa. Nebst einer Anleitung zur zweckmässigen Organisation von Kinder-Krankeninstituten und Kinderspitälern, mit Beiträgen zur Geschichte und Reform sämmtlicher Spitäler im Allgemeinen* (Wien, 1848).
15. Rauchfuss, 'Kinderheilanstalten'.
16. ibid.
17. F.Nightingale, *Notes on Hospitals*, 3rd edn (London, 1863), p. 124.

18. See P. Wunderlich, 'Arthur Schlossmann (1867–1932) und die Kinderheilkunde in Dresden', in H. Schadewaldt (ed.), *Düsseldorfer Arbeiten zur Geschichte der Medizin*, vol. 27 (Düsseldorf, 1967), pp. ix–xxiv.

19. J.G. Rey, 'Anstalten und Einrichtungen für Kinder', in Philipp Biedert (ed.), *Das Kind, seine geistige und körperliche Pflege von der Geburt bis zur Reife* (Stuttgart, 1906), 176–88.

20. *Monatsschrift für Kinderheilkunde* (Beiträge der Jahresversammlung 1928 der Deutschen Gesellschaft für Kinderheilkunde in Hamburg) 41 (1928), 227–306.

21. E. Feer, 'Bau und Einrichtung der Kinderkrankenhauses', in op. cit., 227–41.

22. A. Schlossmann, 'Uber die Versorgun infektionskranker Kinder', in op. cit., 261–300.

23. *Das Krankenhaus. Zeitschrift für das gesamte Krankenhauswesen.* Sonderheft: *Das Kind im Krankenhaus*, 49 (1957), Heft 9, 366–436.

24. G. Fanconi, 'Der Bau von Kinderkrankenhäusern ausserhalb Deutschlands', in op. cit., 370–1.

25. J. Wolff and H. Sahl, 'Das Kinderkrankenhaus', op. cit., 372–416.

26. G. Bessau, 'Das Ambulanzproblem', in *Monatsschrift für Kinderheilkunde*, 301–6.

8

'Fame and fortune by means of bricks and mortar': the medical profession and specialist hospitals in Britain, 1800–1948

Lindsay Granshaw

Early nineteenth-century medical specialists in Britain were often regarded by others in their profession as little more than quacks. They guarded their secret potions jealously, it was said, and sought to make large amounts of money out of the gullible. Yet by the time of the First World War specialists were among the leaders in the profession, associating with royals, and vying with each other in the possession of expensive cars. (Albeit some cynics remarked that they kept their remedies to themselves, and made large amounts of money out of the gullible.)[1]

How did the specialist establish himself on the pinnacle of the profession? Or was he already there, at least in the eyes of the public, if not in those of fellow doctors? Certainly there were a number of well-established specialists in the early nineteenth century with upper-class patrons.[2] But the power and position of specialists as a group was largely a later thing – and in Britain the special hospitals played a key role in that transition. Many of these mostly nineteenth-century creations enabled medical men, in the *British Medical Journal*'s words, to 'step to fame and fortune by means of bricks and mortar'.[3] That they were such a route to power, prestige, and wealth is underlined by the vociferous opposition they encountered from much of the medical profession in the mid-nineteenth century.

Certainly the developments in the theory and practice of medicine emanating from Paris in the early nineteenth century, shifting focus from the body as an indivisible whole to a composite of parts, emphasizing particular organs as the seats of disease, did nothing to hinder the growth of – often specialized – hospitals.[4] However, founders of the hospitals rarely made reference to such changing ideas, and the hospitals usually preceded the development of specialist fields. In most cases, too, they preceded the development of specialized instruments; the invention of particular tools cannot be seen as the reason for the massive expansion in the number and range of special hospitals.[5] It was in the assistance that the hospitals provided to the upwardly-mobile doctor that the key to their foundation can be found.

Special hospitals played a larger part than simply allowing their founders to establish their own reputations. They enabled those on the edge of the profession to gain a crucial place within it. They helped to crystallize the divisions between hospital doctors and general practitioners. They provided a central focus for the profession's struggle to oust lay control from hospitals.[6] In most instances, too, special hospitals were medicalized earlier than general hospitals – medical men spent longer there, patients underwent more medical intervention (especially surgical), and regulations were geared far more to medical work.[7] Condemned by most of the profession when first established, by the end of the century those who might realistically aspire to be leaders in the profession applied to join the staffs of the special hospitals. It was from the special hospitals, too, that textbooks, articles, and novel procedures appeared, defining new fields and emphasizing – always – the necessity of taking specialist advice.

But first it is important to stress that whatever medical men may have thought of so-called quacks in the eighteenth century, the public did not necessarily agree. As Roy Porter has argued, the regulars might talk of how quacks undermined the profession, but that did not stop them prospering; the public seemed quite happy to use their services, or to spread their custom between various practitioners, regular or otherwise.[8] The specialists in the early nineteenth century were very anxious, however, to reject the label of quackery, and they in their turn condemned those whom they considered to be quacks.[9] None of this professional rivalry necessarily had a major impact on potential patients. Quacks prospered – or not – along with the rest.

Thus, specialization had long been the means by which outsiders in medicine might seek to rise. However, it took a much more institutionalized form in the nineteenth century, as institutions themselves became more important to the nascent medical profession. Hospitals in the nineteenth century became the profession's training ground, the main area in which lay control was rejected, the workplace of the medical elite, and, later, the places in which 'scientific medicine', so important to the image of the profession, could in theory be practised.[10] Given the increasing importance of hospitals to the British medical profession, it is not surprising that the new specialists took the hospital route in their attempts to establish themselves.

The middle and upper classes were treated at home in the eighteenth and nineteenth century; hospitals were supposed to be only for the 'deserving poor'. They were supported through philanthropy, and lay men and women received social kudos along with such governors' rights as patient admission and staff selection. This powerful lay influence far from deterred medical men from hospital involvement: rather it encouraged them. They were anxious to secure hospital positions, with the important contacts with the rich and powerful that these brought.[11]

By the end of the eighteenth century there were a number of hospitals in Britain, mostly in the major towns. Set up by laymen, they reflected the growth of the bourgeoisie with its interest in philanthropy. Such hospitals usually excluded certain types of patients, such as lunatics, incurables, and women in childbirth, but at mid-century a few hospitals such as lying-in charities were set up for some of these excluded groups.[12] Again, they were largely lay foundations.

From the last third of the eighteenth century there was a new development – the foundation of medical institutions, mostly outpatient dispensaries, by medical men. The first, the Aldersgate Street Dispensary, established by John Lettsom in 1770, set a trend. Lettsom, a Quaker, was disaffected with the medical establishment that dominated London medicine, and his two foundations, the dispensary and the Medical Society of London, were expressions of that dissatisfaction.[13] A number of dispensaries were set up, particularly in the cities, at the end of the eighteenth century and into the nineteenth century, mostly by medical men.[14]

The specialist hospitals of the nineteenth century usually began as outpatient dispensaries and were an outgrowth of this development. The pattern of their establishment and their use by both the medical men and patients differed significantly from that of the general hospitals. It was crucially important that they were set up not by lay philanthropists but by medical men. Almost invariably these medical men were ambitious entrepreneurs, but something of outsiders, unable to secure the central positions that they desired within the medical profession. Professionalization was one method of assuring position in a rapidly changing world, a route taken by the doctors. As they sought to control entry to their group and to monitor behaviour within it, they also reinforced their tenet that it was inappropriate to advertise. Ways around that had always been found, and a hospital position served as just such a good advertisement, since patients knew that a hospital doctor had at least the right connections.[15] Hospital positions, though, were available only to a few. For doctors to secure hospital positions in the early nineteenth century, it was necessary either to gain medical patronage or to 'buy' the governors who voted in hospital elections, and that could be a very expensive business. At the Aldersgate Street Dispensary in 1824, for example, two competing applicants paid 600 guineas between them in the hope of being elected as surgeon – and of course one failed and had to try again. These were men who were just starting out in practice.[16]

The medical routes to public notice were largely monopolized by those who were already moving in the right social circles. There were other ways – the brass plates, notices giving a change of address, joining the masons (an increasingly useful route to prosperity it seemed), joining local societies and clubs.[17] Unable to advertise directly, it was those who were outside the inner circles but whose intention was to gain admission who took the route of specialization. Upwardly mobile entrepreneurs were as evident in the medical profession as in other social strands of nineteenth-century life. The foundation of special hospitals became a way for some of these medical men to break through.

The template for nineteenth-century special hospitals was Moorfields, set up by John Cunningham Saunders in 1804 as the London Dispensary for the Relief of the Poor Afflicted with Ear and Eye Diseases.[18] Saunders was able and ambitious but his family did not come from sufficiently influential circles. However, he was by no means a complete outsider and had established a foothold on the bottom of the hospital ladder. What was critical was that he could not then climb all the way up it. Saunders was born not in London but in Devon, in 1773. He was apprenticed locally to a barber surgeon. Having served his five years, he came to London to walk the wards so that he could practise in the metropolis, the aim of many an ambitious provincial surgeon. He became house-pupil to Astley Cooper, then a lecturer at St Thomas's, no doubt paying for the privilege.[19] Through Cooper's patronage he secured the position of demonstrator of anatomy at St Thomas's. He also acted as Cooper's dresser. So far, Saunders was doing very well. However, in 1800 Astley Cooper was appointed on his uncle's retirement as surgeon at Guy's, the hospital which both partnered and rivalled St Thomas's.[20] Cooper took on Benjamin Travers as his apprentice, a favoured position from which the patron often arranged promotion. In due course Travers became a surgeon at St Thomas's.[21] (In later years Astley Cooper similarly favoured a range of former apprentices as well as relatives.[22]) John Cunningham Saunders can therefore have had little realistic prospect of Cooper's patronage for the more important positions, and in 1801 he left London for the provinces. However, he soon decided to return to his earlier ambition of securing a practice in the capital, and resumed his position as demonstrator of anatomy at St Thomas's.[23] Saunders was to move no further up the hierarchy.

Astley Cooper had a particular interest in the anatomy of the ear, and Saunders exploited his connection with him by emphasizing a degree of specialization in diseases of the ear, on which he published a book.[24] Saunders then went a stage further in this professional manner of self-advertisement: he established his dispensary for treating ear and eye diseases. Within a few months it was concentrating on eye diseases alone, and Saunders had converted his dispensary into an infirmary with a few beds. He now began to compile a book on diseases of the eye, based upon the cases he saw at his hospital.[25] This is a pattern also seen in later establishments; the medical men wrote what they emphasized were 'practical treatises' (which were accessible both to an educated public and to other doctors) which served to stress their specialist skills, and to differentiate them from the quacks with their secret remedies. However, before Saunders' book could be published, he died, at the age of 37, in 1810.[26]

The early success of John Cunningham Saunders' enterprise acted as immediate encouragement to other establishments. A colleague of Saunders enlisted the help of a banker in setting up an eye hospital in Exeter in 1808, this was followed by Dr. Goldwyer setting up a hospital in Bristol (1810), Dr Sims in Bath (1811), Mr. W.J. Wilson, an oculist, in Manchester (1814), a surgeon, Ryall, setting up an eye and ear hospital in Dublin (1814), and Dr Guthrie establishing a second London eye hospital (1816). Thus, all were set up by medical men. In the subsequent two decades, eye hospitals were established in Shrewsbury, Liverpool, Plymouth, Newcastle, Norwich, Birmingham, Glasgow, Brighton, Edinburgh, Aberdeen, Weymouth, and Sunderland.[27]

Besides the eye hospitals, there were a handful of other infirmaries which specialized in the treatment of other parts of the body. For example, in 1814 Dr Isaac Buxton set up in London what became the Royal Hospital for Diseases of the Chest, and an orthopaedic hospital was set up in Birmingham in 1817. However, the few other specialist institutions established between 1815 and 1835 were far outnumbered by the highly successful formula, the eye hospital.[28] From the 1830s that began to change. One of the next group of hospitals, diversifying away from eye hospitals and again acting as an exemplar for later establishments, was the Fistula Infirmary, which became St Mark's Hospital in London.[29]

As in the case of Moorfields, the Fistula Infirmary was founded by a surgeon from the provinces, in this case Bath. Frederick Salmon had been apprenticed to a local surgeon-apothecary, then came to London in 1817 to complete his training at St Bartholomew's, where he walked the wards, with ninety-two other pupils, behind John Abernethy.[30] Salmon then paid him more than 8 guineas to become his house surgeon, before trying to set up a practice in London. Failing to get on the staff of the Aldersgate Street Dispensary, in 1825 he learned that Abernethy was intending to retire from Bart's and endeavoured to secure his support to be his replacement. It then emerged that Abernethy had made an arrangement with another former pupil for him to take his position, on the written understanding that he in turn passed the position on to Abernethy's young son. In the ensuing controversy, fuelled by the newly-established *Lancet*, Abernethy certainly came under criticism, but Salmon did not gain thereby – he did not secure appointment.[31] Salmon finally succeeded in being appointed at the Aldersgate Street Dispensary in 1827, only to lose the position again in 1833 when all the staff resigned in protest at the controlling hand of the lay governors.[32]

Frederick Salmon had already begun to specialize – in the treatment of rectal diseases – and had published two books on the subject.[33] (Significantly he published nothing further after he had established his hospital; his fame as a rectal specialist was now such that he did not need to do so, and he left that to others on the staff of his hospital in later years.) Salmon had joined a businessmen's club in the City of London, where he had established his practice, and it was from there that he recruited his philanthropic helpers. The founders of specialist hospitals discovered, to the irritation of others in the profession, that there was no shortage of lay philanthropic help in getting their institutions going – if they showed the right entrepreneurial skills.[34] The equally upwardly mobile middle-class traders, lawyers, and businessmen regarded public philanthropy as confirming or conveying on them recognition of their position in the social scale.

Salmon established his institution as a tiny dispensary in one room in the City of London. His enterprise flourished and in the 1850s a thirty-bedded hospital was built. By the time of Salmon's death in 1868 there were four surgeons on the staff. Founded as the Benevolent Dispensary for the Relief of the Poor Afflicted with Fistula, Piles, and other Diseases of the Rectum and Lower Intestines, it had by the early 1850s become St Mark's Hospital.[35] (It had become commonplace for the special hospitals to take saints' names – any saint's name – as they sought greater respectability.[36])

The 1830s saw, besides the Fistula Infirmary, the establishment by local doctors of an Eye, Ear, and Throat Infirmary in Edinburgh, and the Hospital for the Cure of Deformities by Drs W.J. Little and Quarles Harris (later the Royal, then the Royal National, Orthopaedic Hospital), and the Metropolitan Institution for Diseases of the Ear, Throat, and Vocal Organs, founded by Drs Ordwin, Walsh, Everett,

Streeton, and Stephenson. In the 1840s and 1850s the trend
became even more marked, with the foundation in London of
two hospitals for consumption including the Brompton
Hospital, the Women's Hospital in Soho, the Cancer
Hospital, the Hospital for Sick Children, Great Ormond
Street, and several hospitals for skin diseases, diseases of the
chest, and orthopaedic problems.[37] Outside London more
eye hospitals were set up, as well as hospitals for women and
children, ear and throat complaints, consumption, and a
dental hospital. By the early 1860s there were at least sixty-
six special institutions in London alone.[38]

Special hospitals were relatively easy to establish: the practitioner usually rented a house or just a couple of rooms, and
installed a few beds in the care of a residential 'matron' and
perhaps a house surgeon. The success or failure of the institution then usually turned on whether the founder could attract
and then retain sufficient charitable interest. Many little
institutions went under within a few years of being set up, or
else their founders secured other appointments and let their
enterprises fold. Attracting patients never seemed to be a
problem, and this patient demand underlay the overall
success of the specialist hospital movement.[39]

Patients might be happy, but the medical profession was
not. They held very mixed feelings about the specialists and
their hospitals, with the disruption of the *status quo* that this
implied. Those at the top of the medical hierarchy resented
their positions being undermined. As teaching became
increasingly important at the general hospitals, it was argued
that the proliferation of special hospitals drew away interesting cases from the schools. General practitioners had even
greater reason to fear the special hospitals. They argued that
it was not just the very poor who were turning to the multi-
plying hospitals but those who were slightly better-off – in
other words, their own patients.

Defending both hospital doctor and general practitioner,
the *British Medical Journal* made its attitude very clear in a
campaign it ran against special hospitals in the early 1860s.
As it put it:

> it would appear that [these] hospitals . . . were effected
> solely on the behalf of suffering humanity . . . . Anyone
> who knows anything of the working of our metropolitan

charitable institutions is fully aware how far this is from the real – and we must add . . . the vulgar – truth.[40]

Most of the specialist hospitals were established through 'the energetic action of some individual'.[41] They would begin as a dispensary; an energetic surgeon then 'makes up his mind to step to fame and fortune by means of bricks and mortar'.[42] First he must decide on some 'striking specialty' such as the treatment of 'inverted eyelashes'. A quiet house was taken in a side street,

> patrons and patronesses are canvassed for, and in an incredibly short space of time a goodly sprinkling of the aristocracy have been found to pledge themselves to serve suffering humanity and Mr. —, in the matter of inverted eyelashes.[43]

'Carefully got up statistics' would then prove that every tenth person was suffering from this terrible disease, with 20,000 cases treated a year, and the dispensary would need to be expanded into a hospital. Although inverted eyelashes could be treated 'in the old established hospital close at hand', this would never be realized by the gentlemen and ladies

> who so obsequiously follow the lead of the ambitious Mr. —, who is determined that there shall be a building devoted to nothing but misplaced eyelashes and perhaps – but this is of course quite under the rose – to himself.[44]

To the *British Medical Journal*, special hospitals served no useful purpose at all. They starved the general hospitals of the kind of cases which were so instructive to medical students, they destroyed 'that unity of disease which the philosophic mind should always keep in mind'; and they squandered public funds.[45] Special hospitals 'will never furnish great surgeons, or advance the art beyond mere manipulative smartness'.[46]

No sooner had the *British Medical Journal* issued this complaint than it heard that a 'hospital for stone' was about to be established.[47] The British Medical Association (BMA) initiated – with some dissension – a petition against all special hospitals. One dissenter had himself condemned special hospitals six years earlier, but he had subsequently joined one; he now maintained that he would 'give up his post tomorrow if he saw an indication of liberal reform in the greater institutions'.[48] In other words, if he could gain an appointment at a major hospital, his allegiance to special hospitals would immediately evaporate. From his new position he now held that opposition stoked up by the *British Medical Journal* was selfish, exclusive, and hypocritical. However, a more typical view was put by another practitioner who argued that special hospitals were established for one purpose only – the self-interest of their founder. 'It was true that the gentlemen engaged in these hospitals got their names spread all over England, but in the meantime the profession was being ruined.'[49] He complained that they drew patients from all over the country, yet made no investigation whatsoever of whether they were indeed worthy recipients of charity; in other words, whether they were too poor to have afforded to pay a local doctor. The only permissible special institutions, it was maintained, were those which treated cases which were not admitted to general hospitals. An example quoted was epilepsy: Brown-Séquard had moved from Paris to become a surgeon at the National Hospital for the Paralysed and Epileptic, Queen Square; as a rationalization or not, he argued that 'when cases of epilepsy were received into general hospitals, he would resign his situation at once'.[50]

Opposing the new hospital for stone, a manifesto was signed by many of the senior physicians and surgeons on the staffs of general hospitals, stating that they were of the opinion

> that much detriment to the public and the medical profession arises from the modern practice of opening small institutions, under the name of hospitals, for particular forms of disease, in the treatment of which no other management, appliance or attention is required than is already supplied in the existing general hospitals.[51]

They emphasized that a hospital for the treatment of stone and diseases of the urinary organs was 'especially unnecessary'.[52]

The subject continued to be much debated, with a few protagonists arguing that medical knowledge had advanced to a stage where specialization was necessary, others that special institutions were far more expensive in their care for patients than the general hospitals. The hospital for stone went ahead and in 1864 was named St Peter's Hospital. The *British Medical Journal* wondered whether the particular saint had been selected as a joke. The hospital was also dedicated to the treatment of urinary diseases. 'Urinary diseases!' exclaimed the journal: 'all the medical world knows what *they* mean in the eyes of the enlightened public'.[53] Indeed the surgeons at St Peter's in the later nineteenth century had flourishing venereal disease practices among the aristocracy – one, Sir Alfred Cooper, father-in-law of Lady Diana Cooper, travelled round London in what was known as his 'clap trap'.[54]

St Peter's Hospital was set up at a turning point for special hospitals. There was considerable pressure on their founders and their members of staff to abandon their enterprises – pressure which came from both hospital doctors and general practitioners. The general hospitals were just beginning to try to undermine the specialist institutions by appointing specialists themselves, at least in the treatment of eye diseases, and setting aside beds for special cases. However the development of specialist hospitals seemed unstoppable. Many hospital doctors themselves already had profitable associations with them. Most crucially, public support, both from patients and philanthropists, was considerable, even if the controversies of the 1860s show clearly the pulls in the different directions.

St Peter's illustrates the case well. St Peter's had two founder surgeons, Armstrong Todd and Thomas Spencer Wells. Todd seems to have been the mover behind the project. He was Irish and had graduated from Dublin. He became surgeon to the Marylebone Dispensary, but he held no higher position – he was typical of other hospital founders. Wells was not. He was far better known. He was already actively involved in another special hospital, the Samaritan Hospital for Women. However, his operation of ovariotomy was far from accepted, and he stood somewhat outside the medical elite at the time. His public profile, though, was high and he served as a useful publicist for the new hospital. It was Wells who was given the task of drawing up the circular which set forth the advantages of the new specialist hospital.

At this stage, he clearly felt that it was appropriate to be involved in such an enterprise. Within two years, though, he had resigned; St Peter's had become the focus of too much professional discontent.[55]

A second case at St Peter's shows the outcome eventually going the other way. In 1864 Walter Coulson, then surgical registrar at St Mary's Hospital, became surgeon at St Peter's. Coulson's uncle was a prominent and successful medical practitioner, with an interest in urinary diseases. Armstrong Todd at St Peter's, having lost Spencer Wells, encouraged Coulson to join him. The surgical staff at St Mary's immediately condemned St Peter's as 'useless and mischievous, an injury to the schools and an insult to the hospitals'.[56] Coulson saw where his greater interest lay at that stage and resigned his position at St Peter's; he was duly rewarded in 1866 by being appointed assistant surgeon at St Mary's. However, he then resumed his position at St Peter's, and his colleagues at St Mary's were up in arms. They wrote to the medical press in protest. Coulson responded by pointing out that two of the St Mary's surgeons were on the staff of the Lock Hospital and that one of these, James R. Lane, was on the staff of St Mark's as well.[57] Reflecting the gravity of the row, Lane promptly resigned from St. Mark's. The *British Medical Journal* recorded that Lane had 'withdrawn' from the office of surgeon at St Mark's, adding that 'The institution is one which finds small favour in the eyes of the profession now.'[58] Reflecting reality, though, the journal remarked that there would be applicants for the vacancy, 'unenviable as the post may now be generally considered'[59] – such was the demand for such positions, whatever the medical establishment might say.

Coulson did not see special hospitals in the same light as the *BMJ*, however. He refused to be dislodged from St Peter's, remaining there until his death in 1889. St Peter's became embroiled in similar controversies: a Middlesex surgeon, Thomas Nunn, was elected to the staff in the same traumatic year, 1866, but resigned barely a year later because of pressure from the Middlesex. In doing so he recorded that he resigned 'in order to prevent being forced into open rupture with several of my colleagues at the Middlesex Hospital with whom I have been connected nearly twenty years'.[60]

The poor view of special hospitals among the establishment was expressed by the medical press in the obituaries of Frederick Salmon in 1868. The *Lancet* was somewhat more favourable than the *British Medical Journal*, reflecting a gradually differing readership; it recorded the establishment of St Mark's thus: 'The step met with great professional opposition; but by indomitable perseverance, obtaining large funds from the public for the support of the institution, he ultimately succeeded'.[61] Specialization had clearly resulted in great material benefits to Salmon, and the *Lancet* noted that he 'had a large share of private practice in the diseases which he made his especial study'.[62] The *British Medical Journal* hardly beat about the bush:

How far the course which he took was prompted by difficulties in pursuing a useful and honourable career in a general hospital, where his labours would have been more useful and more instructive, it is now difficult to say. It was, we fully believe, contrary to the best interests both of the profession and of the public; and the success of St Mark's Hospital was of unfortunate omen, and has since borne fruit in encouraging similar enterprises.[63]

For the *British Medical Journal* and those whom the journal sought to represent, however, it was already a lost cause. The pressures supporting specialist hospitals were proving far stronger than those restraining them. The staff who joined well-established, wealthily-patronized hospitals were now rarely outsiders. Some resigned their special hospital positions after a few years, when they were well-established in private practice, while retaining their general hospital positions. Occasionally, though infrequently, they gave up their general hospital position and retained only their specialist affiliation. The variety of patterns can be seen at St Mark's. Peter Gowlland, for example, reacted very differently from his immediate contemporary, James Lane; where Lane, under pressure from St Mary's, gave up the position at St Mark's, Gowlland on the other hand relinquished his London Hospital position to concentrate only on rectal diseases – and died a rich man as a result.[64] A few prominent men did not seek a teaching hospital position even though they would have stood an excellent chance of obtaining one. The leading surgeon at St Mark's with the largest practice in rectal diseases in London, William Allingham, author of the main textbook on the subject, winner of numerous prizes during his training at St Thomas's, member of the Council of the Royal College of Surgeons, never held a position at a teaching hospital.[65]

Mixed feelings about specialist hospitals continued to be voiced in the last third of the nineteenth century. When the House of Lords in the 1890s conducted an enquiry into the state of the metropolitan hospitals, many of the medical men giving evidence argued against specialist institutions: such hospitals drained resources from more worthy recipients, let alone stealing their patients.[66] However, despite such rhetoric, there is much evidence that the professional elite were now exploiting the special hospitals. A new pattern in the use of the specialist hospitals by the doctors was emerging. While some of the surgeons and physicians emphasized one specialty only, by the turn of the century those climbing the ladder turned from one specialty to another, in rapid succession. In many cases, biographies and histories indicate that they made no contribution to any specialty. However, they did develop thriving private practices and frequently gained appointments at the teaching hospitals after they had gained experience at the specialist institutions.

Taking a sample of 500 medical men between 1850 and 1950 who were Fellows of the Royal College of Surgeons, therefore recorded in Plarr and likely to be among the elite, the changing pattern in associations with special hospitals can be seen. Plarr under-estimates, since there are a number within the sample where the 'life' does not mention a link with a special hospital which other sources reveal. After all, even if a medical man regarded it as important to his initial career to join such a hospital, at a later date he might obscure this, or others would find it insignificant, and obituaries would fail to record an early association. However, within that constraint, instructive information emerges. In the 1850s about 20 per cent of those in Plarr are recorded to have had some association with a special hospital. Often this was a temporary link, although some founders of hospitals are numbered amongst them. Between the 1860s and the 1880s the proportion rose to 25 per cent, but from the 1890s right through and into the National Health Service it rose to just under 60 per cent.[67]

Thus it was not just the outsiders in the profession who were using the special hospitals, but many of those who could reasonably expect bright futures. Certainly some with humble origins still found the specialist hospital route profitable, but others hardly needed such a boost, and yet sought such positions. Examples illustrating these points can be given. Someone who started on an outside track, Sir John Bland-Sutton, but who became a much famed early twentieth-century cancer surgeon at the Middlesex Hospital, came from a large family in which 'money was not too abundant' and had to teach to keep himself afloat.[68] He did not have powerful connections, and

> he climbed the ladder by ordinary steps, slowly at first as a junior demonstrator of anatomy, then as curator of the hospital museum, next as assistant surgeon to a small special hospital, finally as assistant surgeon, surgeon and consulting surgeon to his own hospital, the Middlesex.[69]

The assumption was that his special hospital appointment was part of his rise to fame and fortune.

Sir Henry Butlin, surgeon at St Bartholomew's and subsequently President of the Royal College of Surgeons, again from inauspicious origins, had traced a similar path.[70] Percy Furnivall, Sir Henry's son-in-law, and well-connected, in the 1890s acted as clinical assistant to a children's hospital, an eye hospital, and a throat hospital, joined the staff of the Metropolitan Hospital, then St Mark's, until finally securing a position at the London Hospital, after which he dropped his remaining specialist positions. He hardly needed a boost to his position, and yet he saw the special hospital affiliation as dispensable but important.[71]

Perhaps most revealing is the Bickersteth family, of Liverpool, who became prominent in the medical profession in the nineteenth century. An eighteenth-century Bickersteth had come from a distinguished social background, and had had a large medical practice in Kirkby Lonsdale, Westmorland. His son, Robert (1787–1857), trained in the best school of the time, Edinburgh, then went to London, before returning north to become surgeon to the Liverpool Infirmary in 1810, which he used as a base for building up a very successful practice.[72] Robert Bickersteth's son, Edward (1828–1908), followed him through Edinburgh, went on to St Bartholomew's, then made a medical tour of Dublin and did what all bright, wealthy young doctors hoped to do, spent some time in Paris before returning to Liverpool where he succeeded his father as surgeon to the Infirmary in 1857.[73] Edward Bickersteth's son, Robert Alexander (1862–1924), took the route that had become the most select in the closing decades of the nineteenth century. He was sent to Eton, Cambridge, and then St Bartholomew's, where he qualified in the early 1890s. With everything in his favour, he chose as his next step to act as clinical assistant first at the Throat Hospital, Golden Square, and then at Moorfields. Only after this did he return to Liverpool, where he took up the position of surgeon to the Royal Liverpool Infirmary. Here his interest was in yet a third specialty, urology. It had clearly been seen both by Bickersteth and his advisers that part of his training should be gained at the special hospitals.[74]

The surgeons who joined the specialist institutions at the end of the nineteenth century fell into two main categories: those who regarded them as stepping stones to large private practices or general hospital appointments; and those who were the more dedicated specialists. It was the latter group that now pushed their chosen fields outwards, publishing first for general practitioners, warning them of the dangers of non-specialist treatment, and then by the early twentieth century for colleagues in their own fields. Journals, clubs, and societies began to be set up in the different fields. It was these specialists, too, who developed new operations, differentiated between diseases, and devised novel instruments.[75]

This evolving pattern did not stop members of the medical profession retaining their very mixed feelings about the idea of specializing at all. As if in pursuit of the image of the classically-educated nineteenth-century doctor with the Renaissance mind, many of the most socially prominent medical men continued to strive for success in general surgery or general medicine, whatever the financial rewards of specialization.[76] The First World War acted as a further stimulus to specialization and to the importance of the special hospitals to medical men. Many doctors went to France, finding on their return that former patients and medical contacts were lost. Specialization was one way of re-establishing a reasonable practice.[77] But the generalist ideal persisted; as one returning surgeon, Sir Charles Gordon-Watson, ruefully saw it, even though he was on the staff of St Bartholomew's, it was his link with a special hospital which was now important:

> How thankful I am that I practised general surgery for many years before the inevitable current of specialisation washed me into this back water. There save for an occasional excursion into the main stream, I must needs stay 'put' to the end, though not unthankful for the rewards that it brings and the benefits that I have been able to hand out to many sufferers.[78]

Clearly, if he had been able to, he would have stayed a general surgeon.

It was the National Health Service, set up in 1948, though, that took at face value the criticisms of the special hospitals. Organized around district general and general teaching hospitals, with specialist departments, many of the specialist hospitals were swallowed up.[79] As ever, the medical profession seemed to agree that specialist institutions were not wanted. As the *Lancet* put it in 1961:

> the small special hospital, which was so perfect an instrument sixty years ago, when individuals were developing their subjects on their own, is no longer the ideal place in an era in which teamwork and the laboratory have taken the place of the single-handed clinician or surgeon.[80]

Ironically, there seemed to have been no period, despite the *Lancet*'s assumption, when special hospitals were agreed to be useful institutions. And yet special hospitals had served the interests of those excluded from elite positions, whose abilities as entrepreneurs rivalled any others in Victorian society. As social changes disrupted the *status quo*, they fought for advancement through establishing their own institutions, adopting the forms of regular medicine. The battles against such specialization were intense, but general practitioners were in a weak position to resist, and although hospital surgeons and physicians for many years opposed special hospitals, the younger generations who formed the future elite found them useful. Their success – based on popular support – was by and large so great that it only took a generation or so before those who could expect to be the elite in the profession were laying aside former disapproval and seeking to join the specialist institutions. Many remained remarkably ambivalent about specialization, so that in the 1870s and 1880s specialist positions were usually relinquished once a surgeon or physician was well established. By the end of the century that was less likely to be the case – an increasing number of those on the staffs of the specialist hospitals now stayed with that specialty throughout their working lives, originating in their fields so that in turn they attracted new entrants into these areas. But for many others, though specialization seemed part of their career pattern, they retained the earlier disdain for such 'narrow-mindedness'. They joined the staff, hoping to enhance their reputations and develop a clientele of patients in a particular field, at least as a starting point, but a main aim of many was to be considered a generalist. Praised or berated, by the end of the nineteenth century and certainly in the twentieth century, therefore, special hospitals were – like the general hospitals earlier in the century – serving the interests of the elite.

Notes

1. For the flourishing twentieth-century specialists, see R. Pound, *Harley Street* (Michael Joseph, London, 1967).

2. R. Porter, 'Before the fringe', in R. Cooter (ed.), *Alternatives; The Social History of Alternative Medicine* (Macmillan, London, 1988).

3. 'Hospital distress', *British Medical Journal*, no. 1 (1860), 458.

4. For varying accounts of the impact of Paris medicine, see M. Foucault, *The Birth of the Clinic. An Archaeology of Medical Perception*, trans. A.M. Sheridan (Tavistock, London, 1976); E. Ackerknecht, *Medicine at the Paris Hospital, 1794–1848* (The Johns Hopkins Press, Baltimore, 1967); and T. Gelfand, *Professionalizing Modern Medicine; Paris Surgeons and Medical Science and Institutions in the 18th Century* (Greenwood Press, Westport, Connecticut, 1980).

5. G. Rosen, *Specialization of Medicine* (Froben Press, New York, 1944) particularly emphasized that instruments played a major role in the development of specialized medicine.

6. See M. Jeanne Peterson, *The Medical Profession in Mid-Victorian London* (University of California Press, Berkeley, 1978) for the

battles against lay control. For professionalization, see E. Freidson, *Profession of Medicine* (Dodd, Mead, New York, 1970); E. Freidson, *Professional Powers. A Study of the Institutionalisation of Formal Knowledge* (University of Chicago Press, Chicago and London, 1986); I. Waddington, *The Medical Profession in the Industrial Revolution* (Gill & Macmillan, Dublin, 1984); N. Parry and J. Parry, *The Rise of the Medical Profession* (Croom Helm, London, 1976). For the division between GP and hospital doctor, see F. Honigsbaum, *The Division in British Medicine: A History of the Separation of General Practice From Hospital Care, 1911–1968* (Kogan Page, London, 1979).

7. L. Granshaw, *St Mark's Hospital, London: A Social History of a Specialist Hospital* (King's Fund Historical Series, London, 1985).

8. R. Porter, 'Before the fringe'.

9. See for example F. Salmon, *Oration on the Necessity for an Entire Change in the Constitution and Government of the Royal College of Surgeons* (Whittaker, Treacher & Arnot, London, 1833). Salmon argues that the College should defend people like himself, though a specialist, and roundly condemned the quacks.

10. For the rhetoric or reality of scientific medicine, see C. Lawrence, 'Incommunicable knowledge: science, technology and the clinical art in Britain, 1850–1914', *Journal of Contemporary History*, no. 20 (1985), 503–20.

11. See, for example, the amounts of money involved in hospital elections in Granshaw, *St Mark's Hospital*, 11.

12. Brian Abel-Smith, *The Hospitals 1880-1948. A Study in Social Administration in England and Wales* (Heinemann, London, 1964); A. Gunn, 'Maternity hospitals', in F.N.L. Poynter (ed.), *The Evolution of Hospitals in Britain* (Pitman, London, 1964), 77–101; J. Woodward, *To Do The Sick No Harm. A Study of the British Voluntary Hospital System to 1875* (London, Routledge & Kegan Paul, 1974).

13. T. Hunt (ed.), *The Medical Society of London 1773–1973* (Heinemann, London, 1972).

14. Z. Cope, 'The history of the dispensary movement', in F.N.L. Poynter (ed.), *The Evolution of Hospitals in Britain* (Pitman, London, 1964).

15. Peterson, *The Medical Profession*.

16. See for example, 'The Westminster Medical Society and the resignation of the medical officers of the Aldersgate Street Dispensary', *Lancet*, no. 1 (1833–4), 218; 'General Dispensary Aldersgate Street', *Times*, 28 October 1833, 3; Veritas, 'Letter to the Editor', *Lancet*, no. 1 (1833–4), 340.

17. Peterson, *The Medical Profession*.

18. 'John Cunningham Saunders (1773–1810)', S. Lee (ed.) *Dictionary of National Biography*, vol. 17 (Smith, Elder, & Co., London, 1909), 815–16.

19. ibid.; B.B. Cooper, *The Life of Sir Astley Cooper*, 2 vols (John W. Parker, London, 1843); R.C. Brock, *The Life and Work of Astley Cooper* (E. & S. Livingstone, Edinburgh and London, 1952).

20. H.C. Cameron, *Mr Guy's Hospital, 1726–1948* (Longmans, Green & Co., London, 1954), 136–8.

21. F.G. Parsons, *The History of St Thomas's Hospital*, vol. 3 (Methuen, London, 1936), 243; E.M. McInnes, *St. Thomas' Hospital* (George Allen & Unwin, London, 1963).

22. Peterson, *The Medical Profession*, 146–7, on Cooper's nephews.

23. *A Treatise on Some Practical Points relating to the Diseases of the Eye, by the late John Cunningham Saunders, Demonstrator of Anatomy at Saint Thomas's Hospital, Founder and Surgeon of the London Infirmary for Curing Diseases of the Eye to which are added, A Short Account of the Author's Life, and his Method of Curing the Congenital Cataract by his friend and colleague, J.R. Farre, M.D.* (Longman, Hurst, Rees, Orme & Brown, London 1816), 6–8; E. Treacher Collins, *The History and Tradition of the Moorfields Eye Hospital: One Hundred Years of Ophthalmic Discovery and Development* (H.K. Lewis & Co., London, 1929).

24. Saunders, *A Treatise*.

25. Farre, *A Short Account*, 14–15.

26. 'John Cunningham Saunders', *Dictionary of National Biography*; Farre, *A Short Account*, 13–35.

27. R. Kershaw, *Special Hospitals* (George Putnam & Sons, London, 1909), 62–4.

28. ibid.

29. Granshaw, *St Mark's Hospital*, 1–48.

30. Sir L. Harvey, *Journal*, 279, St Bartholomew's Hospital Archives, G/54.

31. 'Vacancy at St Bartholomew's', *Lancet*, vol. 12 (1826–7), 399–400; F. Salmon, 'Letter to the Editor,' *Lancet*, vol. 12 (1826–7), 474-5.

32. Granshaw, *St Mark's Hospital*, 13–14.

33. F. Salmon, *A Practical Essay on Stricture of the Rectum* (pr. James Bullock, London, 1828); Salmon, *Practical Observations on Prolapsus of the Rectum* (Whittaker, Treacher & Arnot, London, 1831).

34. Granshaw, *St Mark's Hospital*, 16–21.

35. Op. cit., p. 39.

36. See, for example, All Saints' Hospital, established by an Irish surgeon, Edward Canny Ryall, whose family seemed to have a tradition of setting up such hospitals, and who was said to have chosen this name because there were no saints' names left.

37. Kershaw, *Special Hospitals*, 62–4.

38. Information from *London Medical Directory* and *Medical Directory* of various years.

39. Frequently the development of hospitals is seen as medicine, or profession, propelled. The importance of patient demand should not be underestimated.

40. 'Hospital distress', *British Medical Journal*, no. 1 (1860), 458.

41. ibid.

42. ibid.

43. ibid.

44. ibid.

45. Op. cit., 459.

46. ibid.

47. ibid.

48. 'Annual meeting of the British Medical Association', *British Medical Journal*, no. 2 (1860), 627.

49. Op. cit., 628. There was great concern that charity was being 'abused' by those able to pay a GP for treatment. For charity abuse, see H. Burdett, *Hospitals and Asylums of the World*, 4 vols (1891–3); H. Burdett, *Cottage Hospitals, General, Fever, and Convalescent. Their Progress, Management, and Work in Great Britain and Ireland, and the United States of America*, 3rd edn (The Scientific Press, London 1896), 42.

50. 'Annual meeting of the British Medical Association', *British Medical Journal*, no. 2 (1860), 629.

51. *British Medical Journal*, no. 2 (1860), 582.

52. ibid.

53. 'A special hospital', *British Medical Journal*, no. 2 (1864), 582.

54. ibid.

55. C. Morson, *St Peter's Hospital for Stone* (S. Livingstone, Edinburgh and London, 1960), 15–17.

56. 'Mr Walter Coulson and the Hospital for Stone', *British Medical Journal*, no. 2 (1866), 703.

57. Op. cit., 704.

58. 'Note', *British Medical Journal*, no. 1 (1868), 561.

59. ibid.

60. Morson, *St Peter's Hospital*, 21.

61. 'Frederick Salmon', *Lancet*, no. 1 (1868), 68.

62. ibid.

63. 'Frederick Salmon', *British Medical Journal*, no. 1 (1868), 476.

64. Granshaw, *St Mark's Hospital*, 46–8, 73.

65. Op. cit., 51–2, 74.

66. Third Report from the Select Committee of the House of Lords on Metropolitan Hospitals, *British Parliamentary Papers*, 13 (1892), lix–lxvii.

67. *Plarr's Lives of the Fellows of the Royal College of Surgeons of England*, rev. by Sir D'Arcy Power with W.G. Spencer and G.E. Gask, 2 vols (pr. John Wright & Sons, Bristol, 1930). Continued as Sir D'Arcy Power and W.R. Le Fanu, *Lives of the Fellows of the Royal College of Surgeons of England, 1930–1951* (London, The Royal College of Surgeons, 1953).

68. 'Sir John Bland-Sutton (1855–1936)', *Plarr's Lives* (1953), 90.

69. ibid.

70. 'Sir Henry Butlin (1845–1912)', *Plarr's Lives* (1930), 178.

71. 'Percy Furnivall (1868–1938)', *Plarr's Lives* (1953), 311–12; Granshaw, *St Mark's Hospital*, 162–3, 172.

72. 'Robert Bickersteth (1787–1857)', *Plarr's Lives* (1930), 96; for Edinburgh, see G.B. Risse, *Hospital Life in Enlightenment Scotland.*

Care and Teaching at the Royal Infirmary of Edinburgh (Cambridge University Press, Cambridge, London, and New York, 1986).

73. 'Edward Bickersteth (1828–1908)', *Plarr's Lives* (1930), 95–6; C. Newman, *The Evolution of Medical Education in the Nineteenth Century* (Oxford University Press, London, 1957).

74. 'Robert Alexander Bickersteth (1862–1924)', *Plarr's Lives* (1930), 97.

75. See, for example, Granshaw, *St Mark's Hospital*, 108–9, 124–31.

76. Peterson, *Medical Profession*; Lawrence, 'Incommunicable knowledge'.

77. See, for example, R. Stevens, *Medical Practice in Modern England: The Impact of Specialisation and State Medicine* (Yale University Press, New Haven, 1966); Granshaw, *St Mark's Hospital*, 185–6.

78. C. Gordon-Watson, *Forty Years in Surgical Harness*, typescript, St Bartholomew's Hospital Medical College Library, 4–5.

79. Ruth Levitt, *The Reorganised National Health Service* (Croom Helm, London, 1979); Ruth Hodgkinson, *The Origins of the National Health Service: The Medical Service* (Wellcome Institute, London, 1967); John Pater, *The Origins of the National Health Service* (King's Fund Historical Series, London, 1981).

80. 'A new postgraduate centre?', *Lancet*, no. 2 (1961), 1,269.

9

From Friedenheim to hospice: a century of cancer hospitals[1]

Caroline C.S. Murphy

Archaeological evidence shows that cancer, like the poor, has always been with us. Special cancer hospitals, however, are a far more recent phenomenon – though nothing like as new as the professional group of cancer specialists now known as oncologists.[2] Although the nineteenth-century origins of cancer hospitals may appear similar to those of other special hospitals, their emphasis on terminal care is more reminiscent of the hospice tradition of religious foundations. Unlike many of the other special hospitals, they did not primarily promote themselves as new centres for the development of scientific medicine. Plans made by the cancer hospitals in the 1890s for the establishment of 'hospices' – freed from any religious connotations under the name of 'Friedenheims' – illustrate recognition of the particular needs of the dying, though in the event they came to nothing. The competing demands for the support of clinical laboratory research into cancer were given priority, in the hope that discovery of a cure would remove the need for such 'Friedenheims'; this shift in emphasis has had lasting influence on provision for cancer and cancer patients.[3]

By the turn of the century, the pervasive influence of post-Bernardian scientific medicine effected a change in emphasis in the care offered by cancer hospitals. In the twentieth century they became centres for the development of surgical and radiotherapeutic treatments for cancer, while abandoning the medical treatments developed in the nineteenth century. The need for specialist care of the dying was eclipsed for three-quarters of a century, during which it was thought that the main priority in cancer was more research to uncover its uniquely obscure cause and thereby a cure. In the 1960s and 1970s the suffering of the dying, abandoned by the medical system, was given unprecedented publicity. The professional medical establishment had become geared to successful cures, and was seen to have lost the ability to cope with death. The hospice movement, operating in Britain independently of the NHS, put care of the dying firmly back on to the clinical agenda. Significantly, perhaps, the hospice movement does not yet appear to be aware of its stillborn precursor of a century ago.[4] This chapter cannot provide a comprehensive picture of the history of cancer hospitals; it does, however, hope to show how the demands of those dying of cancer have influenced the development of a very small group of special hospitals.

The Catholic religious tradition of provision of care for the sick and dying gave rise to the great charity hospitals of Britain, which fell into lay hands after the Reformation and the dissolution of the monastries. The establishment of scientific, rational medicine in the hands of licensed doctors and – in the aftermath of Florence Nightingale and her generation – professional nurses produced a change of emphasis in the way medicine was practised. Treatment of the patient with a view to curing a specific disease superseded the more traditional holistic approach to care of the body as the temporary vessel of the immortal soul. Having lost the support of the church, however, voluntary hospitals gained financial support on the basis of impressive statistics, preferably including few deaths. Excision of cancers has always been one of the more common forms of operative surgery, despite Hippocrates' admonition that the cancer patient would do better if left alone.[5] Although the histological nature of the variety of growths diagnosed as cancers in the past is now a matter of speculation, it is the case that 'cancer' patients were regularly admitted to the surgical wards of general hospitals.[6] At the same time, one of the devices used to 'massage' the hospital statistics was the exclusion from the wards of those with 'inoperable' cancers. This meant that there was no access to professional nursing care for those with advanced cancers who could not afford to pay.

Whatever doubts there may now be about the inaccurate diagnoses of leg ulcers, syphilitic sores, and mammary cysts as 'cancer', it is certain that by the late nineteenth century cancer had a reputation as being malign, painful, evil-smelling, and deadly. There were many theories of its cause, and plentiful 'quack' cures were available. The most consistent line adopted by the orthodox medical profession was that cancer could be cured with the knife if treated early enough. Just as long-standing as this surgical belief has been patients' fear of operations and the dread that the diagnosis 'cancer' meant certain and painful death.

With general hospitals unwilling to take in patients with advanced cancer, where were such patients to go and who was to treat them? The majority died at home in the care of their families, with scant help offered by GPs, who saw cancer only rarely during careers dominated by the treatment of contagious diseases. For those with large houses, secure incomes, and servants to change the linen and deal with the more distressing symptoms of the disease, this was manageable. Poor law infirmaries provided care for those accepted into the charge of the parish as paupers, but the 'respectable poor' faced the prospect that the diagnosis of cancer would break up families unable to provide adequate care. If it was the family breadwinner who was ill (often the case when the cancer was a direct result of industrial exposure to carcinogens), the whole family could be reduced to pauperism. The death of the head of the household in the poor law infirmary would then leave his bereaved family stigmatized as paupers.[7]

The inadequacy of the provision of treatment for those suffering from cancer meant that there was nowhere in the country where cancer (a disease taking many forms) could be studied. This was a fact that came home very forcibly to Dr William Marsden, the founder of London's Royal Free Hospital, when his wife died of cancer of the ovary in 1852. There was nothing that he could do for her while she was alive, but after her death he established a cancer hospital, which, like his general hospital, was also 'free' (no admission tickets were required). He hoped that by bringing a large number of cancer cases together, doctors specializing in the treatment of cancer would produce new, more effective, treatments. The hospital's basic role was to provide care until death; as a result, the small new hospital had a higher death rate than most of the larger established infirmaries. An early approach to Queen Victoria in search of patronage for the new hospital was turned down on the grounds that the disease was provided for in the general infirmaries. The first few annual reports produced by the hospital emphasized the preponderance of patients who had previously been turned away as 'untreatable' from such establishments. This evidence of the hospital's distinctive role was probably important in its eventual success in securing royal patronage.[8]

The London Cancer Hospital, now known as the Royal Marsden Hospital, was actually the second special cancer facility established in the capital. At the end of the eighteenth century, a cancer ward had been established at the Middlesex Hospital with money given by Samuel Whitbread. That cancer ward was established specifically for the care of the moribund – those with 'inoperable' cancer – who were excluded from care in the rest of the hospital and the rest of the London teaching hospitals.[9] The cancer ward had no imitators and produced few cancer specialists, though it was useful to the Middlesex Hospital in providing cancer patients for teaching the medical students about the then 'rare' disease. Care for the dying was a luxury that could only be afforded if there was a generous benefactor able to provide a large capital sum. As we shall see, Samuel Whitbread started a tradition of brewers supporting the care and treatment of cancer, a tradition that lapsed for some time after his death but was continued in the twentieth century.

While both the London Cancer Hospital and the Middlesex cancer ward offered care for the dying, only the Cancer Hospital produced its own medical 'cure' for cancer. William Marsden and his son Alexander developed the use of an 'arsenical mucillage' as a form of (reportedly painless) caustic which could be applied directly to a superficial tumour, causing it to slough off. This treatment, very much the product of a world in which the application of caustics, blisters, and leeches was the mainstay of practical medicine, did not enhance the standing of the Cancer Hospital.[10] At the Middlesex, the surgical tradition was perhaps too powerful to allow any such developments, though various medical treatments were tested on cancer ward patients – tests which in retrospect make very interesting reading.[11]

During the mid-nineteenth century, specialist hospitals based on the application of new scientific ideas and methods were proliferating in London. In developing the use of caustics, and continuing the traditional use of dangerously poisonous heavy metals, the Marsdens were not very 'progressive'. This did not mean that their hospital was without its imitators. Six years after its establishment, the Leeds Hospital for the Skin, Cancerous and Scrofulous Affections was opened, but only remained in operation for thirty-two years – the duration of its founder's career.

Granshaw has observed that in London most of the nineteenth-century specialist hospitals were established by medical men, while the eighteenth-century general hospitals had had lay origins.[12] The cancer hospitals founded in various British cities follow this pattern. Between 1857 and 1886, medical men in Leeds, Liverpool, Manchester, and Glasgow established cancer hospitals, all of which had failed by the outbreak of the Great War. Such failure was to be the fate of many nineteenth-century special hospitals on losing their founders. The cancer hospitals which failed did not act as proving-grounds for a specialty of cancer treatment. They were regarded by the medical profession as something far closer to 'quack' emporia where medical cure-alls were applied to superficial complaints of an uncertain nature. Medical cures for cancer were regarded as little more than wart charms, not as valuable contributions to scientific medicine.

The influence of surgeons on the development of cancer treatments is well illustrated by the experience of one of their number when he adopted a non-surgical method of treating cancer. Hugh Murray, who had worked as an assistant to Lister before receiving further training in Germany, established the Glasgow Cancer and Skin Institution in 1886. While Marsden claimed not to be competing with the established infirmaries, Murray specifically offered a medical alternative to the normal surgical treatment of cancer. Murray received no support from other Glasgow medical men who, it was reported, opposed him bitterly when he abandoned the knife for medical treatment. But he did have support from politically influential members of the citizenry in his regard for 'the knife treatment of cancer as the reproach and opprobrium of surgery'.[13] This support took the practical form of subscriptions when, in 1889, Dr Murray sought to expand his hospital. Unfortunately for Murray, some of his subscribers were those who supported the orthodox use of surgery in cancer. By 1893 they had replaced him as medical superintendant of 'his' hospital with an innovative surgeon, George Beatson. The Glasgow Cancer Hospital then took its place as a respected part of the Glasgow medical establishment – accepted as a place for surgical teaching – but it had problems attracting enough patients with 'true' cancer to be subjected to such surgery. Hugh Murray, on leaving the Glasgow Cancer Hospital, successfully ran his Glasgow Cancer and Skin Institution, for outpatients only.

The Glasgow Cancer Hospital did not remain unique as a cancer hospital recognized as a part of the local medical establishment. The Manchester Cancer Hospital was established adjacent to the Royal Infirmary by the executors of the Whitworth estate, under the chairmanship of a Manchester businessman, academic, and politician, Chancellor R.C. Christie.[14] In some ways, this hospital was very like the much larger London Cancer Hospital, providing for the care of the dying who were above the pauper class for whom the infirmary would not provide: unlike the London, however, it was not necessarily free. From the Hospital's foundation, it was intended to learn more about the nature of cancer in order to improve its treatment; the Hospital was immediately accepted as a useful addition to Manchester's hospital provision.

The London Cancer Hospital remained somewhat on the fringes of orthodox London medical practice at the end of the century, after the death of its founder William Marsden. One reason for this was the idiosyncratic (and high) profile of the hospital's consulting surgeon, Herbert Snow. Snow published extensively on the subject of cancer treatment and was a regular contributor to the correspondence columns of the *BMJ*.

In 1890 he published 'On the re-appearance (recurrence) of cancer after apparent extirpation, with suggestion for its prevention; and general remarks on the operative treatment of malignant growths', which was reviewed in the *BMJ* with his 'The palliative treatment of incurable cancer, with an appendix on the use of the opium pipe'.[15] The reviewer applauded Snow's advocacy of early excision as the best treatment for cancer and his belief in cancer as a 'local disease' rather than the product of heredity. Where the reviewer differed with him was in his attribution of 'too much influence on such conditions as mental distress and worry and general debility' as the causes of cancer. Snow had used opium in the relief of pain in cancer patients since 1876, because of his belief that the disease had neurotic origins; opium-smoking was *recommended* as a means of establishing an opium habit. In 1893 Snow combined the use of opium and cocaine for pain relief; he published his successful results in 1896.[16] His mixture formed the basis of the Brompton cocktail, which was to play such a large part in Cicely Saunders' establishment of hospice care for the dying about seventy years later. In the 1890s, though, it appears to have attracted little interest.

At this time, radical cancer surgery such as Halsted's radical mastectomy, oöphorectomy, and Wertheim's hysterectomy were becoming established parts of general surgical practice.[17] These operations could not be carried out in private houses; they became common in voluntary general hospitals. Those cancer hospitals which were not free were able to charge surgical patients for the use of 'pay beds' in rooms alongside their charity wards. The extra pressure that the increased use of radical surgery placed on the available beds was doubtless in some part responsible for the decision reached independently by the London, Manchester, and Glasgow cancer hospitals to establish 'Friedenheims'. A Friedenheim – a 'home of peace' for the dying – had been established for terminal TB patients in Germany in the 1880s (though the word never seems to have reached a German dictionary). The *Medical Directory*, however, shows that the first British Friedenheim, the Princess Alexandra's Friedenheim, was opened in Upper Avenue, Swiss Cottage (now the site of the Camden Local History Library) in 1889.[18]

The cancer hospitals in three of Britain's largest industrial cities planned to open such homes in the country, where their patients would go, not to convalesce, but to die in peace and comfort. While all three hospitals did increase their provision for surgical treatment, none of them ever opened a Friedenheim. As belief in the new, more aggressive surgery strengthened, and the methods of physiological research repeatedly proved their success in the control of infectious diseases, investment in homes for the hopeless seemed increasingly inappropriate. In 1902 the Imperial Cancer Research Fund (ICRF) was established in the belief that, given £½ million and twenty years, cancer would be cured as a result of the work of scientists in its laboratories.[19] The cancer hospitals, recognizing that research would attract greater support than the care of the dying, all shelved their Friedenheim plans and opened research laboratories.

Those cancer hospitals which adopted the new scientific approach to the disease tended to be those which survived into the twentieth century; those which were not able to adopt the new approach failed. There was one exception to this: St Catherine's Home for Cancer and Incurables in Bradford continued to provide a home for the dying well into the twentieth century. The Leeds Hospital for the Skin, Cancerous and Scrofulous Affections, the Manchester Hospital for the Skin, Cancer and Scrofula and All Chronic Diseases, and the Liverpool Tumour Hospital had all folded around 1889.[20] What remained of Hugh Murray's Glasgow Cancer and Skin Institution was to suffer directly from the influence of the ICRF.

In 1911 the Fund's Director, E.F. Bashford, included Murray as one of the cancer quacks castigated in his article 'Cancer, credulity and quackery' in the *British Medical Journal*.[21] Murray took no action concerning the article (he was old and died in 1914), but Dr Robert Bell of the Battersea Anti-Vivisection Hospital sued Bashford for libel over his description as a 'quack'. Bell was another surgeon who relinquished surgery, and was later to establish cancer wards for the dietetic and medicinal treatment of cancer. The court did not accept Bashford's argument that Bell's refusal to act on the result of mouse experiments and use surgery amounted to quackery, and Bashford was ordered to pay £2,000 damages.[22] After this courtroom defeat, Bashford did not remain in his position at the ICRF for long; he retired prematurely. Ironically, although Bashford's claim that surgery was the sole treatment for cancer was rejected by the court, the medical profession accepted that surgery should always be used as the first and main treatment for the disease, except in the case of superficial and skin cancers, for which a third alternative to the traditional choice of surgical or medical treatment became available.

Radiology and radiotherapy

X-rays were discovered at the end of 1895 and were first used in the treatment of cancer in 1896, though such early experiments in no way constituted an effective cancer treatment regime. Radioactivity was discovered in 1897 and radium in 1898: X-ray and radium therapy, however, took some time to become established as more than 'scientific' quack nostrums, fit only to be dismissed with such chemical nostrums as trypsin, arsenic, mercury, and potassium iodide.[23] The discovery of X-rays and their therapeutic use followed Finsen's successful development of ultraviolet light treatment in Denmark. UV was particularly useful in the treatment of skin diseases such as lupus (TB of the skin) and skin cancer. When it was established that X-rays, like UV, were constituents of health-giving sunlight, both forms of rays were used by dermatologists. The lead in this development in dermatology came from the London Hospital, which had benefited from an unwanted gift of a large UV treatment apparatus from Princess Alexandra in 1900.[24] The use of these different ray therapies in the treatment of skin cancer and other skin conditions continued the traditional association of cancer and skin which can be seen in the names of the nineteenth-century institutions. The accurate diagnosis of superficial cancers and their separation from non-cancerous conditions was a problem compounded by the tendency of syphilitic sores and leg ulcers to become 'malignant'. It was only with the development of reliable pathological techniques that accurate diagnosis and a specific definition of malignancy became possible.

From the time of their discovery, the main use of X-rays in medicine has been diagnostic. In those hospitals which had a medical electrician, this diagnostic work fell to him, leaving dermatologists such as James Sequira, at the London Hospital, to develop X-ray cancer treatments. In Manchester, X-ray treatments were successfully developed by the dermatologist at the Skin Hospital, where the Cancer Hospital sent appropriate patients. The Cancer Hospital found the technical difficulties of running their own X-ray plant too great to justify its use on the small number of patients involved at the small hospital.[25] In Glasgow, the medical electrician at the Royal Infirmary, Dr J. Macintyre (primarily an otolaryngologist), had an 'electric pavilion' before X-rays were discovered. He was so successful in his development of X-ray cancer treatments that no attempt was made to emulate him at the small Cancer Hospital down the road.[26] In all three cities, the cancer hospitals concentrated in the first decade of this century upon developing their research laboratories and their surgical facilities. These attracted patients who were not of the 'hospital class', as well as terminal charity cases, who were still turned away at the general infirmaries. Patients accommodated in 'home' beds until death accounted for a decreasing proportion of the work of the cancer hospitals. In Glasgow, a domiciliary service provided patients with, *inter alia*, coal, food, inflatable pillows, and clean bed linen, to ease dying at home. In the hospitals, the dying patients increasingly gave way to patients admitted for aggressive treatment aimed at cure; the treatment was often a combination of surgery and radiotherapy.

Radium (which was found to have a half-life of nearly 2,000 years) spontaneously produces the radioactive gas radon. For many years radon, rather than radium, the rarest and most valuable element in the world, was usually used for medical treatments. Radon gas, which was recommended for a vast range of conditions, was taken in a solution of water, directly inhaled, or sealed into tubes and implanted in body cavities. In the late 1890s naturally-occurring radon solutions were discovered to have been in use at spas for centuries before the discovery of radiation. The use of this discovery in advertising by both spas and industrial producers of radium products did not enhance the position of radium in the pharmacopoeia: Marie Curie's claim that it was a cancer specific did, however, increase patient demand for radium treatments.[27]

Gamma rays, like UV and X-rays, were found naturally in health-giving sunlight; they were regarded as natural and healthy like the other forms of physical therapy, such as electricity, heat, light, water, and massage. Radium institutes were established in most of the European capitals. It appears to have been King Edward VII who was directly responsible for the establishment of the London Radium Institute – Britain's first. He was himself successfully treated with radium (nearly 300 mg of salt were used), and he insisted that such treatment be available to his subjects. In both London and Manchester, brewers were the major supporters of outpatient radium institutes, which were, in a sense, radium dispensaries.[28] Just prior to the Great War, radium institutes were established in London and Manchester; radium supplies were also purchased for various cities around the UK, including Glasgow, Sheffield, Dublin, Plymouth, and Hull.

Although radium was rarely mentioned without reference to the belief that it might cure cancer, the majority of patients treated with radium before 1920 were suffering from arthritic and other chronic but not cancerous conditions. The only cancer hospital with more than a few milligrams of radium was the London Cancer Hospital, but new radium treatments were largely developed at the radium institutes, which increasingly specialized in cancer treatment.

After the Great War, the newly-formed Medical Research Council distributed radium for use in a multi-centre research scheme for the development of cancer treatments. The centres chosen were virtually all large general hospitals; only tiny amounts went for research to Lord Rutherford at the Cavendish Laboratories and to the London Radium Institute. Small amounts went to St Mark's and St Peter's, both of which had added 'cancer' to their titles before the outbreak of the war. The cancer hospitals were excluded from the scheme, apparently on the grounds that they were small – government radium would be in danger of being under-used. In the event, the radium was under-used in the large general hospitals which did receive it. One of these was the Middlesex Hospital, where the eighteenth-century cancer wards had been transformed from a charitable home for the dying into a centre for treatment and research.[29]

Despite the snub they received from the MRC, the small charitable institutions did not abandon cancer research and treatment, but terminal care became less important. In Manchester, the Radium Institute successfully developed a treatment regime for cancer of the mouth and throat. Working in co-operation with the nearby cancer hospital, they were able to develop inpatient treatments. Patients receiving these treatments tended to take beds which would previously have been used for terminal care, a change which was not universally welcomed by those on the hospital board. The poor law infirmaries had improved considerably in the first thirty years of the twentieth century, but they certainly did not provide ideal care for terminal cancer patients.[30]

During the economic stringencies of the 1920s and 1930s there was little money available for the expansion of the cancer hospitals, but there were demands for an increased radium supply, especially after the success of the MRC scheme. Until the mid-1920s, radiation was often only recommended as a palliative in those cases where surgery had failed. Primary radiation therapy could only be developed on those patients who adamantly refused surgery.[31] During the 1920s successive falls in the price of radium made it an increasingly popular object of medical patronage. By the end of the 1920s hospitals – large and small, all over the country – were seeking to secure their own supplies for cancer treatments.

Cancer therapy or radiotherapy

After a radium census in 1929, a national radium supply was purchased, to avert the consequences of virtually every hospital having its own inadequately-managed, extremely dangerous radium. A National Radium Trust, acting through a National Radium Commission, supplied radium to a series of National Radium Centres. Each centre was based on a teaching hospital and a university physics department; cancer hospitals were not even considered when the structure was drawn up. The only national radium centres to include pre-existing radium institutes and/or cancer hospitals were at Manchester and Liverpool. In London, which did not have to follow this pattern of regional centres – in deference to the anarchic free-for-all between the competing teaching hospitals – the Cancer Hospital was by no means the pre-eminent centre for radiotherapy. Bart's, the Middlesex, and the Westminster fought for this distinction; at the Cancer Hospital radiotherapy received scant regard, but it did benefit from the increased supplies of radium.[32]

Increased confidence that radium offered a cure for cancer is shown by the Mount Vernon Hospital's decision to change from a TB sanatorium to a specialist radiotherapeutic cancer hospital. Another cancer hospital established in London during the early 1920s was the Marie Curie Cancer Hospital, staffed by women for the treatment of women cancer patients.[33] This hospital was a particularly successful participant in the MRC radium research scheme, developing the first successful treatment for cancer of the uterus. These two new cancer hospitals were like almost all the other remaining cancer hospitals – centres for the development of radium therapy. Even the relatively small Glasgow Cancer Hospital opened its own radium institute; the emphasis of the hospital had changed from care of the dying to radical aggressive surgery and radiotherapy.[34]

The success of the new cancer treatments based on the integration of surgery and radium therapy was demonstrated in the terms of the 1939 Cancer Act. This established a financial structure for the provision of radium treatments for cancer patients throughout the country. This structure was needed despite a fall in the price of radium (as Canadian radium came on the market), because high-energy radiation-beam therapies became established in the late 1930s.[35]

In 1939 the Second World War intervened, preventing the implementation of the Cancer Act, whose provisions were superseded by those of the National Health Service Act of 1946. Much to the regret of many involved with it, this brought an end to the National Radium Commission; there would no longer be an independent body monitoring and controlling the medical use of radionucleides.[36] By this time, radium was beginning to be replaced by radio-cobalt and iridium, isotopes which did not continually produce a dangerous radioactive gas like the radon produced by radium. Under the NHS, most cancer hospitals lost their 'special' designation and were gradually integrated into large general hospitals. Radiotherapy became a regional specialty which, like plastic surgery, was to be made available at one site – usually a general teaching hospital – within every region.

Significantly, the discussions concerning the possibility of a role for the NRC in the NHS had centred on the question of the extent to which radiotherapy could be regarded as 'cancer therapy'. It was tempting before the Second World War to present radiotherapy as the cancer therapy applicable wherever surgery could not offer a cure. This was not the full story, though. Radiotherapy was also used to treat some non-malignant conditions, and some practitioners were worried that, if radiotherapy were only presented as cancer therapy, some patients would avoid treatment for fear of stigma. There were also some forms of cancer which neither surgery nor radiotherapy could hope to cure.

In the wake of the Second World War, the medicinal treatment of cancer was reintroduced. The aggressive cancer chemotherapeutic use of nitrogen mustards and their derivatives were actually a direct consequence of a military accident, but the new antibiotics and synthetic hormones helped to open up new potential aggressive treatments aimed at cure.[37] This made sense of the location of cancer patients in large general hospitals where teams of surgeons, physicians, and radiotherapists could develop appropriate courses of treatment for their patients. Terminal care was not, however, regarded as a specialty, and no special provision was made for the dying. Part of the reason for this can be seen in the speech Bevan made on presenting the NHS Bill to Parliament. He described how he 'would rather be kept alive in the efficient if cold altruism of a large hospital than expire in a gush of warm sympathy in a small one'.[38] That is all very well where there is the prospect of recovery. The health service he created had little room for the dying – the embarrassing evidence of the failure of medicine to make man immortal. His despised 'gush of warm sympathy' was missed, once reorganization and rebuilding had done away with the small hospitals (especially the cottage hospitals). During the first twenty years of the NHS, it became increasingly common for people to die in hospital, on general wards, away from the support of their families, under the care of medical staff ill-equipped to cope with death.[39]

The hospice reborn

In the white heat of the technological revolution of the 1960s, death came to be seen as the great 'medical failure' rather than a natural part of life, to be coped with rather than ignored. New, more aggressive cancer treatments were developed which left patients and relatives wondering whether the treatment was worse than the disease and demanding an answer to the difficult question 'Is a few more weeks of life worth the pain and suffering involved?' This was a question which did not attract strong charitable support from the ICRF or the Cancer Research Campaign, the latter a charity originally conceived as a means of routing money into clinical rather than laboratory research. Research into care for the dying attracted little support from the existing charities. A new cancer charity, the Marie Curie Cancer Relief Fund, was established; this supported home care for the terminally ill.[40] The area which needed most attention – and appeared most intractable – was pain control. Successful research into this problem was carried out, not in a teaching hospital, but in a South London hospice, run by nuns who devoted themselves to easing their patients' passage from the world of the living to that of the dead.

Stoddard, in her book *The Hospice Movement: A Better Way of Dying*, traces the origins of the modern hospice movement to the Dublin Hospice, established by Sister Mary Aikenhead, a Sister of Charity, who had been a co-worker and contemporary of Florence Nightingale.[41] In 1902, the English Sisters of Charity opened St Joseph's Hospice in London; by this time there were already several homes for the dying, including the Hostel of God (founded in 1892, now the Trinity Hospice), St Luke's Hospital (a 'home for the dying poor', founded in 1893, now Hereford Lodge) and the Friedenheim Hospital (founded 1892). Unlike the religious establishments, the Friedenheim Hospital, which later became the Princess Alexandra Friedenheim, is not mentioned in the work of the chroniclers of the hospice movement. 'Friedenheim' was, however, the title chosen by those who wanted to establish homes for the dying attached to new cancer hospitals in the 1890s.[42]

Research into the control of terminal cancer pain started at St Luke's Hospital in 1948, and was developed at St Joseph's Hospice between 1958 and 1965 by Cicely (now Dame Cicely) Saunders – one of those rare creatures, a doctor of medicine who is also qualified as a nurse (and almoner). This work would not have been possible in the USA, because of its dependence on the controlled use of heroin and cocaine, neither legal – even in medical use – in the USA. The value of the combination of these drugs had been established at the London Cancer Hospital by the surgeon Henry Snow. Snow's 'Brompton cocktail' (as the heroin and cocaine mixture was known) was far better received than his controversial observation that cancer was stress-related. This claim had attracted considerable criticism in the pages of the *BMJ*. The problem with terminal pain control, however, was to ensure that the patient was not simply caught on a seesaw between drug-induced oblivion and overwhelming pain. The objective was to keep the patient in a mental condition adequate to continue sharing life, even if only from bed, with family and friends. Cicely Saunders combined the 'Brompton cocktail' of heroin (or morphine) and cocaine in controlled doses with synthetic steroids, anti-inflammatories, cancer chemotherapy, and palliative radiotherapy.[43] The discovery that pain control was possible, though by no means simple, brought about what was possibly the greatest revolution in cancer treatment since the introduction of radium treatments.

In 1967, Dame Cicely Saunders, by now the personification of the hospice movement, established St Christopher's Hospice as the first research and teaching hospice. Her intention was to lay the scientific foundations of terminal care and in so doing make the care of the dying medically respectable. From 1969 St Christopher's ran a domiciliary care service, much like that run by the Glasgow Cancer Hospital before the First World War. In 1974, eighty years after its plan for a Friedenheim was shelved, the Royal Marsden opened a ward – the Horder Ward – to provide specialized care for the dying. From 1975, money became available from the National Society for Cancer Relief for the building of twenty-five-bed terminal-care centres on NHS land. By the mid-1980s the hospice movement has developed so far that it has now declared its aim to be not the provision of hospice beds for all moribund patients, but to have such an effect on attitudes and training that 'no dying patients, anywhere, should fail to find staff with sufficient awareness of their needs either to give help themselves or to call in others where they cannot do so'.[44] The NMTBD ('no more to be done') that was regularly written on the notes of patients failed by radiotherapy should become a thing of the past.

Ironically, it was during this minor revolution in cancer care that Britain's first Friedenheim was closed in bizarre circumstances. In 1958, after staffing difficulties, the 120-year-old buildings of the St Columba's Hospital, as it was called by then, were demolished to make way for the Civic Centre at Swiss Cottage.[45] At this point, St Columba's, which was described by Sir John Fremantle as 'an old voluntary hospital with a remarkably fine atmosphere', was not under threat of closure, though the number of beds was

halved to thirty-five.[46] The building it moved to, The Elms
on Spaniard's Lane, was said to be the second largest house
in London (after Buckingham Palace), but it had no bed lift
– so the upper floors went unused. In 1979 the Kensington,
Chelsea, and Westminster Area Health Authority started
trying to close it, with a view to saving about £200,000 per
year and to realize capital on the sale of the site. At the end
of 1980 the NUPE campaign against the closure of the
twenty-seven-bed hospital for terminally-ill cancer patients
had extended from negotiations with various statutory bodies
to a picketing and leafleting campaign, including a picket of
the TUC Annual Conference. The Health Authority, in its
desire to clear the site, started transferring patients in private
ambulances.[47] After a union official had been injured by one
of these vehicles – and a patient had died in transit – one
driver decided that he could not take the remaining dying
man from his ward. For the first few weeks of 1981, while the
hospice movement was gaining support throughout the world
for specialized supportive care for the dying, one old man lay
dying with his London hospice (one of only seven then run
by the NHS) dying around him on its spectacular 7-acre site,
overlooking the vale where Keats heard his nightingale.[48]
After his death, proposals that The Elms should become a
test-tube baby clinic, an American hospital, or be converted
into flats came to nothing. The building was sold to an Arab
for £2.6 million, but remains unoccupied because of planning
problems over a proposed conversion of the stable block into
a harem.[49]

The London Cancer Hospital had by then established its
specialized ward for terminal care; it had developed its own
proposed Friedenheim site (in Sutton) as a modern cancer
hospital many years previously. The house which had been
offered to the Glasgow Cancer Hospital as a Friedenheim had
burnt down before it was equipped to receive patients, but in
the late 1970s its grounds provided the site for the new Beatson Cancer Research Laboratories when they outgrew the old
Glasgow Cancer Hospital. The foundations of the old
building are now grassed over, overlooked by the veterinary
school, where AIDS vaccines are being developed. We live in
the remains of our history, just as much in the field of cancer
treatment as elsewhere. The demands for terminal care were
never pushed out by the putative success of research into the

cause of cancer. What may seem rather ironic is the way in which palliative care has come to regain the respectability it lost from the 1940s to the 1960s.

When Beatson took over the Glasgow Cancer Hospital from the unorthodox Hugh Murray in the 1890s, he gained international acclaim for his introduction of the ovariectomy as a treatment for breast cancer in pre-menopausal women. After the deaths of all the patients with whom he had had impressive results for several years, he wrote a disclaimer of this 'cure for cancer'. He could not recommend it; it was only palliative. When artificial female hormones became available, they were used to produce 'premature menopause' in much the same way that Beatson had brought it about surgically. When radium implants were first developed, they were only recommended as palliatives, to be used for the relief of local pain and symptoms. The 'real' treatment was surgery. One of the important elements of modern terminal care is, once again, palliative radiotherapy. It is reasonable to speculate that by the end of this century therapeutic spa treatments using radioactive muds and waters will have been reintroduced from the continent as part of the complete care of the cancer patient.

This may only be speculation, but it is certain that while general hospitals have extended the treatments they offer to cancer patients, the role of the special cancer hospital has in some important respects come full circle – from terminal care to aggressive treatment and back to terminal care – in the course of a century. If the lessons learned by hospices can be successfully introduced into general hospital practice, it will be in a sense a re-run of the passage of radiotherapy from special cancer hospitals into the general hospitals. This illustrates how small specialist centres have developed in the past and can still develop new aspects of patient care that may then usefully be taken up into more general use by the large institutions.

Notes

1. Dr Murphy is now the Education Officer (Ethics) of the Royal Society for the Prevention of Cruelty to Animals. This work was financed by the Wellcome Trust through a post-doctoral Fellowship

and postgraduate scholarship and by the Science and Education Research Council – Social Science Research Council joint committee postgraduate scholarship.

2. M.B. Shimkin, *Contrary to Nature* (US Department of Health, Education, and Welfare Public Health Services, National Institute of Health, Washington, 1977), 19–20. J. Austoker, 'Cancer research left to charity', *New Scientist*, no. 1,582 (1987), 28–9 and *A History of the Imperial Cancer Research Fund 1902 to 1986* (Oxford University Press, 1987).

3. C.C.S. Murphy, 'A history of radiotherapy to 1950: cancer and radiotherapy in Britain 1850–1950', PhD thesis, University of Manchester Institute of Science and Technology (1986), *passim*.

4. D. Winn, *The Hospice Way* (Macdonald, London, 1987), 23–4; S. Stoddard, *The Hospice Movement: A Better Way of Caring for the Dying* (Jonathan Cape, London, 1979) *passim*; and C. Saunders, D. Summers, and N. Teller (eds), *Hospice: the Living Idea* (Edward Arnold, London, 1981), *passim*.

5. Shimkin, *Contrary to Nature*, 24. In G.E.R. Lloyd, *Hippocratic Writings* (Penguin, London, 1978), 230, this aphorism – section VI, number 38 – is translated as 'It is better not to treat those who have internal cancers since, if treated, they die quickly; but if not treated they last a long time.'

6. G.B. Risse, *Hospital Life in Enlightenment Scotland: Care and Teaching at the Royal Infirmary Edinburgh* (Cambridge University Press, Cambridge, 1986), 164–6.

7. J. Woodward, *To Do The Sick No Harm: A Study of the British Voluntary Hospital System to 1875* (Routledge & Kegan Paul, London, 1974), 51 and 134. See also Murphy, 'History of Radiotherapy', 1.1–1.12.

8. F. Sandwith, *Surgeon Compassionate: The Story of Dr William Marsden* (Peter Davies, London, 1960), 193–261.

9. E. Wilson, *The History of the Middlesex Hospital* (Churchill, London, 1845), 17.

10. A. Marsden, *A New and Successful Mode of Treating Certain Forms of Cancer* (J. Churchill, London, 1869).

11. Minutes of the Cancer Investigation Committee of the Middlesex Hospital, 24 May 1904. See also J.W.G. Myler, 'Some empirical methods adopted in the treatment of inoperable cancer and their results', *Archives of the Middlesex Hospital*, vol. 2, March (1904), 65.

12. L. Granshaw, *St Mark's Hospital, London: A Social History of a Specialist Hospital* (King's Fund Historical Series, London, 1985), 6.

13. *The Glasgow Cancer and Skin Institution Annual Report* (1891), 11. See also G.T. Beatson (Sir), *A Short History of the Glasgow Royal Cancer Hospital* (The Glasgow Royal Cancer Hospital, 1930), 1.

14. T. Macdonald, 'Christie Hospital and Holt Radium Institute: foundation, development and achievements 1892–1962', M.Sc. thesis, University of Manchester Institute of Science and

Technology (1977).

15. H. Snow, 'On the re-appearance (recurrence) of cancer after apparent extirpation, with suggestions for its prevention; and general remarks on the operative treatment of malignant growths' and 'The palliative treatment of incurable cancer, with an appendix on the use of the opium pipe', *British Medical Journal*, vol. 2 (1890), 689–90.

16. H. Snow, 'Opium and cocaine in the treatment of cancerous disease', *British Medical Journal*, vol. 2 (1896), 718.

17. Murphy, 'History of radiotherapy', 1.23–1.28.

18. See the *Medical Directory* 1894–1913 under London: Special Hospitals.

19. Anon (probably J. Craigie), *Imperial Cancer Research Fund 1902–1952: Fifty Years of Cancer Research* (supplement to ICRF Annual Report, 1952), and C.E. Dukes, 'The origins and early history of the Imperial Cancer Research Fund', *Annals of the Royal College of Surgeons*, vol. 36 (1965), 325–9.

20. Information from various editions of the *Medical Directory* and from the area health authorities.

21. E.F. Bashford, 'Cancer, credulity and quackery', *British Medical Journal*, vol. 1 (1911), 1,221–30.

22. R. Bell, *Reminiscences of an Old Physician* (John Murray, London, 1924), 241–4 and Appendix. See also Medico Legal, 'Bell *v.* Bashford and the British Medical Association', *British Medical Journal*, vol. 1 (1912), 1,403–7 and 1,461–7.

23. Murphy, 'History of radiotherapy', 3.31–3.42. See also L.D. Longo, 'Electrotherapy in gynaecology: the American experience', *Bulletin of the History of Medicine*, vol. 60, no. 3 (1986), 340–66.

24. M. Rowbottom and C. Susskind, *Electricity and Medicine: History of Their Interaction* (San Francisco Press, 1984), 229–33. See also A.E. Clark-Kennedy, *The London: A Study in the Voluntary Hospital System 1740–1948* (Pitman Medical Publishing, London, 1963), 142–3. This equipment is on display in the Wellcome Galleries at the Science Museum, London.

25. Murphy, 'History of radiotherapy', 3.26.

26. A.L. Goodall, 'John Macintyre, pioneer radiologist 1857–1928', *Surgo*, Whitsun (1958), 119–26.

27. R. Reid, *Marie Curie* (Collins, London, 1974), 126, 133, and 224.

28. Murphy, 'History of radiotherapy', 3.43–3.63.

29. Op. cit., 5.1–5.14.

30. J.V. Pickstone, *Medicine and Industrial Society: A History of Hospital Development in Manchester and its Region, 1752–1946* (Manchester University Press, 1985), 256–64; G.E. Birkett, *Radium Therapy: Principles and Practice* (Cassell, London, 1931).

31. G.L. Keynes, *The Gates of Memory* (Oxford University Press, 1983), 211–16.

32. F.G. Spear and K. Griffiths, *The Radium Commission: A Short*

History of its Origins and Work 1929–1948 (HMSO, London, 1951).

33. Murphy, 'History of radiotherapy', 5.25–5.30.

34. Beatson, *Glasgow Royal Cancer Hospital* 7–9.

35. E.R. Landa, 'The first nuclear industry', *Scientific American*, vol. 247 (1982), 154–63.

36. Murphy, 'History of radiotherapy', 7.55–7.61.

37. G.B. Infield, *Disaster at Bari* (Hale, London, 1974), *passim*.

38. B. Abel-Smith, *The Hospitals 1800–1948: A Study in Social Administration in England and Wales* (Heinemann, London, 1964), 481.

39. Marie Curie Memorial Foundation, *Report on a National Survey Concerning Patients Nursed at Home* (Marie Curie Memorial Foundation, London, 1952), *passim*; and H.L.G. Hughes, *Peace at the Last – A Survey of Terminal Care in the United Kingdom* (The Calouste Gulbenkian Foundation, London, 1960), *passim*.

40. B.J. Lunt, *Terminal Cancer Care: Specialist Services Available in Great Britain in 1980* (Wessex Regional Cancer Organization, Southampton, 1980).

41. Stoddard, *The Hospice Movement*, 65.

42. Murphy, 'History of radiotherapy', 1.39–1.40.

43. R.G. Twycross, 'Relief of pain' in C. Saunders (ed.), *The Management of Terminal Malignant Disease* (Edward Arnold, London, 1984), 82–3.

44. C. Saunders, 'Evolution in terminal care' in Saunders (ed.), *Management of Terminal Malignant Disease*, 216.

45. *Hampstead and Highgate Express*, 11 July 1958.

46. *Hampstead and Highgate Express*, 14 Oct. 1955; see also *Hampstead and Highgate Express*, 14 Dec. 1979, 29 Aug., 24 Oct., 19 Sept., and 7 Nov. 1980.

47. *Morning Star*, 22 Oct. 1980.

48. *Hampstead and Highgate Express*, 21 Nov. 1980.

49. *Hampstead and Highgate Express*, 9 Nov. 1981; *Daily Telegraph*, 3 Dec. 1981. These newspaper cuttings are part of the special collection about St Columba's in the Camden Local History Library.

10

Managing medicine: creating a profession of hospital administration in the United States, 1895 – 1915

Morris J. Vogel

Hospitals are ₹mong the most complex of modern social institutions. They have assumed responsibility for the care of individuals confronting extreme crises. They mobilize some of society's most advanced intellectual and technological resources, and command substantial and growing proportions of the common wealth. And they are directed through formal bureaucratic structures and sophisticated management techniques that befit their roles and resources.

It is difficult to recall that not much more than a century ago hospitals did little more than provide settings in which physicians practised a minimally interventionist medicine on the small minority of the sick and injured who sought institutional treatment. Concentrated as they were in larger urban centres, the nation's few hospitals were outside the experience and even the imagination of most Americans. Furnishing room, board, and attention primarily to the socially marginal, hospitals were themselves marginal, little more than homes for the sick homeless. They furnished no special medical technologies, no therapies not otherwise available in the ordinary patient's home.[1]

The hospital was like the home in its informal administration as well. Though physicians increasingly involved themselves in determining institutional priorities, major decisions remained in the hands of lay trustees, the charitably-inclined individuals whose benefactions underwrote institutional expenses but whose primary responsibilities were focused elsewhere. The authority of hospital superintendents and the other managers who directed day-to-day operations rarely extended beyond control of the

243

domestic staff and the purchase of food, coal, and other household provisions.

The American general hospital began to assume its modern form and significance at the turn of the twentieth century. The hundred or so institutions of the early 1870s grew to around 4,000 by 1910. By that date, towns of 10,000 residents might reasonably expect to have hospitals within their limits or nearby, and hospitals were regularly admitting middle-class patients who, a generation earlier, would have spurned their services.[2] Physicians had begun to reorganize their practices around the institution and the skilled nursing, laboratories, specialized facilities, and newly-developing medical technologies it offered. Patients were now more likely to be hospitalized for episodes of acute illness than for chronic care or recuperation, and their treatment was correspondingly more active and interventionist. Costs, as a consequence, were rising dramatically and in many cases outstripping the resources of private charity. The transformed institution could no longer be managed as informally as its predecessor.[3]

It was against this backdrop that the Association of Hospital Superintendents of the United States and Canada (which changed its name in 1906 to the American Hospital Association) first met in 1899. Eight superintendents – all but one from Cleveland, where the group met, and Detroit – and a publisher, whom the group elected to honorary membership, convened for two days in September to draft a charter for a national organization that would bring superintendents together regularly for the interchange of ideas about hospital management.[4]

The involvement of Del Sutton, the publisher, suggests that the organization was not a fore-ordained necessity. Sutton, who had been campaigning for a superintendent's group since he had begun *The National Hospital Sanitarium Record* in 1897, had a financial stake in creating the Association. Sutton intended his new journal as an advertising vehicle for suppliers to the growing hospital market. He had begun with a special relationship with the makers of Imperial Granum Food, a processed wheat food for convalescents, before the Association's charter meeting adopted his *Record* as its official organ. In his formal address to the second meeting in 1900, Sutton revealed something of his interest in the hospital market. Noting that the previous three years had seen the founding of 1,000 new hospitals, Sutton pointed out that vast sums were now spent in building and supplying hospitals. The *Record* published abbreviated accounts of Association proceedings for three years before the Association undertook this task itself in 1902. Sutton's journal survived until 1915, changing its name several times before it was purchased by the Association and discontinued in favour of the Association's newly-established *The Modern Hospital*.[5]

While Sutton had his own agenda in promoting the Association, he and the small group at the first meeting had struck a responsive chord. Thirty-one superintendents attended the 1900 meeting, forty-seven came in 1901, and more than 100 registered for the fourth meeting in 1902. By its tenth meeting in 1908, the new association had more than 450 members from across the United States and Canada.[6] These men and women joined together for a variety of reasons. The superintendents resembled other groups of Americans – managers, professionals, and the like – in new, rapidly growing, or evolving fields who affiliated with one another in new organizations to seek common answers to common problems, fellowship with others similarly situated, and ways of enhancing their status and self-esteem.[7]

The first generations of hospital superintendents had not been selected for their presumed technical competencies; indeed, they were meant to learn their craft on the job. Presiding over essentially domestic arrangements, the early nineteenth-century superintendent's chief qualifications had been his probity and his willingness to spend his life within the confining walls of the hospital. It is little wonder that retired ships' captains – men who had assumed responsibility for the fortunes of others – were heavily represented among *ante-bellum* stewards and superintendents. The role was that of a caretaker; superintendents were not expected to initiate or innovate.[8]

By the end of the nineteenth century, hospital superintendents had generally changed little in background and training from their predecessors. To be sure, a significant proportion of superintendents were now women, matrons or head nurses with responsibility for predominantly smaller hospitals, or religious superiors in charge of Catholic institutions. These women resembled their male counterparts in that they were chiefly qualified by virtue of being presumed satisfactory caretakers. But the radical transformation of the hospital then underway posed new challenges and created new opportunities and roles for superintendents.

Among the larger hospitals particularly – where change was likely to be most dramatic – superintendents had begun to look to each other informally for advice by the close of the nineteenth century. Circular letters had inquired about such newly-pressing issues as facilities for middle-class patients or whether physicians were permitted to charge fees for inpatient care. Superintendents had also started to tour other institutions – with the Massachusetts General and the new Johns Hopkins as favourite destinations – to familiarize themselves with the state of the managerial art. Superintendents from several Boston hospitals had met informally to discuss common concerns, and in New York City an ongoing hospital conference brought together representatives of forty institutions.[9] The annual meetings of the American Hospital Association extended and institutionalized these informal practices. Formal papers, scheduled discussions, and face-to-face contact allowed superintendents to share the specialized knowledge of their craft and to seek guidance on subjects they found puzzling. Furnishing occasions for the exchange of institutional and personal experience, the new association and its regularly scheduled meetings made superintendents part of a national movement and fit their concerns into the early twentieth-century campaign for scientific management.[10]

Much of the discussion addressed the modernization of the hospital. Whether superintendents actively directed their institutions or merely gathered information for their trustees, they had to consider a broad range of new issues. Asepsis and the other demands of scientific medicine required, for example, that many older buildings be modified or replaced, and that the design of new structures accommodate current technologies. In many cases, superintendents found that they could no longer simply manage inherited physical plants, but they had to represent their institutions in architectural collaborations that balanced the needs of physicians and the financial resources of the institution.[11] The growing clinical orientation of medical education likewise imposed demands on hospitals, sometimes requiring superintendents to weigh the competing needs of medical staff, patient care, and teaching, and make appropriate recommendations to trustees.[12]

The aspect of the hospital's transformation in which the superintendent figured most conspicuously was the cost squeeze. Mounting expenses forced the modernizing hospital to look beyond the charity of its narrow circle of traditional donors. No longer could it rely as completely on informal appeals spearheaded by trustees. The fact that hospitals were attracting increasing numbers of middle-class patients expanded the possibility for financial support. By the early twentieth century, organized fund drives – in which superintendents co-operated with professional managers – were appealing to a broadened base of community support.[13]

But it was especially with their individual payments for patient care that the middle classes came to take on the burden of hospital funding. The hospitalization of the middle classes changed the nature of the traditional institution as fundamentally as scientific medicine. And superintendents took on much of the burden for fashioning the hospital's response to this growing patient class. Doctors bore the primary responsibility for attracting these paying patients through referrals, but it was largely left to domestic and nursing staffs under the superintendent's direction to adjust the day-to-day life of institutions originally intended for the poor to the care of middle-class patients and the recognition of their needs. Superintendents also had to implement cost accounting procedures to determine to what extent hospitals were subsidizing or profiting from paying patients.[14] At the same time, superintendents – much more than physicians – were expected to defend the interests of the hospital's original constituency of poor patients, whose care was coming now more often to be thought a drain on funds rather than the sacred duty it had been a half-century before.[15] Strains in the historic obligation to provide charitable care for the poor were evident, for example, in the obsessive concern with medical abuse. The accusation that patients who could afford to pay imposed on hospital charity by seeking free treatment had been heard before, but it acquired special urgency as middle-class patients began to seek hospital treatment and hospitals came to depend on their fees. Association meetings regularly featured papers demonstrating the pervasiveness of this practice and presenting stratagems to limit it.[16]

One is struck by the apparent trivia often exchanged under Association auspices. Some details seem to be no more than housekeeping hints. But even much of this mundane detail was motivated – and perhaps even necessitated – by the changing nature of the hospital. Superintendents wanting to remain current about techniques for maintaining asepsis, for example, had to concern themselves with flooring materials installed in operating rooms and with the way wards were swept. Hospitals competing for middle-class patients had to serve meals attractive to middle-class palates. And given the steeply-mounting expenses of the modernizing hospital, it is understandable that prudent administrators would also consider domestic economies.[17] J.T. Duryea, general medical superintendent of hospitals in Brooklyn, New York, struck perhaps the Association's keynote in his presidential address to the fourth annual convention. Arguing that superintendents could learn from each other's methods in managing the myriad details of their complex institutions, he declaimed, 'Show us how you keep your census high and your cost per diem low.'[18]

Association sessions were extraordinarily earnest in their consideration of such details of domestic management as the proper temperature to store lemons, how to mark sheets, and the importance of buying only foods in season. Underlying much of this concern was the effort to reduce expenses. Session after session added to the array of cost-cutting techniques: superintendents explained how to clean and re-use soiled gauze (furnishing softer and more absorbent bandages in the bargain); and how they confronted surgeons with comparative counts of instruments used (and therefore needing costly cleaning and sterilization) in operations.[19] The obsessive commitment of some turn-of-the-century superintendents to exaggerated and almost ludicrous economies must be understood as more than simple efforts to keep expenditures in check. Association activists should be recognized as ideologues, converts to the doctrine of efficiency then gaining broad social currency.

Superintendents joining together in the Association shared a sense of their mutual cause. Running through their early deliberations was the notion that they confronted common problems and would therefore profit by looking beyond their local communities and their personal experiences. It made little sense for an individual administrator to develop a solution to a problem that had already been resolved elsewhere. But the point of these meetings was not merely the exchange of information, important as that was. In their frequent reiteration of the complaint that they too often had to rely on their own judgement, superintendents made clear that they were searching for a body of objectifiable data, of certifiable knowledge.[20] The 'facts' of an administrative science would not only aid decision-making, but would also serve as the base of specialized knowledge on which superintendents could establish their claims to professional expertise. A seeming jumble of simple domestic wisdom, basic administrative procedure, construction technology, organizational schemes, customer relations, and professional aspiration was at its core an effort to work out a system of managerial science addressed to the special problems of the modern hospital. In this regard, as in their commitment to a cost-cutting efficiency, superintendents were full participants in the scientific management crusade of the early twentieth century.[21]

Like self-consciously scientific managers and technical experts in other fields, superintendents sought to forge a professional identity. A collective organization was an important strategy in this regard; meetings, journals, management handbooks, and courses of study offered more than an opportunity to share technique. The very fact that the superintendents developed a specialized organization at whose meetings they devoted themselves to the pursuit of arcane knowledge and worthy public ends signalled professionalism. Joining together allowed hospital administrators to define the special competencies required for the practice of their craft and to certify mutually that Association members were expert in the enterprise of hospital superintendency.[22] Within its first decade, the Association had developed standards for membership which, while generously inclusive, required that applicants be voted into fellowship in the Society. The appearance of organizations promoting and staking public claims about the expertise of their members and the public good they served was a salient characteristic of turn-of-the-century America. Following the lead of engineers, social scientists, and – most conspicuously – physicians, hospital administrators sought to capitalize on the authority American society increasingly granted those professing technical expertise.[23]

While discussions at early Association meetings generally proceeded from a widespread consensus that it was desirable to enhance the status and authority of superintendents, papers and recorded debates revealed less ·unanimity on specific agendas to meet these goals. For one thing, turn-of-the-century administrators came from a variety of backgrounds. A small but significant minority – some of whom directed the large and important urban hospitals – were physicians. Relatively secure in their credentials, they emphasized the importance of medical qualifications in carrying out administrative tasks. Male lay superintendents, on the other hand, tended to regard the business sense that had commended them to like-minded trustees as the most important skill for the roles they already had and for the increased authority most prized.[24] These men generally took the lead in Association discussions that treated the household arrangements at the core of early twentieth-century hospital administration as subjects for technical management analyses.[25] Management science may have been doubly attractive to these male lay superintendents because it offered the possibility of escaping the stigma of tasks broadly defined as feminine – a fact that could hardly go unnoticed in a field, many of whose practitioners were women. Women superintendents – a near majority at most early meetings – on the whole absented themselves from recorded discussions about exercising or augmenting the institutional power of the superintendency. This last fact may owe to internalized social and cultural constraints about appropriate public postures for women. The apparent reluctance to discuss power may stem equally from the specific institutional settings in which most women superintendents worked. Concentrated in smaller hospitals, they presided over comparatively simple bureaucracies which in many cases merely paralleled the nursing hierarchies through which they had risen to institutional responsibility.[26]

Particularly in the larger and more bureaucratically complex hospitals, superintendents professionalizing their craft and marking out spheres of authority had to contend with power wielded by others who already played important roles in the hospital. Notable in this regard were the trustees. They had created the superintendency, delegating authority to a steward or caretaker they hired and over whom they exercised oversight. Superintendents derived their power from the trustees; they owed deference in return. It was not uncommon for lay superintendents especially to share their trustees' world view and notions of the hospital as a moral universe rather than a bureaucratic organization. This complex relationship showed strains as superintendents tried to function more as executives and less as caretakers. Even George H.M. Rowe, who enjoyed exceptionally good rapport with the governing board of his Boston City Hospital, felt the need to point out that a superintendent functioned most effectively when vested with executive authority. In other discussions, one can sometimes detect a pained embarrassment at the low esteem in which trustee boards sometimes held their superintendents. J.T. Duryea complained in his presidential address, for example, that trustees sometimes perceived 'night watchmen or other accidents of employment' as suitable superintendents.[27] The superintendent's chief advantage in expanding his role and his authority *vis à vis* his superiors stemmed from his mastery of institutional detail that left even the most intensely involved trustee dependent on him.[28]

Superintendents were more successful in asserting leadership over their fellow servants within the hospital. Like other nineteenth-century employers, hospitals drew many of their employees – housekeepers, ward attendants, kitchen help, laundresses, and labourers – from a workforce not accustomed to the discipline required in increasingly complex institutions. Association sessions devoted considerable attention to administrative techniques for imposing order on the staff. Clocks, schedules, rules, record-keeping requirements, and printed forms routinized work, leaving ever less to the judgement of individual employees and putting ever more of the institution under bureaucratic control.[29] Even race could be an effective instrument for extending the superintendent's authority; Dr Eugene Elder of the Macon (Georgia) Hospital commended black employees to his fellow superintendents because they were especially easy to control.[30]

Doctors proved the most enduring challenge to hospital administrators. Superintendents based their aspirations to professional status on technical competence and the mastery of a body of arcane knowledge. But the claims of physicians clearly had widespread acceptance; the early twentieth-century reform of medical education, with its increasing emphasis on modern science, extended this advantage. These same changes in medical schooling would, by restricting access to the medical profession and thereby raising the social class origins of practitioners, broaden as well the social superiority that most hospital physicians enjoyed over their administrative counterparts. But it was to the age-old content of medical practice – the almost priestly role of explaining disease and reassuring the sick – that doctors most owed their advantaged position in the culture generally and in the hospital particularly.[31] Superintendents would find it difficult to interpose administrative edicts between doctor and patient.

Only the most eccentric superintendents publicly questioned the autonomy of physicians, but the problem of controlling the medical staff was a frequent undercurrent in Association proceedings.[32] The often-repeated debate over whether superintendents needed to be medically qualified generally returned to the same issue: Would doctor-administrators be better able than laymen to secure the co-operation of hospital physicians?[33] It is tempting to see the conflict between doctors and superintendents over the latter's control of institutional discipline and costs in terms of the professional aspirations of administrators. But the superintendents should not be understood solely as advocates of a modern hospital bureaucracy. Rather, many of them very much remained representatives of the more traditional views of the trustees, speaking as voices from the past against the interest of physicians in transforming the hospital into a modern medical workshop. Superintendents articulated lay concerns that doctors sometimes cared more about disease than about their patients. They were sensitive to the careerism – both intellectual and financial – that physicians sometimes brought into the hospital. And some superintendents expressed reservations about tying the fortunes of hospitals and their patients too closely to the modern teaching and research agendas of medical schools. Yet it was ordinarily only when they spoke for the trustees that most early twentieth-century superintendents could hope to prevail in these clashes of values with physicians.[34]

It was not until the late twentieth-century transformation of third-party payment that the balance of power within the hospital began to shift noticeably from physicians to administrators. Neither the workmen's compensation programmes introduced in the 1910s nor the Blue Cross-Blue Shield plans that began in the 1930s and expanded greatly in the postwar decades significantly altered the internal organization of the hospital. It had indeed been the intent of the Blue Cross system to preserve the institution precisely as it existed.[35] Likewise, the Medicare and Medicaid reforms of the great society were expected to leave the hospital structurally unchanged while making medical treatment more broadly available. But government assumption of responsibility for the health care for millions of elderly and poor Americans led ultimately to substantial change in the health care system.[36]

Massive federal funding channelled through programmes for patient care financed the development and acquisition of expensive new medical technologies, raising expectations and costs throughout the system. The same federal money underwrote dramatic increases in physicians' incomes.[37] An increasing reliance on complex technologies – often operated by non-physicians – further distanced relationships between practitioners and patients. The new level of physicians' incomes did the same. The inflow of federal money would ultimately undermine the cultural authority of doctors by dividing them from those they treated. At the same time, the hospitals in which they practised came ever more under the scrutiny of government officials concerned with what some feared to be costs rising inexorably toward national economic disaster. Regulations imposed by these outside authorities and administered by hospital managers seemed, by the mid-1980s, to be bringing the practice of hospital medicine under bureaucratic control. Doctors – no longer as able as before to argue that their opposition to reform derived from a principled commitment to patient care – were handicapped in resisting the intrusion of cost control and accountability. Joining their managerial colleagues in other areas of late-twentieth-century economic and institutional life, hospital administrators were able to proclaim the triumph of management. It was a victory in a quest not even imagined when their predecessors had embarked on the road to professionalization early in the twentieth century.

Notes

1. The standard histories of the American general hospital are Morris J. Vogel, *The Invention of the Modern Hospital: Boston, 1870– 1930* (University of Chicago Press, Chicago, 1980) and Charles E. Rosenberg, *The Care of Strangers: The Rise of America's Hospital System* (Basic Books, New York, 1987).

2. The usually-cited figure of 178 hospitals in 1873 is in J.M. Toner, 'Statistics of regular medical associations and hospitals of the United States', *Transactions of the American Medical Association*, 24 (1873), 314–33. Toner's list includes fifty-eight institutions iden- tifiable as insane asylums. Edwin H.L. Corwin, *The American Hospital* (Commonwealth Fund, New York, 1946) and Commission on Hospital Care, *Hospital Care in the United States* (Commonwealth Fund, New York, 1947) provide a wealth of data about the institu- tion in the first half of the twentieth century.

3. Vogel, *Modern Hospital, passim*; Rosenberg, *Care of Strangers, passim*.

4. 'Association of Hospital Superintendents, report of the proceedings', *National Hospital and Sanitarium Record*, 3 (September, 1899), 1–3. Summary listings of the Association's first thirty-eight meetings can be found in Bert W. Caldwell, 'American Hospital Association', *American and Canadian Hospitals* (Physicians' Record Company, Chicago, 1937), 11–35. See also Alejandra C. Laszlo, 'The American Hospital Association: emergence of a professional organization, 1899–1914', unpublished paper, Department of History and Sociology of Science, University of Pennsylvania, January, 1986.

5. Within its first year of publication, Sutton shifted the *National Hospital and Sanitarium Record* from its complete identification with a convalescent food to a new product. The journal began to advocate uniform systems of hospital accounting and record-keeping and to carry editorials, endorsements, and advertising for preprinted forms and filing systems designed specifically for hospital use. See, for example, the December 1897, and the February and May 1898 issues in volume 1. Sutton later chronicled his success as a publisher of hospital forms in 'Past, present and future', *The International Hospital Record*, 15 (March, 1912), 7. Sutton sold the *International Hospital Record* to the American Hospital Association, reportedly because he 'found the work too exacting . . . especially in conjunc- tion with his printing business and the publication of his system of hospital records': editorial, 'Announcement of purchase', *The Modern Hospital*, 4 (March, 1915), 183.

6. The *National Hospital and Sanitarium Record* evidently carried the only contemporaneous data for the first three meetings of the Association. See 3 (September, 1899), 1–3; 3 (August, 1900), 33–5; 5 (September, 1901), 3–9. The Association began to publish annual

accounts of its meetings – including lists of those attending – with its fourth annual conference in 1902. Titles vary, and the only original copy of the 1903 volume known to exist – *Proceedings of the Association of Hospital Superintendents of the United States and Canada* (hence *Proceedings AHA*) – is in the Countway Library of Harvard Medical School, Boston, Massachusetts.

7. For the general phenomenon of middle-class occupational organizations, see Robert H. Wiebe, *The Search for Order, 1877–1920* (Hill & Wang, New York, 1967), especially Chapter 5, 'A new middle class', 111–32. For scientific societies, see Margaret W. Rossiter, *Women Scientists in America: Struggles and Strategies to 1940* (Johns Hopkins University Press, Baltimore, 1982), 72–99. Burton J. Bledstein, *The Culture of Professionalism: The Middle Class and the Development of Higher Education in America* (Norton, New York, 1976).

8. Charles E. Rosenberg, 'And heal the sick: hospital and patient in 19th-century America', *Journal of Social History*, 10 (1977), 429–47, especially 437; William H. Williams, *America's First Hospital: The Pennsylvania Hospital, 1751–1841* (Haverford House, Wayne, PA, 1976), 52–4, 110–11, 140–2.

9. Responses from other institutions to an 1894 letter from the Massachusetts General Hospital asking about facilities for middle-class patients are in the Massachusetts General Archives, Private Ward (1894) folder, Phillips House file. On practices in Boston, F.A. Washburn and W.B. Howland, 'The training of hospital administrators', *Transactions of the American Hospital Association* (hence *Trans. AHA*), *12th Annual Conference* (hence *AC*), *1910*, 249–56; on New York, S.S. Goldwater, comment in minutes of the annual meeting, *Trans AHA, 8th AC, 1906*, 43.

10. For the perspective that physicians embracing scientific management brought to their parallel quest, see Ernest Amory Codman's memoir of his efforts to establish the American College of Surgeons in his text, *The Shoulder* (Thomas Todd Company, Boston, 1934), v–xi; epilogue, 1–29. Also Susan Reverby, 'Stealing the golden eggs: Ernest Amory Codman and the science and management of medicine', *Bulletin of the History of Medicine*, 55 (1981), 156–71; J.M.T. Finney, 'The standardization of the surgeon', *Journal of the American Medical Association*, 63 (1914), 1,433–7.

11. Examples include: C.S. Howell, 'Hospital construction', Frank E. Baker, 'Hospital ventilation', and ensuing discussion, all in *Proceedings AHA, 4th AC, 1902*, 141–7, 155–63; A.B. Ancker, 'Notes of the requirements of modern hospital architecture', Frank Miles Day, 'Hospital Architecture', and Henry M. Hurd, 'Modern hospital architecture: the pavilion hospital', *Trans AHA, 5th AC, 1903*, 81–128; Edmund Wheelwright, 'Hospital operating rooms and their accessories', Bertrand E. Taylor, 'The standardizing of hospital construction and equipment', and ensuing discussion, *Trans AHA, 7th AC, 1905*, 77–109. Superintendent (and later AHA

president) Thomas Howell attributed many of the increased costs to extravagance, asking rhetorically if hospitals were over-indulging their mostly poor patients with too much architectural ornament, and wondering whether the institutions were too quick to embrace medical fads like tiled surfaces to promote asepsis; Howell, 'Is the increased expenditure in hospital construction and equipment justified?' *Trans AHA, 7th AC, 1905*, 133–45.

12. J.A. Washburn, 'Medical organization and medical education in general hospitals', E.S. Gilmore, 'The organization of a teaching hospital', and ensuing discussion, *Trans AHA, 9th AC, 1907*, 131–46; Joseph Howland, 'Report of sub-committee on medical organization and medical education', *Trans AHA, 10th AC, 1908*, 353–5.

13. A.S. Kavanagh, 'Hospital support, and how to secure it', and ensuing discussion, *Trans AHA, 9th AC, 1907*, 64–78, 88–91. See also Vogel, *Modern Hospital*, 125–6.

14. C. Irving Fisher, 'Private patients in general hospitals', and ensuing discussion, *Trans AHA, 6th AC, 1904*, 93–104; George H.M. Rowe, 'Presidential Address', *Trans AHA, 7th AC, 1905*, 53–66, especially 57; Louis Curtis, 'The modern hotel-hospital', *Trans AHA, 9th AC, 1907*, 182–8. Thomas Howell, Superintendent of New York Hospital noted that

> very few managers of hospitals which maintain private patient services know whether they are conducting them at a profit, or at a loss, for the reason that they do not insist upon an accurate system of accounting being introduced and maintained. (Howell, 'Cost accounting in hospitals', *Trans AHA, 11th AC, 1909*, 193–205, especially 195)

For the role of physicians in attracting paying patients, see David Rosner, *A Once Charitable Enterprise: Hospitals and Health Care in Brooklyn and New York, 1885–1915* (Cambridge University Press, 1982).

15. Jane Addams, 'The layman's view of hospital work among the poor', *Trans AHA, 9th AC, 1907* 57–63.

16. Examples include: John Peters, 'Dispensary abuse', *Proceedings AHA, 4th AC, 1902* 119–27; Franklin B. Kirkbride, 'Uses and abuses of dispensaries', *Proceedings AHA, 5th AC, 1903*, 172–85; R.R. Ross, 'Presidential address', *Trans AHA, 9th AC, 1907*, 50–6; John Peters, 'The development of the work and the restriction of the abuse of the out-patient department', and Thomas Howell, 'Method of investigating out-patient applicants at Worcester hospitals', both in *Trans AHA, 10th AC, 1908*, 268–73, 280–4.

17. Josephine E. Royan, 'Hospital housekeeping', M.W. M'Kechnie, 'Hospital housekeeping', Maud Banfield, 'The cleaning', and John Peters, 'Hospital dietary', all in *Proceedings AHA, 5th AC, 1903*, 45–80, 151–70; Renwick Ross, 'Artificial refrigeration',

and John H. McCollom, 'The destruction of refuse and disinfection', *Trans AHA, 7th AC, 1905* 209–38; M. Wahlstrom, 'Breakage and loss, and how far should employees be held responsible?' and William O. Mann, 'My experience with floors', *Trans AHA, 9th AC, 1907*, 99–111; John Hornsby, 'Some scientific aspects of hospital administration', *Trans AHA, 10th ACA, 1908*, 219–36.

18. J.T. Duryea, 'Annual address of the president', *Proceedings AHA, 4th AC, 1902*, 20–4.

19. F.A. Washburn, 'Some methods of utilizing hospital waste', Jeremiah Long, 'Engine room economies', and ensuing discussions, *Trans AHA, 7th AC, 1905*, 239–56; R.W. Bruce Smith, 'Waste in hospitals', *Trans AHA, 9th AC, 1907*, 147–54.

20. In his presidential address, Duryea called attention to the need for superintendents to establish an agreed-upon knowledge base:

> The troubles and trials of each of us have individualities not peculiar to all of us. We teach ourselves to meet and master the obstacles that we encounter, and the little crystals of wisdom and direction that come to us from these virtues are the jewels in our crown of rejoicing. In these instances, our methods are not our own, they should belong to all of us. We require them to be individually and mutually successful. We come to these conferences hungry and thirsty for ideas, intelligent, well digested ideas of management, of government, of finance, of construction, of training schools, of our boards, of each other, and we ask them from all of you. (*Proceedings AHA, 4th AC, 1902*, 20–4)

21. The impact of scientific management in the hospital is discussed in Charles E. Rosenberg, 'Inward vision and outward glance: the shaping of the American hospital, 1880–1914', *Bulletin of the History of Medicine*, 53 (1979), 346–91. The broader scientific management movement in the United States was particularly associated with engineer Frederick W. Taylor. One of his briefer explanations of 'Taylorism' is 'A piece-work system', *Transactions of the American Society of Mechanical Engineers*, 16 (1895), 856–903. Critical analyses are in Harry Braverman, *Labor and Monopoly Capital* (Monthly Review Press, New York, 1974), especially Chapter 5, 'The primary effects of scientific management', and David F. Noble, *America by Design: Science, Technology, and the Rise of Corporate Capitalism* (Knopf, New York, 1979).

22. The first issue of *Modern Hospital*, the Association's journal, appeared in 1913. A bibliography of works on hospital construction, management, and the like appeared in the conference proceedings in 1904, even before the publication of the first handbooks of hospital administration: Charlotte A. Aikens (ed.), *Hospital Management* (W.B. Saunders, Philadelphia, 1911); Albert J. Ochsner and

Meyer Strum, *The Organization, Construction and Management of Hospitals* (Cleveland Press, Chicago, 1909); and John Hornsby and Richard Schmidt, *The Modern Hospital* (W.B. Saunders, Philadelphia, 1913). Training emerged as a theme at superintendents' conventions in 1907 when members petitioned the Association to organize a two- or three-week summer course on hospital work. S.S. Goldwater reported to the same meeting, as chair of the Association's Committee on Hospital Progress, the establishment of a chair of hospital management and economics at the new Brooklyn Post-Graduate Medical School and the fact that a New York-area university – evidently Columbia University Teacher's College – was about to establish a department for training hospital superintendents:

> Thus approaches the realization of a hope long cherished by many members of the Association, that the technical training of hospital superintendents might be undertaken by an educational body of dignity, learning, foresight and influence, not for the greater glory of those who are already engaged in the labor of hospital administration, but for the greater efficiency and better social service of their successors. (*Trans AHA, 9th AC, 1907*, 46–7, 151–71)

The Massachusetts General Hospital developed two parallel educational programmes for administrators – a three- to four-month programme for alumni of the hospital's nursing school, and a several-year training rotation in which physicians served on the hospital staff as assistant directors – early in the twentieth century. Detroit's Grace Hospital had a programme for graduate nurses similar to that in Boston: F.A. Washburn and W.B. Howland, 'The training of hospital administrators', *Trans AHA, 12th AC, 1910*, 249--65. See also, Frederic A. Washburn, *The Massachusetts General Hospital: its Development, 1900–1935* (Houghton Mifflin, Boston, 1939), 27.

23. Superintendent Charlotte Aikens complained in 1906 that the Association of Hospital Superintendents was only a paper shell; annual meetings and rotating officers were inadequate to the organization's needs. Properly organized, a superintendents' association could not only promote learning and co-operation among its members, but it could also interpret its mandate more broadly and earn the trust of the public at the same time. A stronger Association could, for example, prevent the 'unnecessary duplication' of hospitals: 'Development of a wider national association', *Trans AHA, 8th AC, 1906*, 150–60, especially 157; Thomas Howell, 'Report of the committee on the development of the association', *Trans AHA, 10th AC, 1908*, 210–18. In 1913 the Association appointed a committee to study the possibility of a permanent headquarters and year-round organization – in part

because of the greater public good that such a reorganization could accomplish: E.P. Haworth, 'What the American Hospital Association can do for the hospitals of America' and ensuing discussion, *Trans AHA, 15th AC, 1913*, 256–73. The Association's first permanent headquarters opened in Philadelphia in 1917: Laszlo, 'American Hospital Association', 38. Professionalizers also realized that they had to earn the public trust by policing their own ranks. For one of the occasional admissions that some superintendents were not adequate to their tasks, see Duryea, 'Annual address of the president', *Proceedings AHA, 4th AC, 1902*, 23. Bledstein argues the link between claims to technical expertise and the exercise of cultural authority with particular vehemence: *Culture of Professionalism, passim.*

24. J.C. Biddle, 'The physician as a hospital superintendent', C.S. Howell, 'The layman as a superintendent', and ensuing discussion, *Trans AHA, 6th AC, 1904*, 47–53, 58–68.

25. See, for example, the presidential address of layman superintendent Daniel D. Test, *Trans AHA, 6th AC, 1904*, 43–6.

26. Membership lists, with professional degrees and institutional affiliations, are published in the annual transactions.

27. George H.M. Rowe, 'Observations on hospital administration', J.T. Duryea, 'Annual address of the president', both in *Proceedings AHA, 4th AC, 1902*, 51–67, 20–4.

28. Herbert B. Howard, long-time administrator of the Massachusetts General Hospital, reminded his peers that trustees depended for information on the superintendent, who has 'entire charge of the details of his institution': Howard, 'The managers and the superintendent', *Proceedings AHA, 4th AC, 1902*, 68–70.

29. See, for example, James B. Woodward, 'Hospital organization' with ensuing discussion, *Proceedings AHA, 4th AC, 1902*, 71–88; C. Irving Fisher, 'Uniformity in hospital financial reports and statistics' and ensuing discussion, *Trans AHA, 7th AC, 1905*, 257–82; R.H. Townley, 'Discipline and organization' and ensuing discussion, *Trans AHA, 8th AC, 1906*, 84–95; M. Wahlstrom, 'Breakage and loss, and how far should employees be held responsible?' and Asa Bacon, 'The selection and management of hospital employees: a comparison of hospital pay rolls', both in *Trans AHA, 9th AC, 1907*, 99–104, 112–19.

30. Eugene Elder, 'The management of the race question in hospitals', *Trans 9th AC, 1907* 127–30.

31. On the impact of reform in medical education on the social status of physicians, see Howard S. Berliner, 'A larger perspective on the Flexner Report', *International Journal of Health Services*, 5 (1975), 573–92; on the hieratic role of physicians, a good place to start is Charles E. Rosenberg, 'The therapeutic revolution: medicine, meaning, and social change in nineteenth-century America', in Morris J. Vogel and Charles E. Rosenberg (eds), *The Therapeutic Revolution: Essays in the Social History of American Medicine*

(University of Pennsylvania Press, Philadelphia, 1979), 3–25.

32. For example, Alice Seabrook, 'Appointment of internes' and ensuing discussion, *Trans AHA 8th AC, 1906* 195–200.

33. J.C. Biddle, 'The physician as hospital superintendent' and discussion, *Trans AHA, 6th AC, 1904*, 47–50, 58–68; Henry M. Hurd, 'The medical organization of hospitals' and discussion, *Trans AHA, 8th AC, 1906* 72–83.

34. George P. Ludlam, 'Presidential address', *Trans AHA, 8th AC, 1906*, 63–71.

35. On workmen's compensation, see Vogel, *Modern Hospital*, 121–4. On Blue Cross, Ronald L. Numbers, 'The third party: health insurance in America', in Vogel and Rosenberg (eds), *The Therapeutic Revolution*, 177–200, especially 182–3; and Rosemary Stevens, *American Medicine and the Public Interest* (Yale University Press, New Haven, 1971), 269–72.

36. Stevens, *American Medicine*, 444–527.

37. On increased expenditures, Numbers, 'Third party', 189; on physicians' incomes, Robert Stevens and Rosemary Stevens, *Welfare Medicine in America: A Case Study of Medicaid* (The Free Press, New York, 1974), 194.

Index

Index

269